I0753211

HISTORIC PHOTOS OF
TUCSON

TEXT AND CAPTIONS BY MIKE SPEELMAN

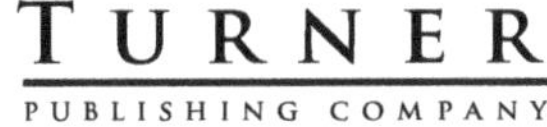

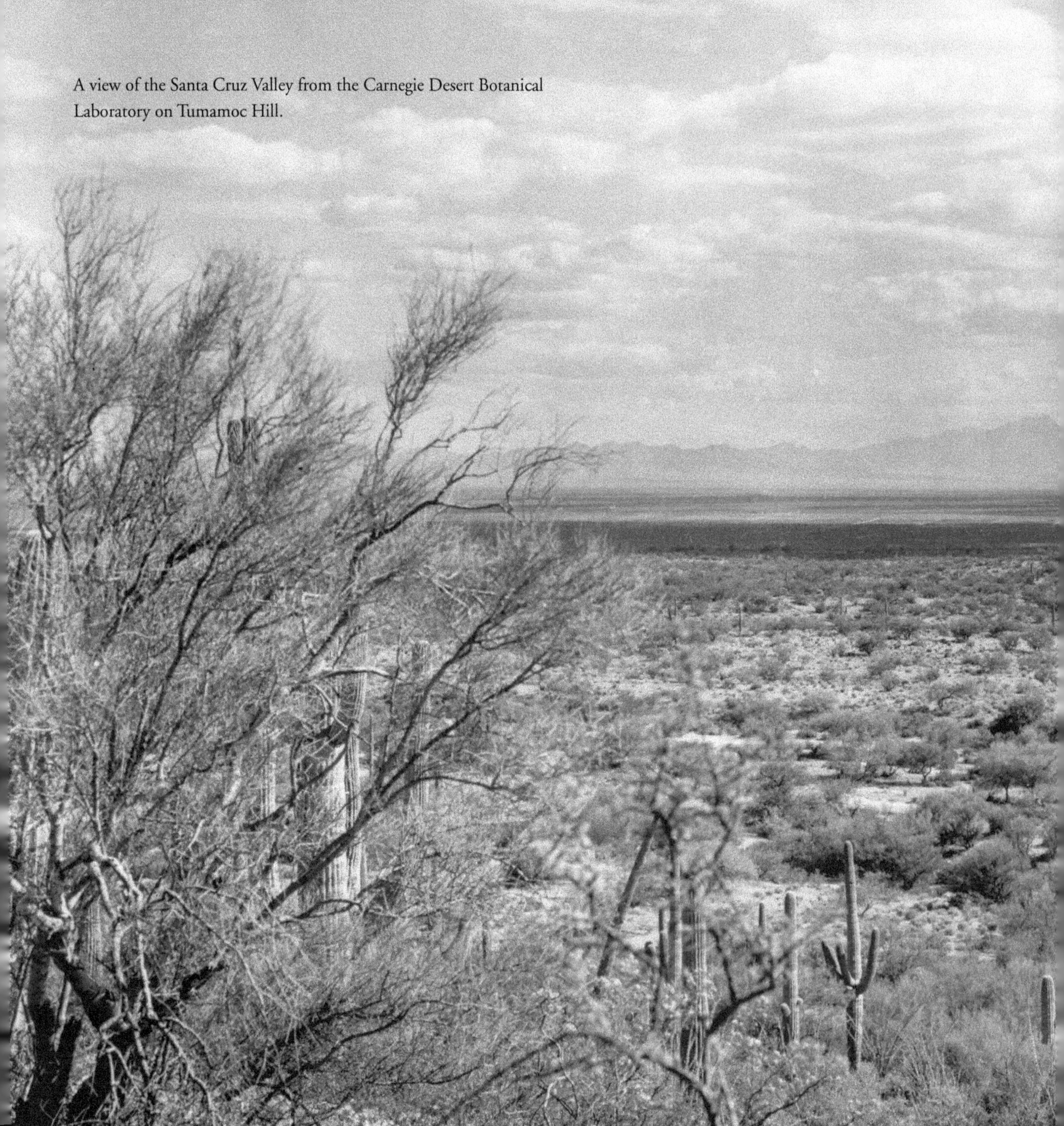

A view of the Santa Cruz Valley from the Carnegie Desert Botanical Laboratory on Tumamoc Hill.

HISTORIC PHOTOS OF
TUCSON

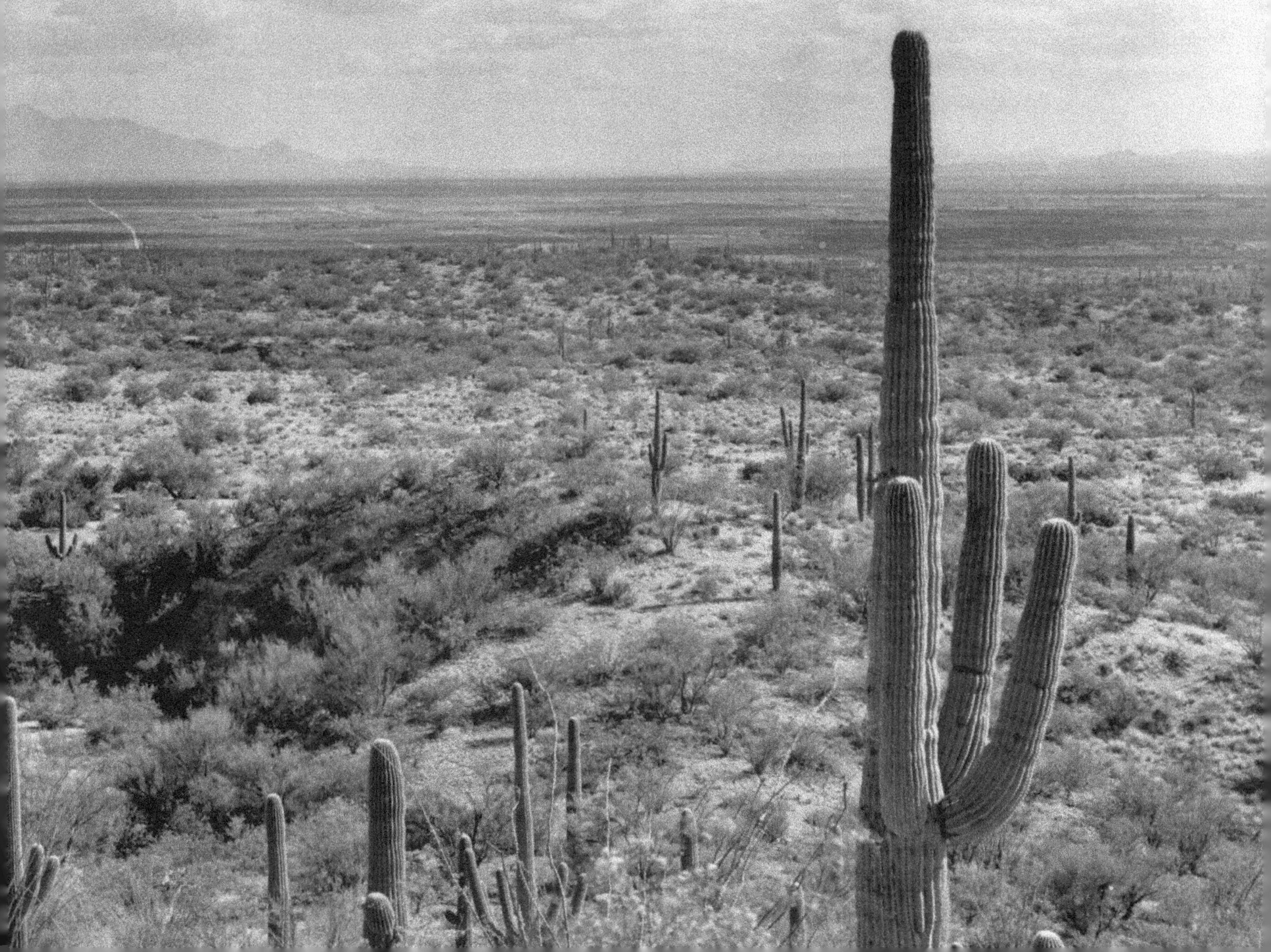

Turner Publishing Company
www.turnerpublishing.com

Historic Photos of Tucson

Library of Congress Control Number: 2007929568

ISBN-13: 978-1-59652-370-8

ISBN 978-1-68336-958-5 (hc)

CONTENTS

The Alianza Hispano Americana float for an Armistice Day parade around 1925.

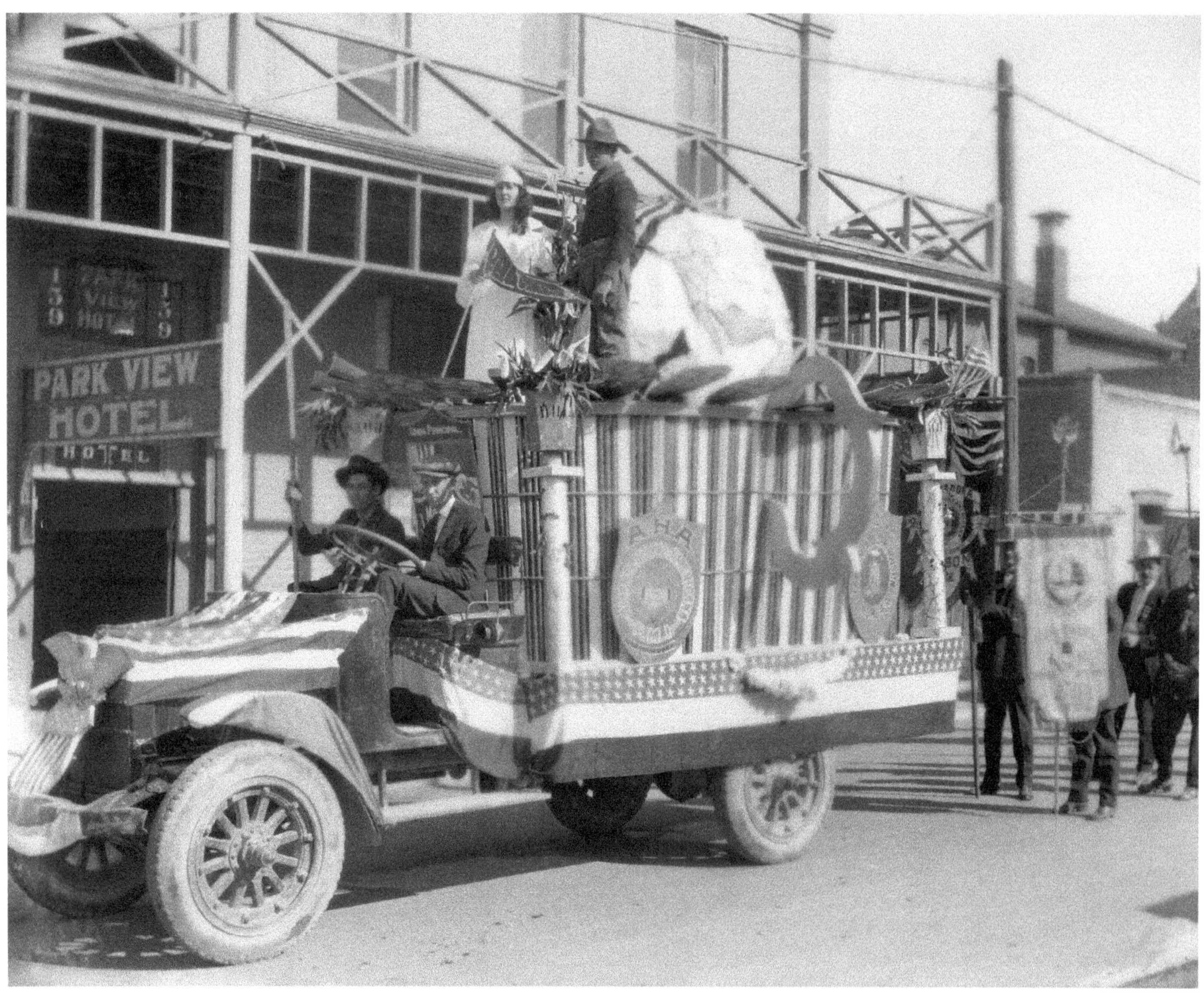

ACKNOWLEDGMENTS

This volume, *Historic Photos of Tucson,* is the result of the cooperation and efforts of many individuals, organizations, and corporations. It is with great thanks that we acknowledge the valuable contribution of the following for their generous support:

Arizona Historical Society
Library of Congress

I wish to acknowledge the informed and patient assistance of the staff of the Research Library of the Arizona Historical Society in Tucson: Kate Reeve, Debbie Newman, Kim Frontz, Dave Tackenberg, Jill McCleary, and Chrystal Carpenter Burke, photo archivist supreme. I couldn't have done it without them.

–Mike Speelman, Author

Preface

Tucson has thousands of historic photographs that reside in archives, both locally and nationally. This book began with the observation that, while those photographs are of great interest to many, they are not easily accessible. During a time when Tucson is looking ahead and evaluating its future course, many people are asking, "How do we treat the past?" These decisions affect every aspect of the city—architecture, public spaces, commerce, infrastructure—and these, in turn, affect the way that people live their lives. This book seeks to provide easy access to a valuable, objective look into the history of Tucson.

The power of photographs is that they are less subjective than words in their treatment of history. Although the photographer can make decisions regarding subject matter and how to capture and present it, photographs do not provide the breadth of interpretation that text does. For this reason, they offer an original, untainted perspective that allows the viewer to interpret and observe.

This project represents countless hours of review and research. The researchers and writer have reviewed thousands of photographs in numerous archives. We greatly appreciate the generous assistance of the individuals and organizations listed in the acknowledgments of this work, without whom this project could not have been completed.

The goal in publishing this work is to provide broader access to this set of extraordinary photographs that seek to inspire, provide perspective, and evoke insight that might assist people who are responsible for determining Tucson's future. In addition, the book seeks to preserve the past with adequate respect and reverence.

With the exception of touching up imperfections caused by the damage of time and cropping where necessary, no other changes have been made. The focus and clarity of many images is limited to the technology and the ability of the photographer at the time they were taken.

The work is divided into eras. Beginning with some of the earliest known photographs of Tucson, the first section records photographs through the end of the nineteenth century. The second section spans the beginning of the twentieth century through World War I. Section Three moves from the 1920s to the 1940s. The last section covers the World War II era to recent times.

In each of these sections we have made an effort to capture various aspects of life through our selection of photographs. People, commerce, transportation, infrastructure, religious institutions, and educational institutions have been included to provide a broad perspective.

We encourage readers to reflect as they go walking in Tucson, strolling through the city, its parks, and its neighborhoods. It is the publisher's hope that in utilizing this work, longtime residents will learn something new and that new residents will gain a perspective on where Tucson has been, so that each can contribute to its future.

Todd Bottorff, Publisher

The San Xavier del Bac Mission complex, known as the White Dove of the Desert, and the vast Santa Cruz River Valley surrounding it, nine miles south of Tucson. Founded by Father Kino in 1692, the mission was built near a Tohono O'odham village.

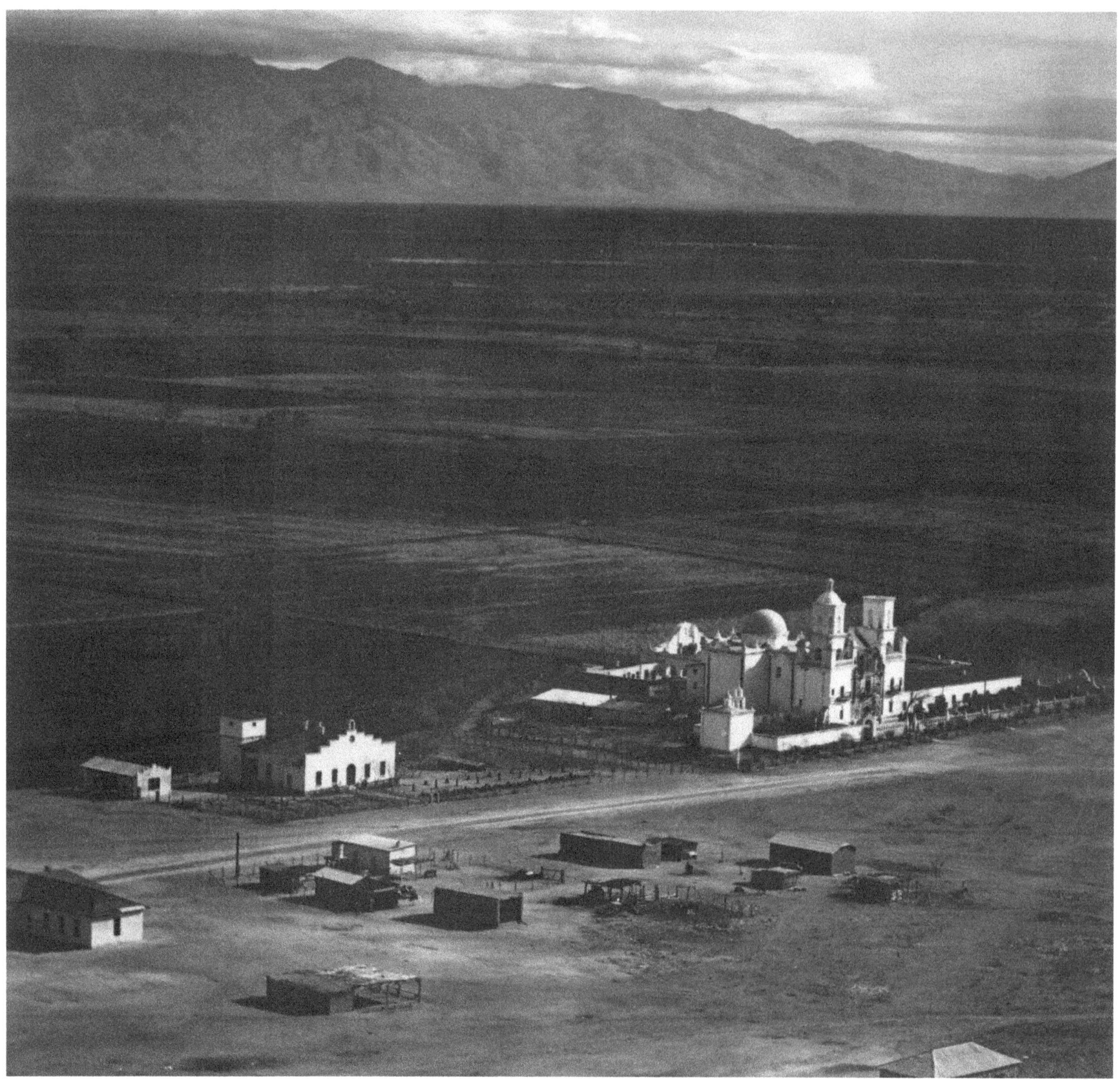

Life on the Southwestern Frontier (1870–1899)

By 1870, Tucson had been part of the Spanish Empire, Mexico, and the United States. Hugo O'Connor, an Irishman in the Spanish Army, founded it as the Presidio San Agustín de Tucson on August 20, 1775. Mexico gained its independence from Spain on September 16, 1821. After a war with the United States between 1846–1848, Mexico signed rhe Treaty of Guadalupe Hidalgo on February 2, 1848, giving the U.S. much of northern Mexico, which did not include Tucson.

Agitation for a southern railroad route free from winter snows and delays led to the Gadsden Purchase, negotiated by James Gadsden, the Minister to Mexico. The agreement, ratified by Congress June 29, 1854, paid $10,000,000 for 29,644 acres in Mexico. Tucson was part of this area, and its residents became American citizens. The town's population in 1860 was 623—few were Anglos—but more than doubled to 1,568 by 1864.

The Arizona Territory split off from New Mexico Territory on February 24, 1863. Tucson was the territorial capital from 1867 to 1877. The population reached 3,224 in 1870, and Tucson was incorporated as a village on May 21, 1871, then as a city on February 7, 1877. Despite these changes, Tucson remained relatively isolated from the rest of the country. Apache raids made life uncertain for miners, farmers, and ranchers. The expense of shipping goods was another obstacle to growth—many necessities sold for the price of luxuries elsewhere. The long-awaited Southern Pacific Railroad arrived on March 20, 1880. Among the changes it brought were Chinese residents to add to the cultural mix. Raiding by Apaches, however, continued into the 1880s, deterring development of Arizona's natural resources. The first telephones were installed in 1881, and gaslights became available in 1882, but the population shrank from 7,000 in 1880 to 5,000 in 1890.

Tucson itself lacked a strong industrial base, acting as supplier and shipper for the core industries of copper, cattle, and cotton. A national economic slump in the early 1890s affected the city, but expectations remained high that the railroad would bring a change in fortunes. As the mythology of the Wild West grew, tourism became a burgeoning industry; people came to the Southwest for its attractions, spurring a need for hotels, restaurants, and other amenities of a modern city.

Ruins of the Convento of the San Agustín de Tucson Mission. Also known as San Cosme de Tucson, it was built around 1800 and stood on the west bank of the Santa Cruz River near Sentinel Peak. Because of attacks by Apaches, this mission was abandoned by 1840.

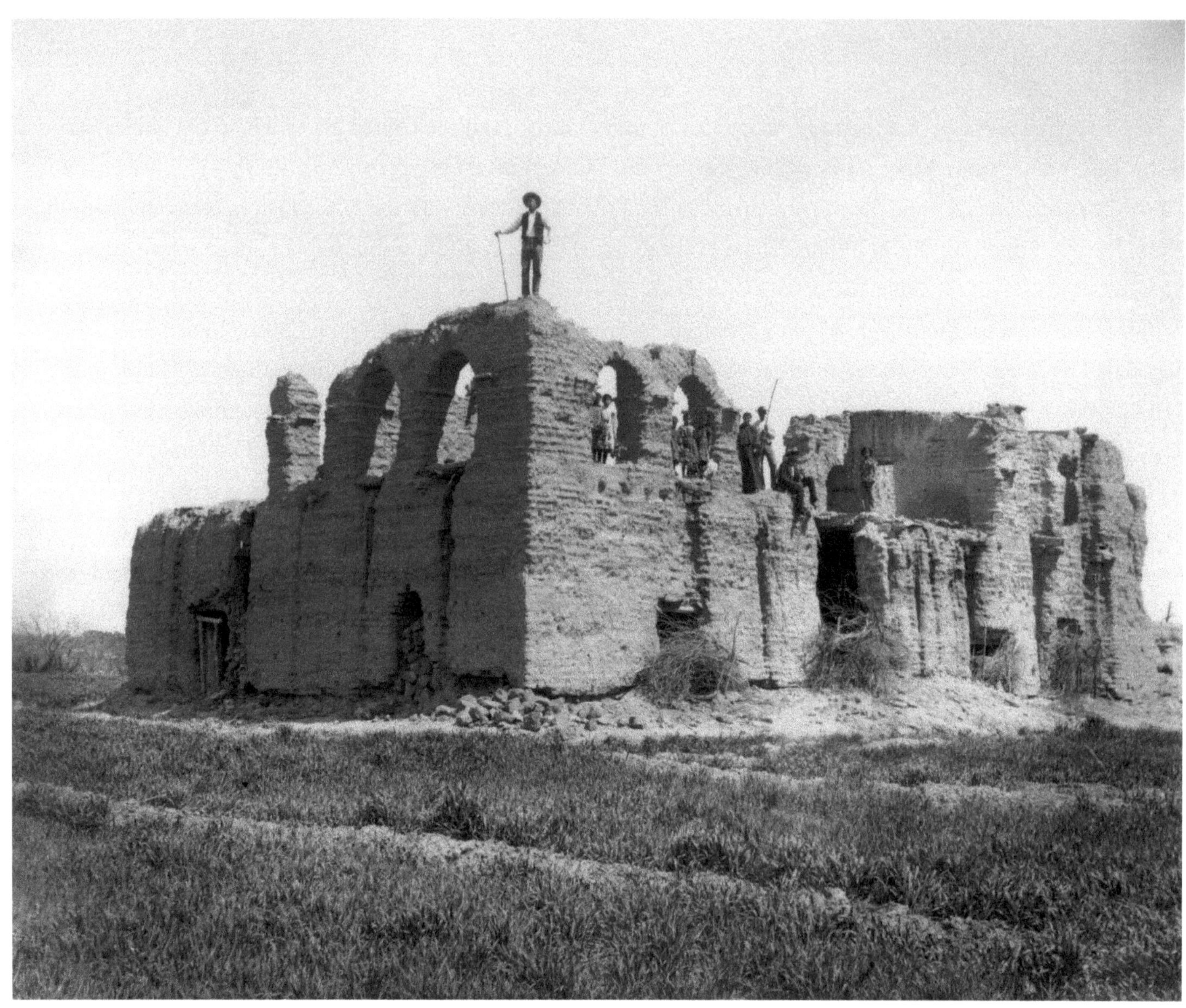

Ruins of the Quartermaster and Commissary buildings of Fort Lowell, ca. 1902. In March 1873, Camp Lowell, named for General Charles Russell Lowell, Jr., moved from Tucson east to the banks of the Rillito River. Designated a fort in April 1879, it was closed in 1892.

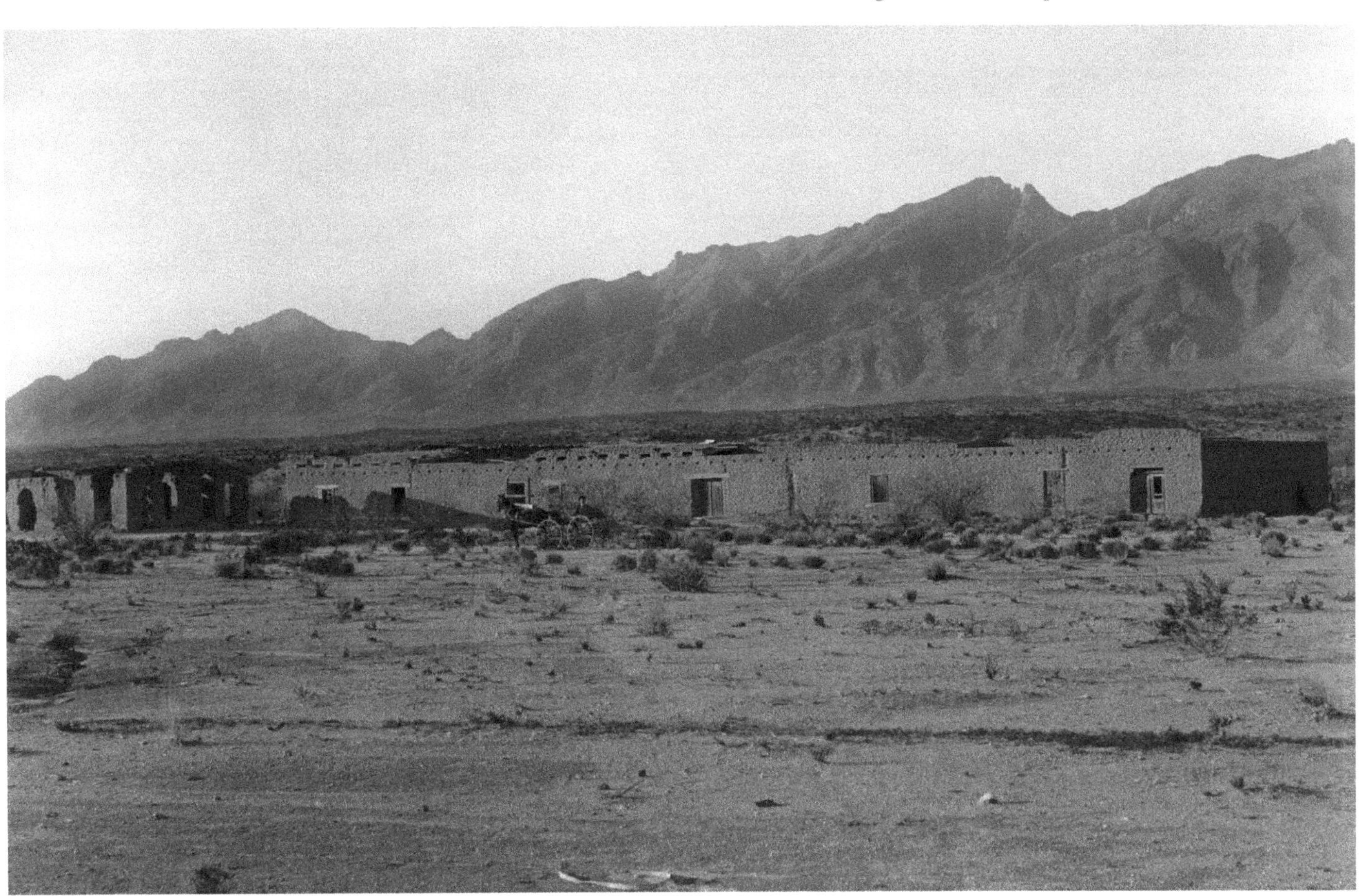

The hospital at Fort Lowell was constructed during 1874 and 1875. It was an adobe building, with cool interior rooms and fifteen-foot ceilings. The wardroom held twelve to sixteen beds and there were smaller rooms for officers and special cases.

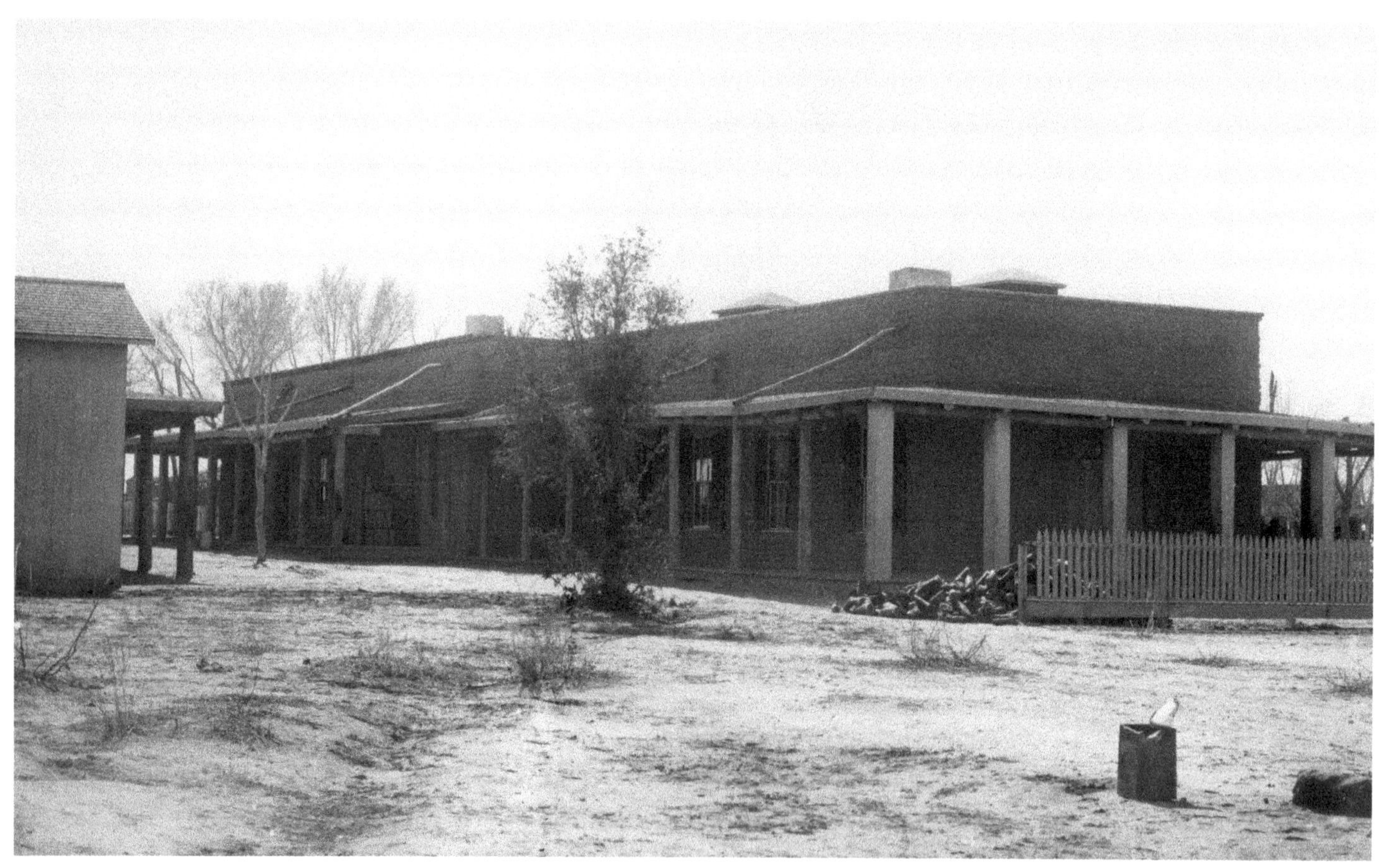

The Fort Lowell Band on the parade ground. Military bands helped relieve the unavoidable boredom of service on the frontier. They were also popular with civilians in nearby Tucson where they often performed outdoor concerts.

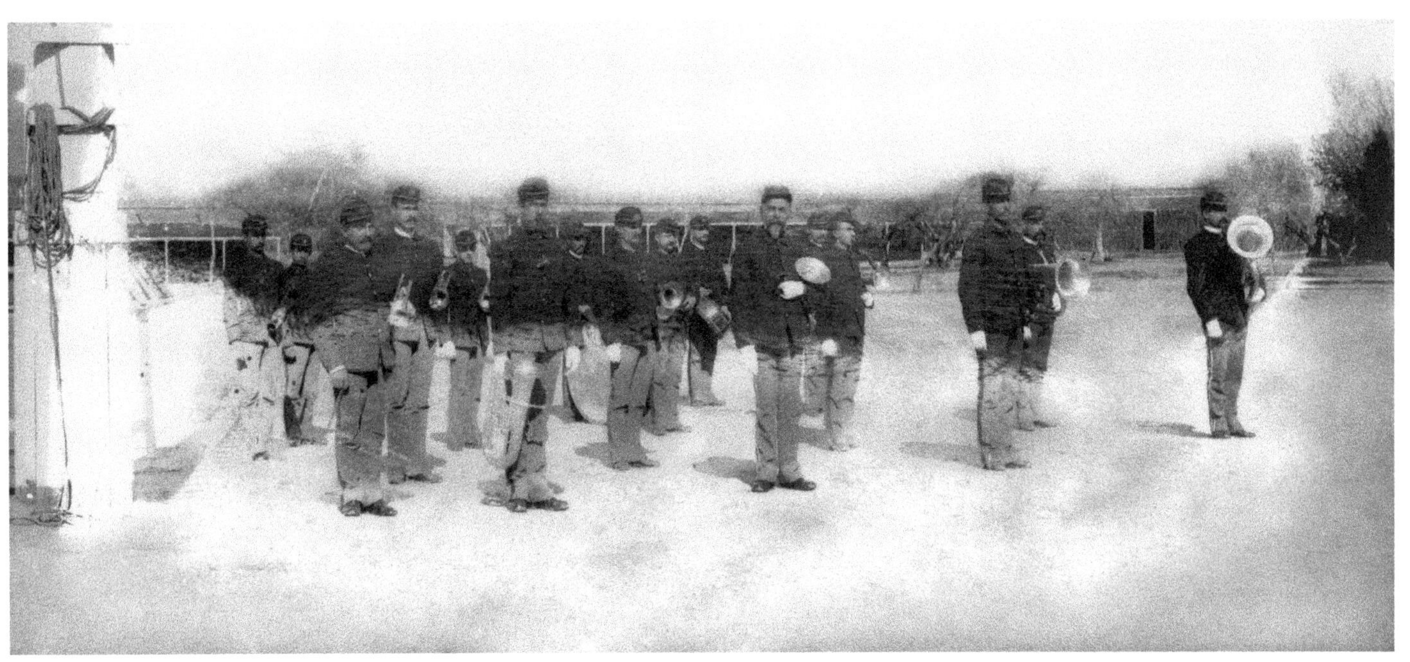

Two riders pose with their horses in a Tucson corral around 1875. As indicated by the sign in the background, Spanish remained the dominant language in daily use in southern Arizona well into the American era.

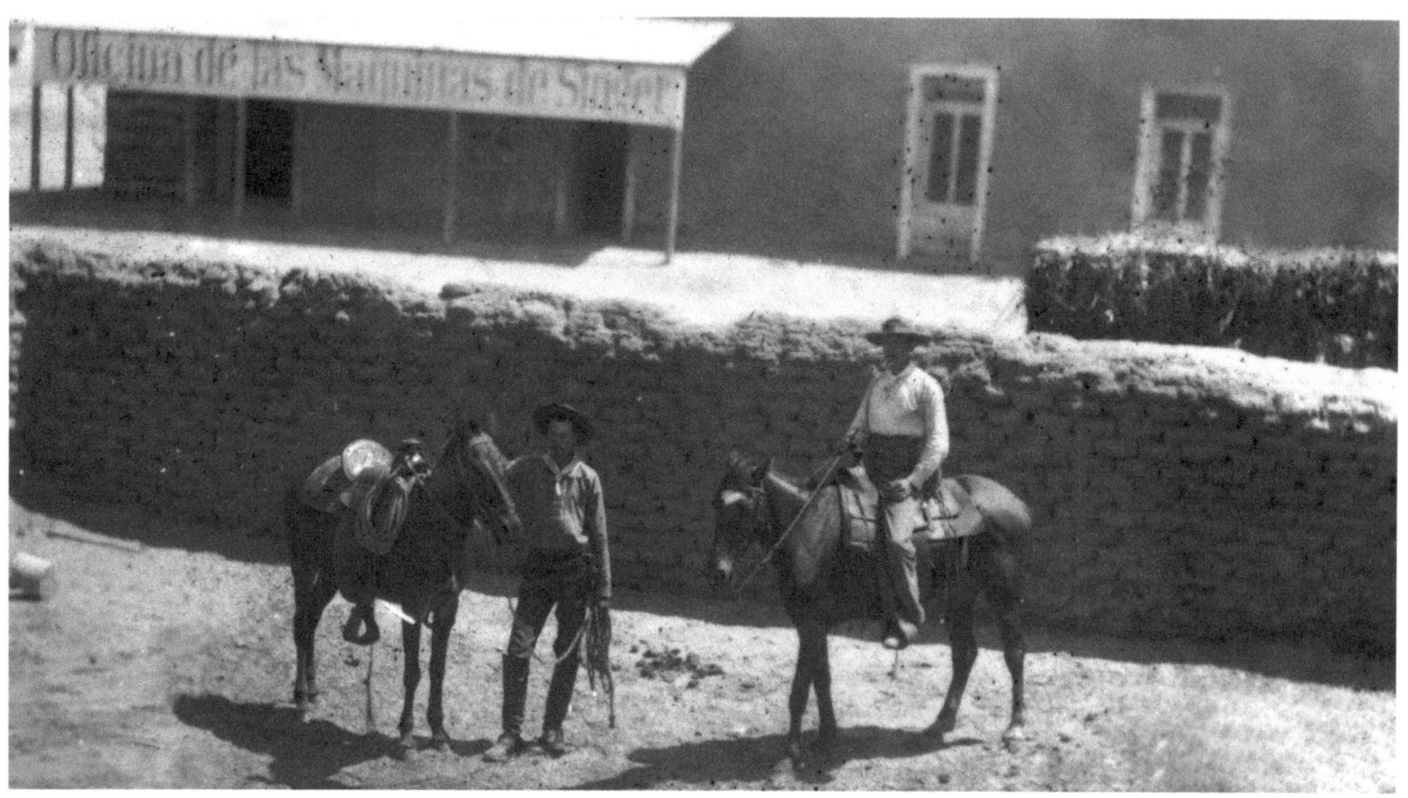

Three pioneer establishments—John Archibald's mercantile store, E. N. Fish's Flour and Feed Store, and the Park Brewery Depot Saloon started by brewer Alex Levin—on the east side of Main Street, looking north (ca. 1878). Main Street was the economic and social center of early Tucson.

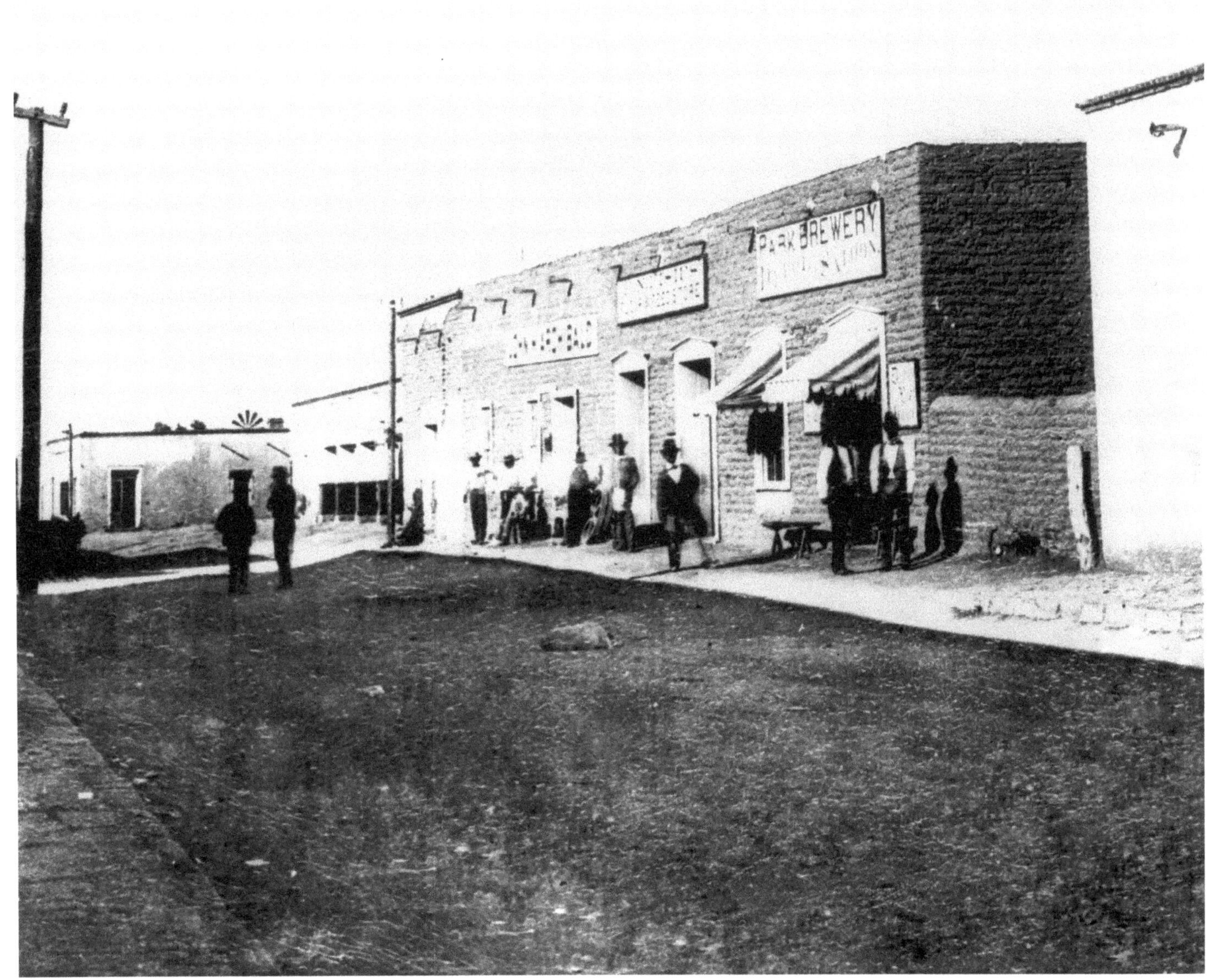

With its arrival in March 1880, the railroad changed the nature of travel and shipping in the southwestern desert. The arduous and expensive journey to reach Tucson was alleviated.

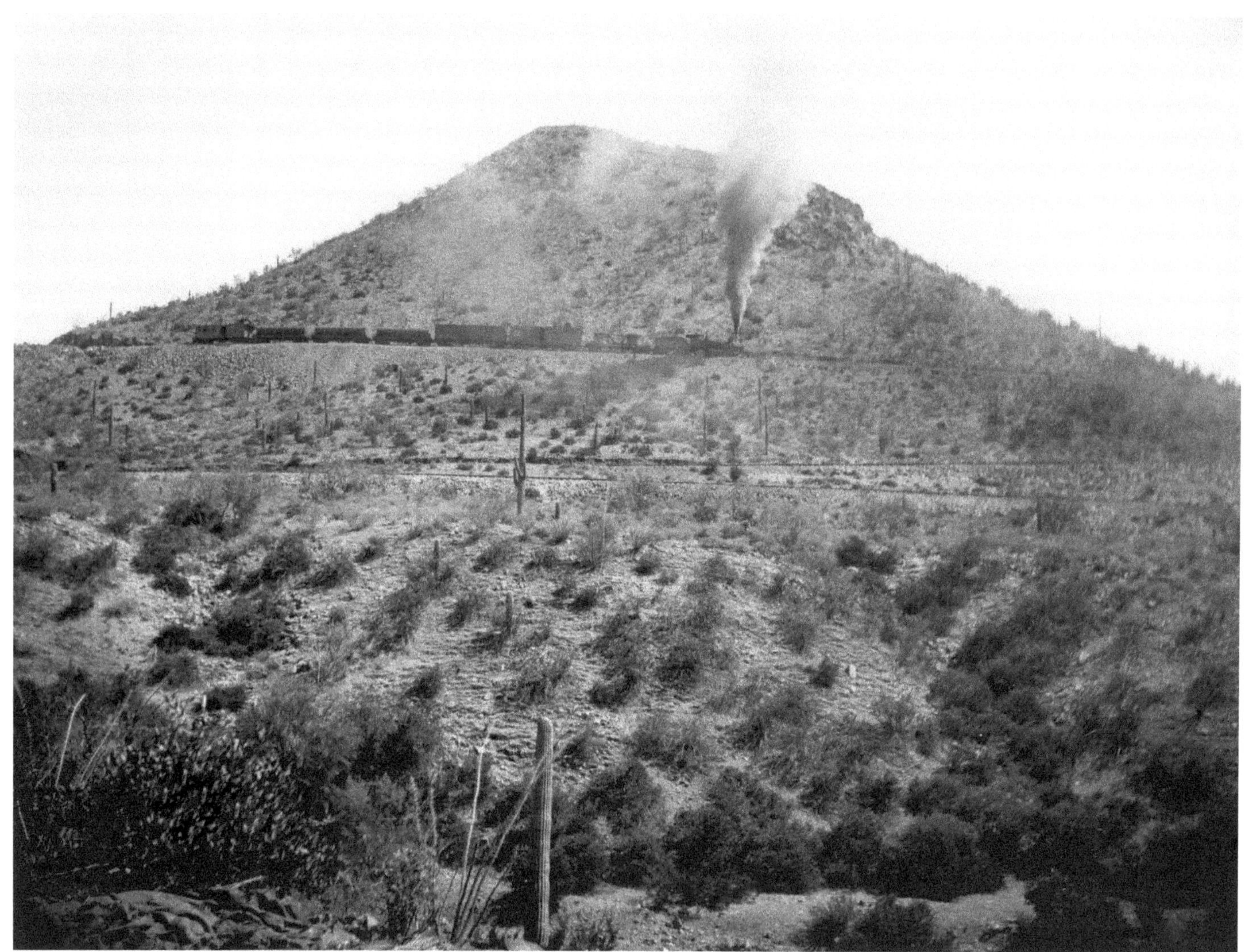

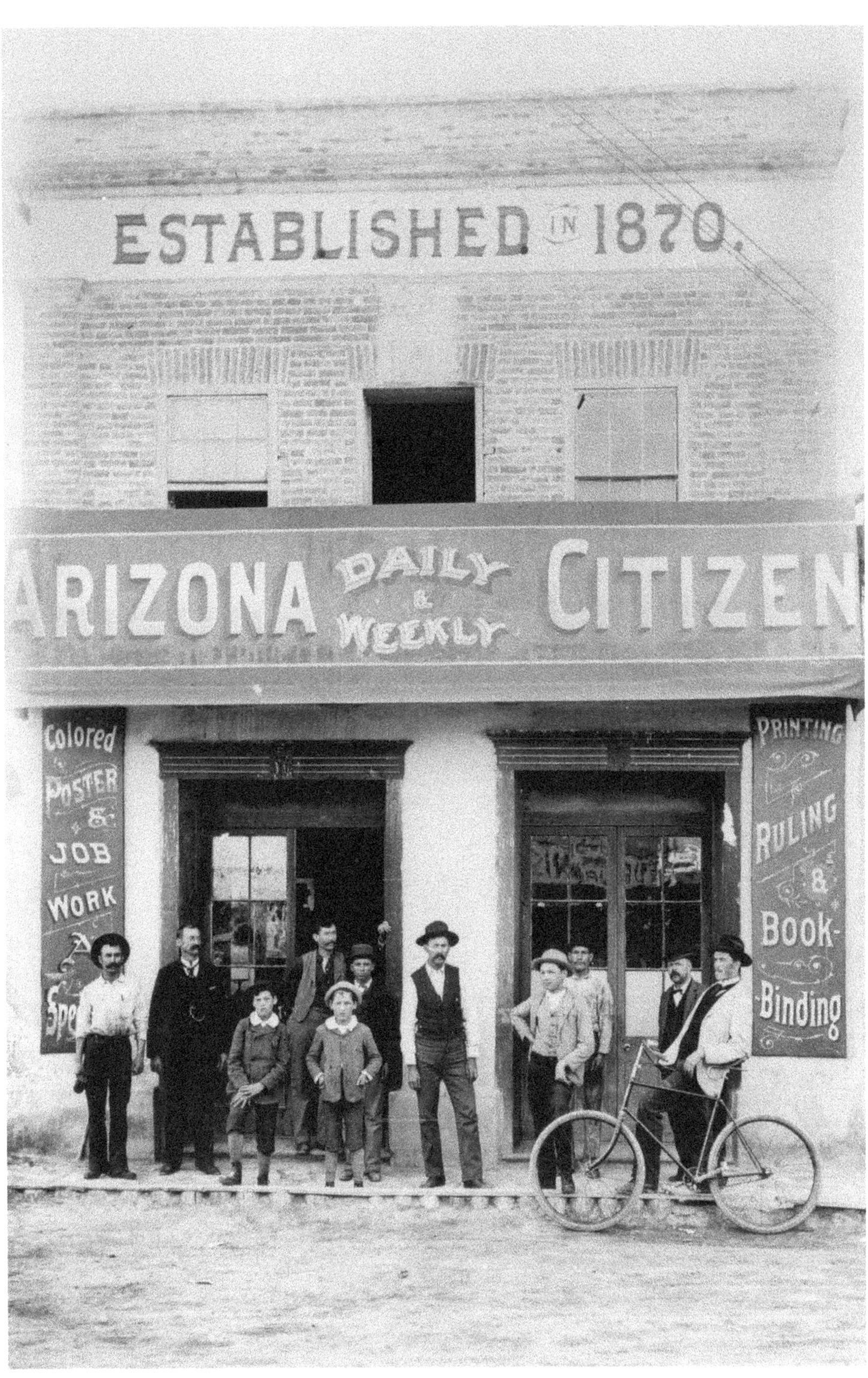

The *Arizona Citizen* began during a heated election campaign in October 1870 to oppose the *Weekly Arizonan,* Tucson's first newspaper. It became a daily in 1879, and is still published today as the *Tucson Citizen.* This office was located at 4 Plaza Square around 1880.

The San Xavier Hotel, built in 1881 for the convenience of train passengers, stood just north of the Southern Pacific Depot. The first hotel to have telephones and electric lights, it was a popular place for balls and receptions. The building was destroyed by fire in 1903.

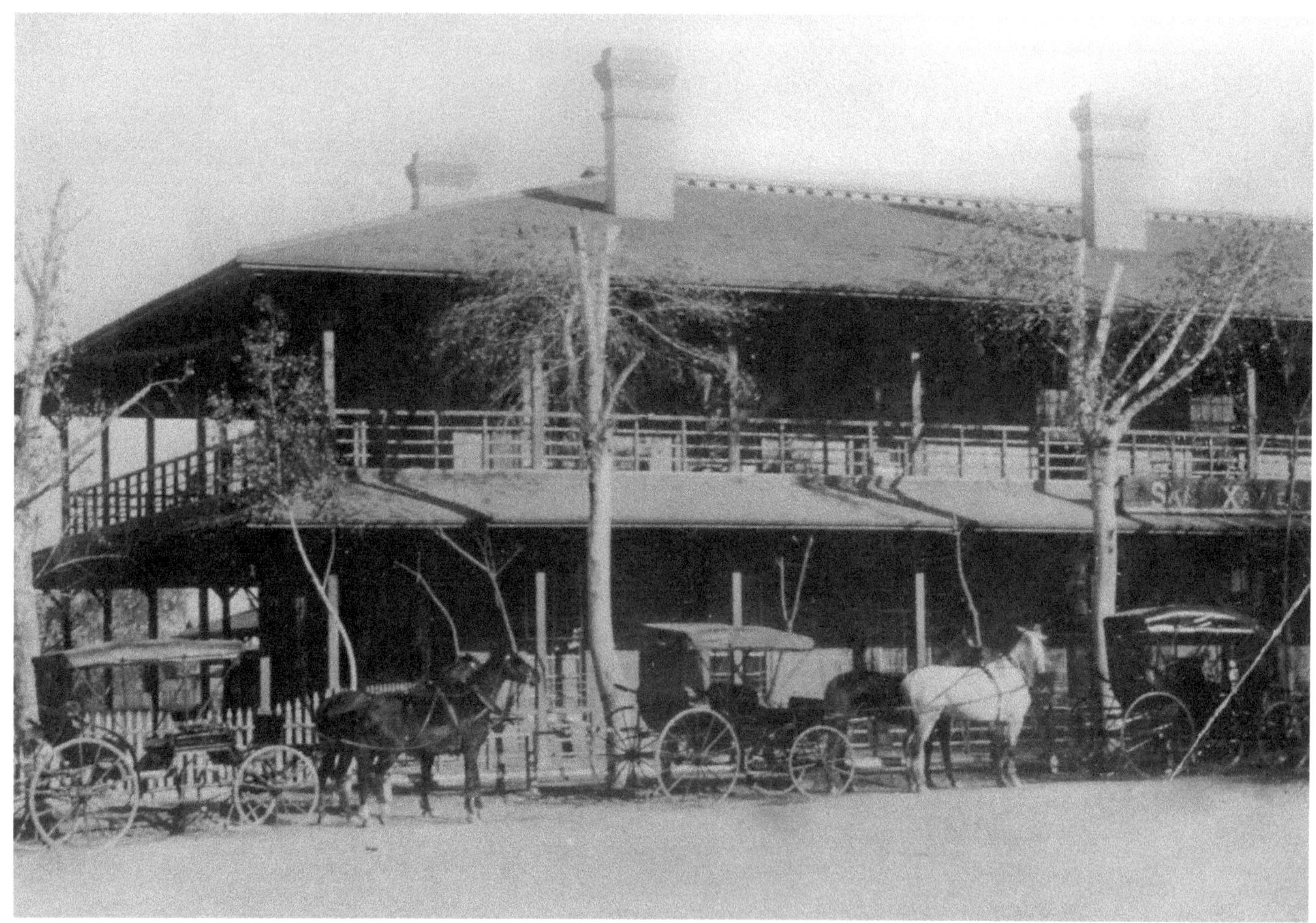

The San Agustín Cathedral and Church Plaza around 1885. Designated a cathedral upon completion in 1868, the brick church had towers added in 1881 and a new façade in 1883. For many years, the Plaza was the site for the often rowdy Fiesta of San Agustín, Tucson's patron saint.

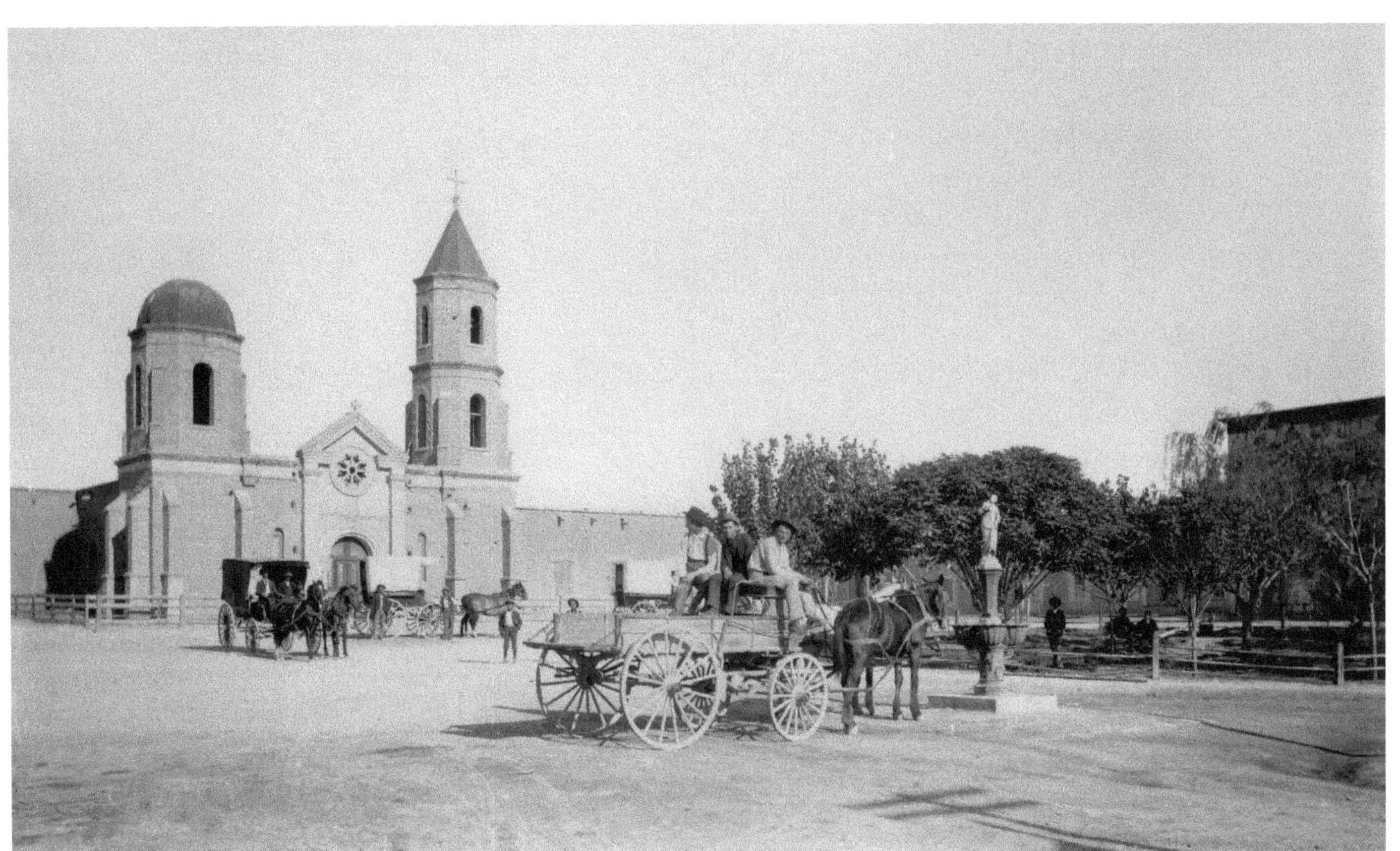

A view into the backyard of the San Agustín Cathedral around 1881. Across the roof can be seen signs for the Helvetia Saloon and the Tucson Restaurant and, further back, the St. Charles Restaurant and M. G. Roca's mercantile store.

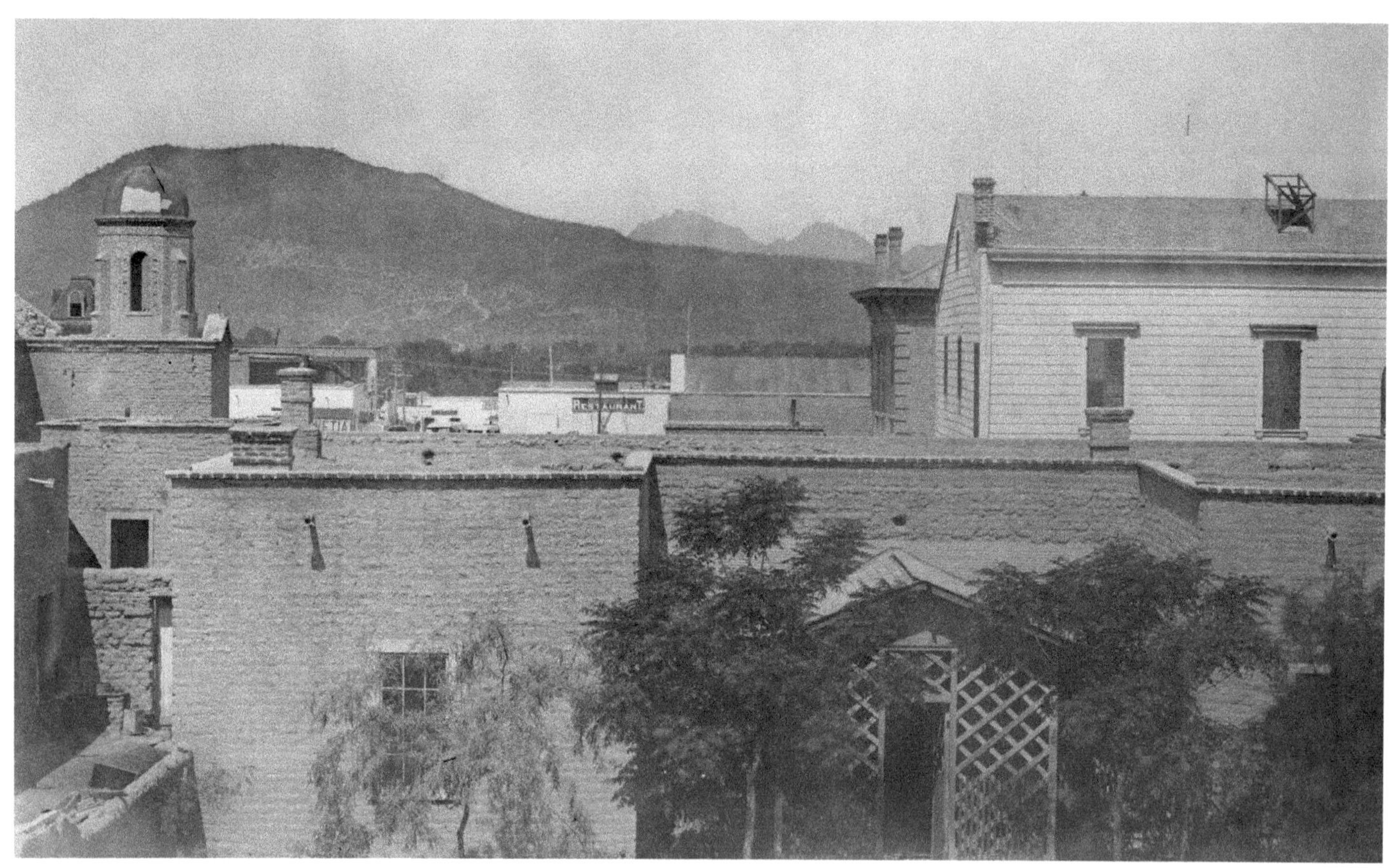

The Cosmopolitan Hotel, at Main and Pennington streets, was built using the southwest corner of the Presidio wall about 1856. Known by various names, it was owned by Hiram Stevens and had become the Cosmopolitan by 1874. The wooden second floor was added in 1883.

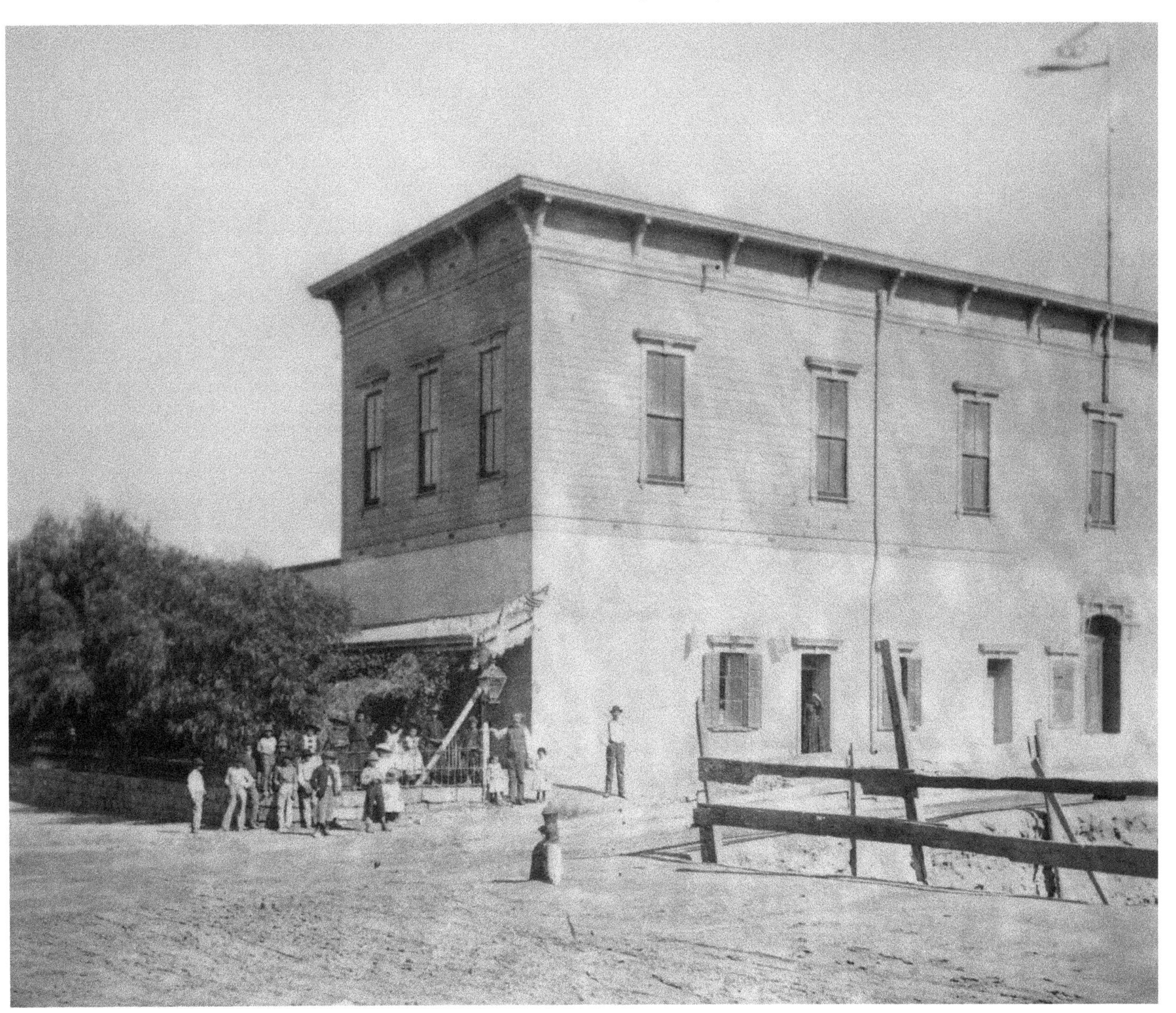

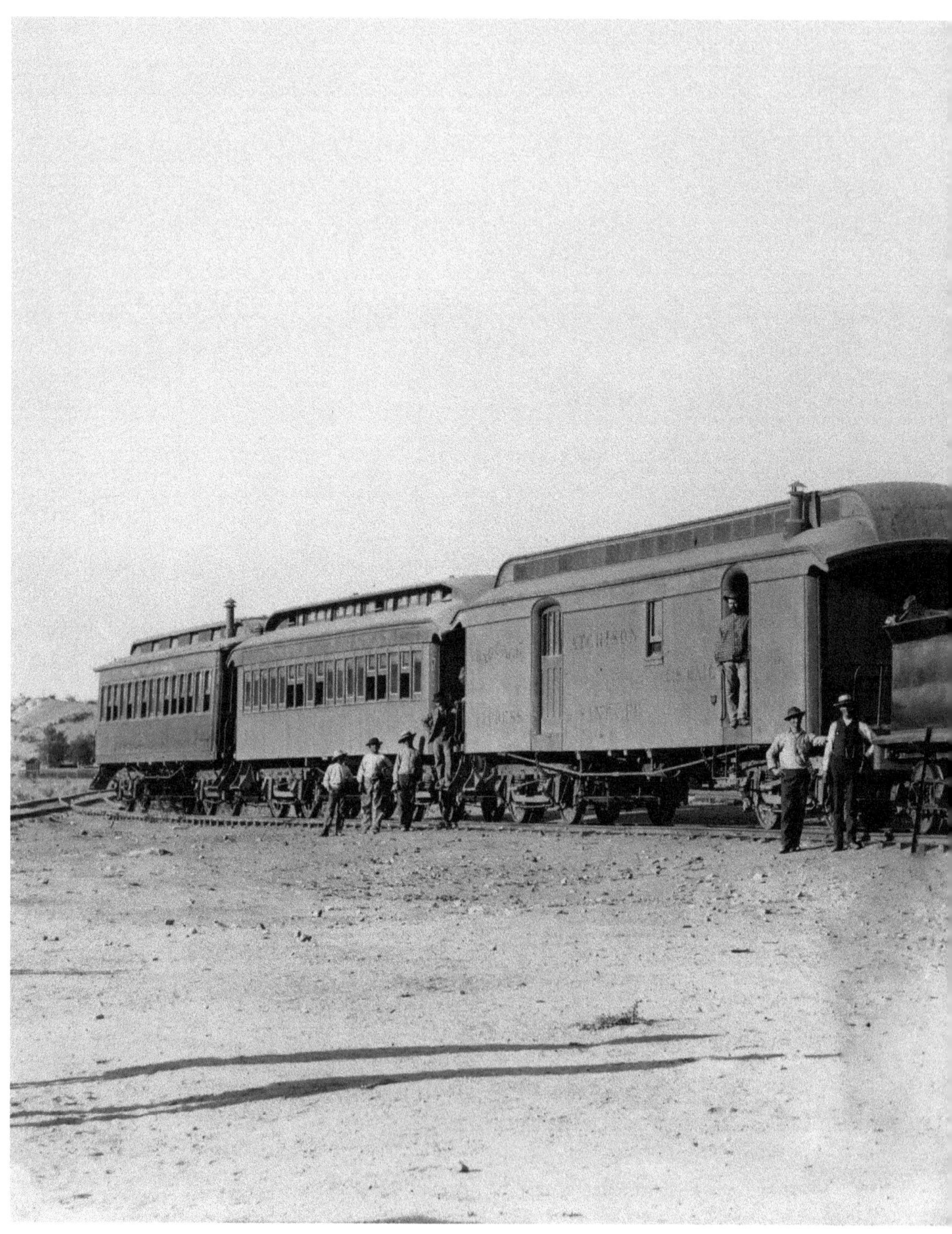

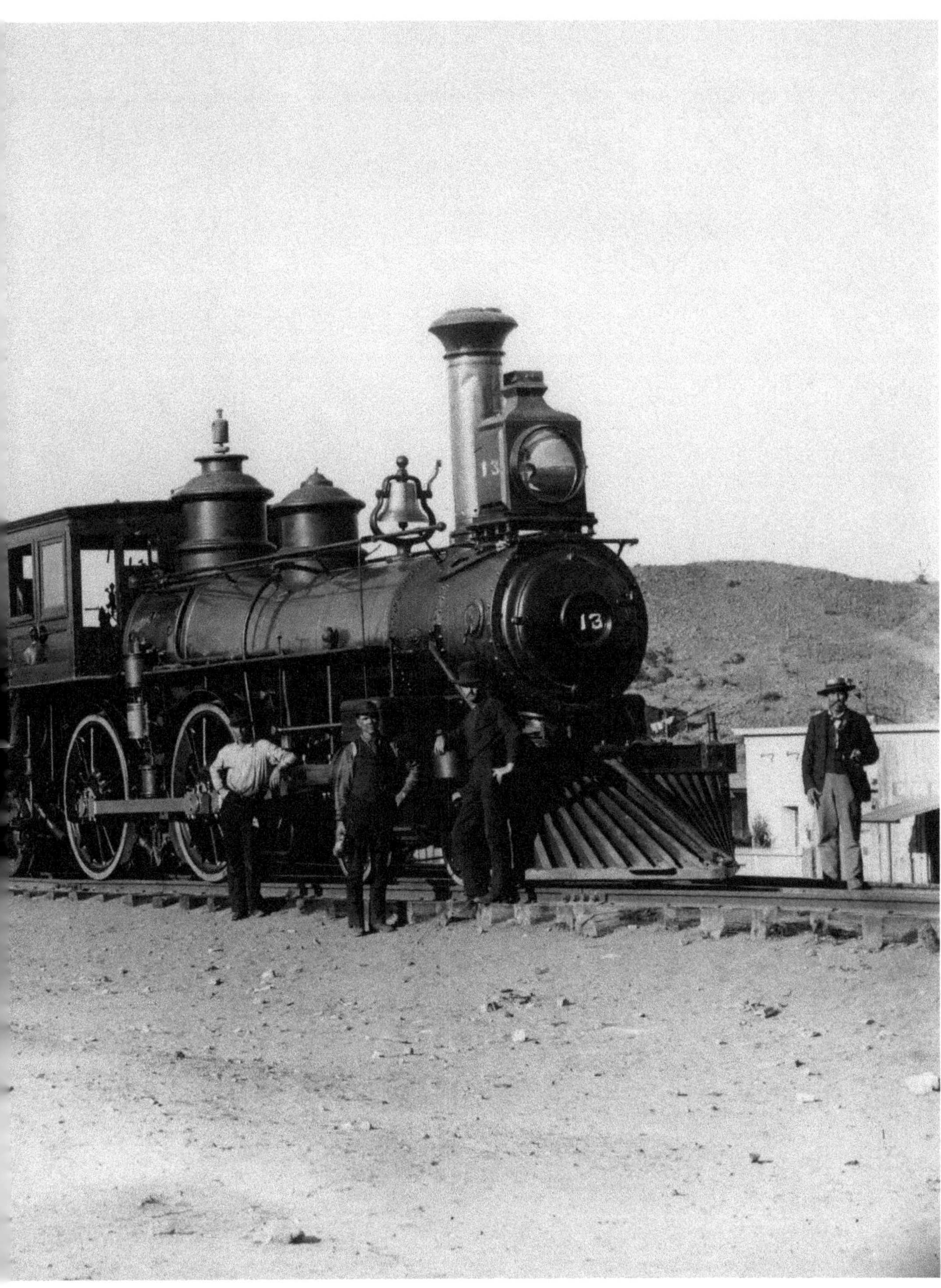

After failed attempts by others to build a railroad in Sonora, the Sonoran Railroad Company began operating in the early 1880s. Eventually running from Guaymas through Hermosillo to Nogales with a spur to Benson, the railroad provided service well into the twentieth century.

Looking west on Congress Street from Stone Avenue (ca. 1884).

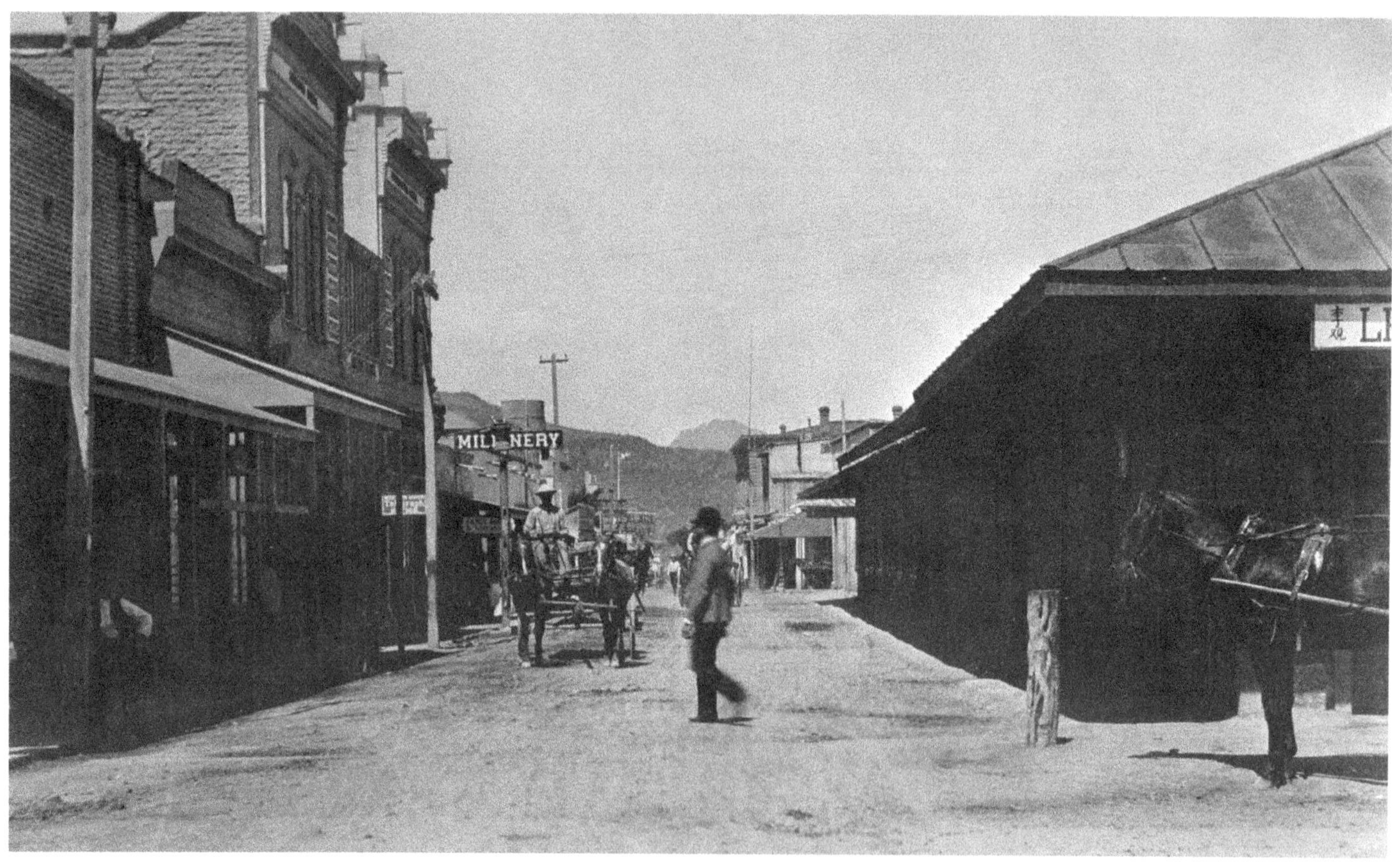

Looking east along Congress (ca. 1885). The building with the extended roof is the Congress Street School, built in 1875. The Lexington Stable is in the distance. Tucson's large single male population created a pressing need for rooming establishments like the Congress Lodging House.

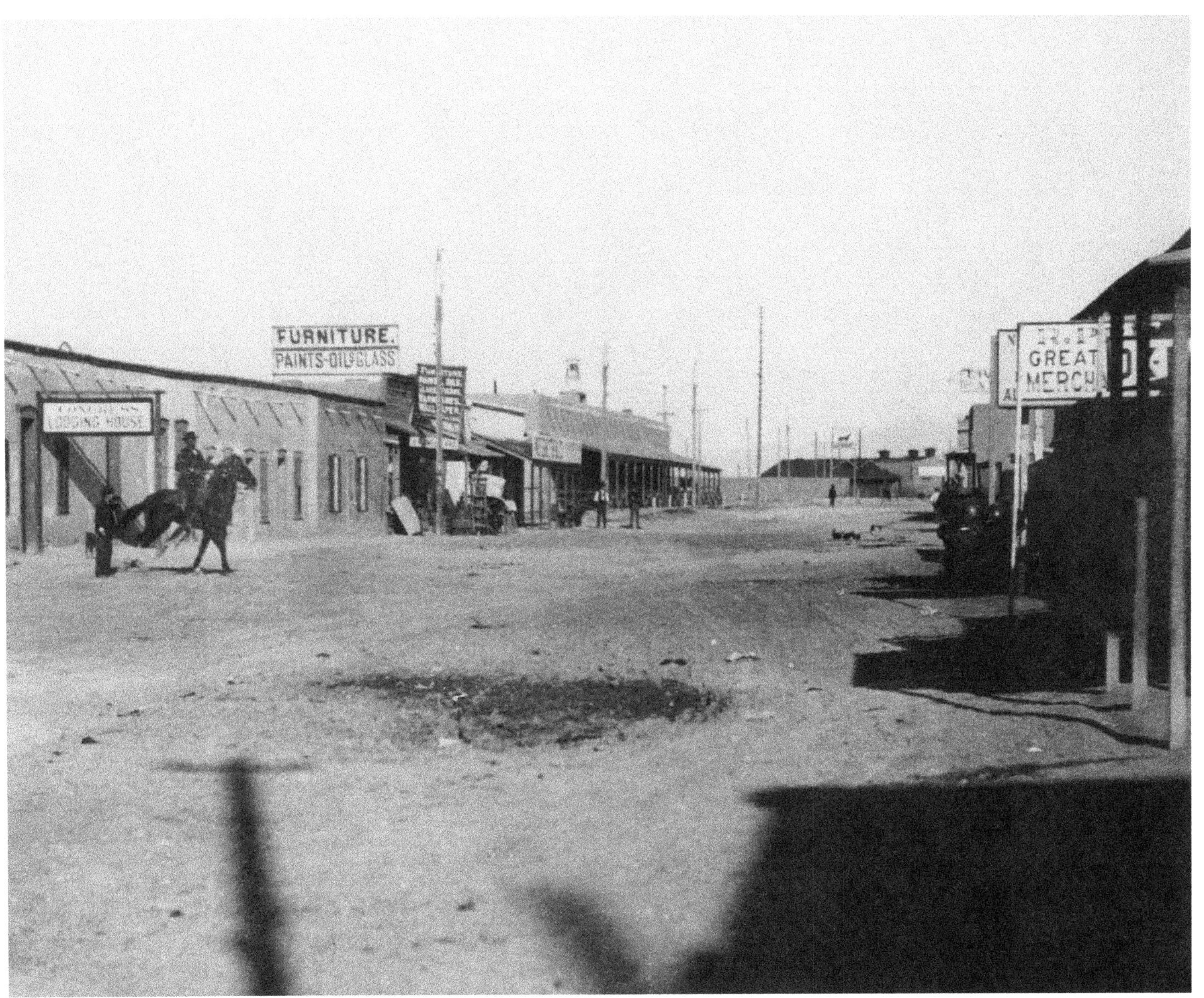

On November 8, 1887, Main Street was decorated for a parade honoring General Nelson A. Miles, commander of Arizona troops, for the surrender of Geronimo. Grateful citizens of Tucson and southern Arizona feted Miles with speeches and a ball, presenting him with a golden sword.

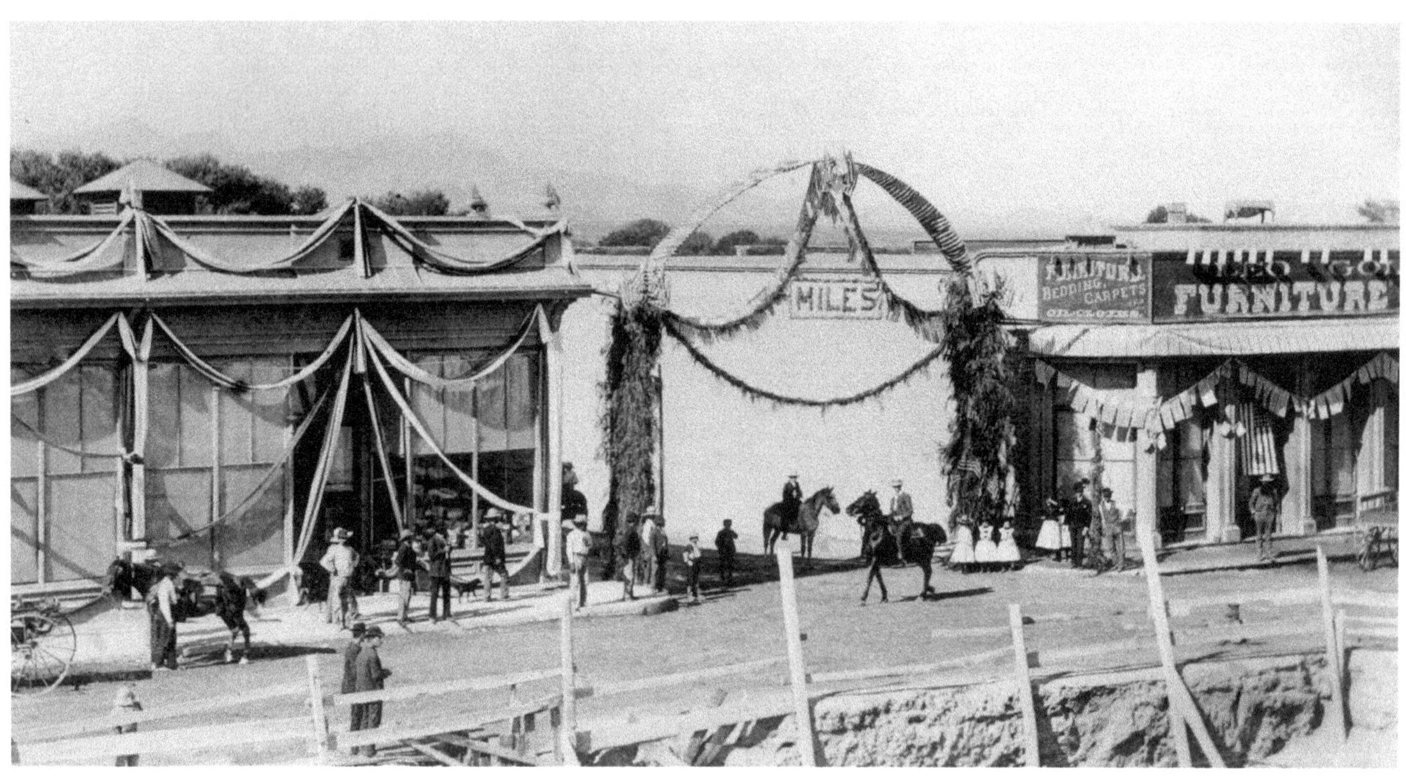

Mac Troy McCleary with Black Beauty, a trotting mare, in front of his home at 241 W. Franklin Street in 1888. In the early 1880s, McCleary was known as a gambler and ran the Shakespeare Club House. Eventually, he became a carpenter and contractor.

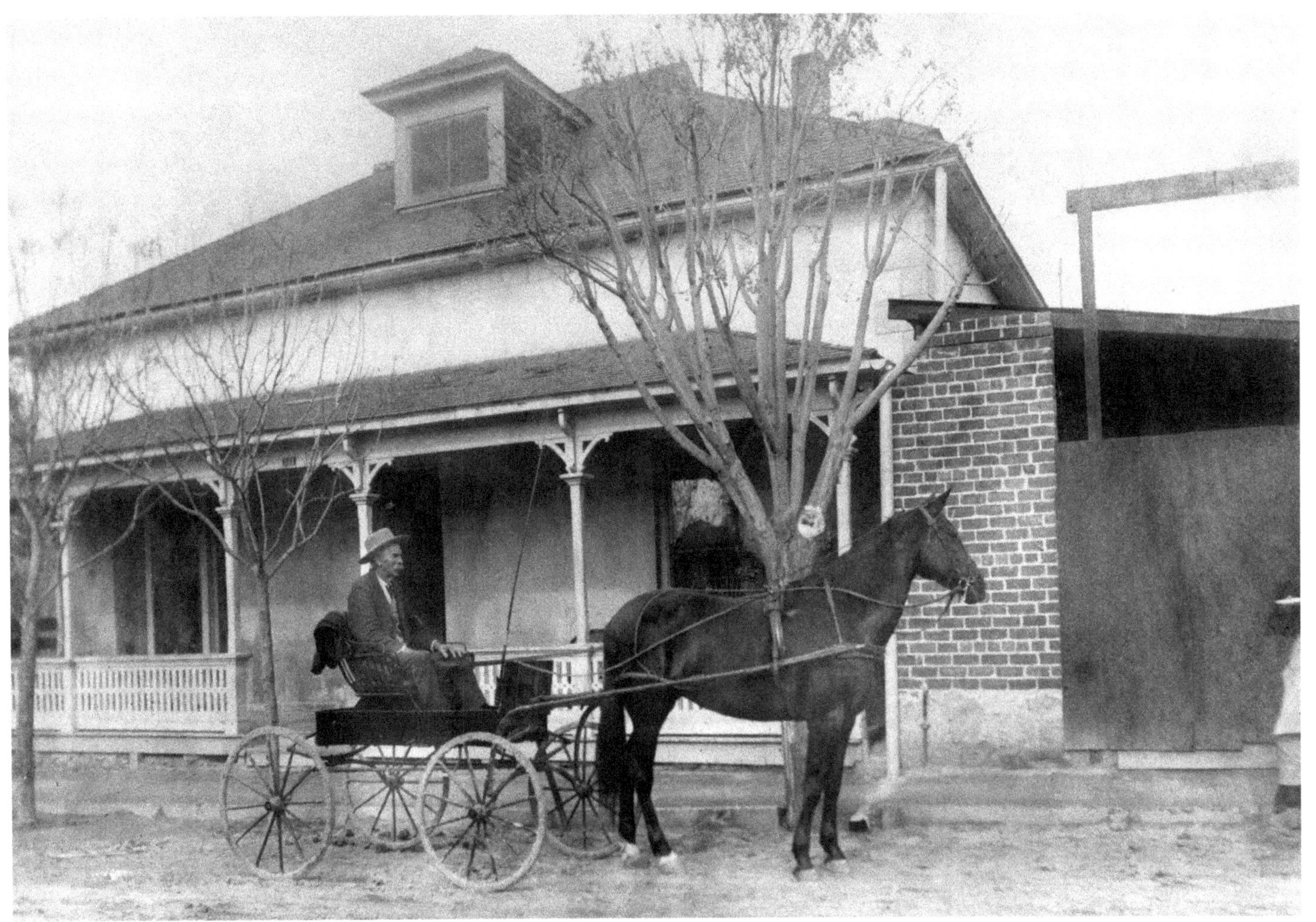

The San Xavier del Bac Mission (ca. 1890).

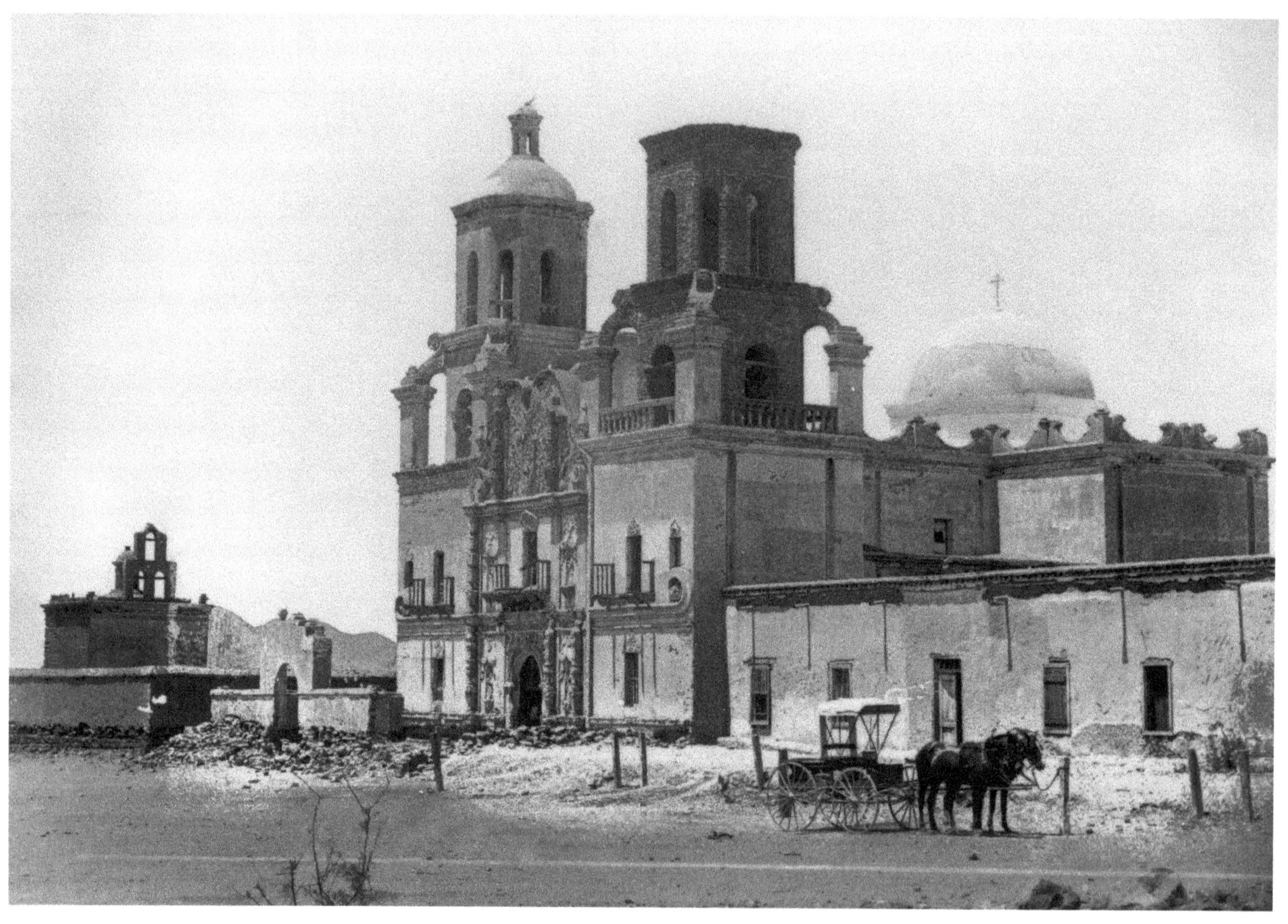

The San Agustín Cathedral and Church Plaza, perhaps just after a mass (ca. 1890).

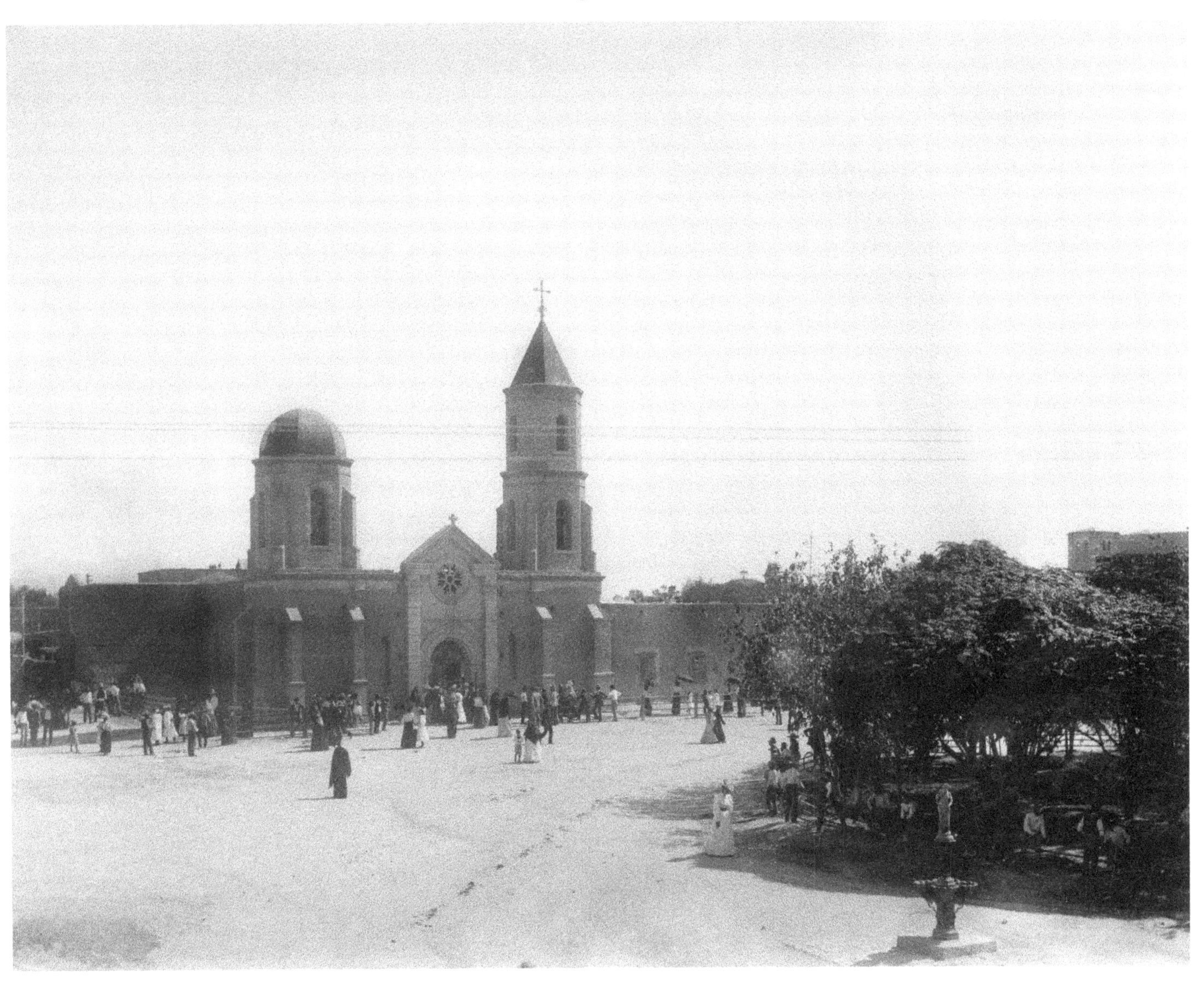

The Southern Pacific Railroad Employees Reading Room on N. Third Avenue, just east of the SP Depot around 1890. Many railroad workers built houses in the vicinity.

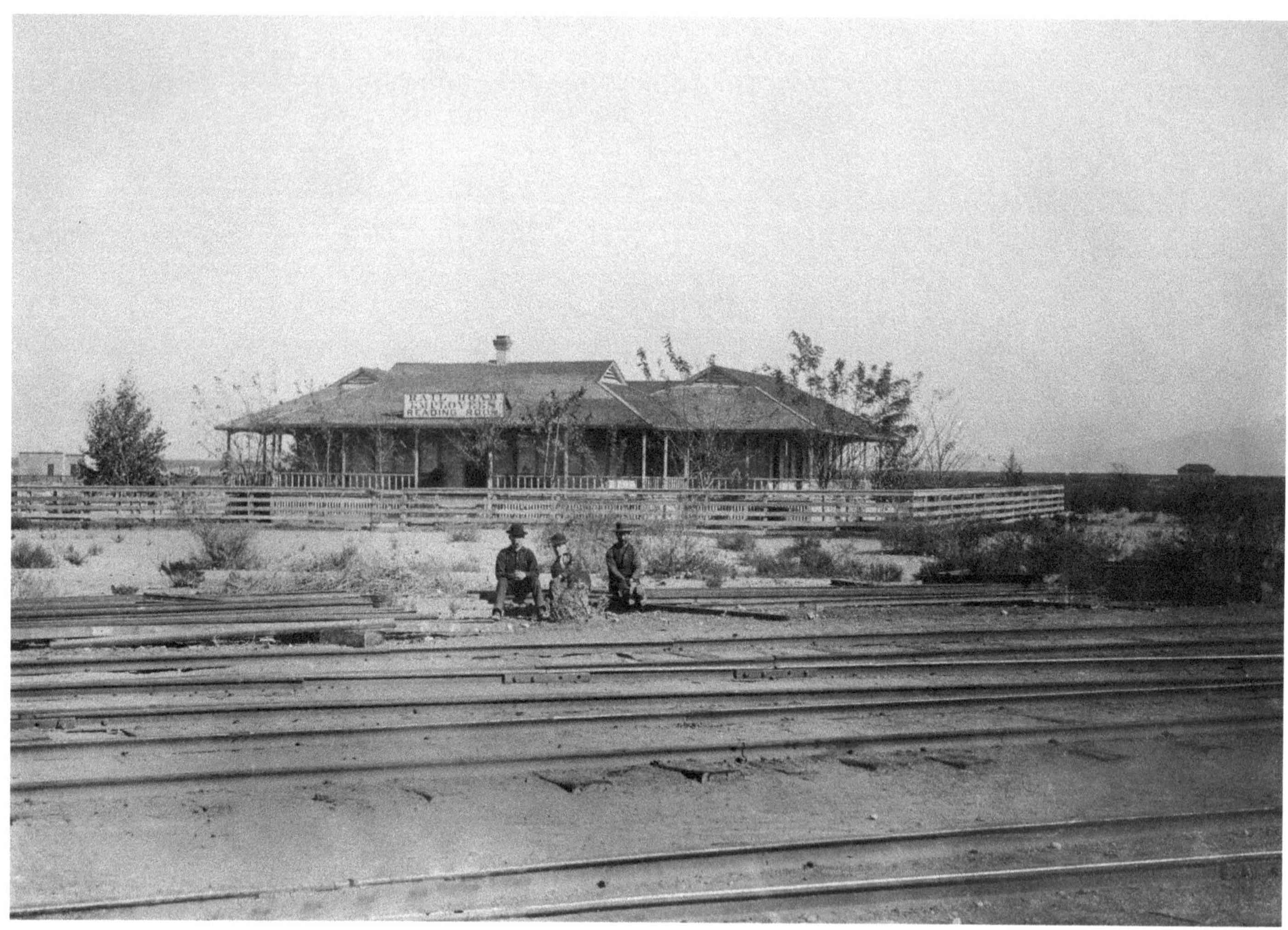

Federico Ronstadt (center, in dark coat) organized the Club Filarmónico Tucsonense in 1889. The Club began a series of weekly outdoor Sunday concerts in 1890 and made a two-week tour of southern California to great acclaim in August 1896. The group disbanded in 1898.

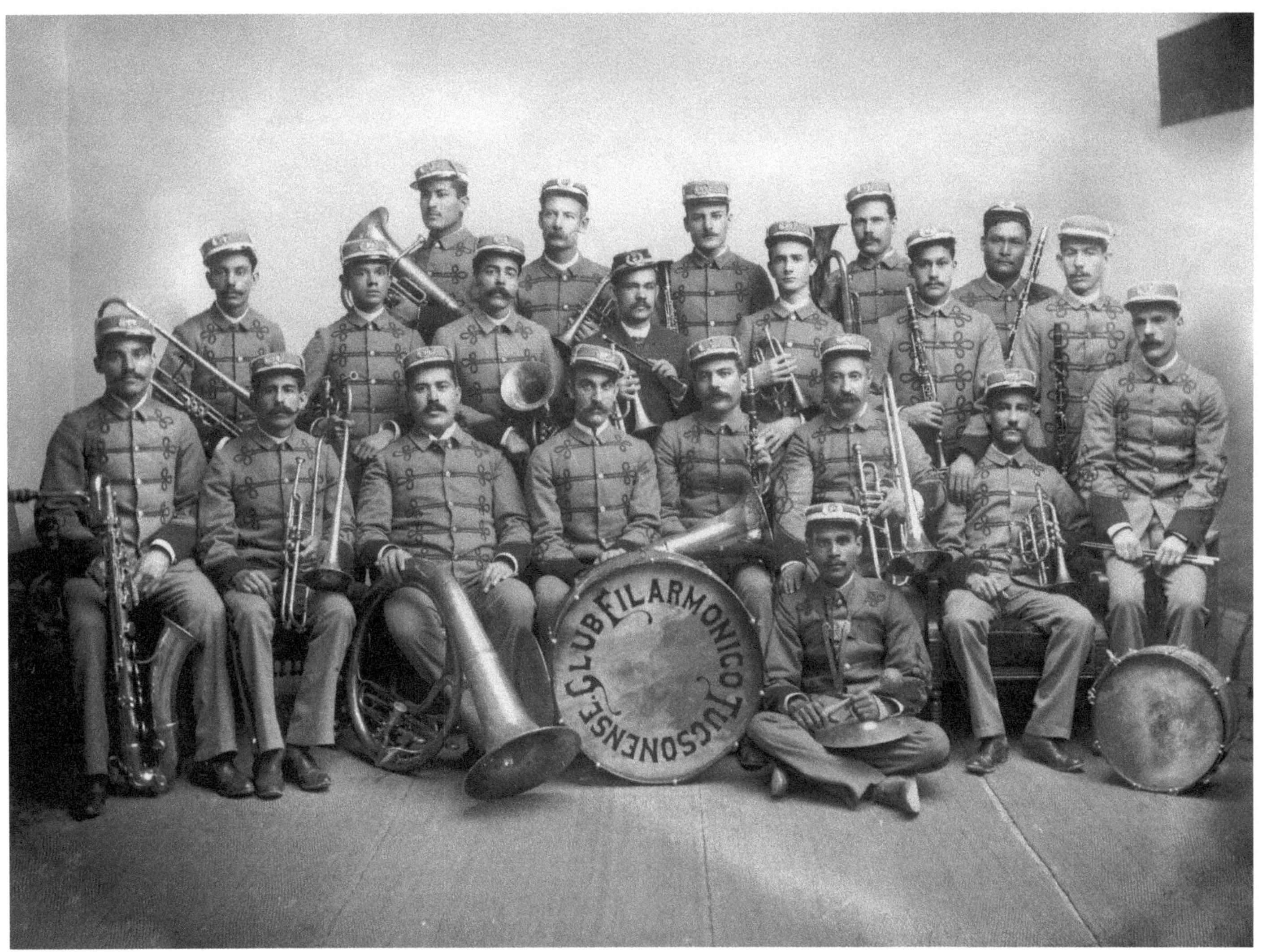

As Tucson began to expand beyond the downtown area, architectural styles began to change, as seen in this neighborhood, looking to the northwest (ca. 1890).

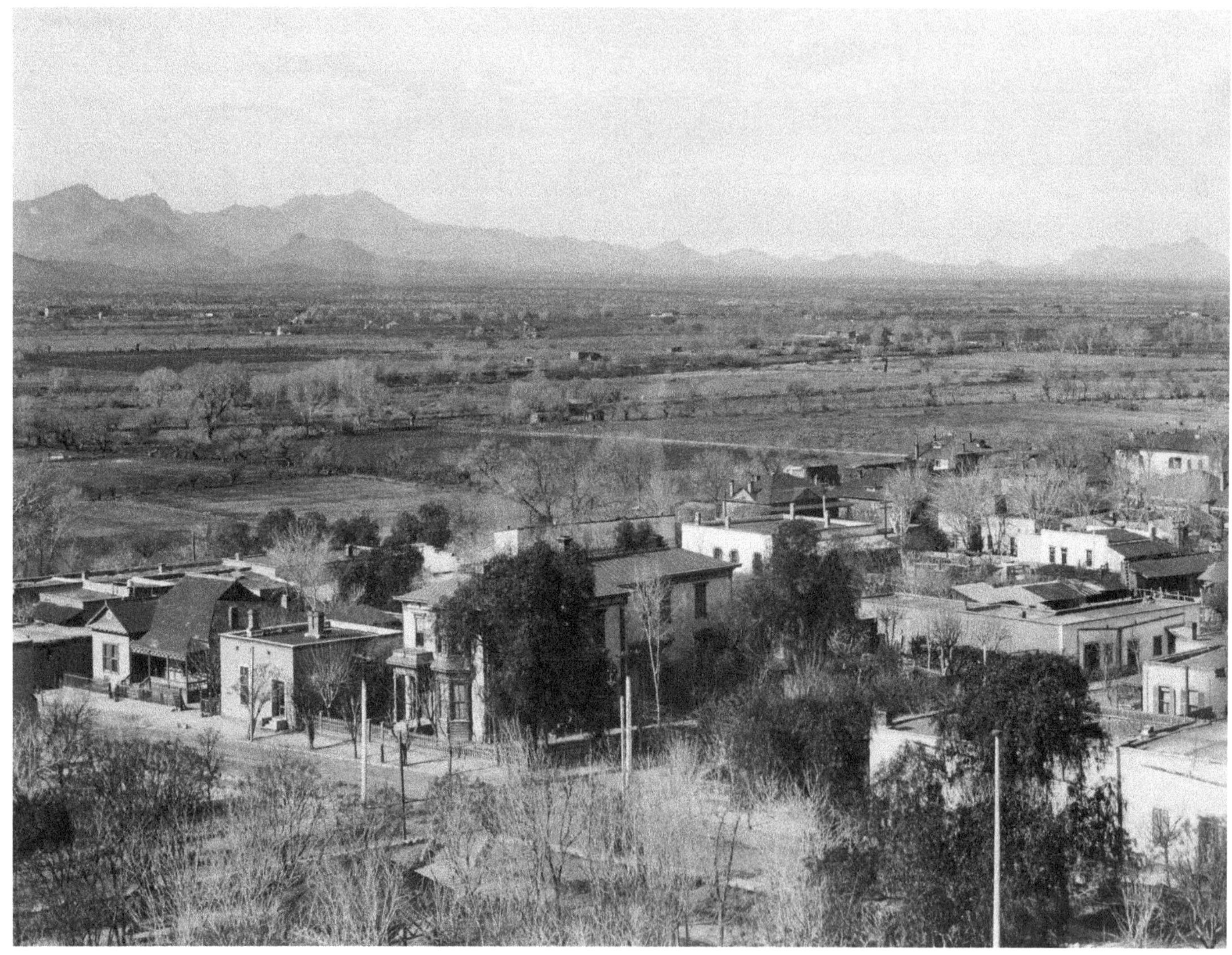

Looking across the rooftops north of East Congress Street at North Stone Avenue (ca. 1893).

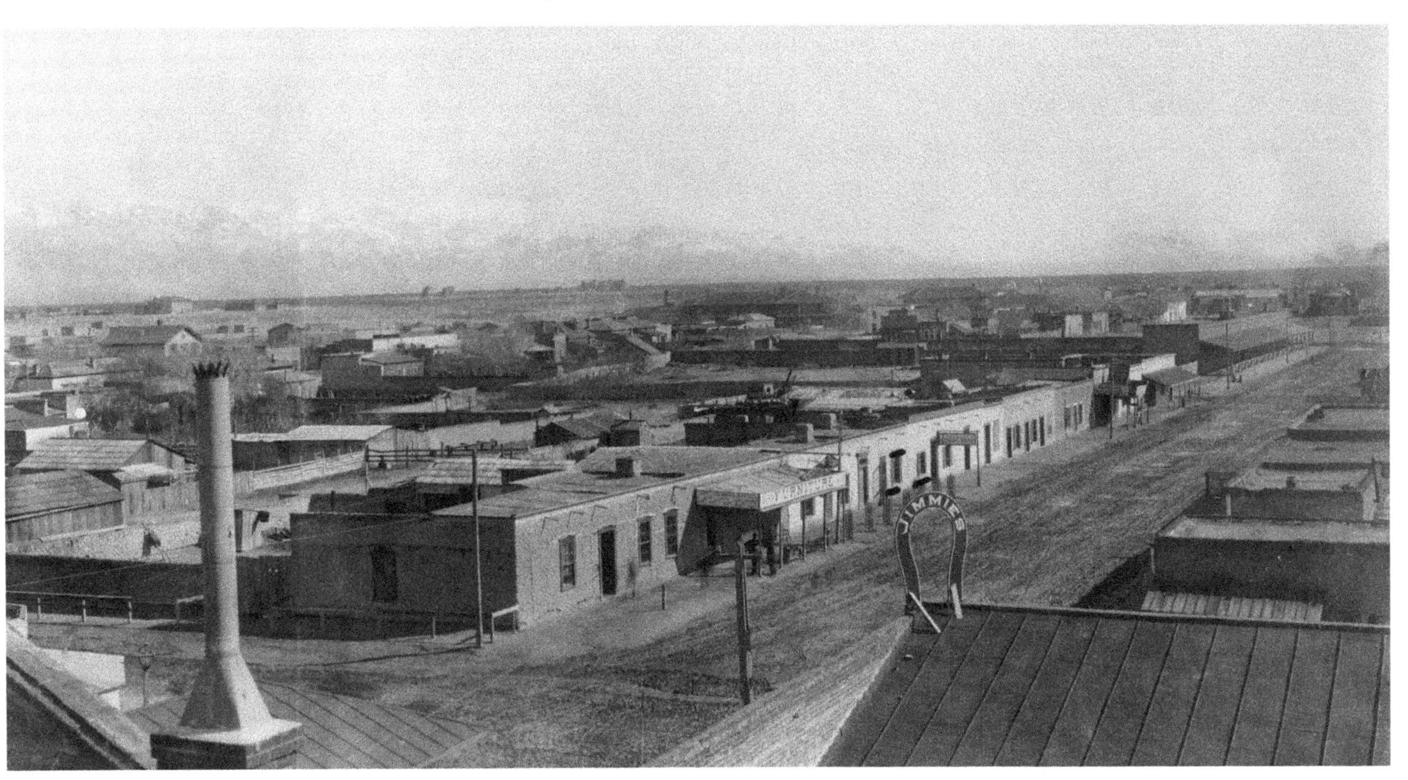

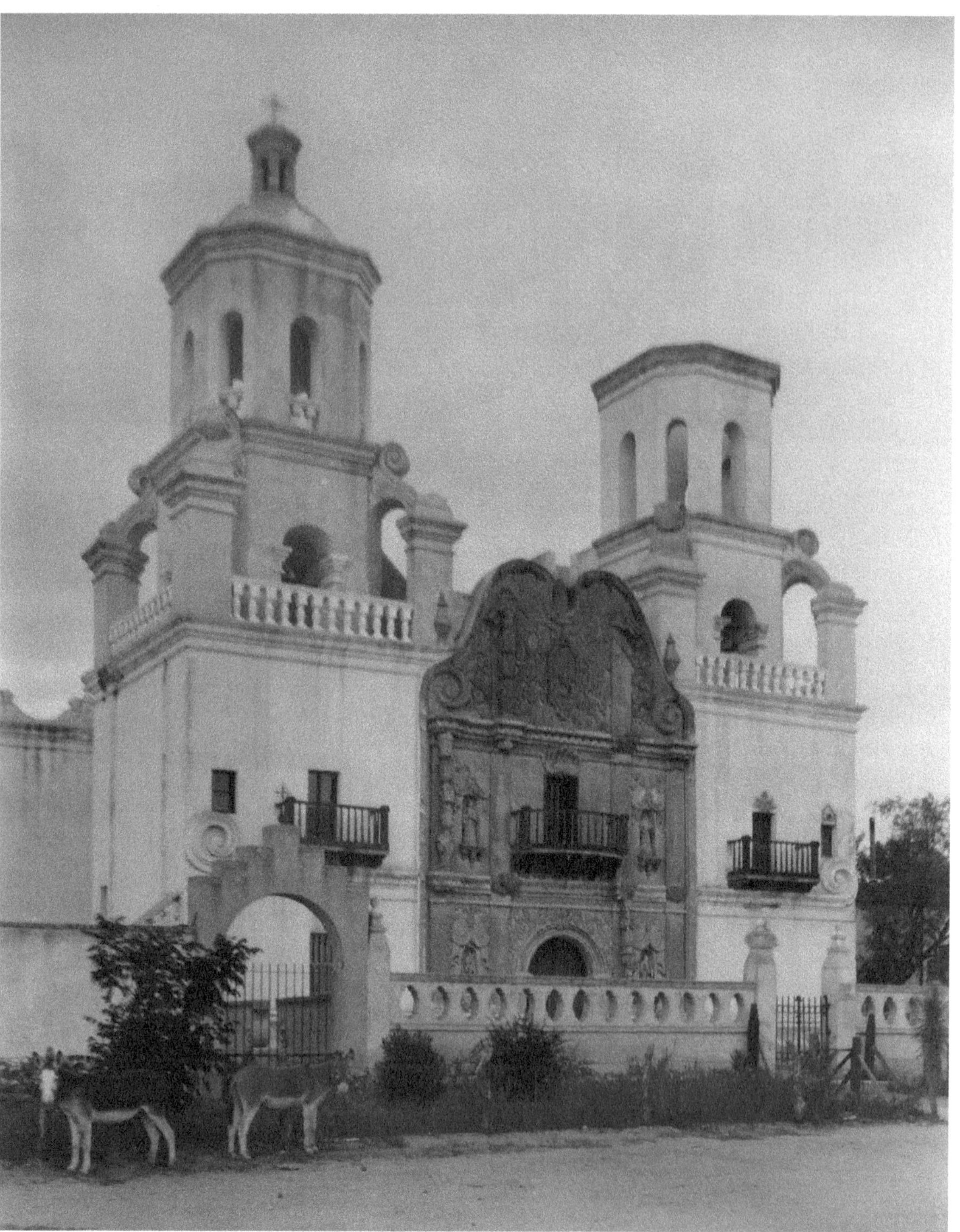

The front of San Xavier del Bac.

A view of the interior of San Xavier del Bac.

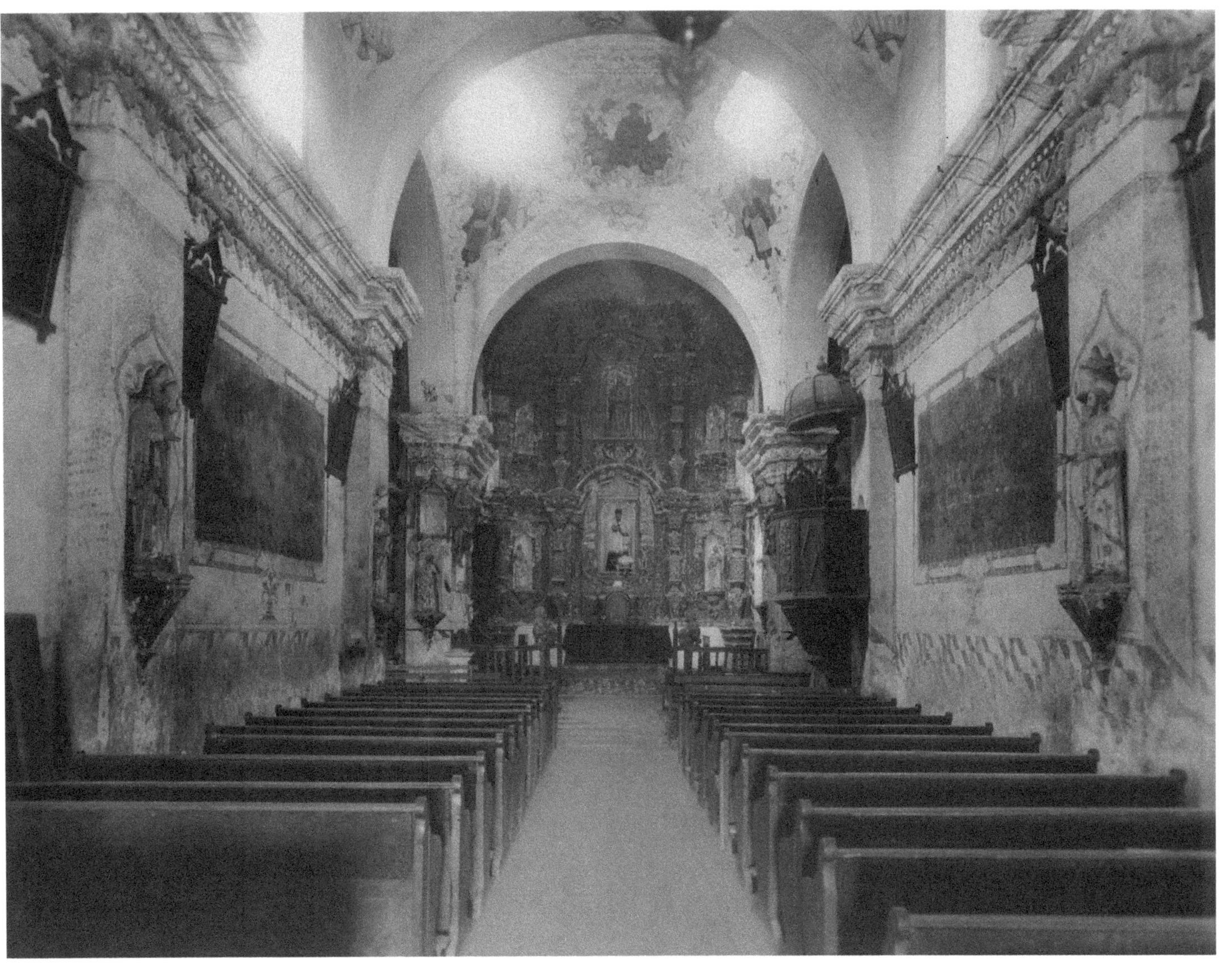

Looking across the rooftops to the southeast. The two-story building in the center background is a public school. The large open area is the Military Plaza where Camp Lowell was once located.

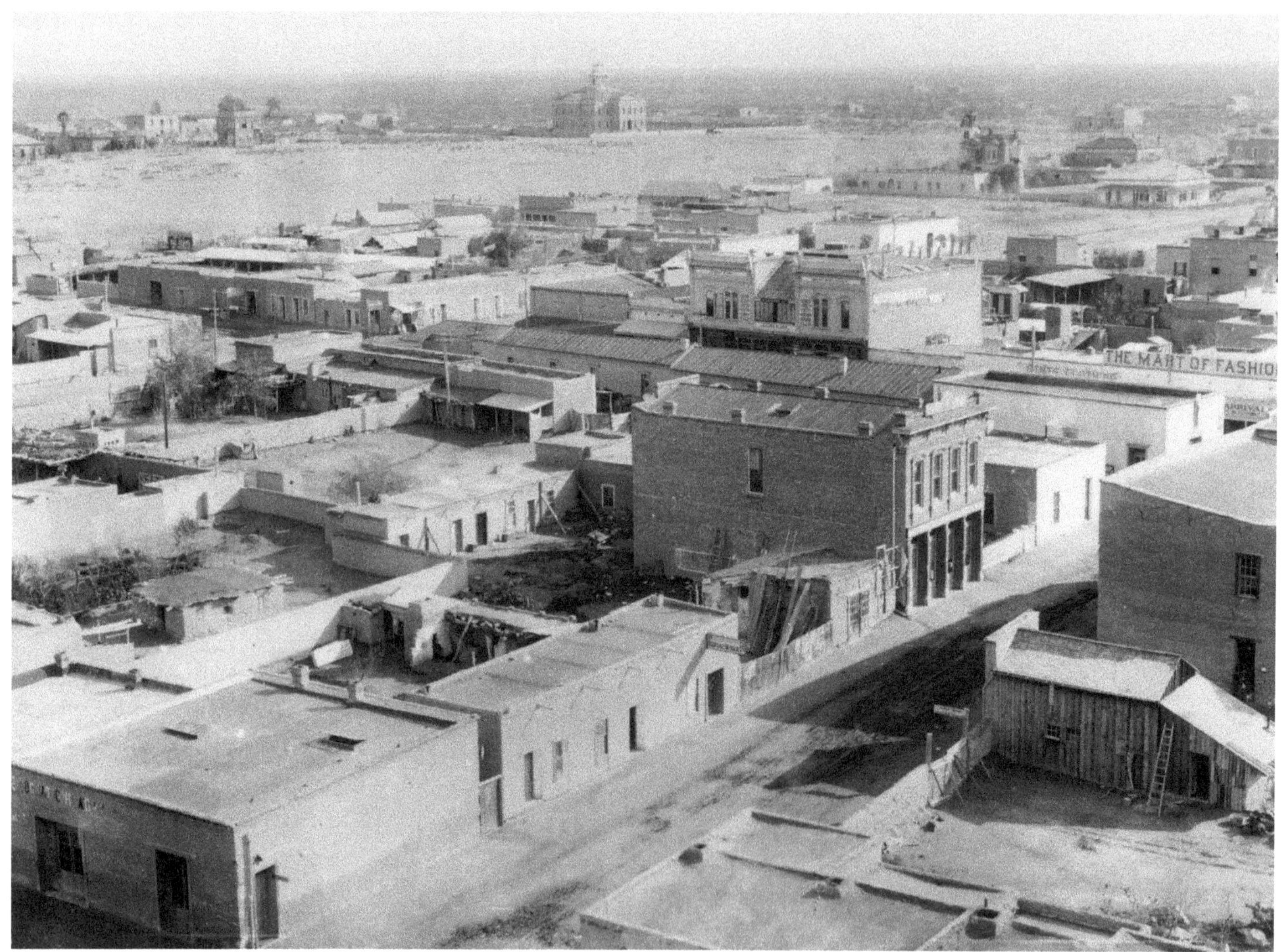

The Hose Company of the Tucson Volunteer Fire Department at a Fourth of July celebration in 1898.

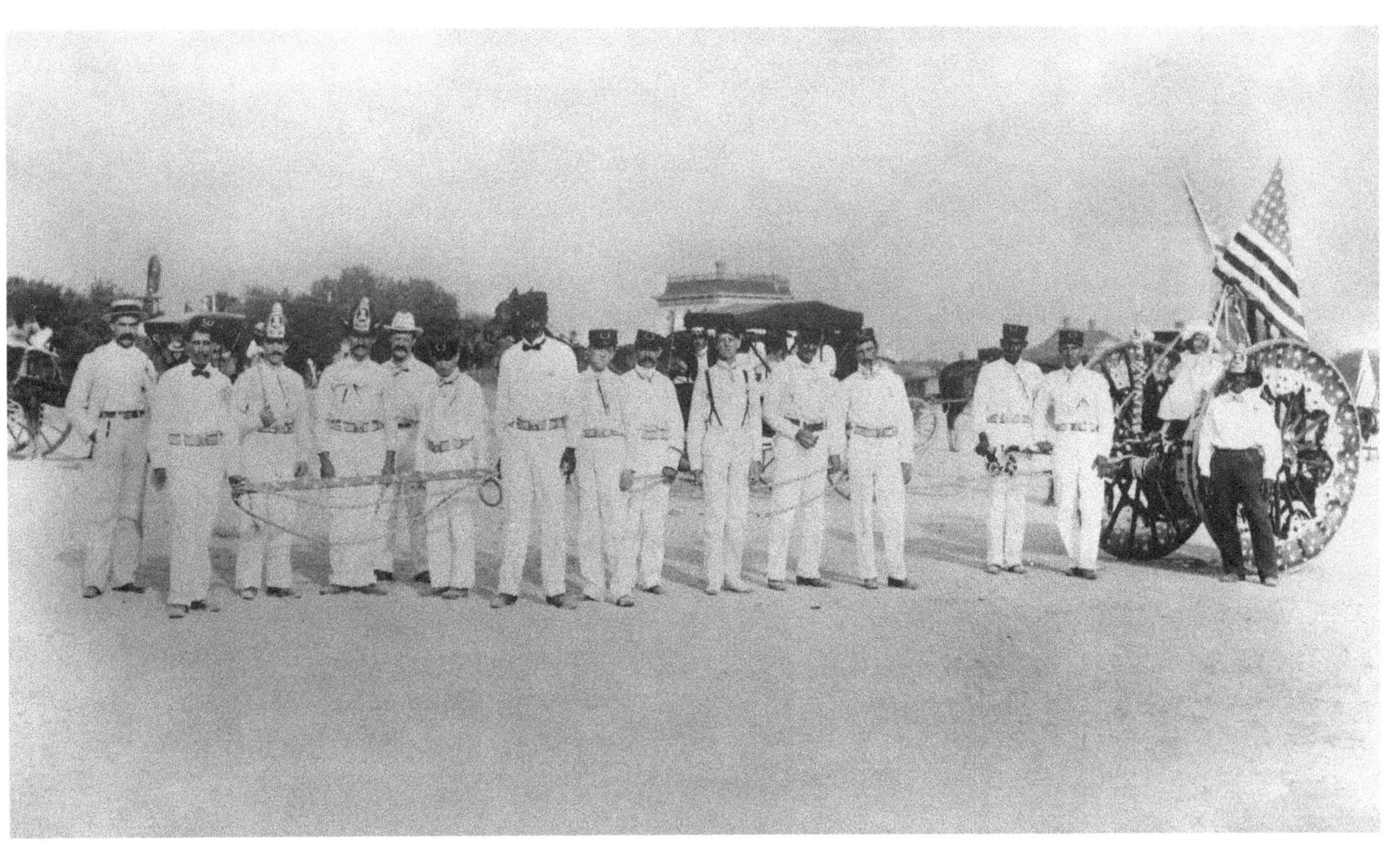

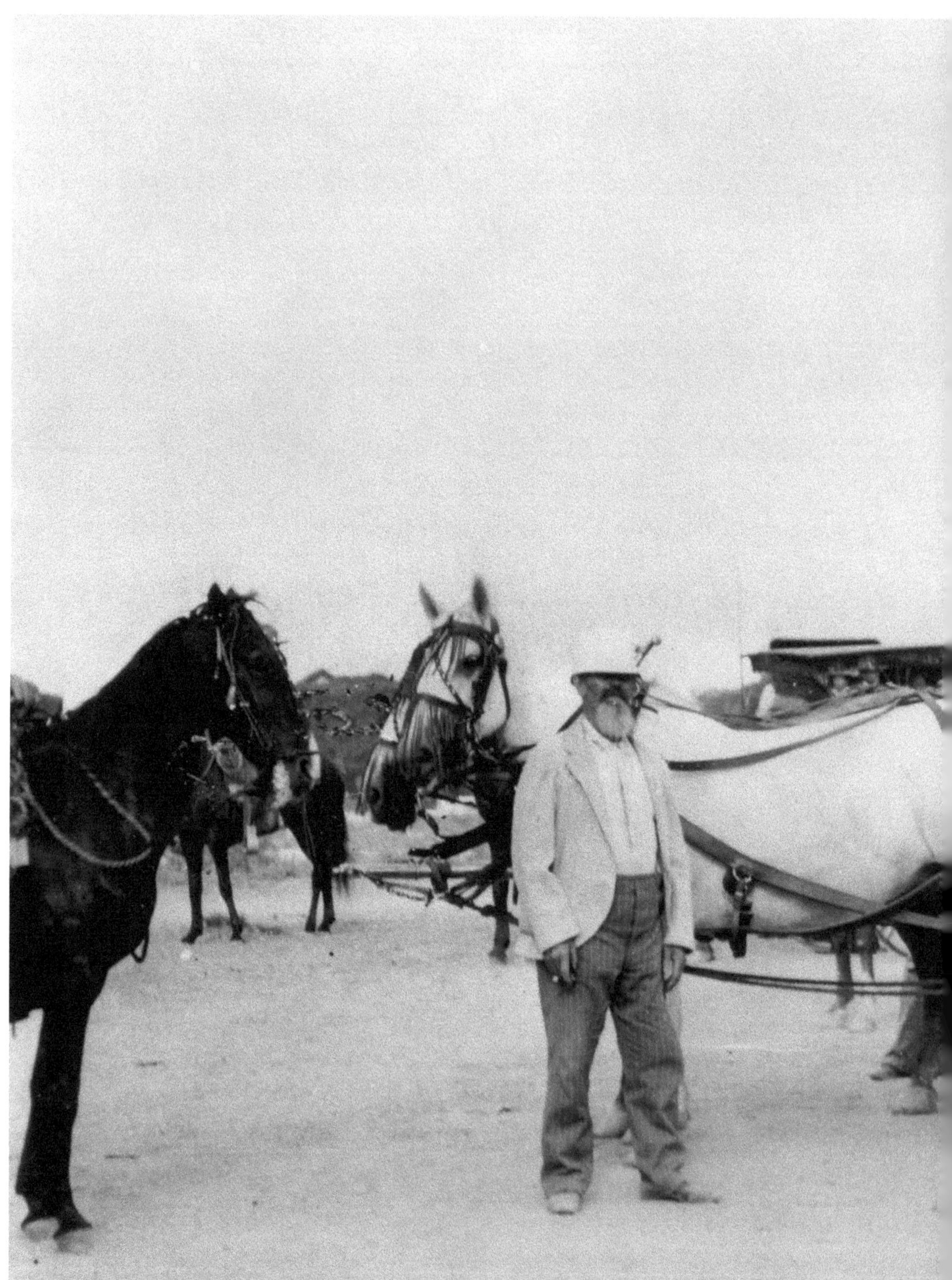

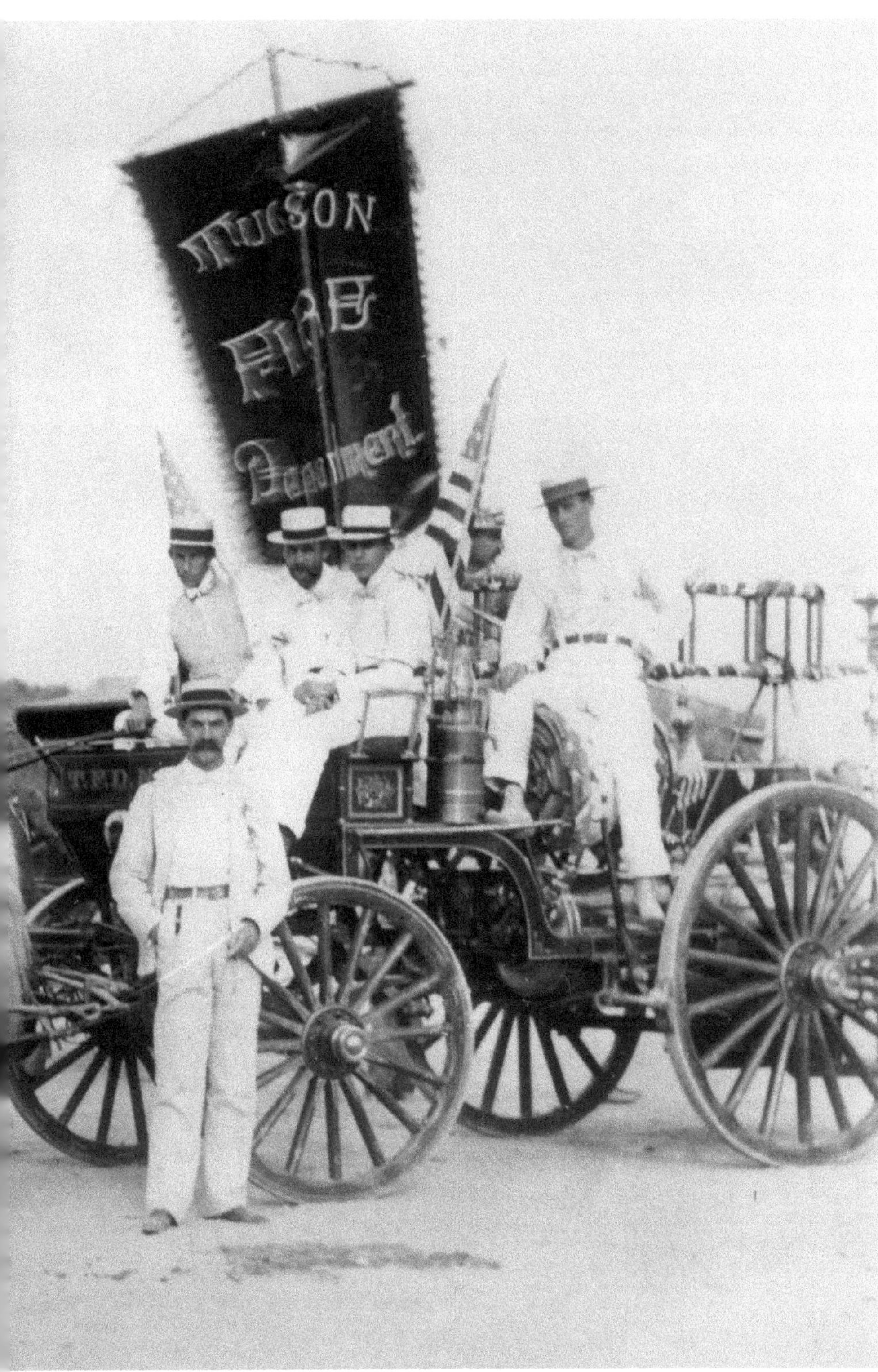

Chemical Wagon #1 of the Tucson Volunteer Fire Department, July 4, 1898.

In October 1899, Andrew Carnegie gave Tucson a $25,000 grant to build a public library, as he did for many communities. The Carnegie Public Library building still stands today at 200 S. Sixth Avenue.

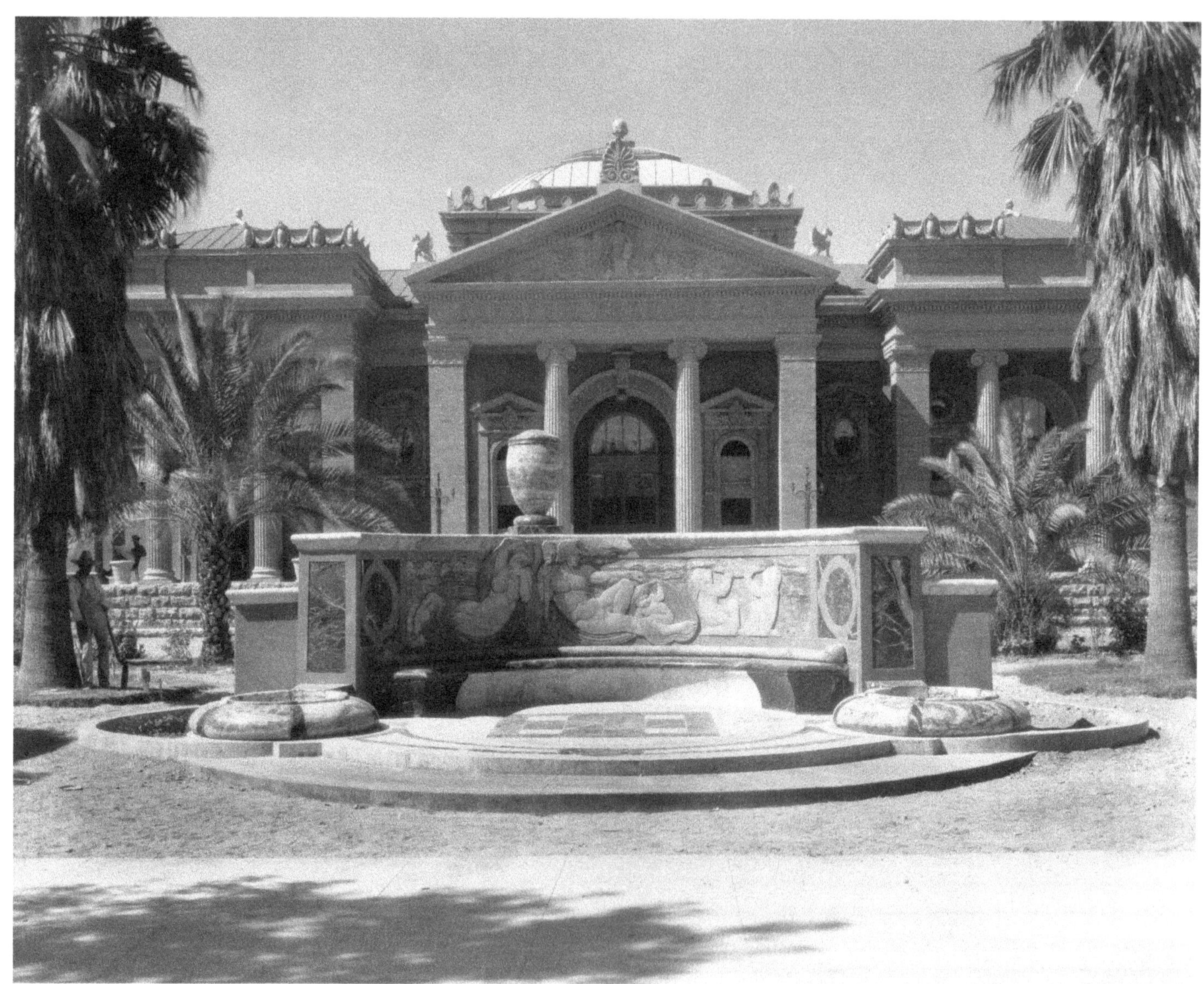

From Territory to Statehood

(1900–1919)

With the new century, Tucson began to shed its frontier trappings in earnest as civic leaders successfully pressed reforms. Downtown urban renewal began when a pie-shaped, three-block section called the Wedge was removed in 1902, making Congress Street wider to accommodate more traffic. Many historic adobe buildings were lost in the process, accelerating the change in Tucson's architectural appearance. Beginning in 1905, increasingly stringent restrictions closed down many of the saloons and gambling halls that seemed endemic to downtown. Controlling prostitution was not as easy; no laws attempting to eliminate it were passed until 1917.

The railroad continued bringing people from around the country. Businesses sprang up to provide services for new residents and for the increasing numbers of tourists. The health benefits of Arizona's warm, dry climate attracted those with tuberculosis; many sanatoriums were built in and around Tucson. The number of cultural and civic organizations grew and new theaters and large halls were built to present vaudeville shows, concerts, and movies. Trolleys with occasionally obstinate mules gave way to electric streetcars in 1906. Evaporative cooling devices began to appear commercially around 1910. The first automobiles came to Tucson in 1900, creating far more dust than wagons had. Streets were sprinkled with water in an attempt to suppress this dust, but oiling soon replaced water sprinkling. In 1911, some downtown streets were macadamized. Paving with asphalt began in 1913.

Arizona was granted statehood on February 2, 1912. Woman's suffrage was added to the State Constitution in 1912 and a Prohibition amendment in 1914. Saloons made the conversion to restaurants or pool halls, many with back rooms for the illicit sale of alcohol. The El Paso and Southwestern Railroad built Tucson's second depot on the west side of town in 1912.

During the Mexican Revolution, 1910–1920, refugees and rebels came to the city for shelter and supplies. Tucson mobilized during World War I, holding Liberty Bond rallies and other events. The Spanish influenza pandemic struck during October–November 1918. With the end of the war, copper mines were suddenly idle, a drought hurt cattle and crops, and Tucson's commerce-based economy suffered from post-war shortages of food and gasoline, but the Union Fiber Company announced its intention to build a factory in Tucson in 1919, one of the few industrial concerns to do so.

These north-facing businesses on Congress Street used canvas tarps both for advertising and to provide relief from the desert's harsh summer sun (ca. 1900).

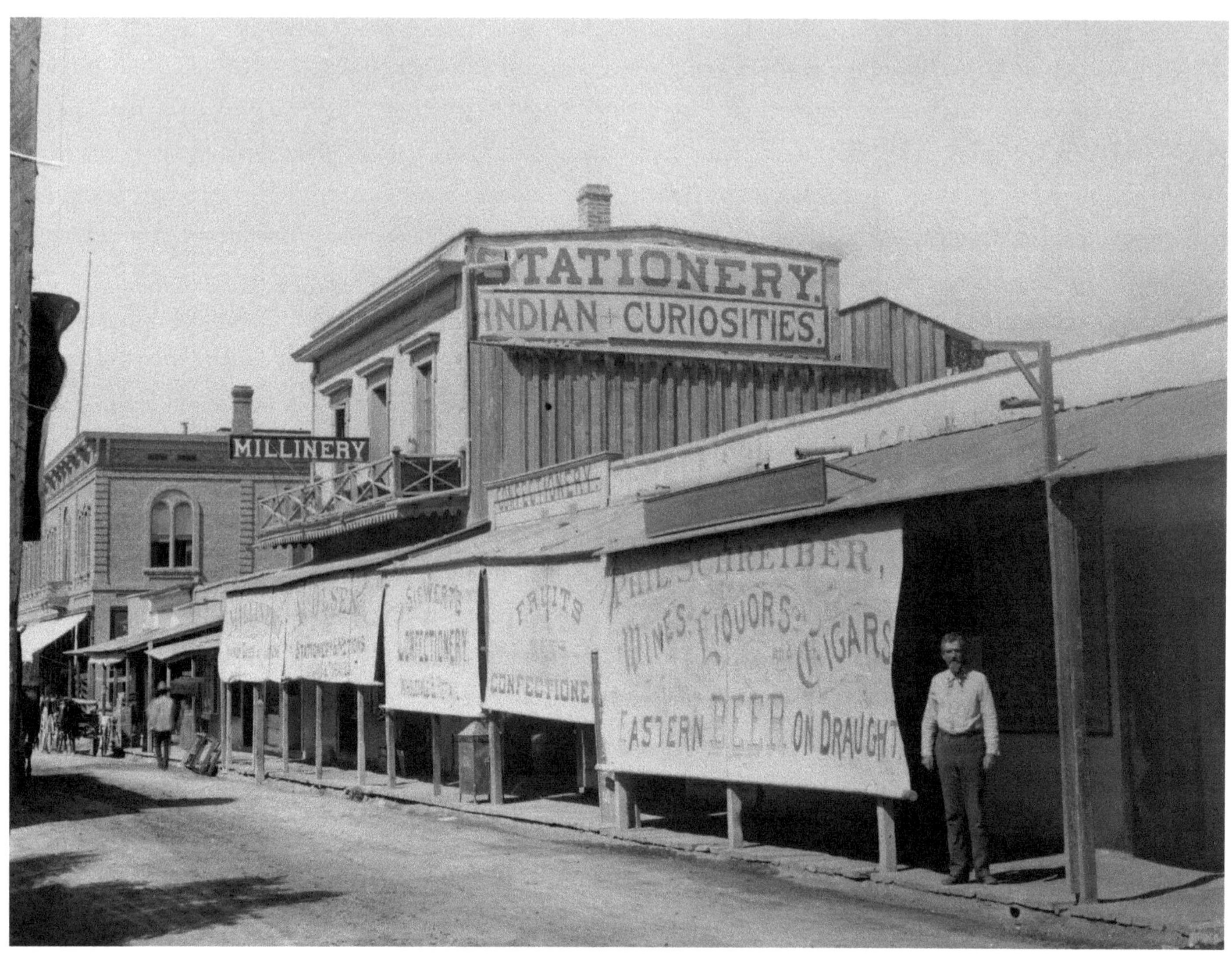

Southern Pacific Railroad employees decorated a work shed for the Fourth of July.

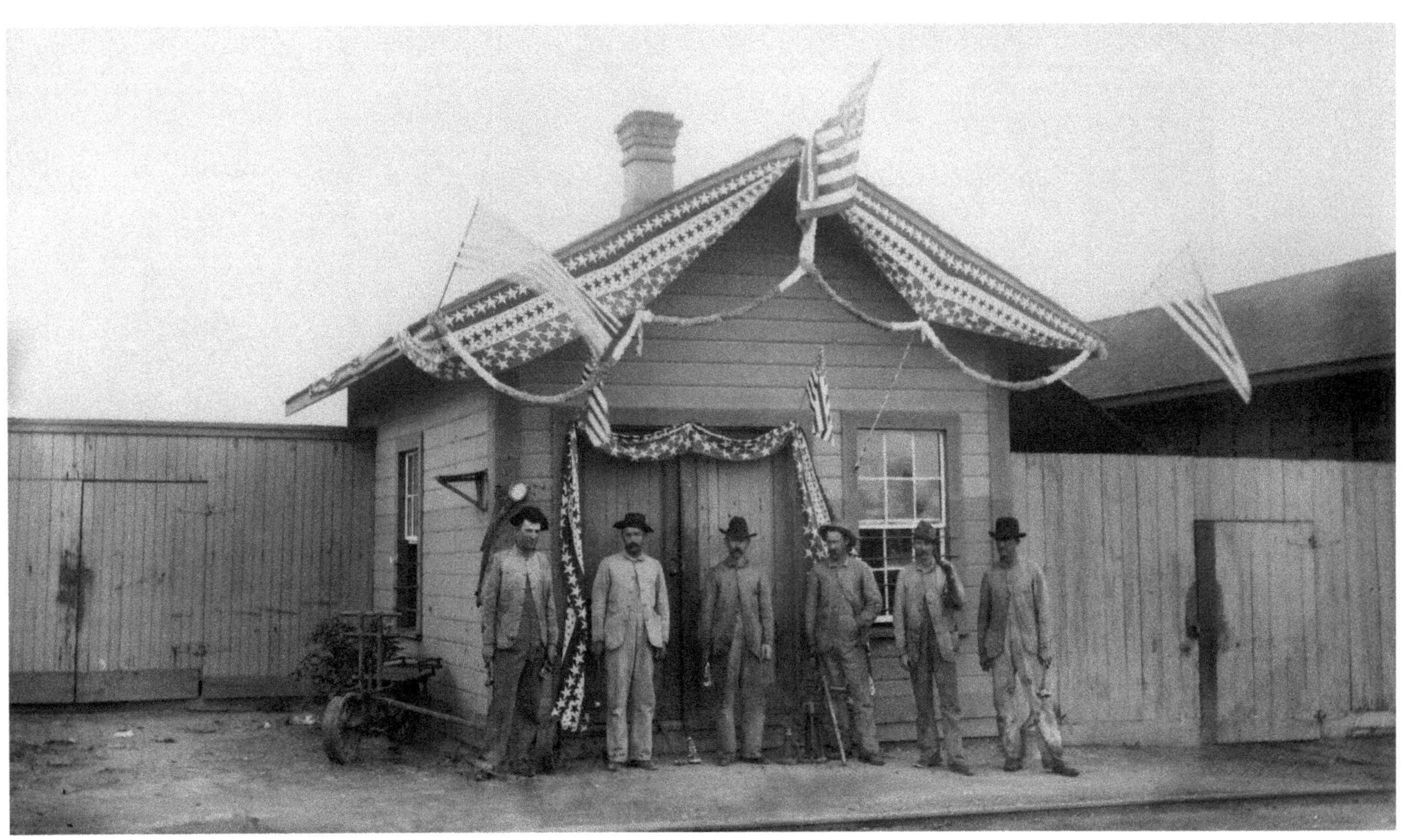

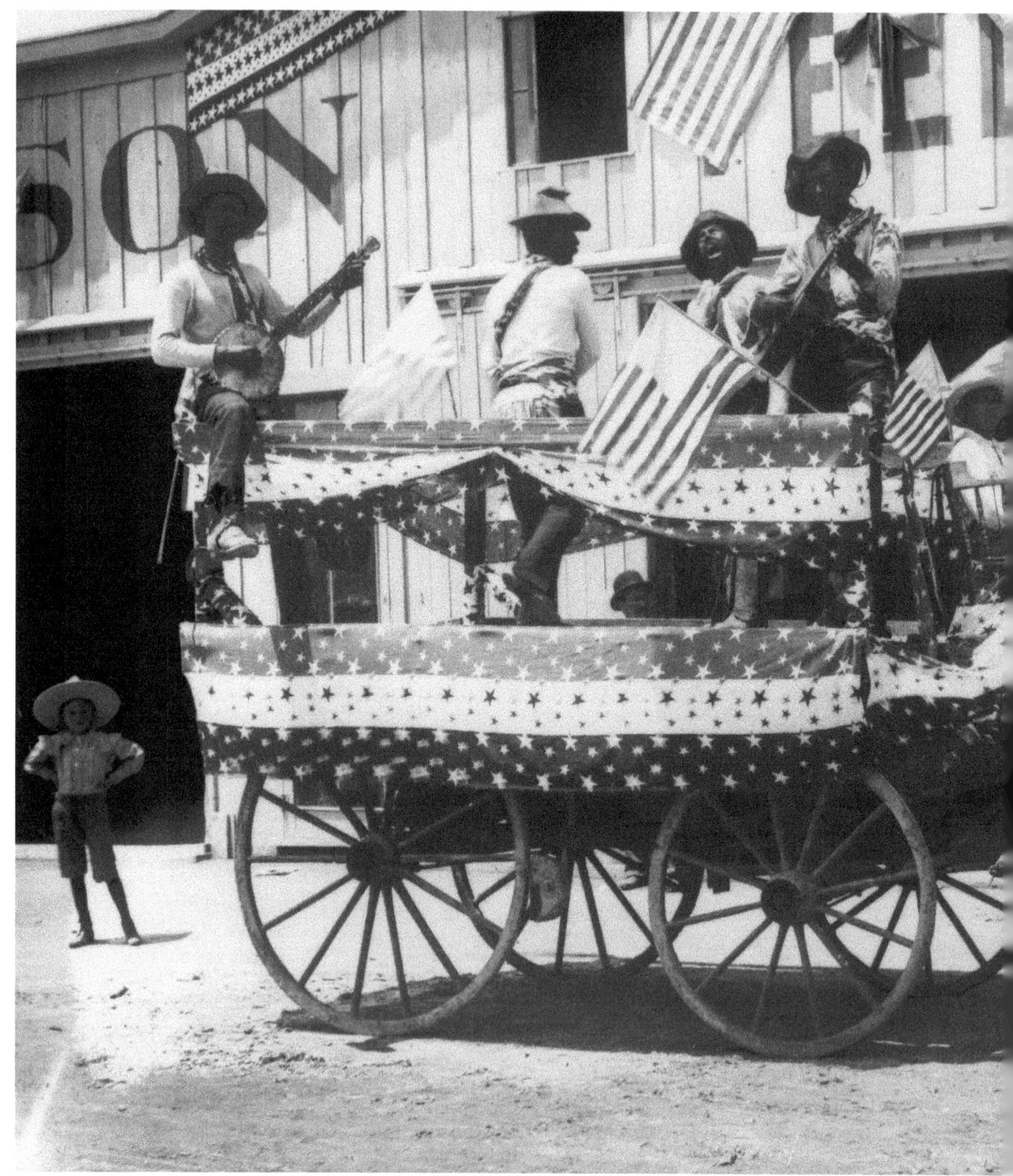

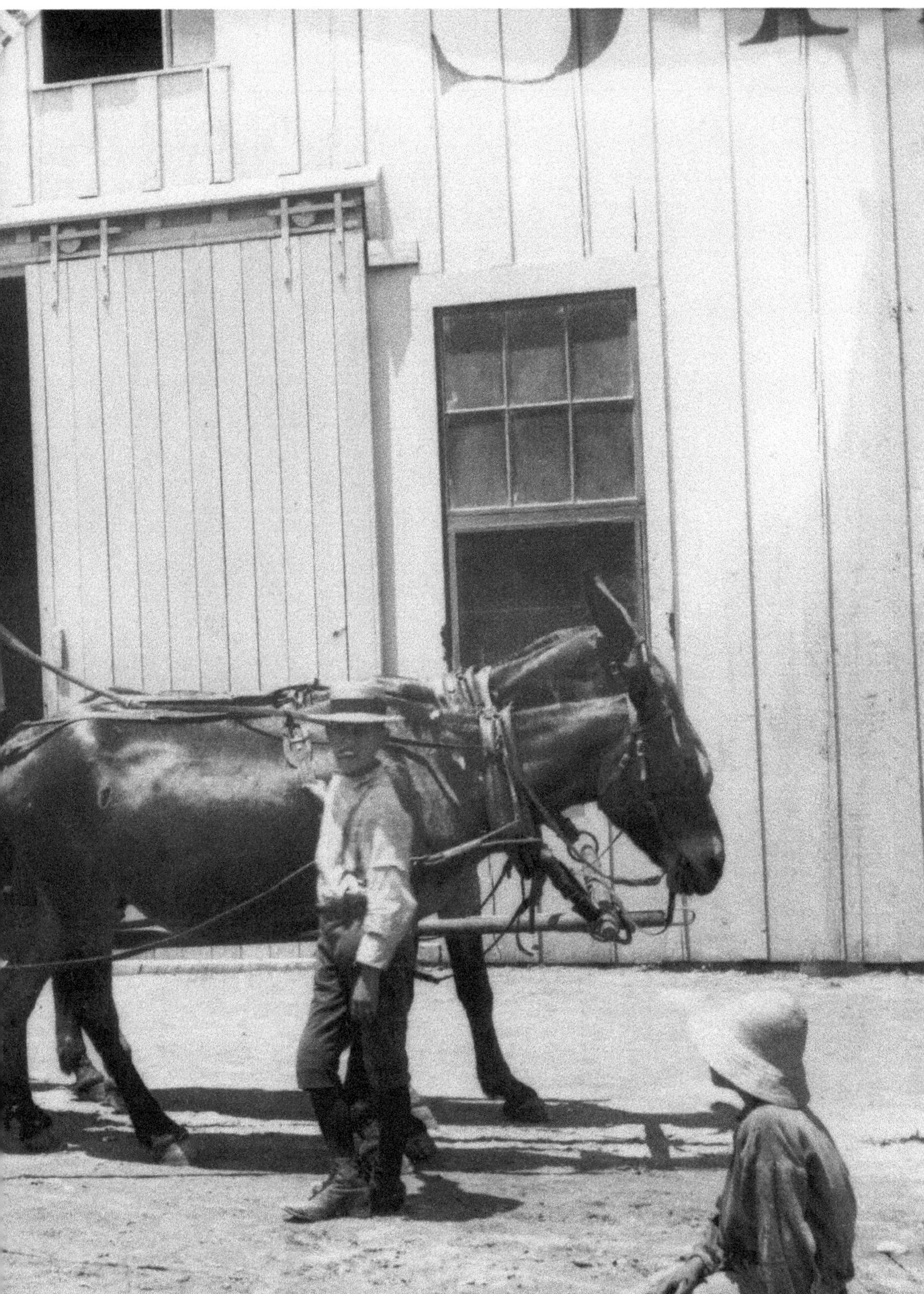

A musical Fourth of July float paused in front of the Tucson Stables, owned by John Barkley (ca. 1900).

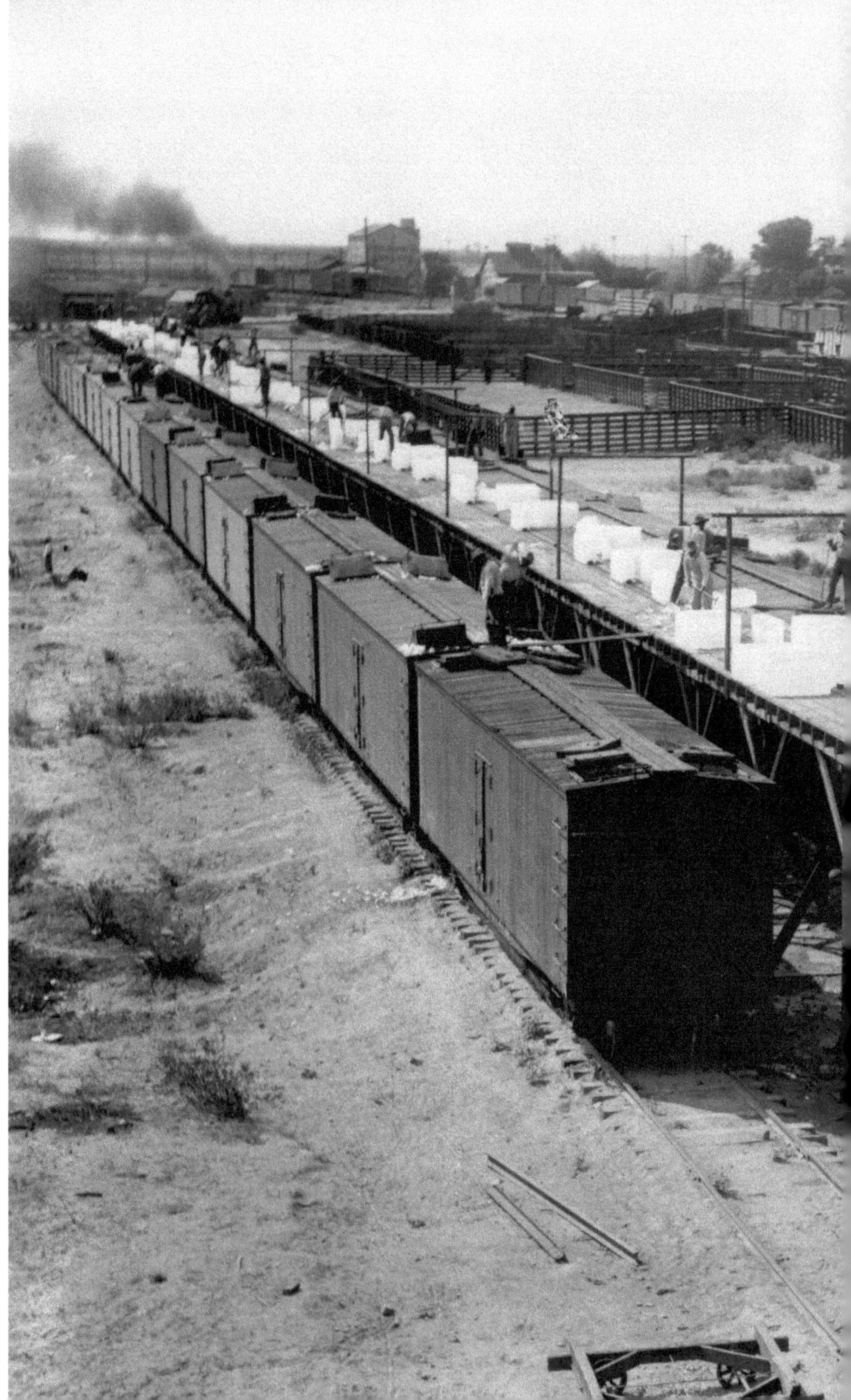

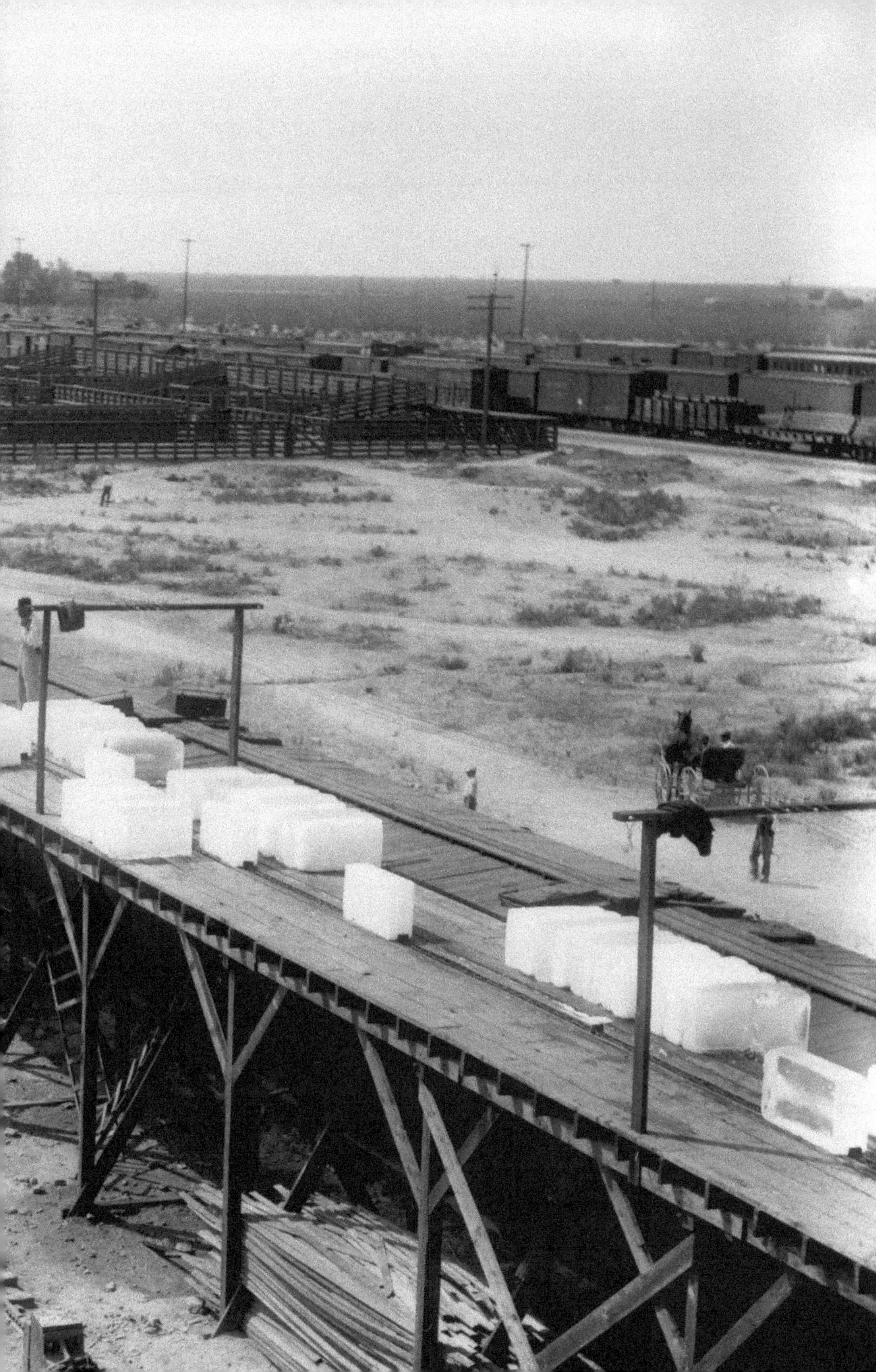

Southern Pacific employees preparing to load blocks of ice into refrigeration cars around 1900. The Tucson Ice and Cold Storage Company made the ice at their plant just east of downtown.

Looking east along Congress Street, not long after a rainstorm (ca. 1900).

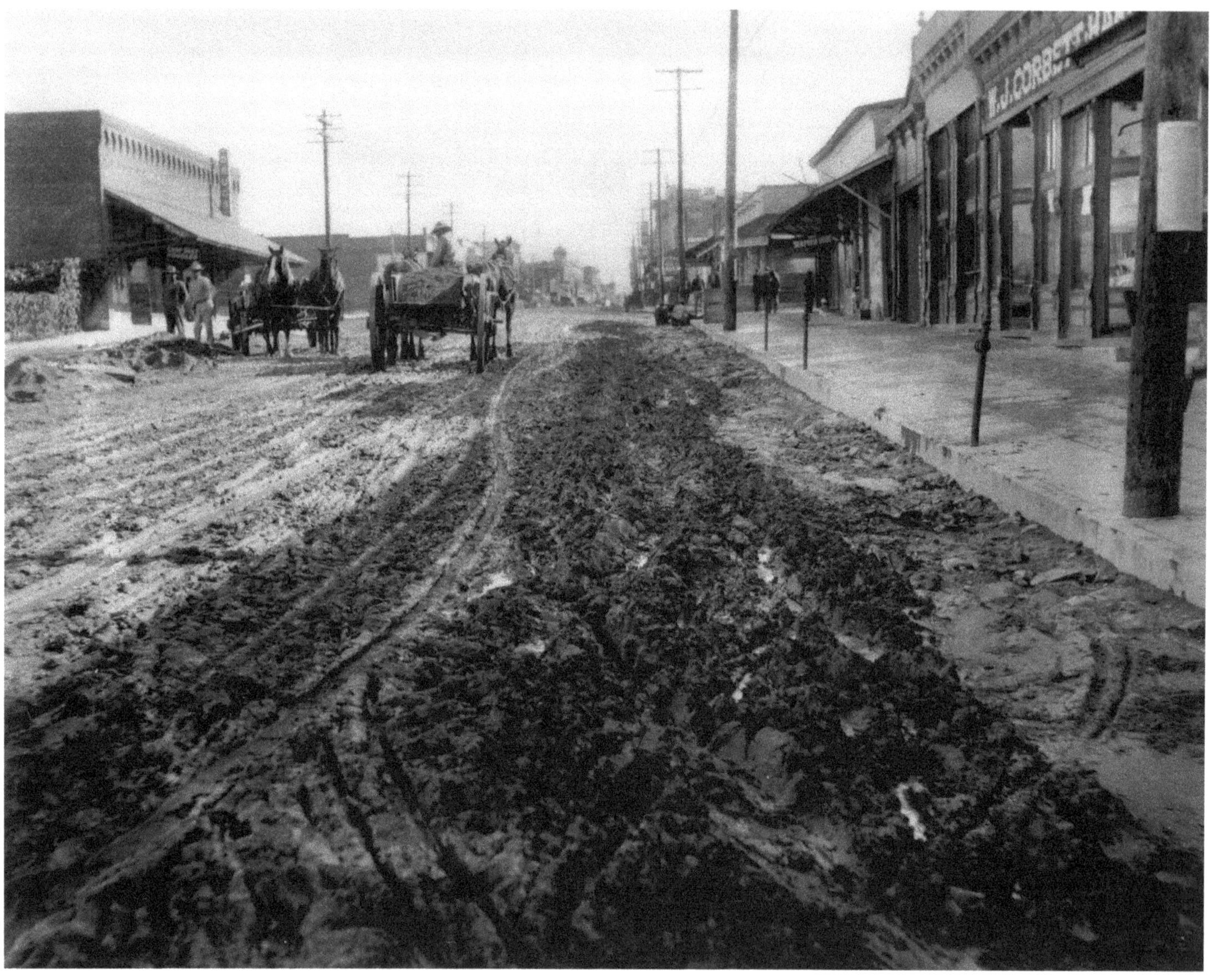

Originally the Reid Opera House, built by gambler Billie Reid in 1886 as a public hall and theater, the building near Pennington and Meyer streets became the Parkview Hotel in 1902. It was torn down in 1958.

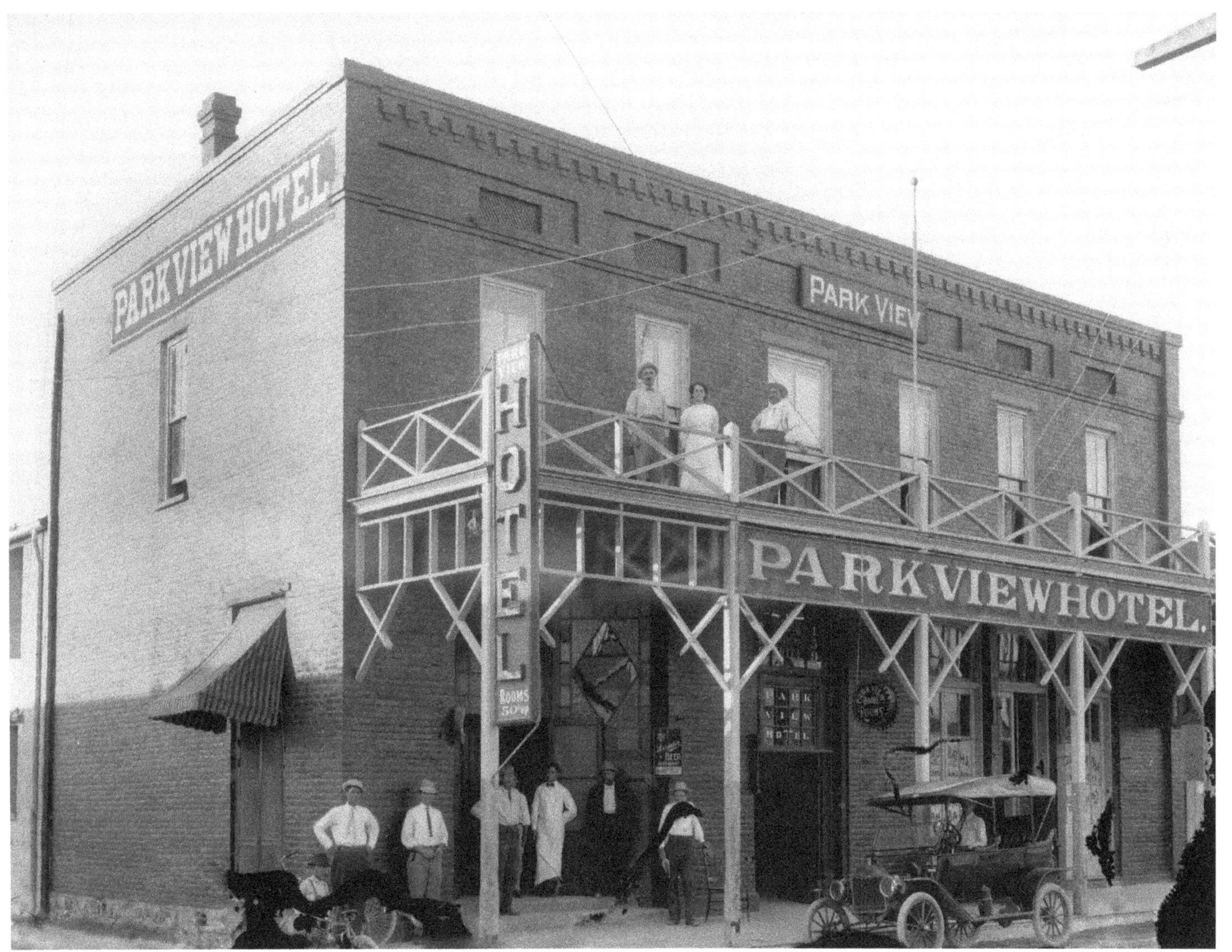

A view looking west on Congress Street from Scott Street (ca.1903). Built around 1897, the Ivancovich & Company roof gave a distinctive look to the Tucson skyline. The Tucson Opera House, with a Tucson Hardware sign painted on its side, was the largest theater of its time.

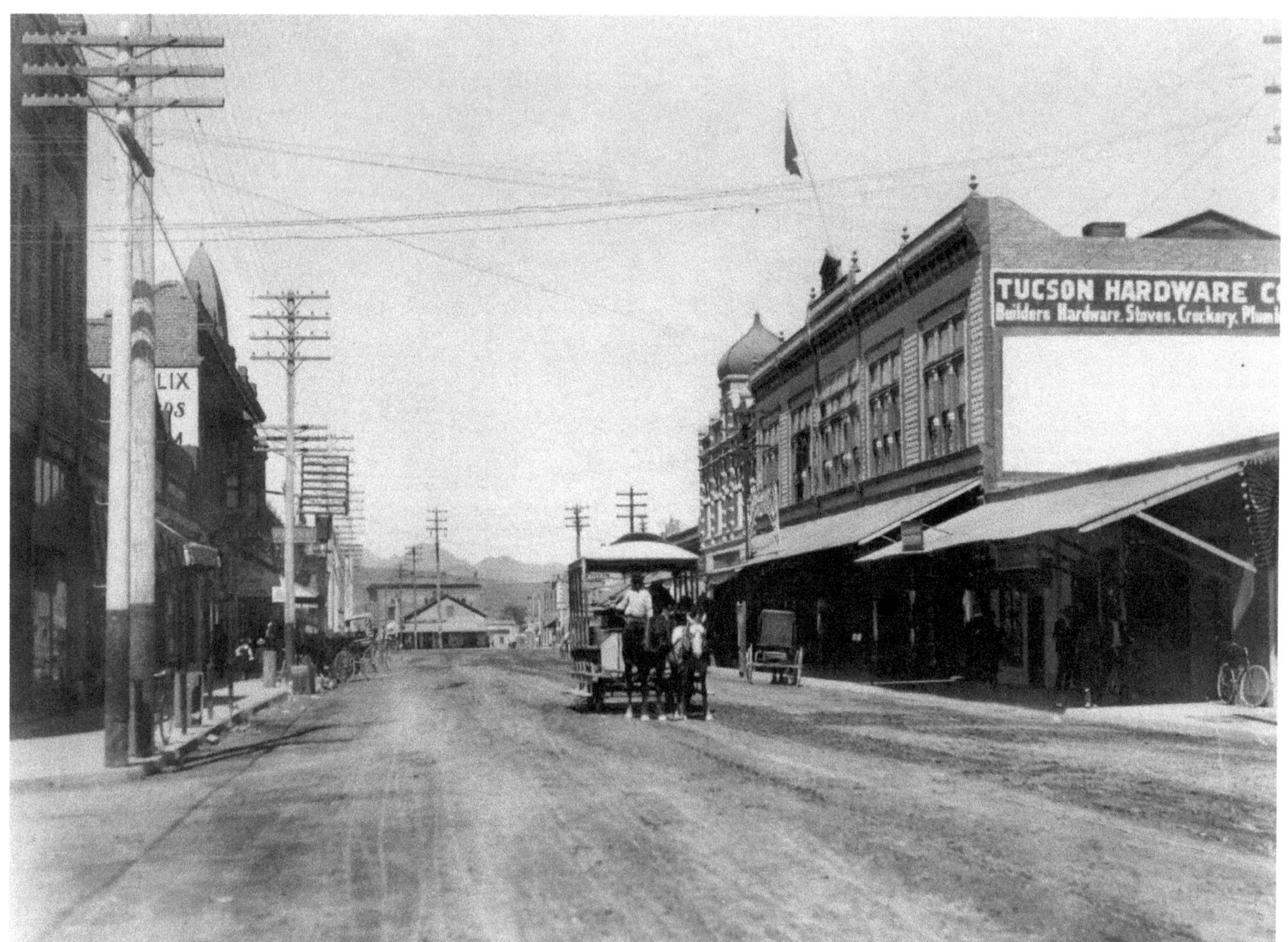

The Owl's Club was formed in 1886 to provide accommodations for well-to-do bachelors and as a place for social gatherings. Previously occupying two other locations, in 1902 members built this building on Main Street near Franklin Street, which housed the club until it disbanded in 1912.

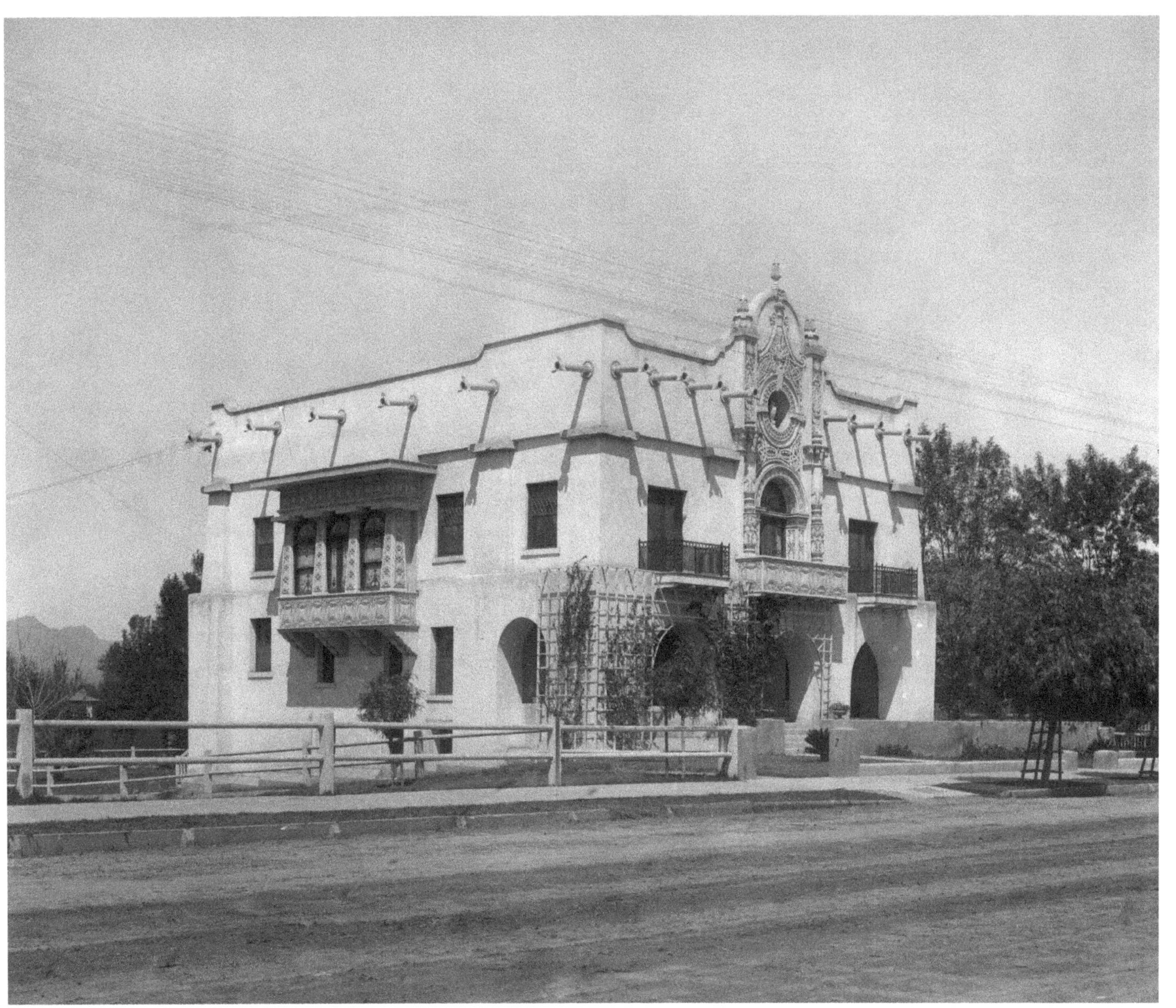

Established in 1903 with a grant from Andrew Carnegie, the Carnegie Desert Botanical Laboratory studied Sonoran plant life for nearly four decades. This is one of the earliest buildings at the site on Tumamoc Hill west of Tucson.

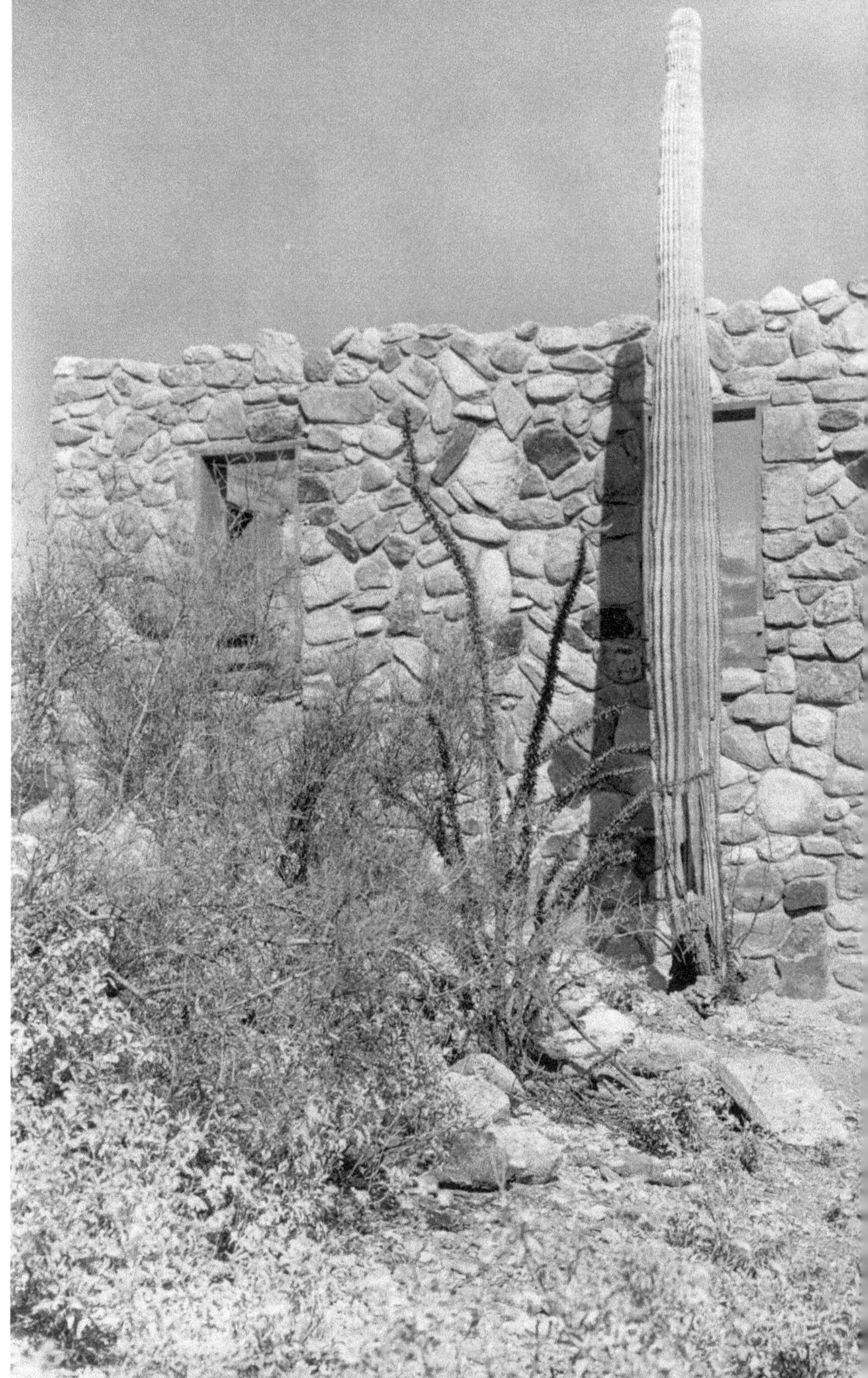

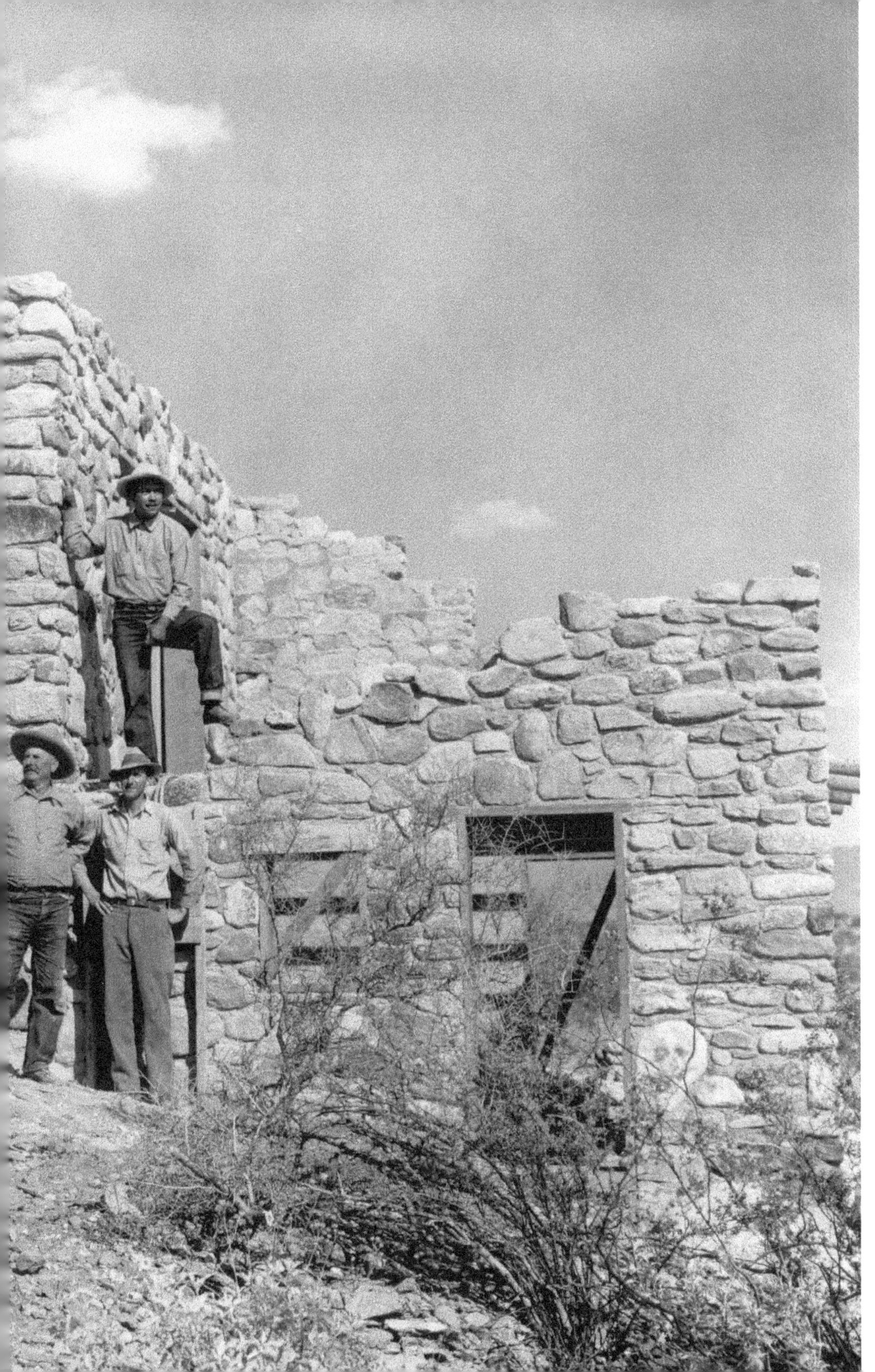

The Santa Rita Hotel was built in 1904 on the corner of Scott Street and Broadway Boulevard, with 200 luxurious rooms. It would remain one of Tucson's favorite hotels for many decades. This view is from around 1925. The rectangular sign at one corner reads "H. A. Smith Arizona&Mexico Lands," while in the alley beyond the Western Union and Wells Fargo offices, a sign on the F. Ronstadt building points to a wagon shop. An electric streetlight hangs over the intersection.

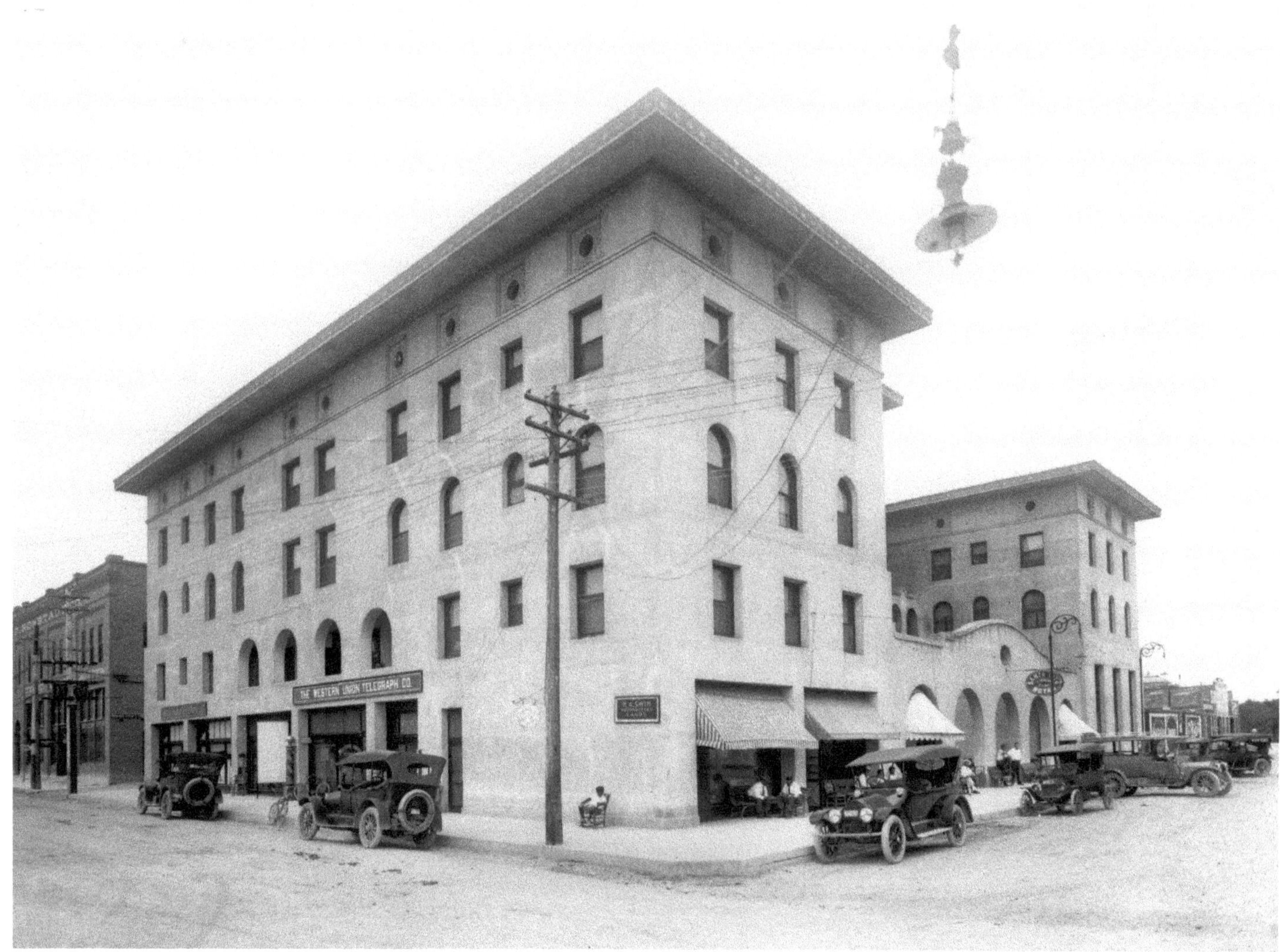

The chauffeur-driven touring cars of the Santa Rita Hotel used to pick up guests at railroad depots and to take them on excursions around the area. Note the Hotel sign offering the "European Plan." The Chas. G. Miller Auto Co. was in the location shown across the street during 1923-1924.

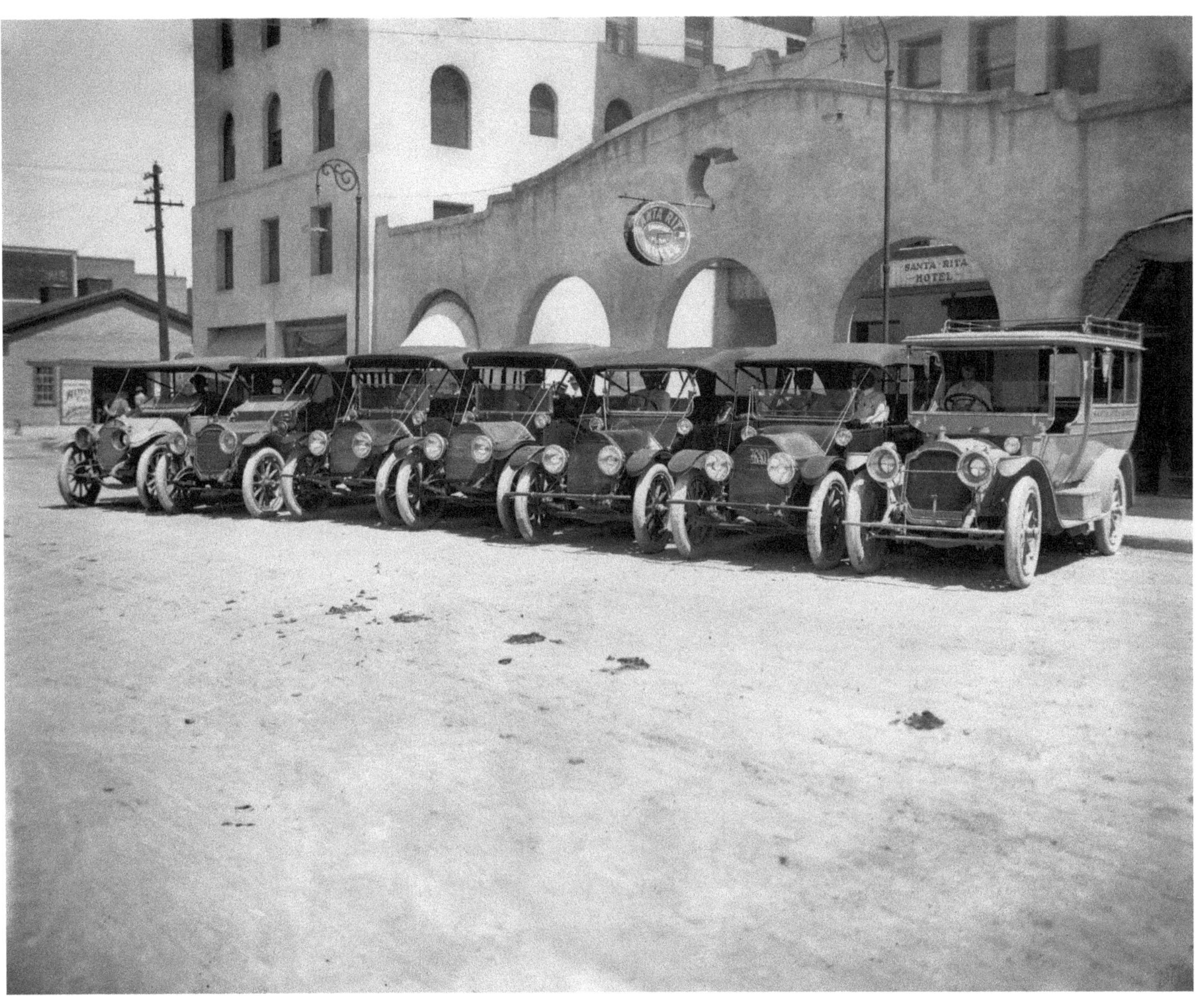

A view from the roof of the Santa Rita Hotel, looking down on the intersection of Stone and Broadway around 1904; the *Citizen* occupies the small building on the corner. The Hotel Hall, the two-story, white building in the center, had been expanded from a private home as the Russ Hotel in 1883. To the right, a grocery store offers German delicacies, wines, liquors and cigars; beyond it is Meyer's Bee-Hive. A rooftop porch for hot summer nights can be seen in the lower left corner.

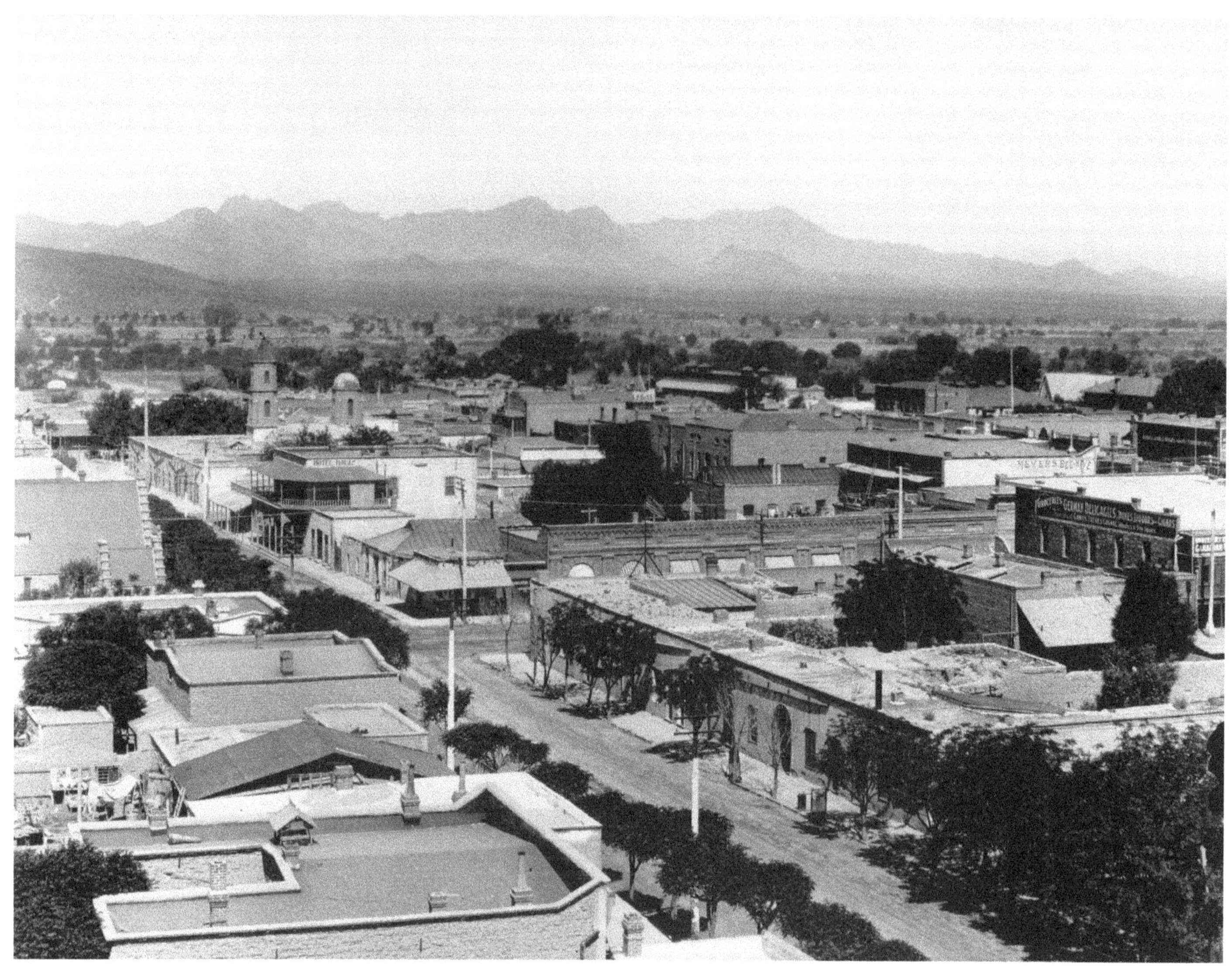

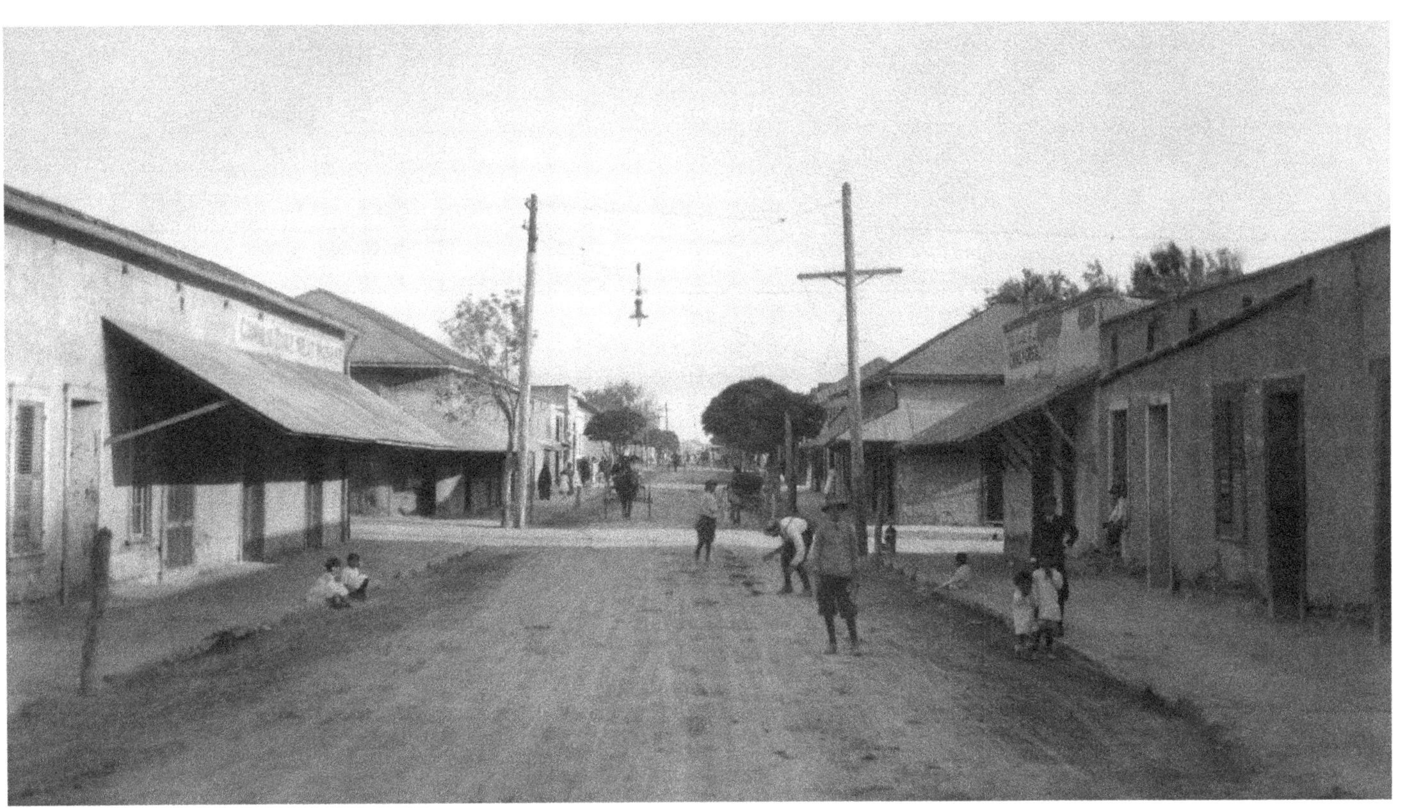

Looking south on Convent Street, across McCormick Street in the heart of Barrio Veijo around 1905. The Camilo Diaz Meat Market, the neighborhood butcher, is on the left. An electric streetlight illuminated the intersection.

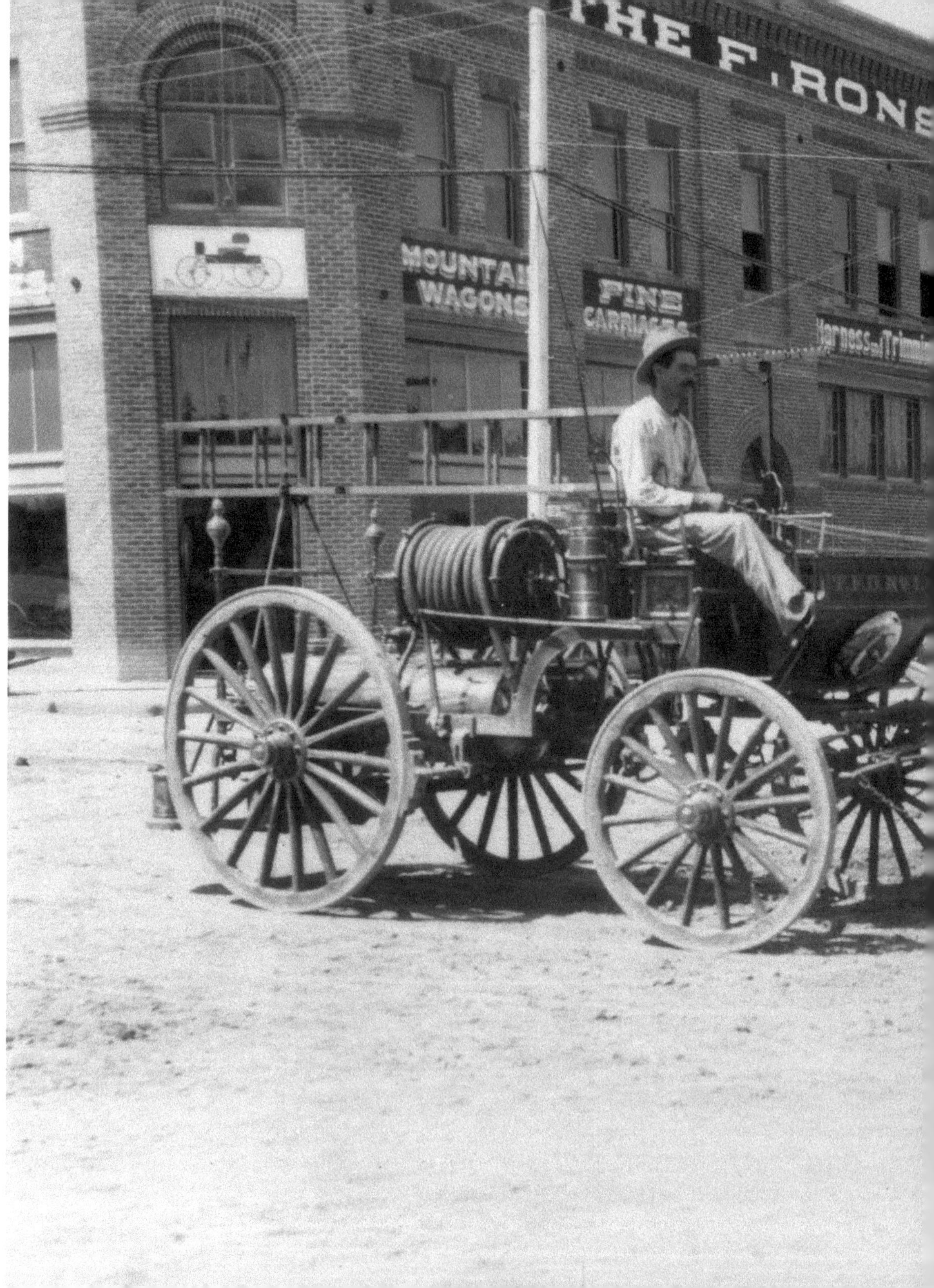

MOUNTAI
WAGONS
FINE

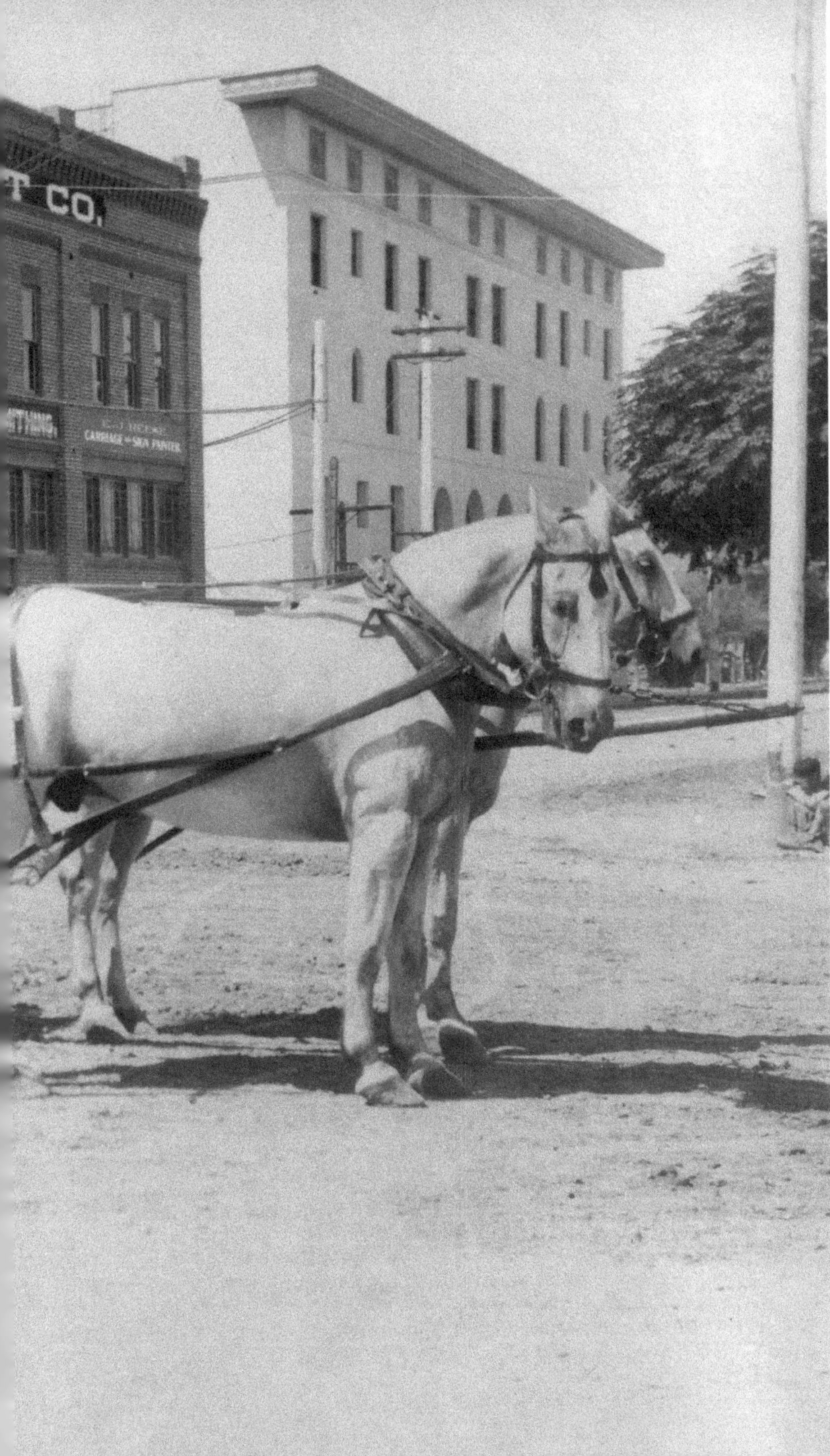

A Tucson Volunteer Fire Department hose and ladder wagon on Broadway Street (ca. 1904). Fire hydrants were installed on the streets beginning in 1883. The F. Ronstadt Co. was well-known throughout the Southwest for the quality of its wagons and carriages. At the far end of the building is E. J. Reese carriage- and sign-painting shop.

The Ramona Hotel at 34 S. Fifth Avenue, across from the Southern Pacific Depot, around 1905. The S. P. Barber Shop offered hot and cold baths to weary travelers.

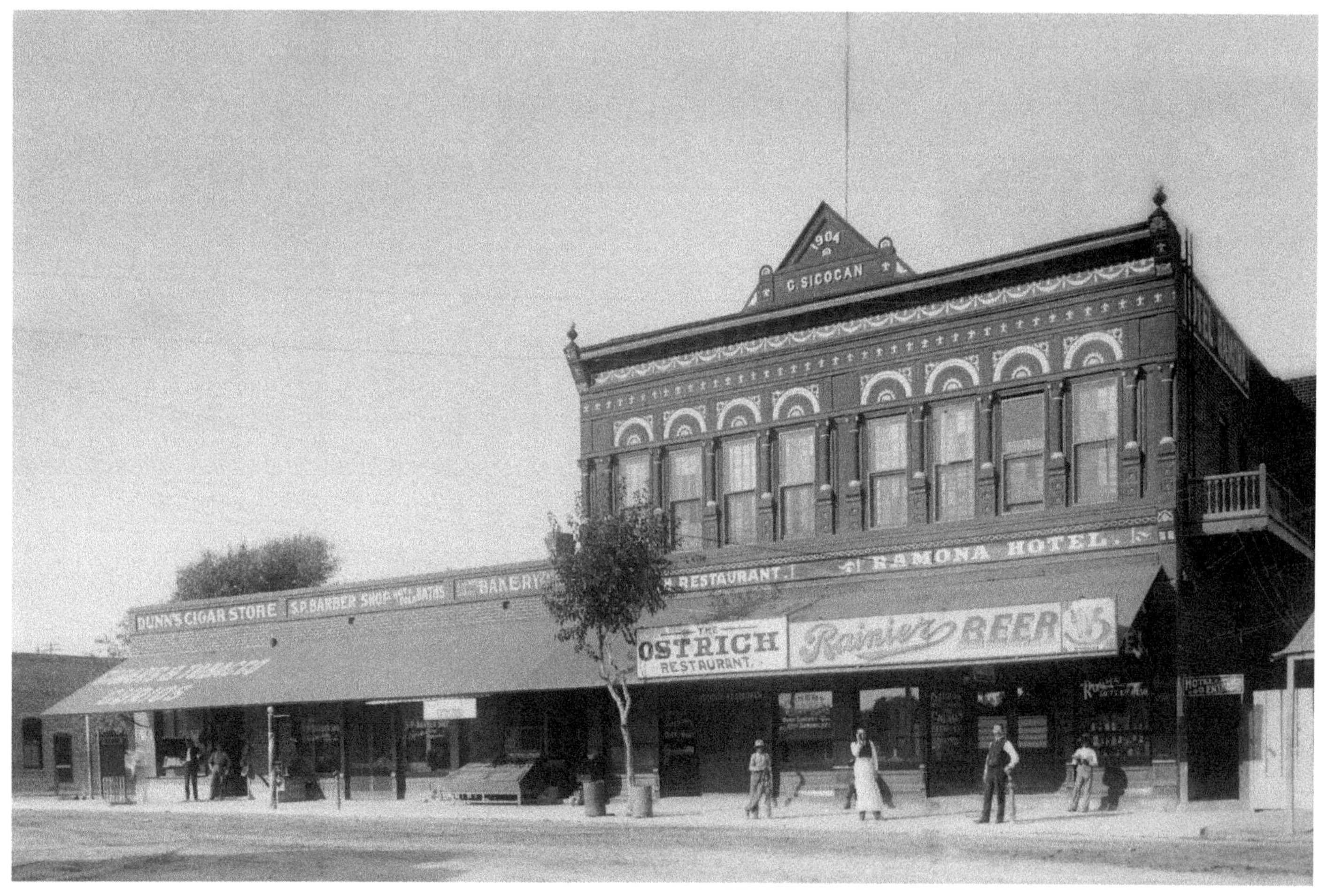

Like many local businesses, the J. Knox Corbett Lumber Co. sponsored a baseball team (ca. 1905). Most games were played on the diamond at the Elysian Field, a south-side park formerly known as Carrillo's Garden.

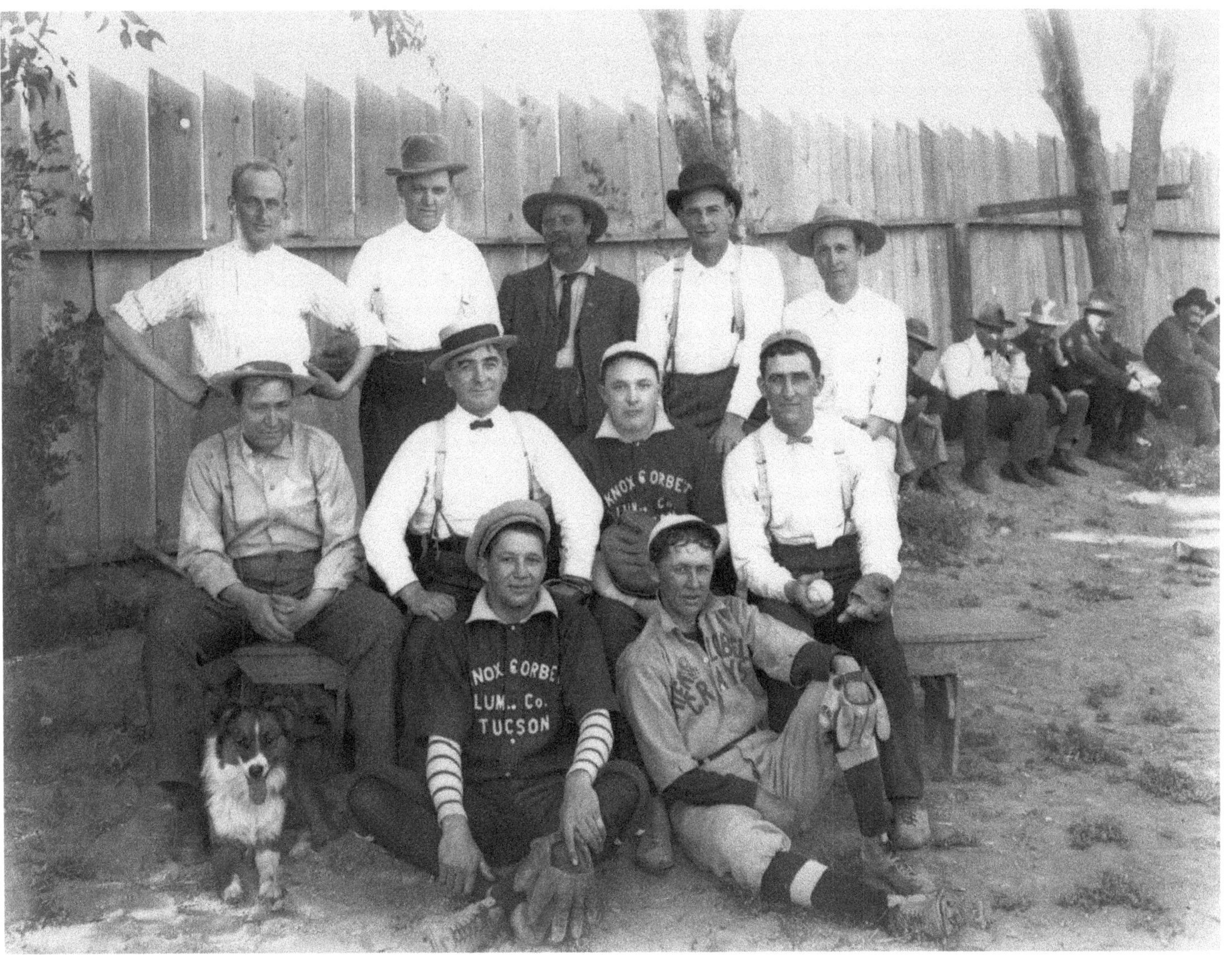

The University of Arizona campus at the Third Street entrance (ca. 1905). A football field, goal posts, and spectator stands can be seen. On the far right is the girl's dormitory and left of it are the East and West Cottages. The President's House is hidden by a large tree.

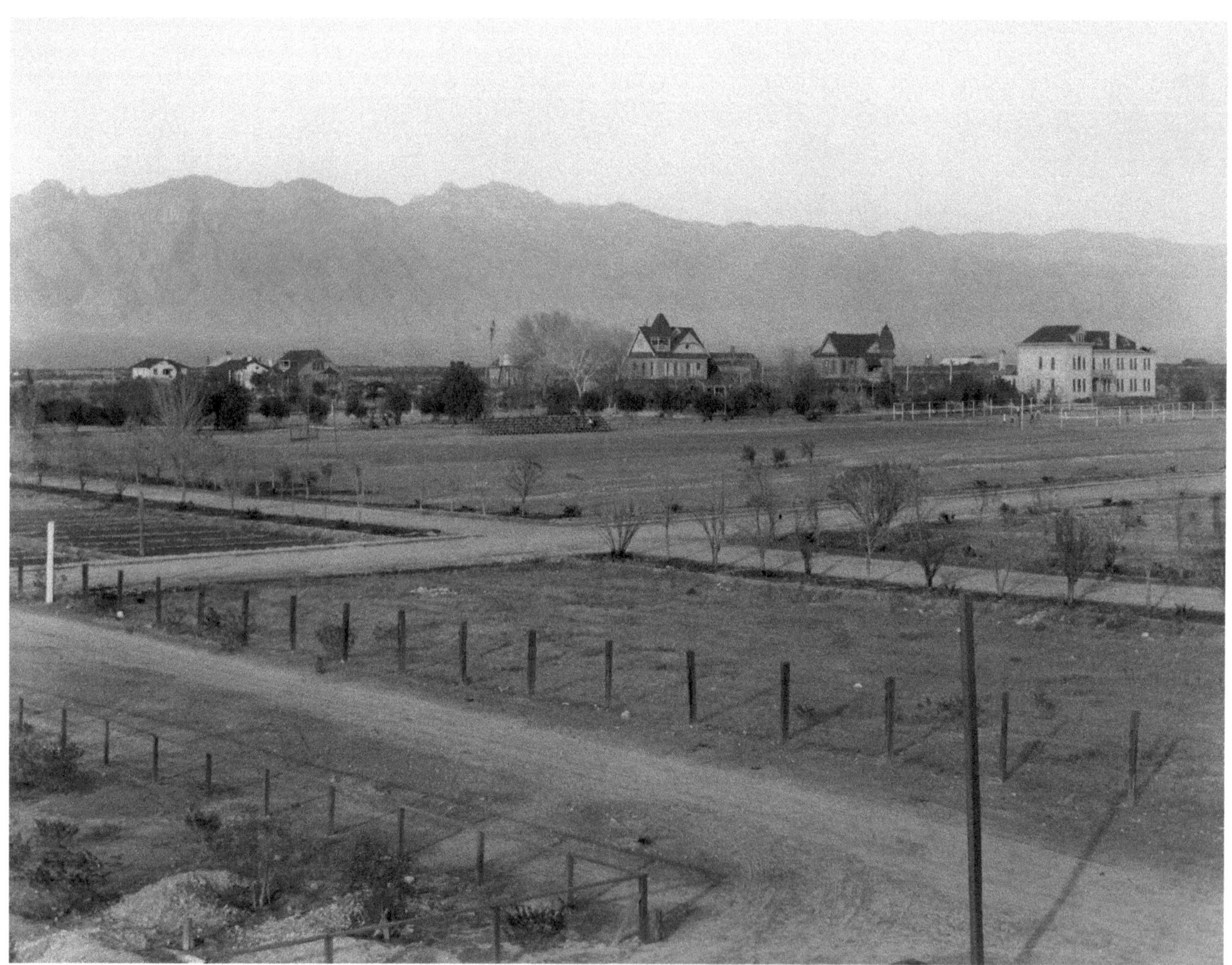

The circular tuberculosis sanatorium at St. Mary's Hospital (ca. 1905). In 1880, the Sisters of St. Joseph built Arizona's first public hospital, west of Tucson, adding the sanatorium in 1900. The order came to Tucson in 1870, opening a school for girls and an orphanage.

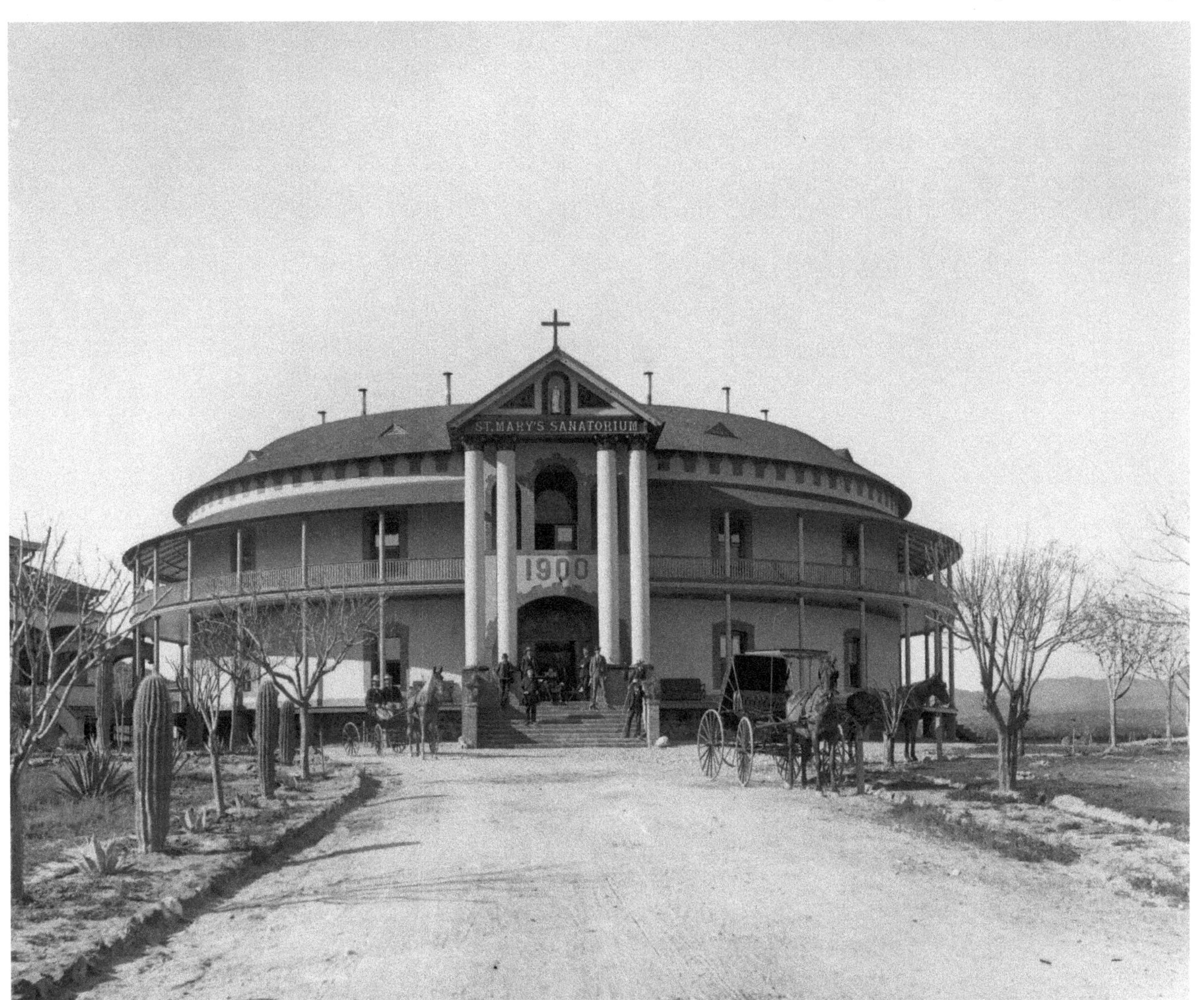

A side view of the front steps of the St. Mary's Hospital Sanatorium (ca. 1918).

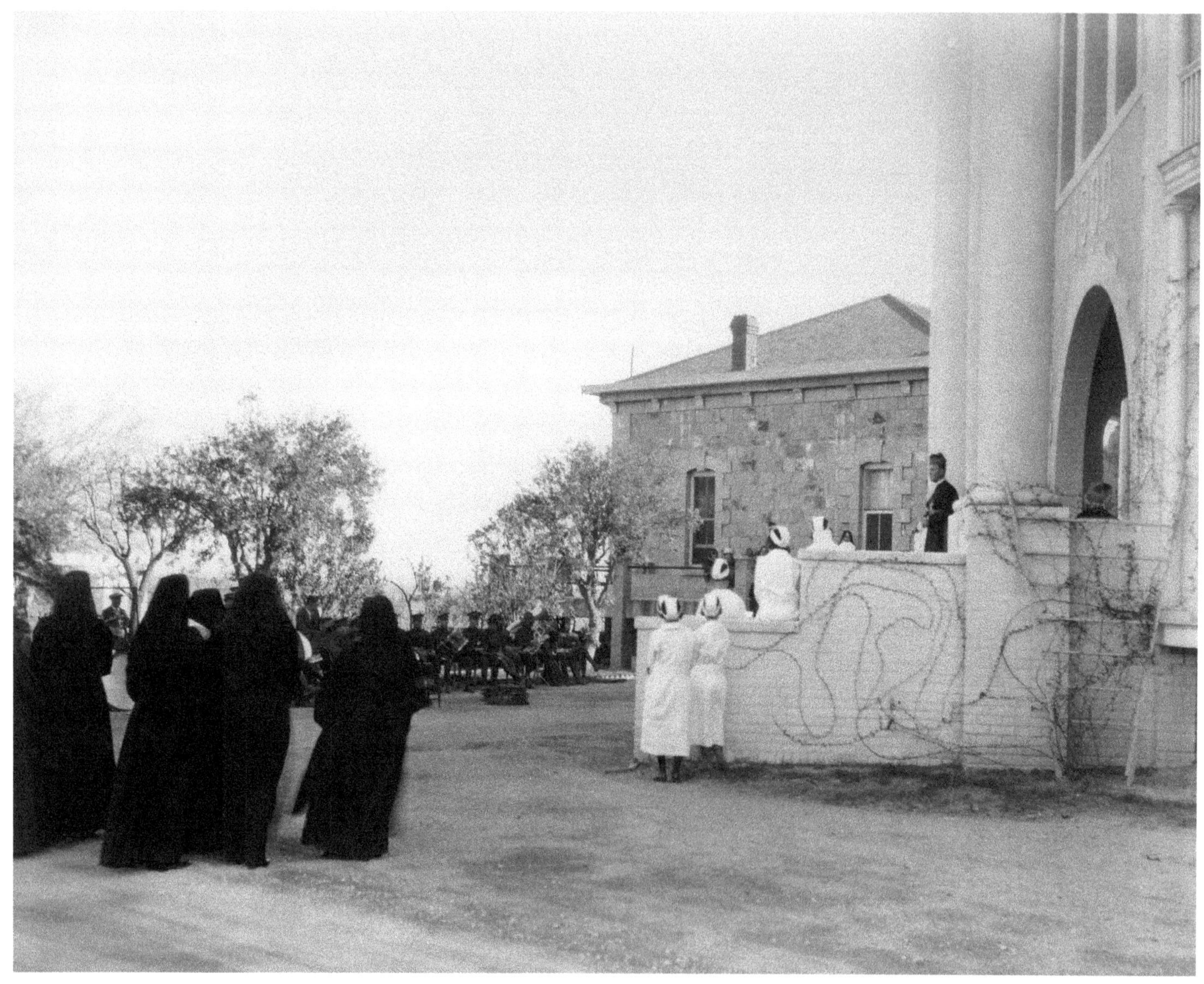

A crew smoothing concrete during the laying of tracks for the electric streetcar along Congress Street (ca. 1906).

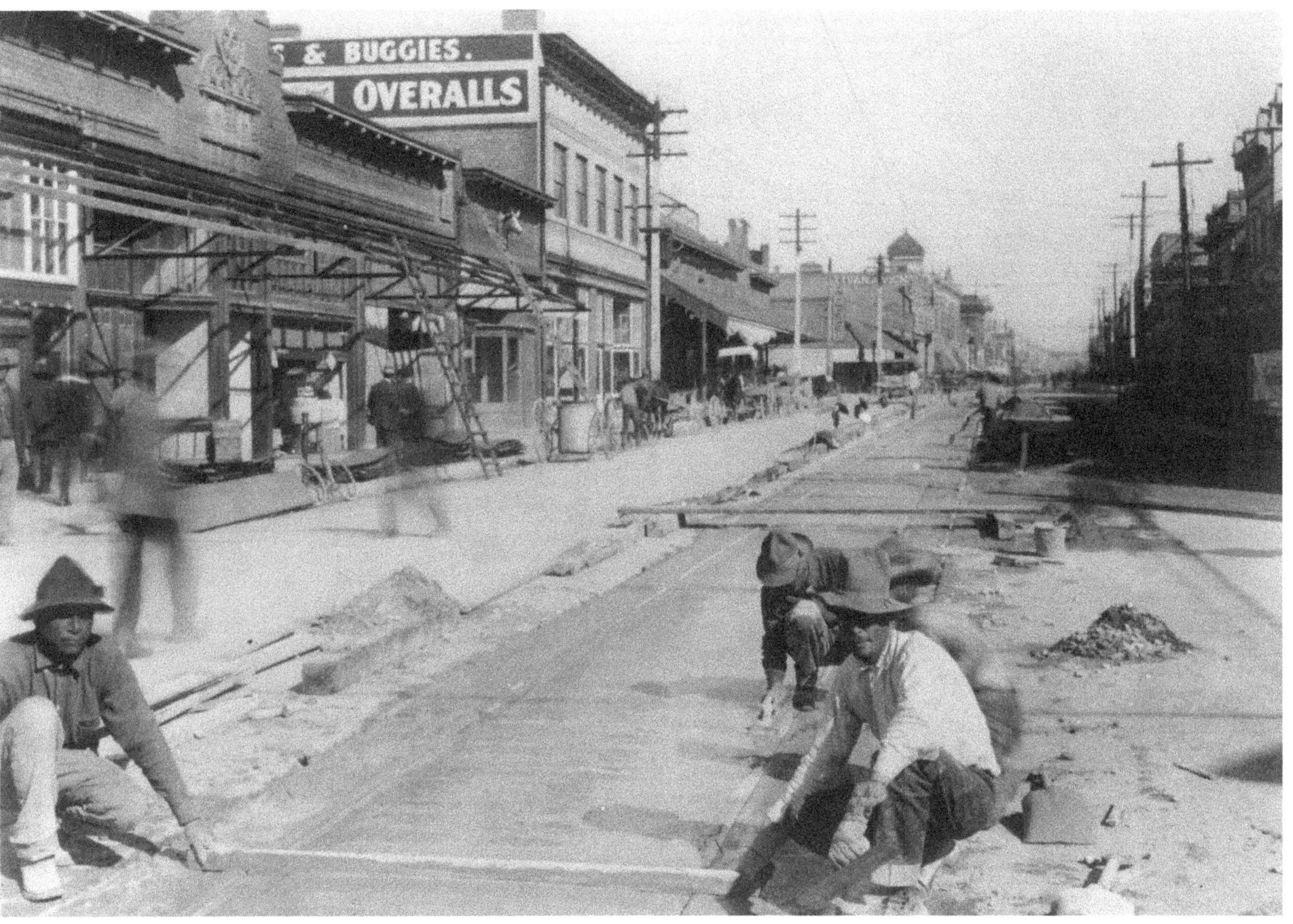

A view of the small community that grew up around the Silver Bell copper mine northeast of Tucson (ca. 1906). Initially discovered in the 1860s, the mine was reactivated in 1902 and worked until 1931.

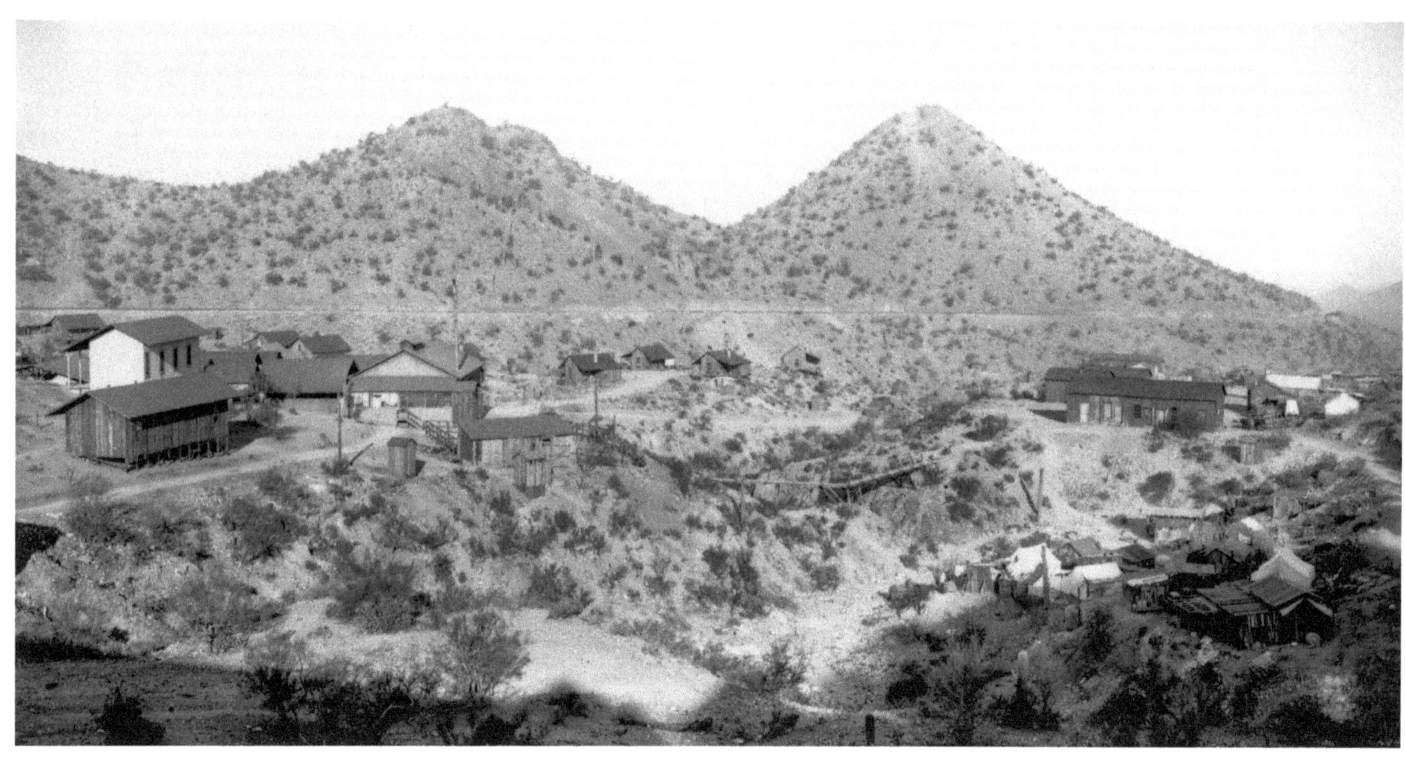

A view of the Silver Bell Mine showing the Union Shaft, the power plant, and a test mill that could process ten tons a day (ca. 1908).

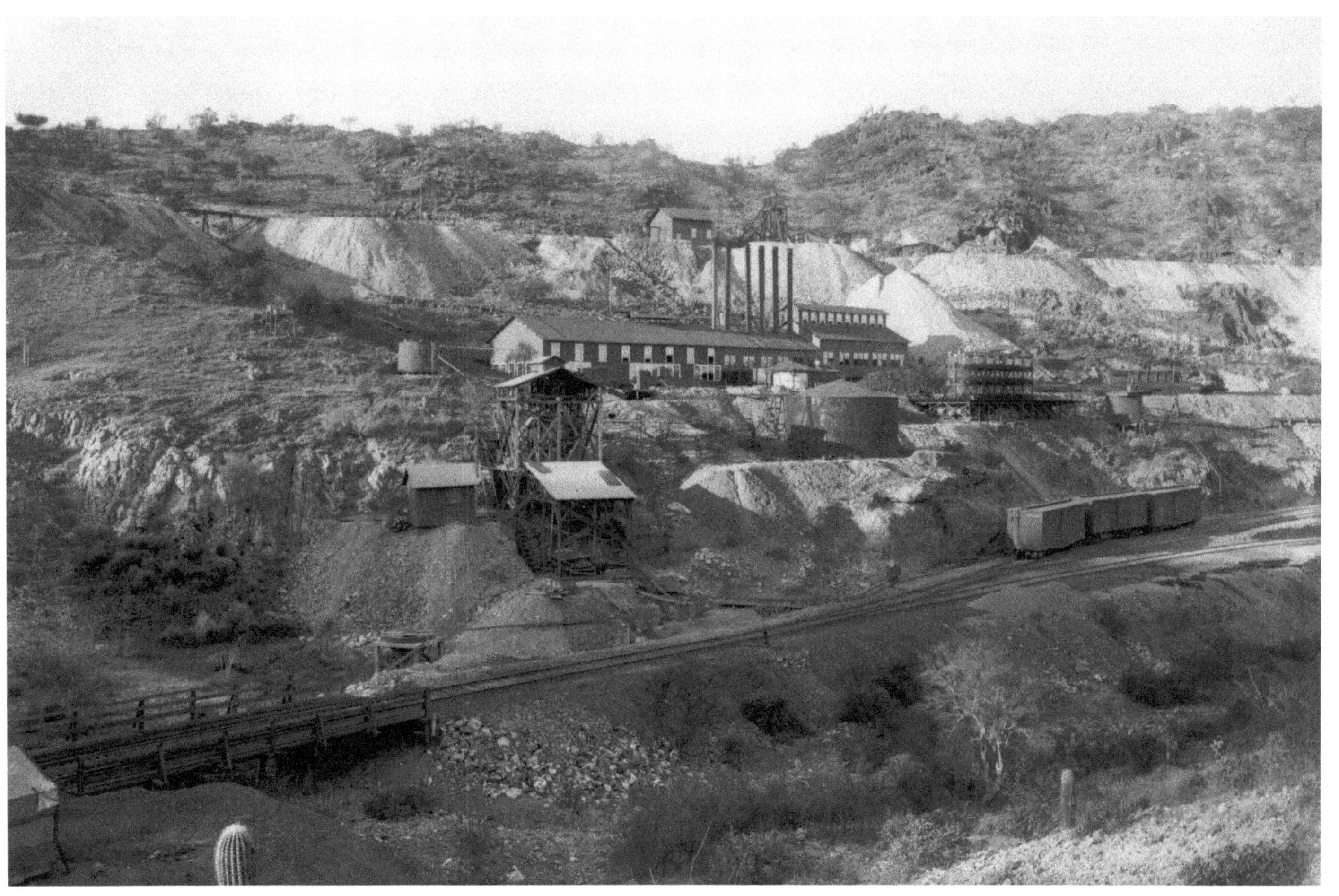

Built in 1907 after the original building burned down, the new Southern Pacific Depot on Toole Avenue is seen here not long after opening. Waiting for passengers along the street were both horse-drawn and motorized taxis.

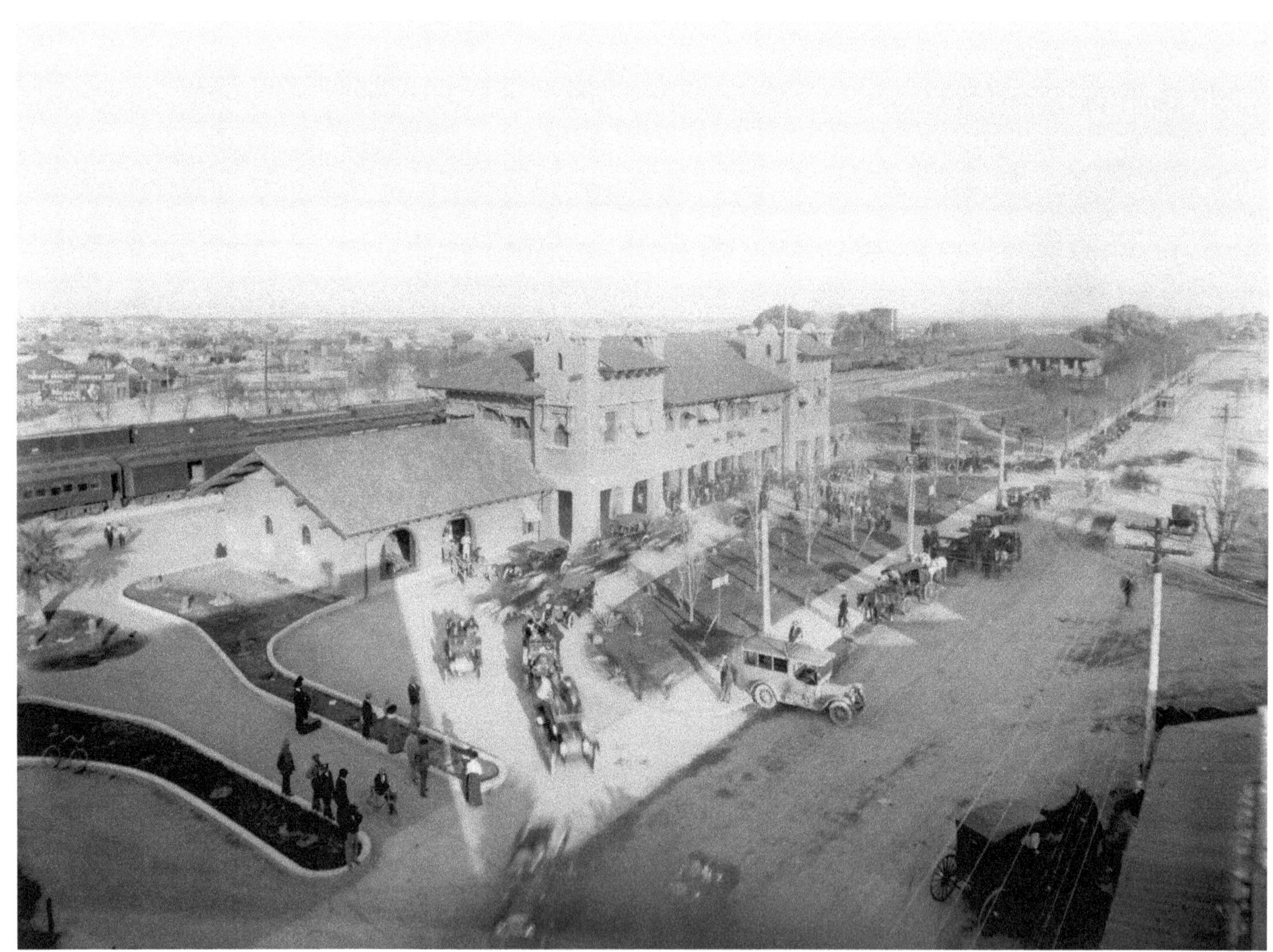

Even Santa Claus had to make concessions to the desert in order to deliver his Christmas presents. A billboard touts a Dec. 14 appearance by the Lewis & Wolf Players. The Southern Pacific Depot is in the background (ca. 1907).

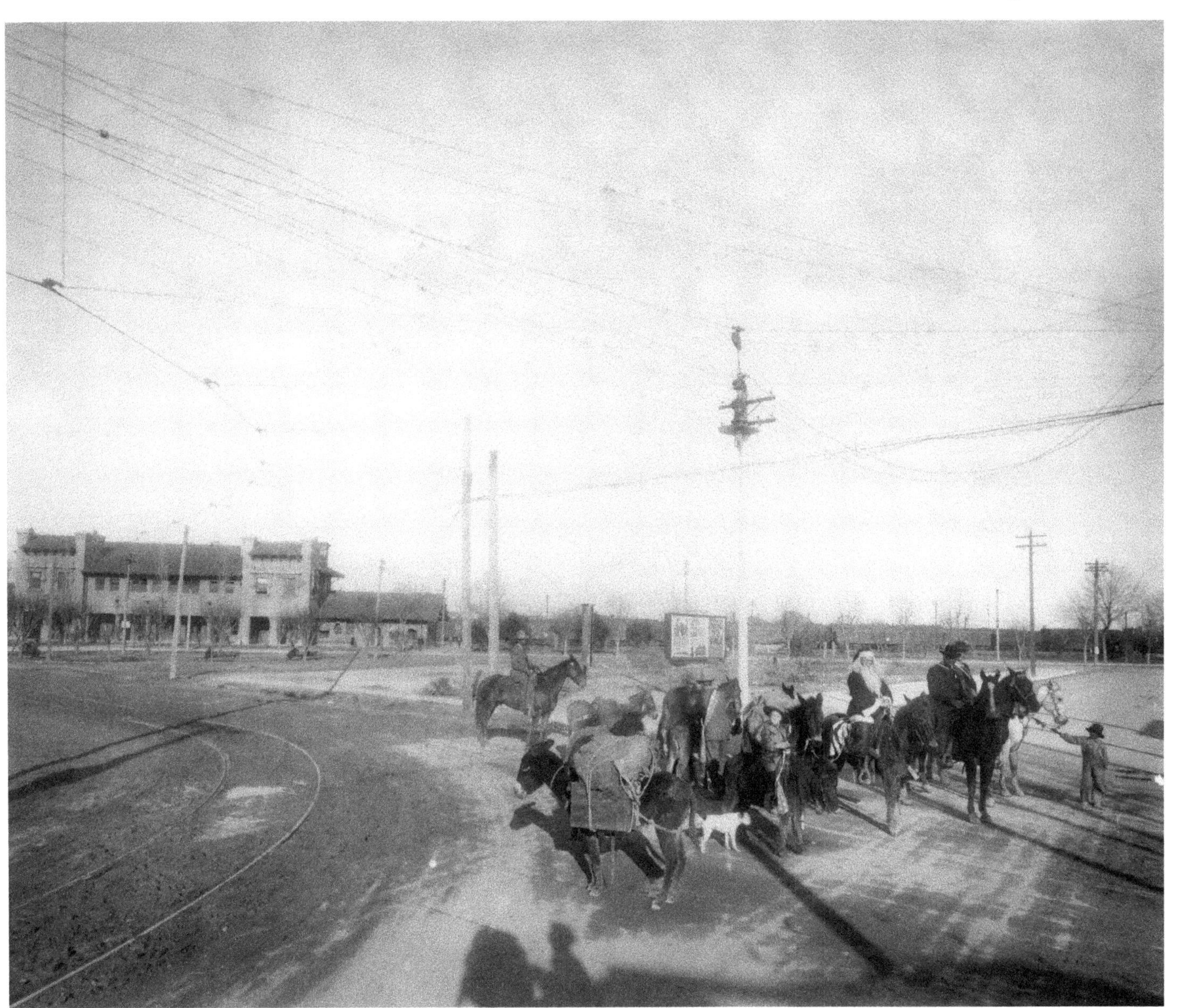

The southeast corner of Congress Street and Stone Avenue around 1908. Formerly the site of a saloon and a jewelry store, a new building was constructed in 1901 to house the Consolidated National Bank.

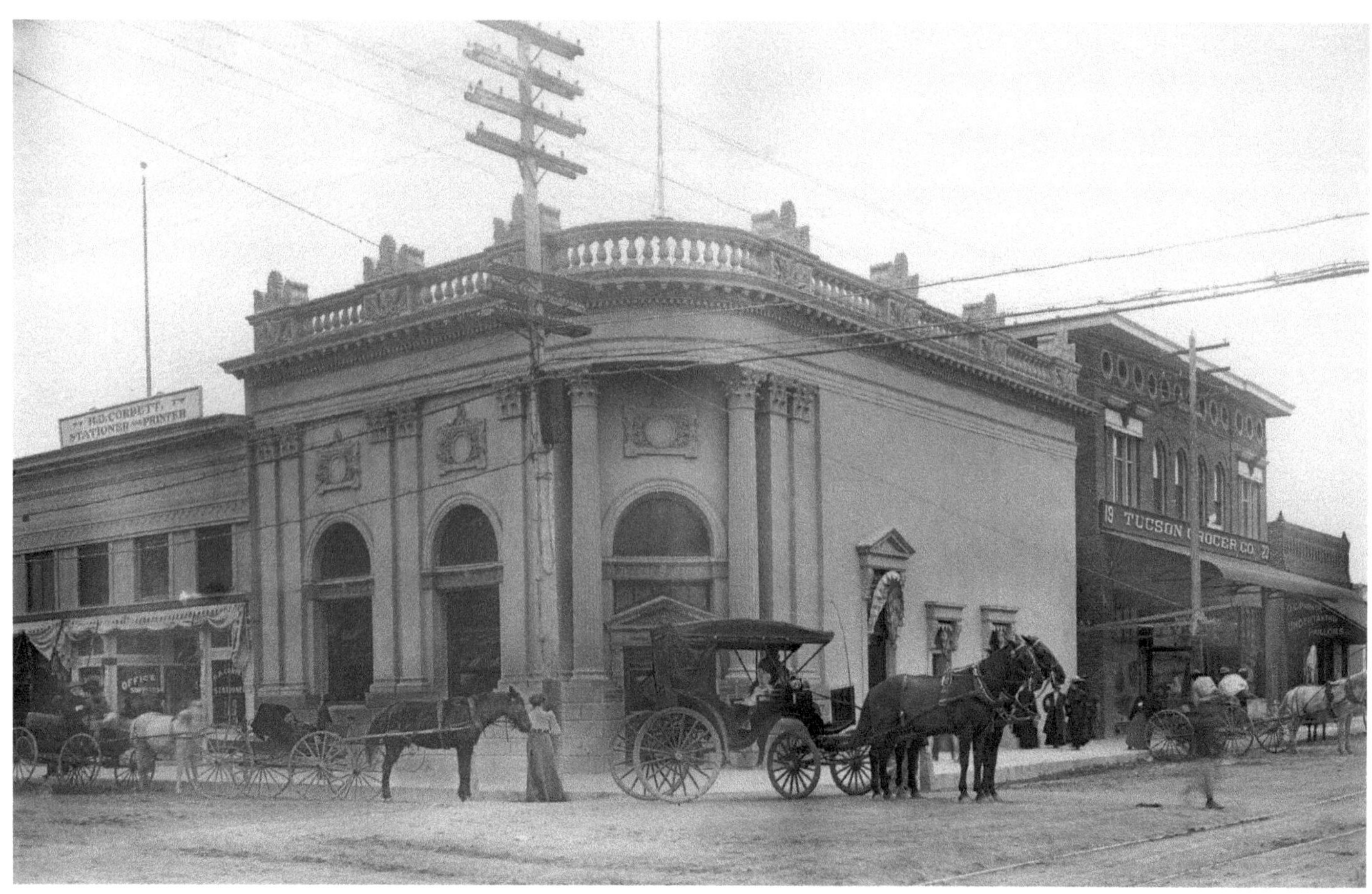

A group of African Americans posed in excursion automobiles before making a trip to San Xavier around 1909. San Xavier was a popular destination for picnickers and sightseers from Tucson and elsewhere.

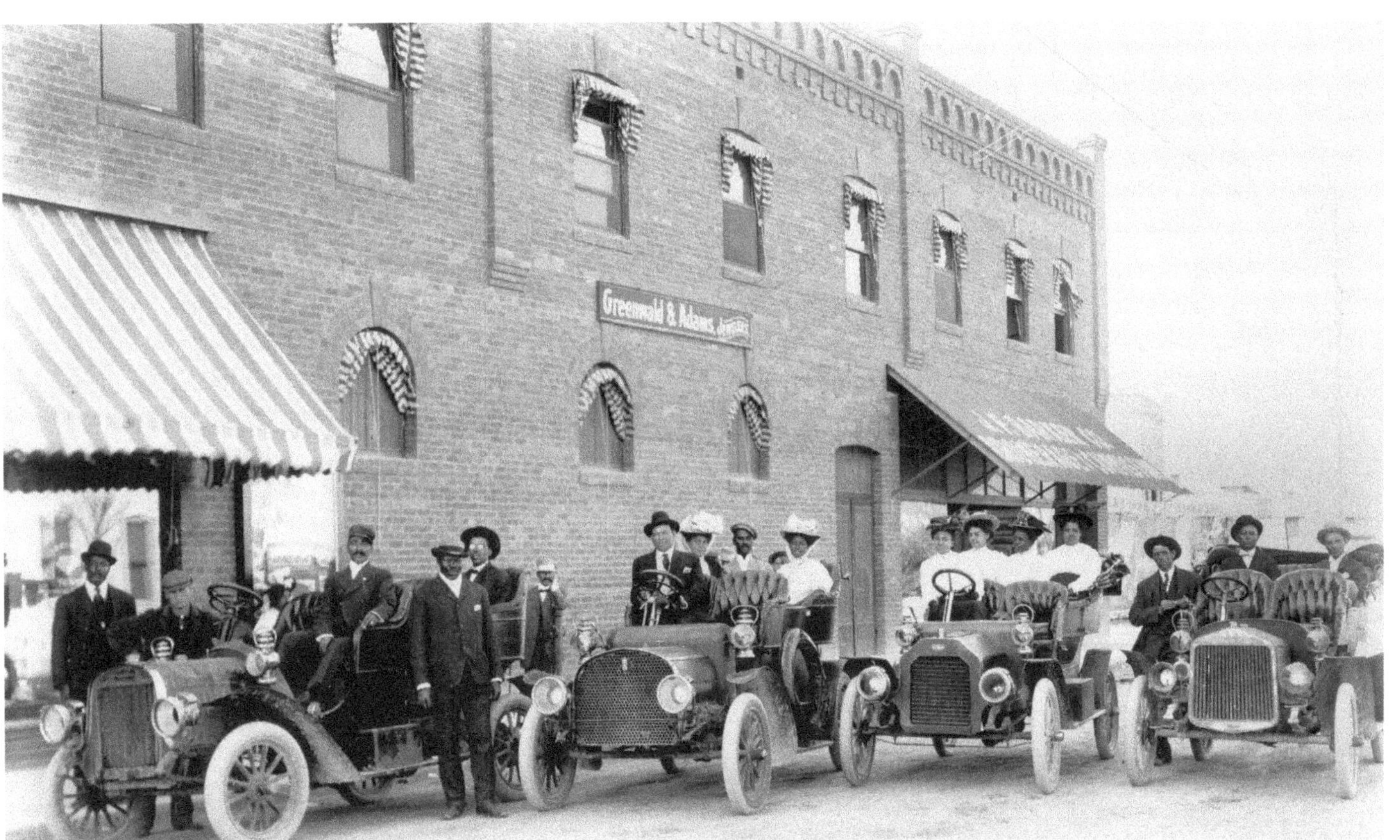

The interior of the Cabinet Club at 68 W. Congress about 1910. The sign behind the bar advertised specialties of the house.

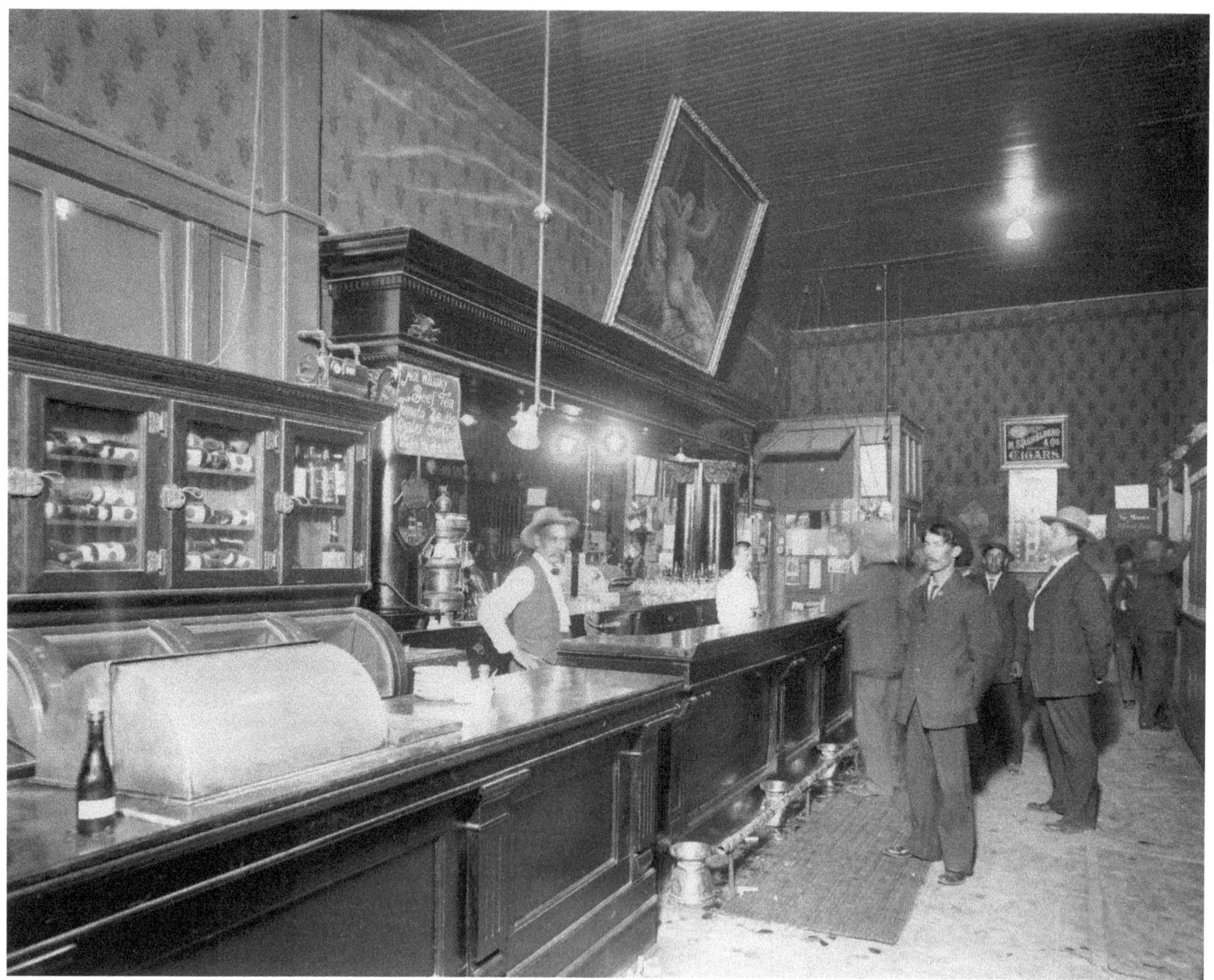

An employee of the Carnegie Desert Botanical Laboratory drove an E-M-F Company "30" automobile while exploring the desert around 1910.

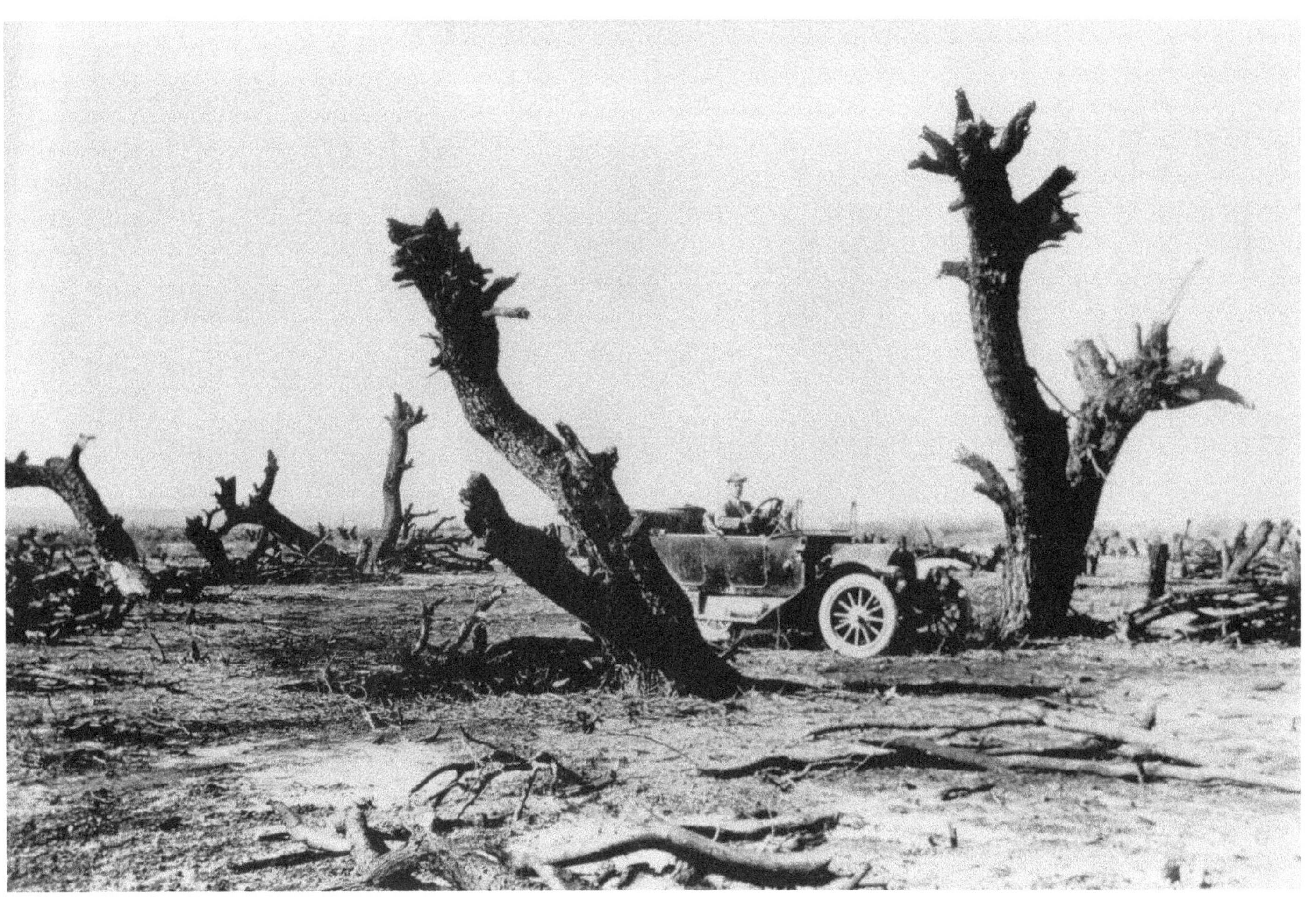

A tried-and-true method for crossing the Rillito after a flood took out the bridge on Oracle Road (ca. 1910).

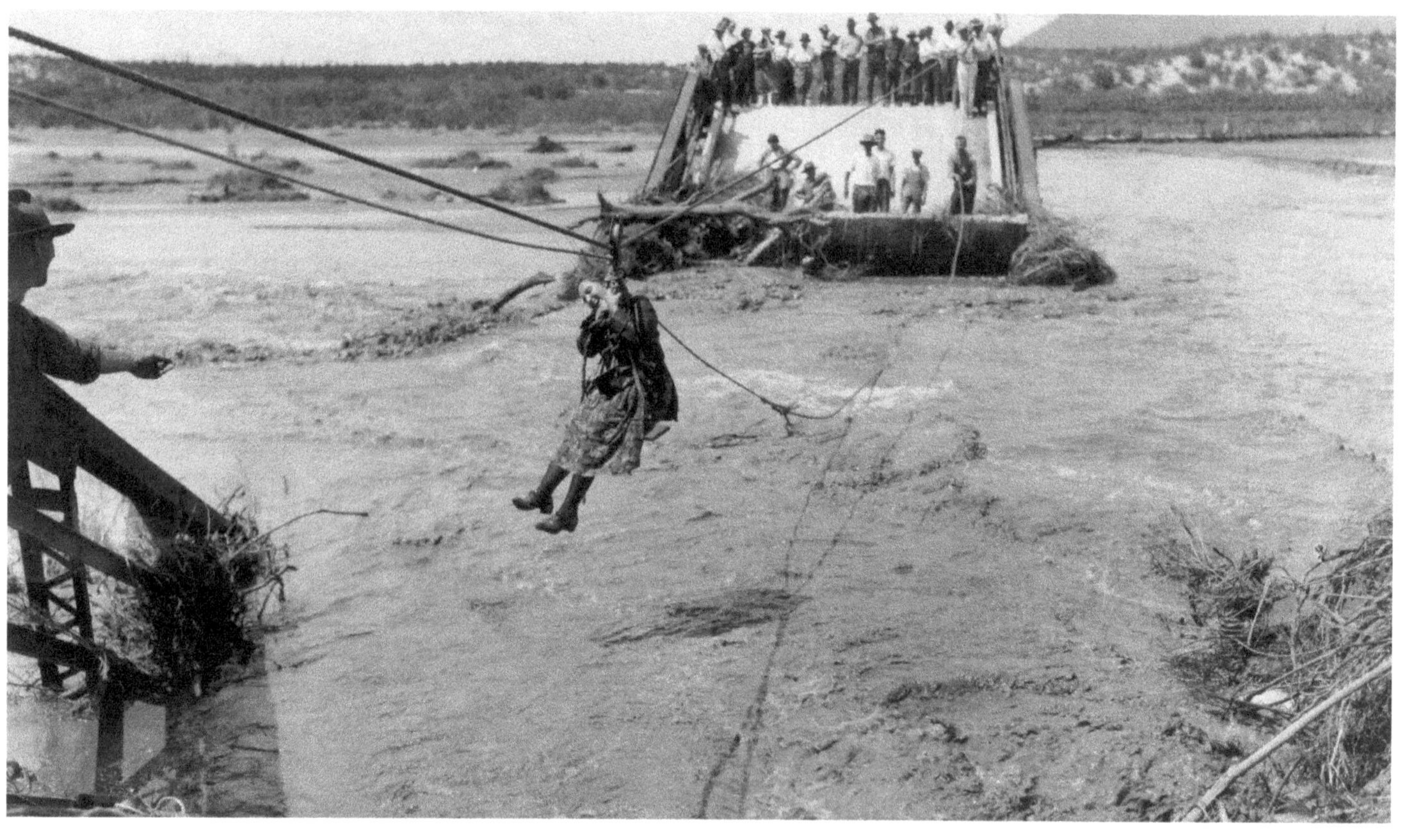

Looking west on Congress Street from Scott Street, with a curio store on the corner (ca. 1910).

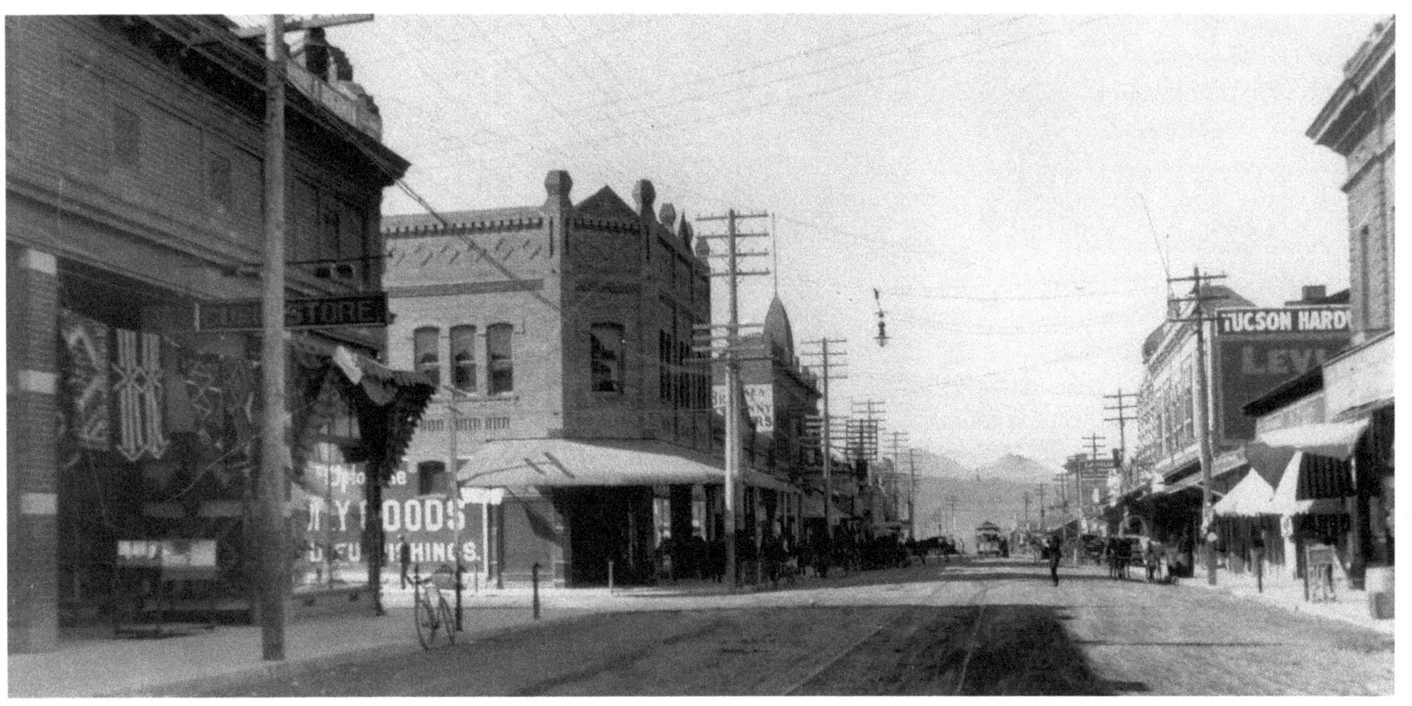

A view of Congress Street from Sixth Avenue looking west (ca. 1910).

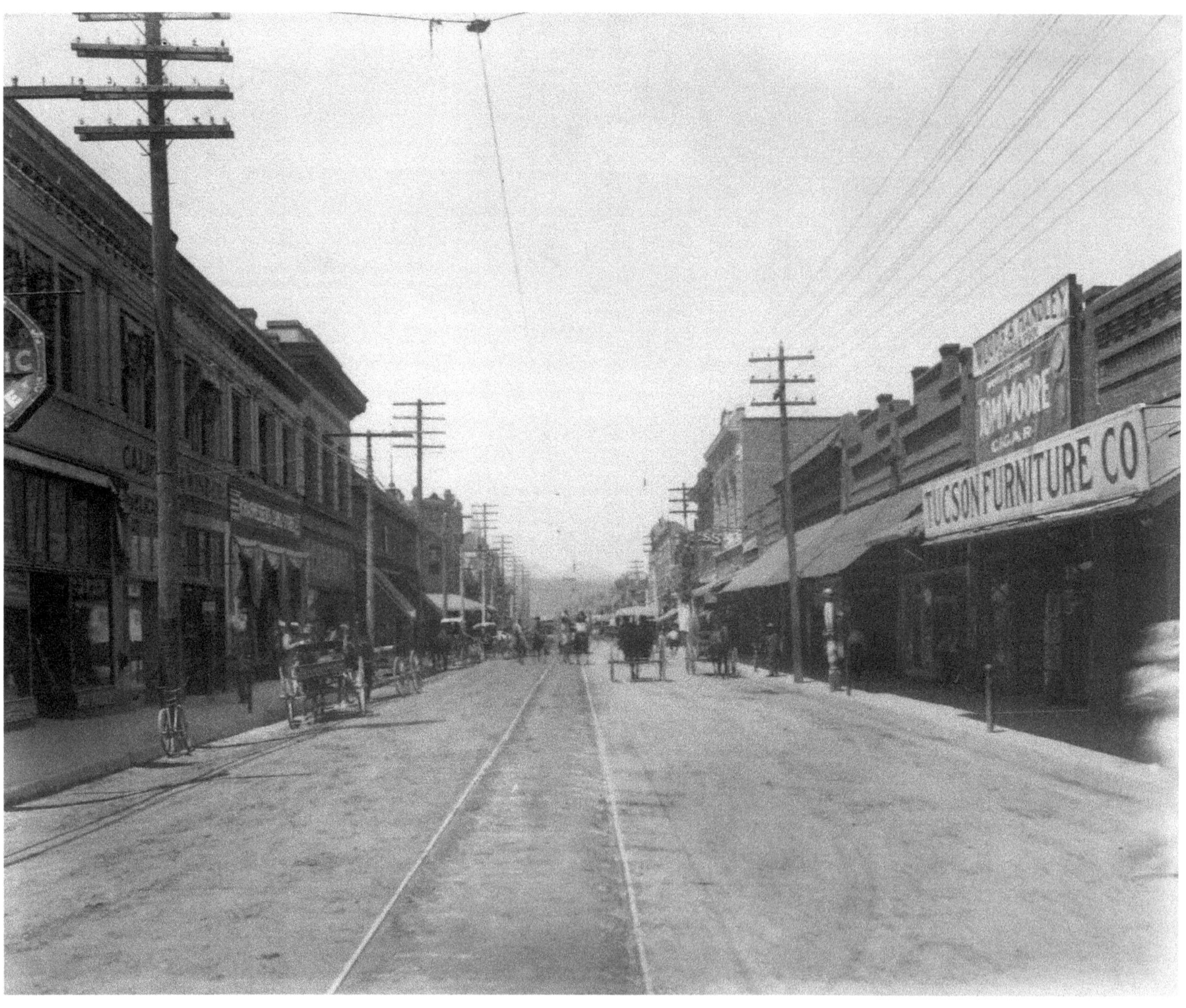

The ruins of the original San Agustín Mission continued to deteriorate. The Santa Cruz River flows in the foreground (ca. 1910).

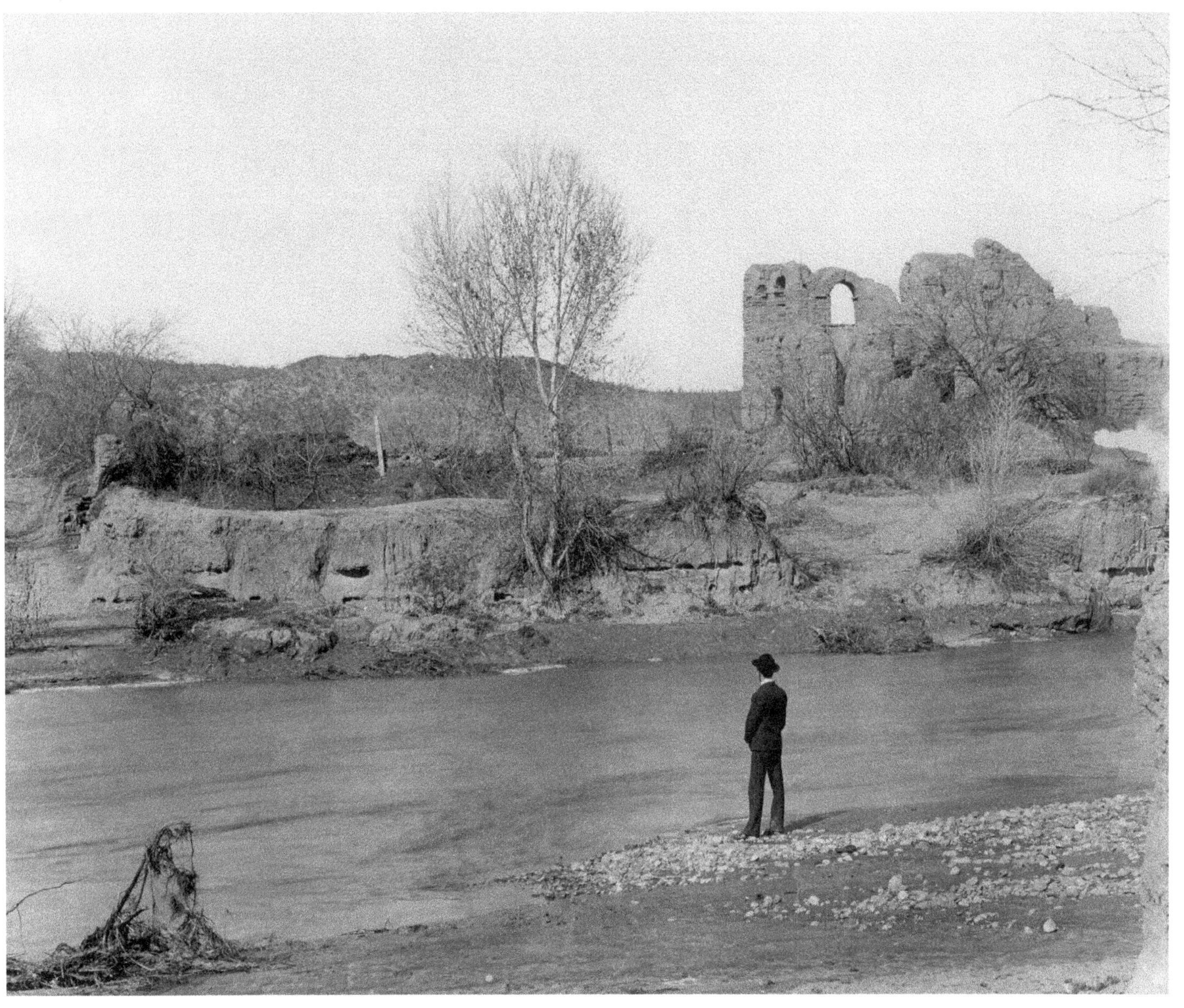

Trolley tracks can barely be seen in the mud at the intersection of Congress Street and Stone Avenue (ca. 1910).

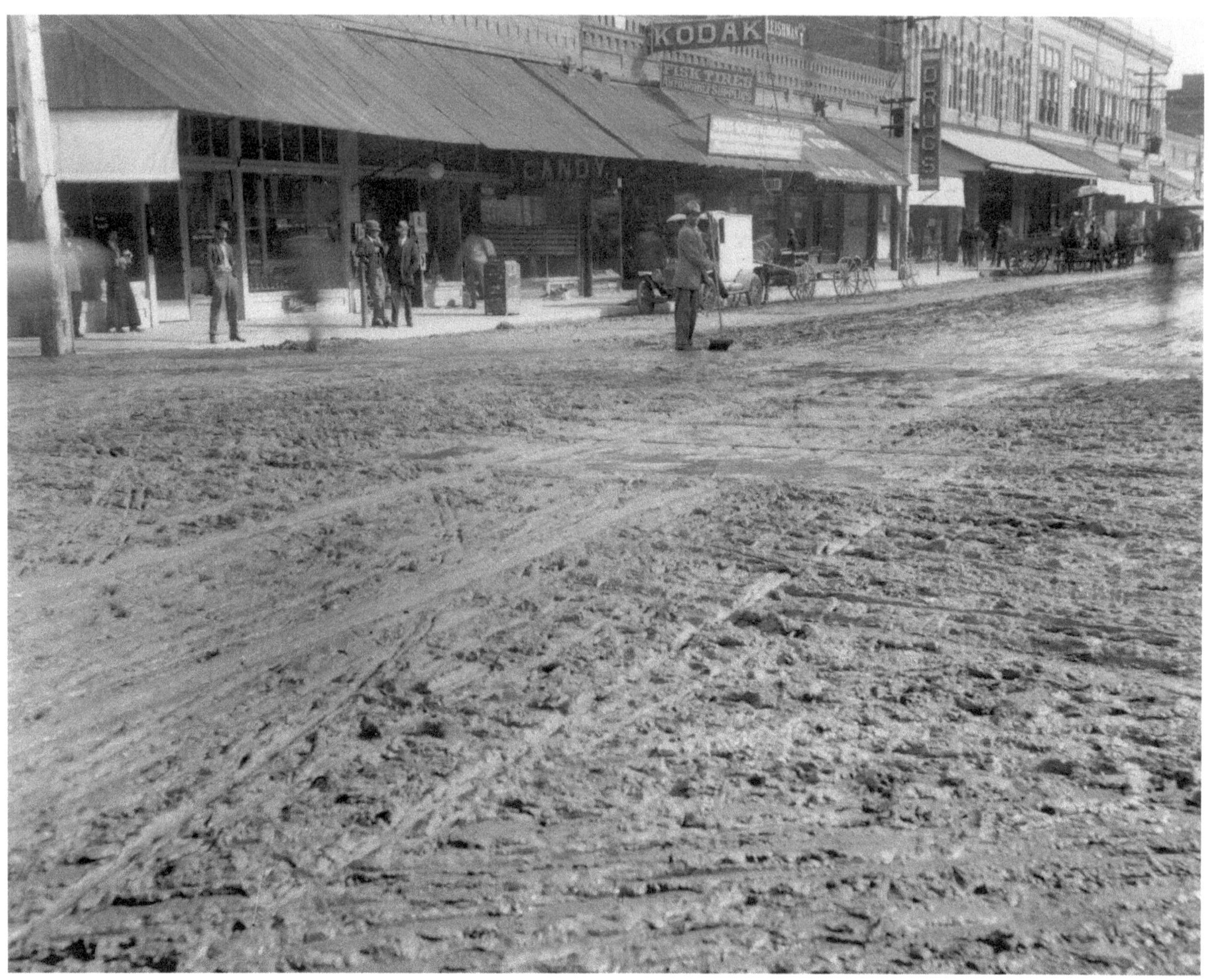

The University of Arizona football team warming up before a game in 1910. Old Main, the University's first building in 1891, is in the background.

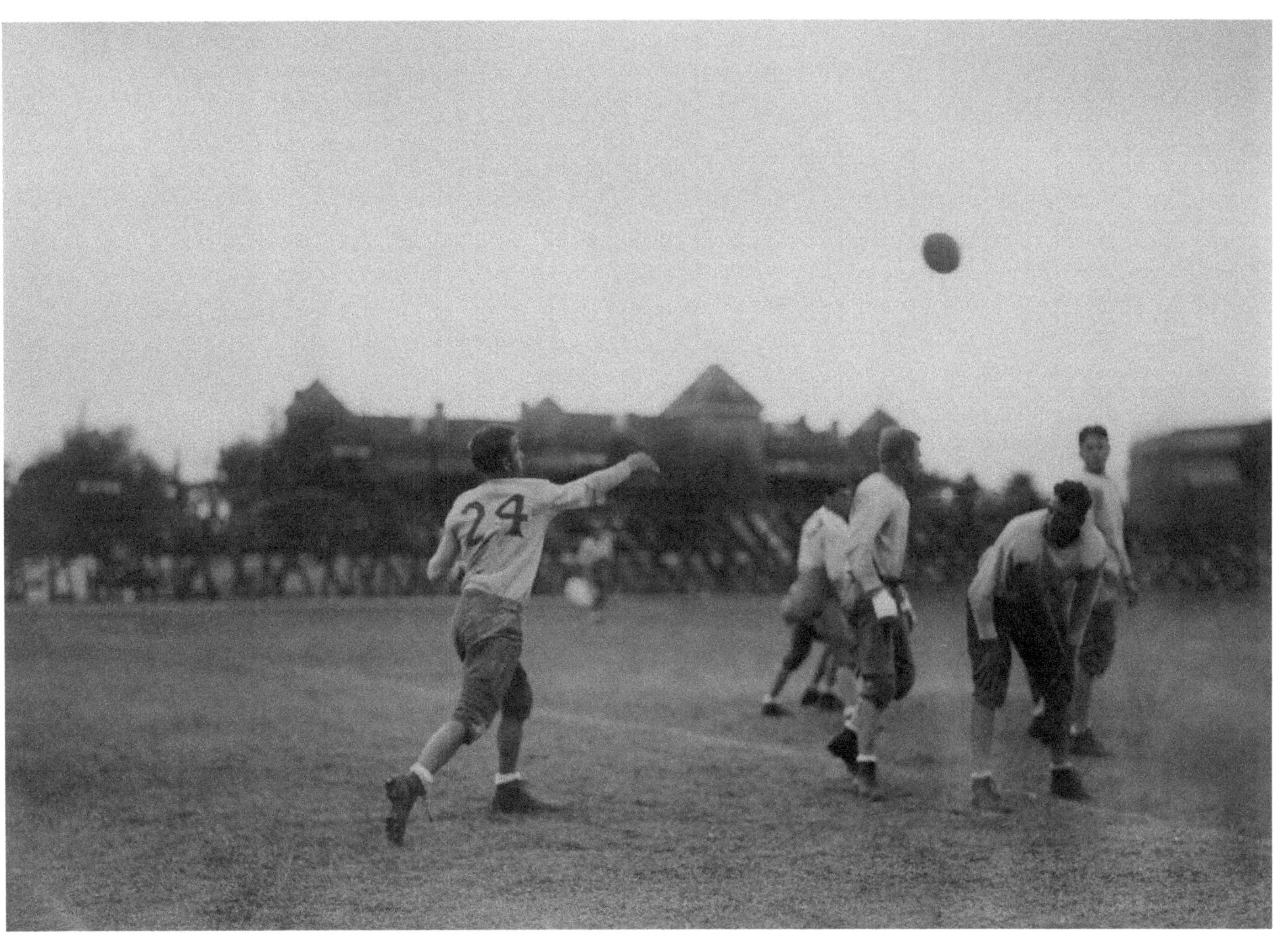

Looking north on Stone Avenue from Congress Street around 1912.

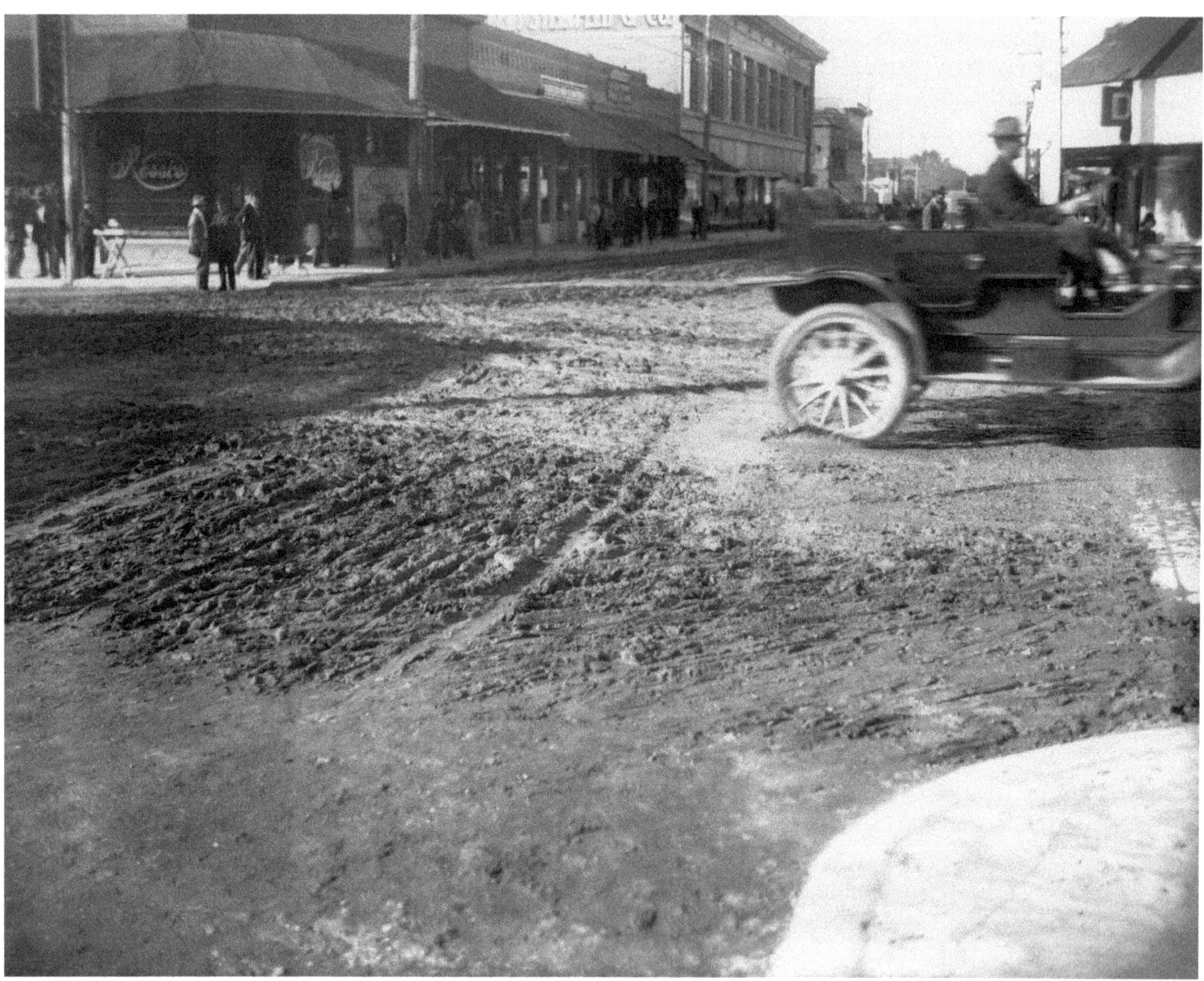

The paving crew at the El Paso and Southwestern Railroad Depot posed for a group picture in 1912.

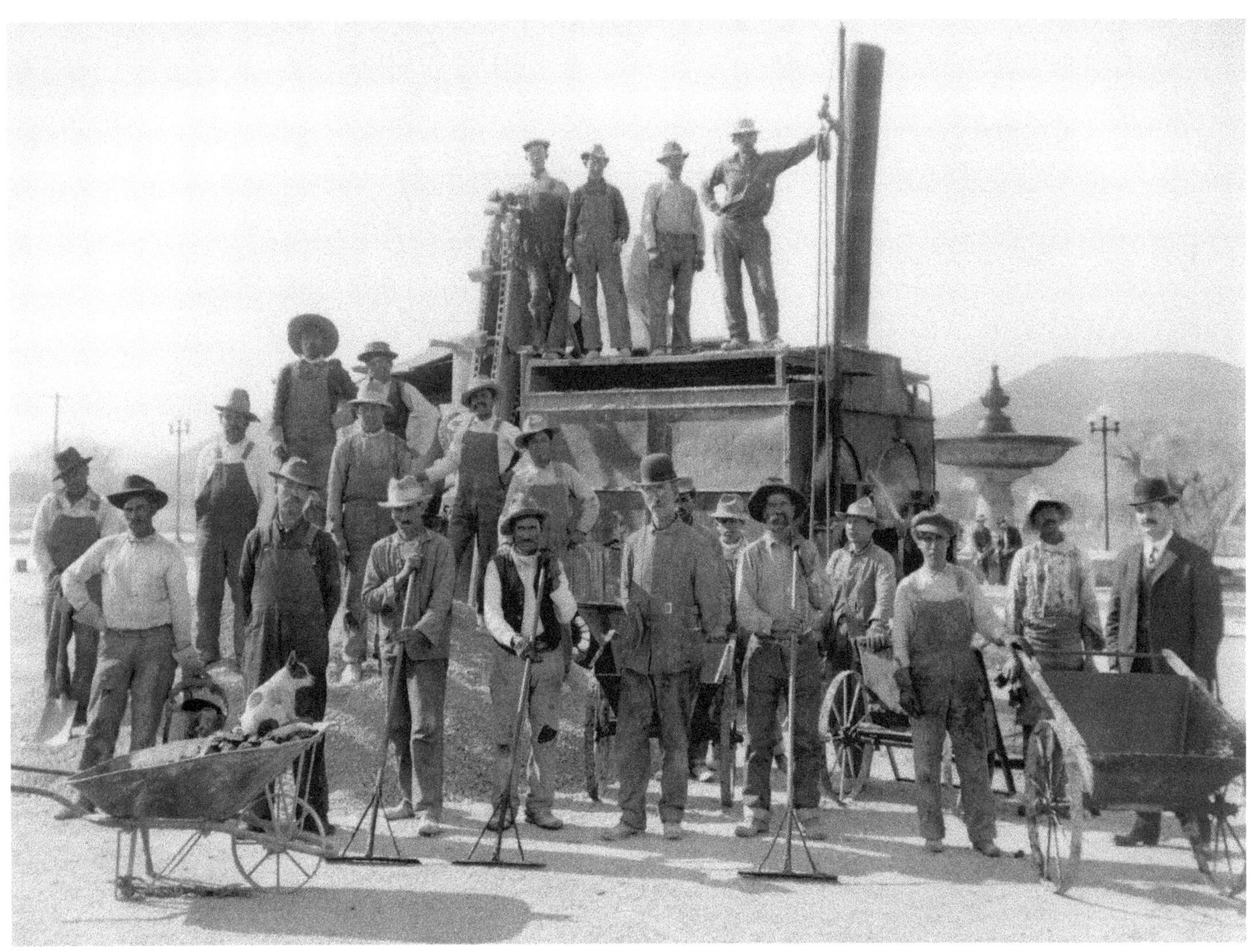

Paving the concourse at the El Paso and Southwestern Railroad Depot, 1912.

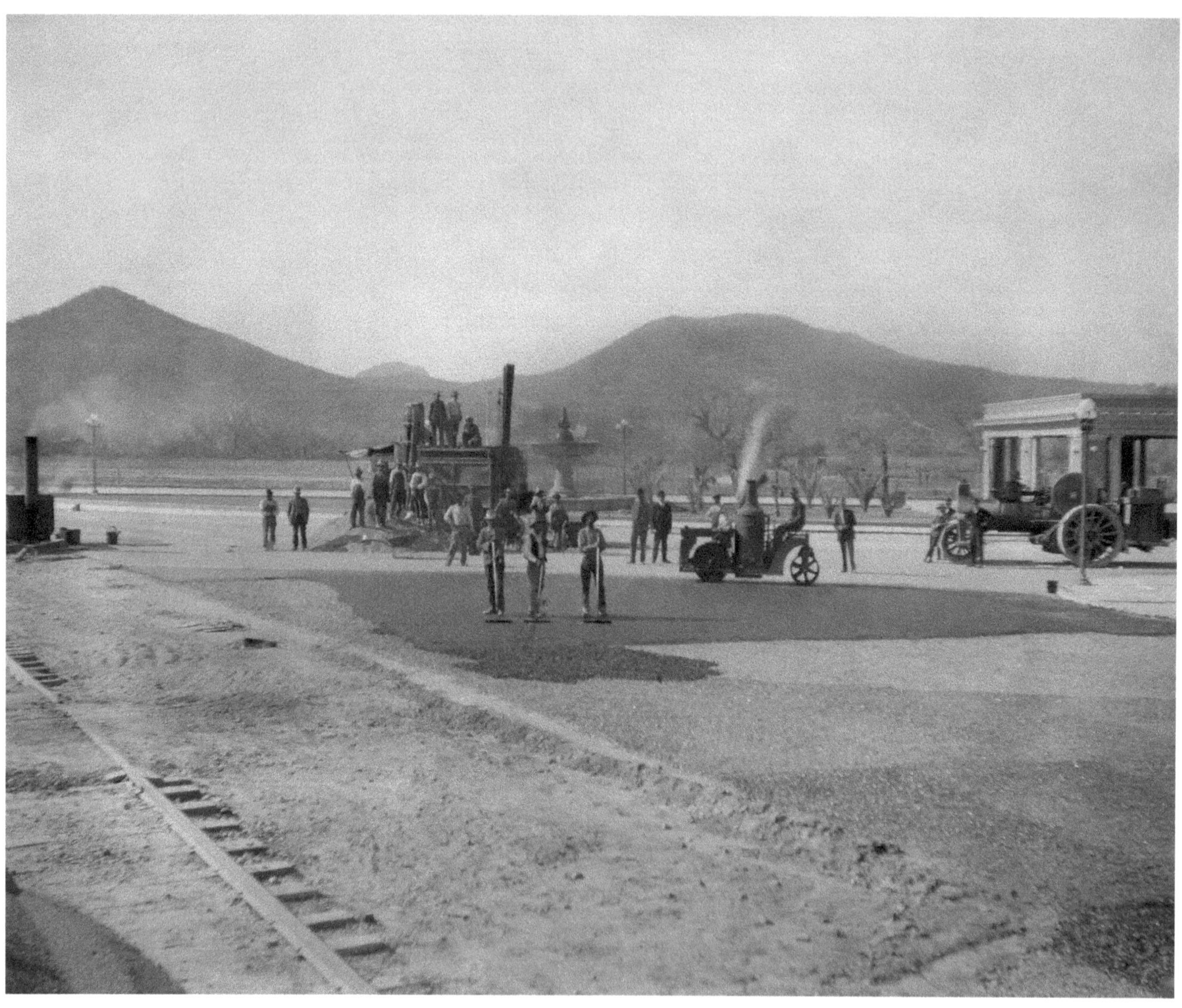

The El Paso and Southwest Railroad Depot, Tucson's second station, around 1913. The adjoining, 2.6-acre Railroad Park was designed by Cammillo Fenzi Franceschi and contained many exotic plants and trees. In the background are Sentinel Peak on the left and Tumamoc Hill on the right.

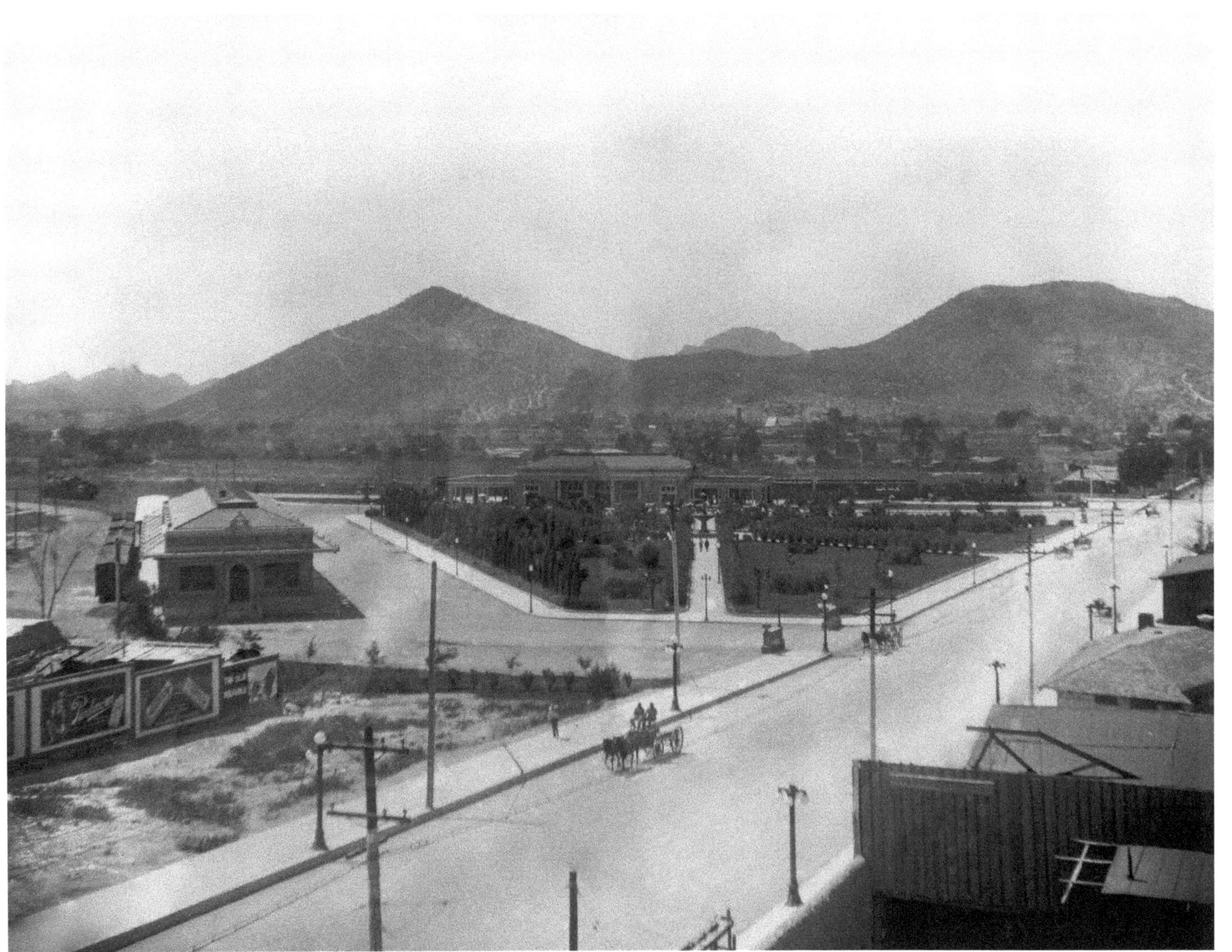

The paving of Congress Street during 1913.

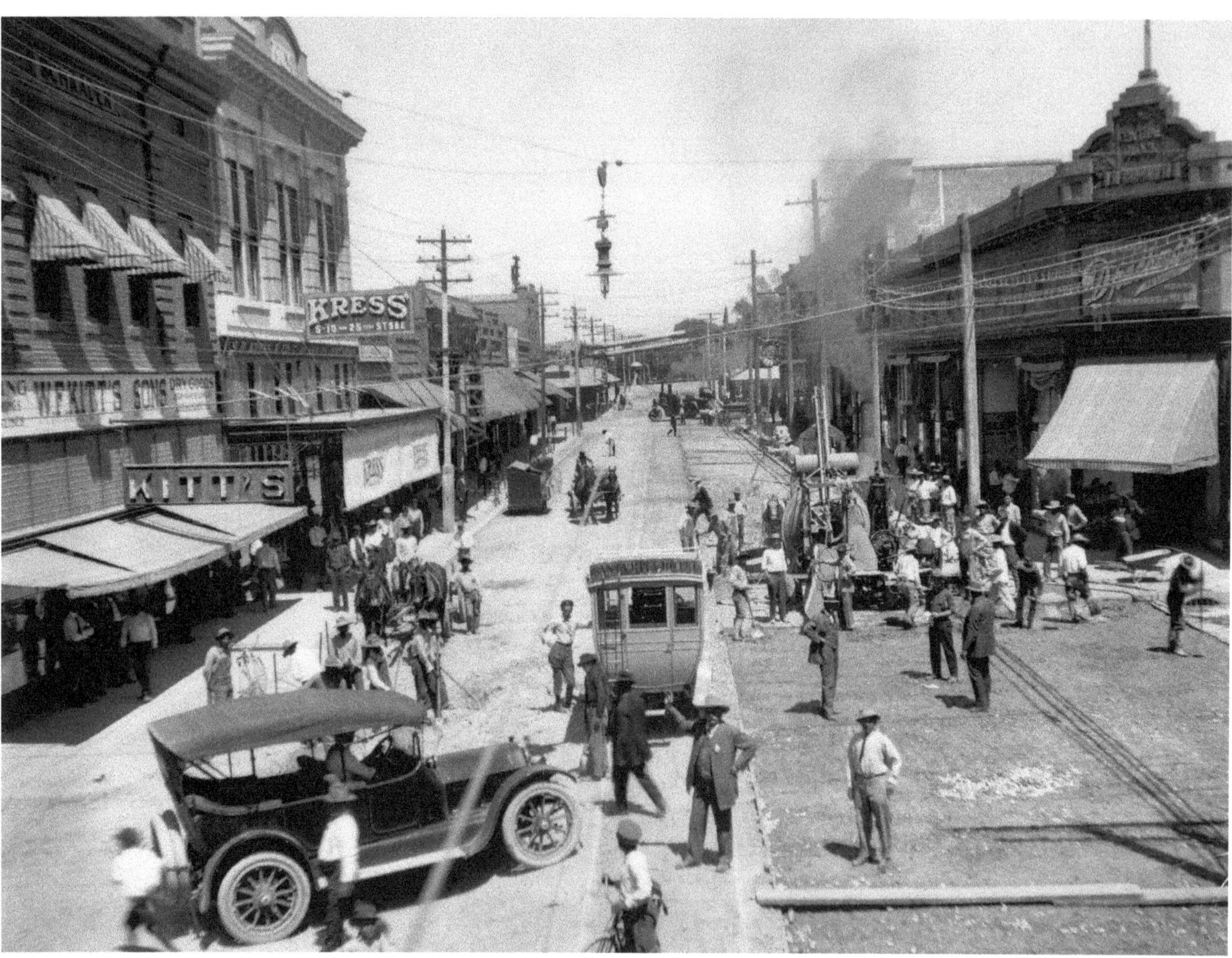

A view of Congress Street after the paving, looking west from Scott Street, around 1913. A trolley crosses Congress at Stone Avenue in the distance. There was still a mix of automobiles and horse-drawn vehicles in the streets.

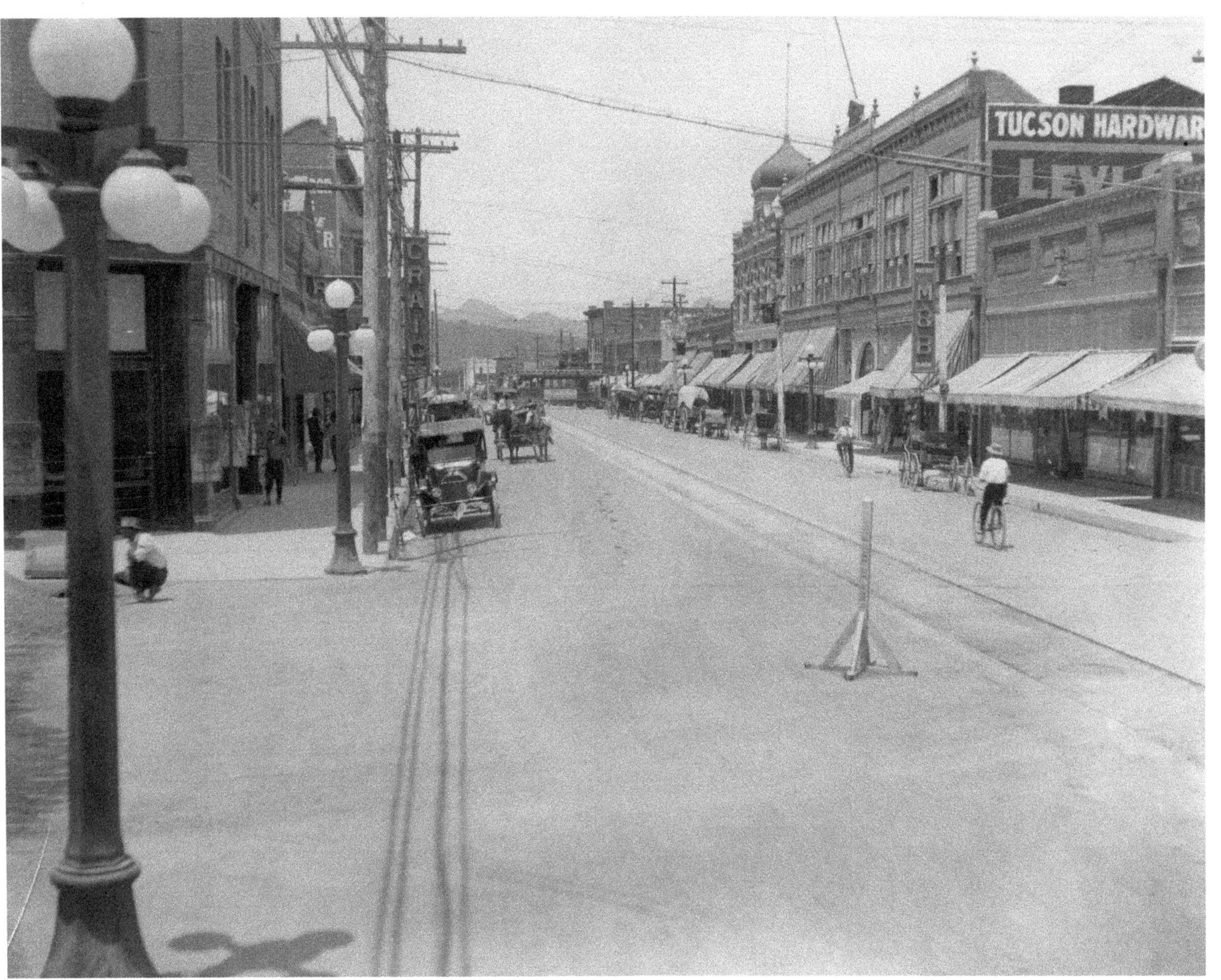

Congress Street looking west from Sixth Avenue after paving (ca. 1914).

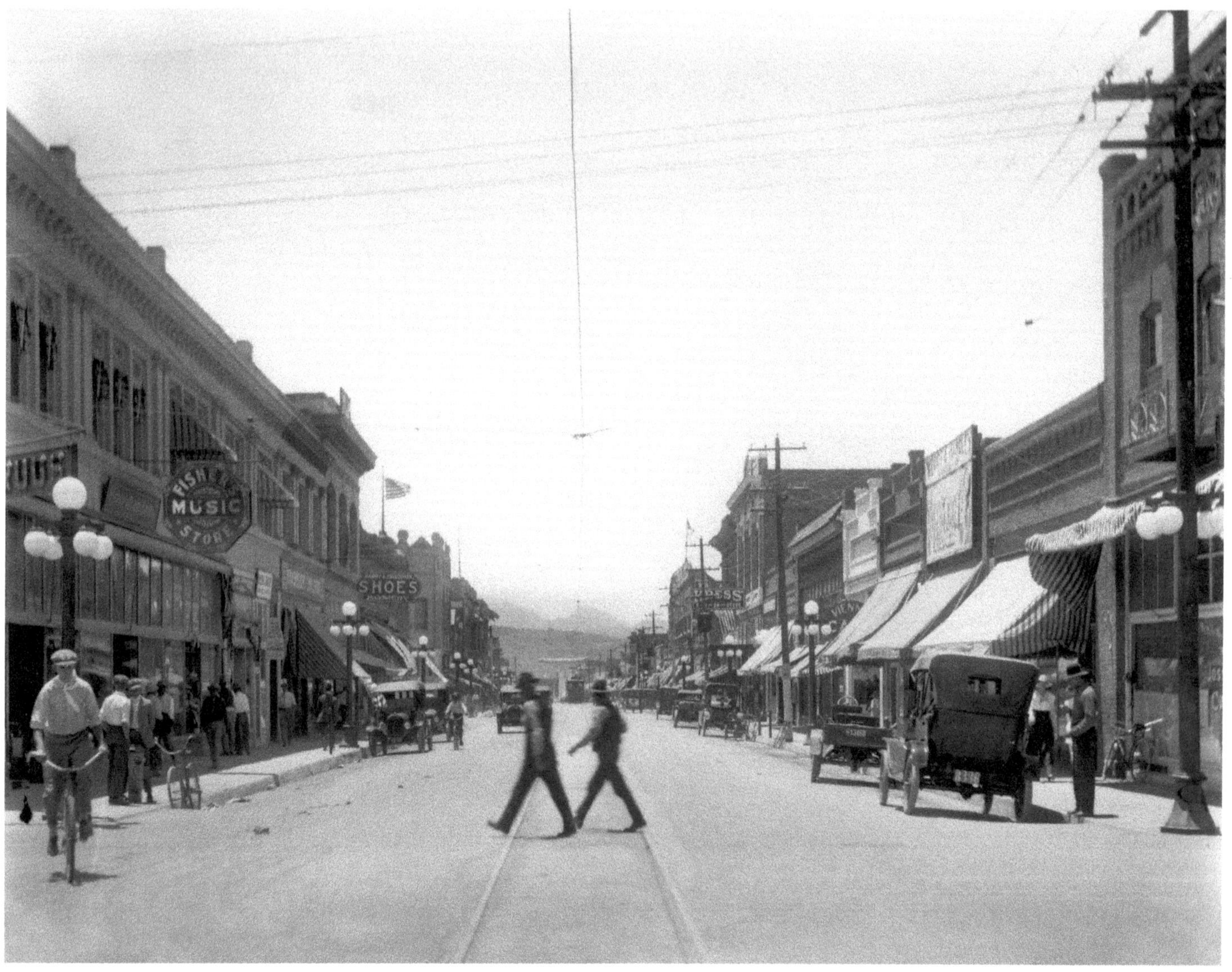

Freight and pickup trucks of local merchants on the concourse in front of the El Paso and Southwestern Depot around 1914.

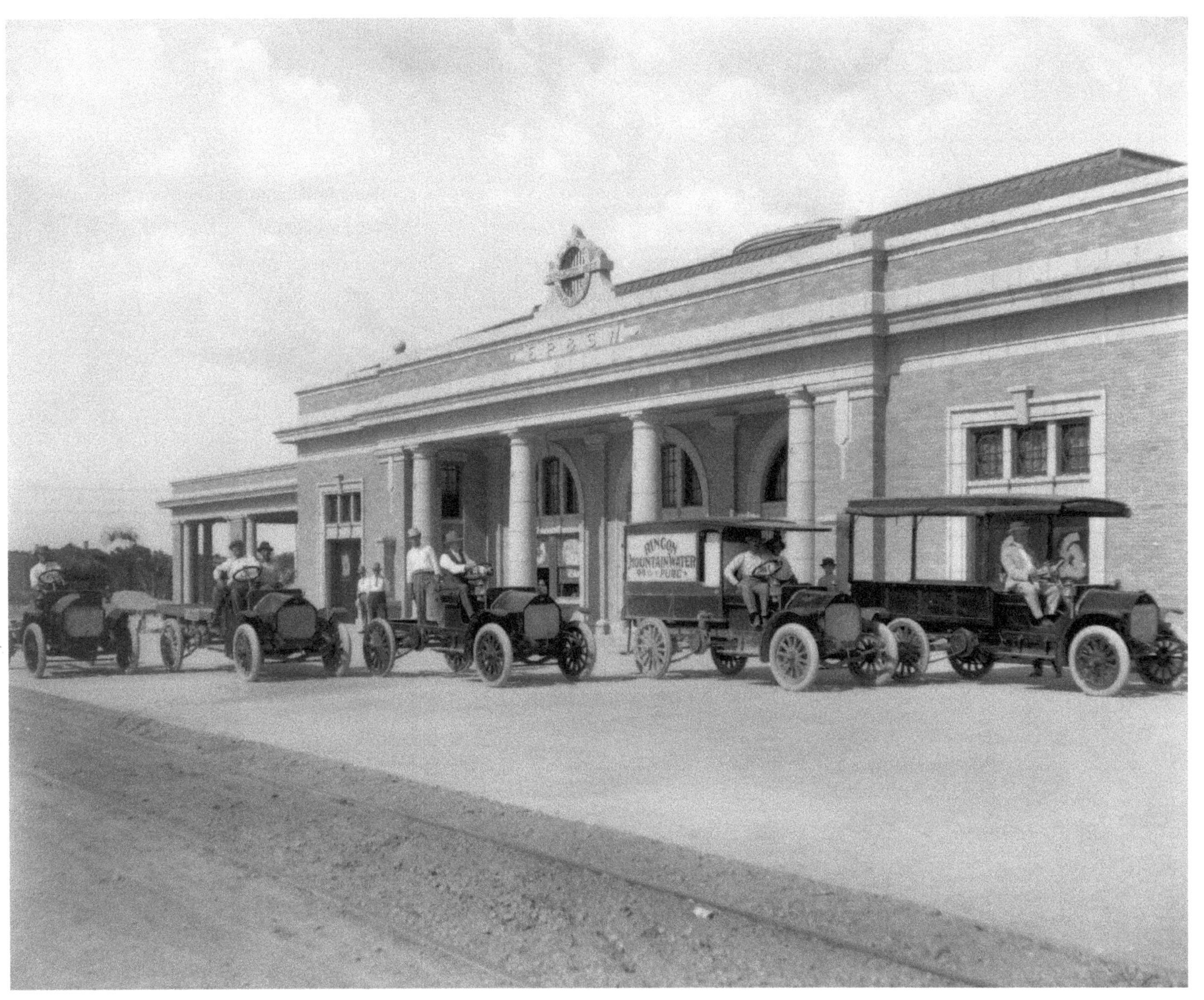

A crowd gathers at the site of a one-car automobile accident on Mesilla Street around 1914. The Chicago Store was *una tienda barata* or a store with low prices. Across Meyer Street was the Lee Kwon & Co. grocery and dry goods store.

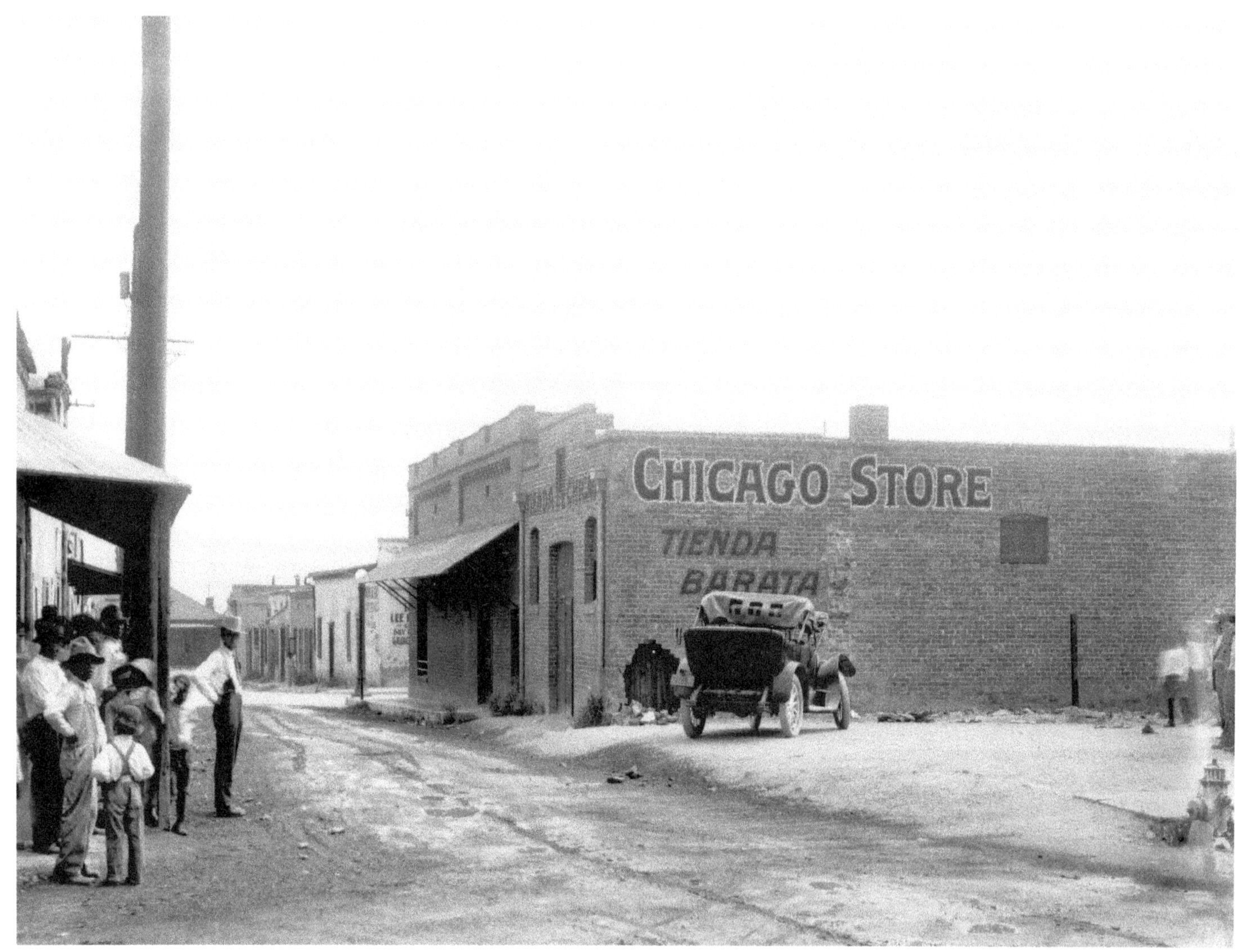

Built in 1913, the Hotel Tucsonia stood at Main Street and Congress Street near the El Paso and Southwestern Depot, seen here about 1915.

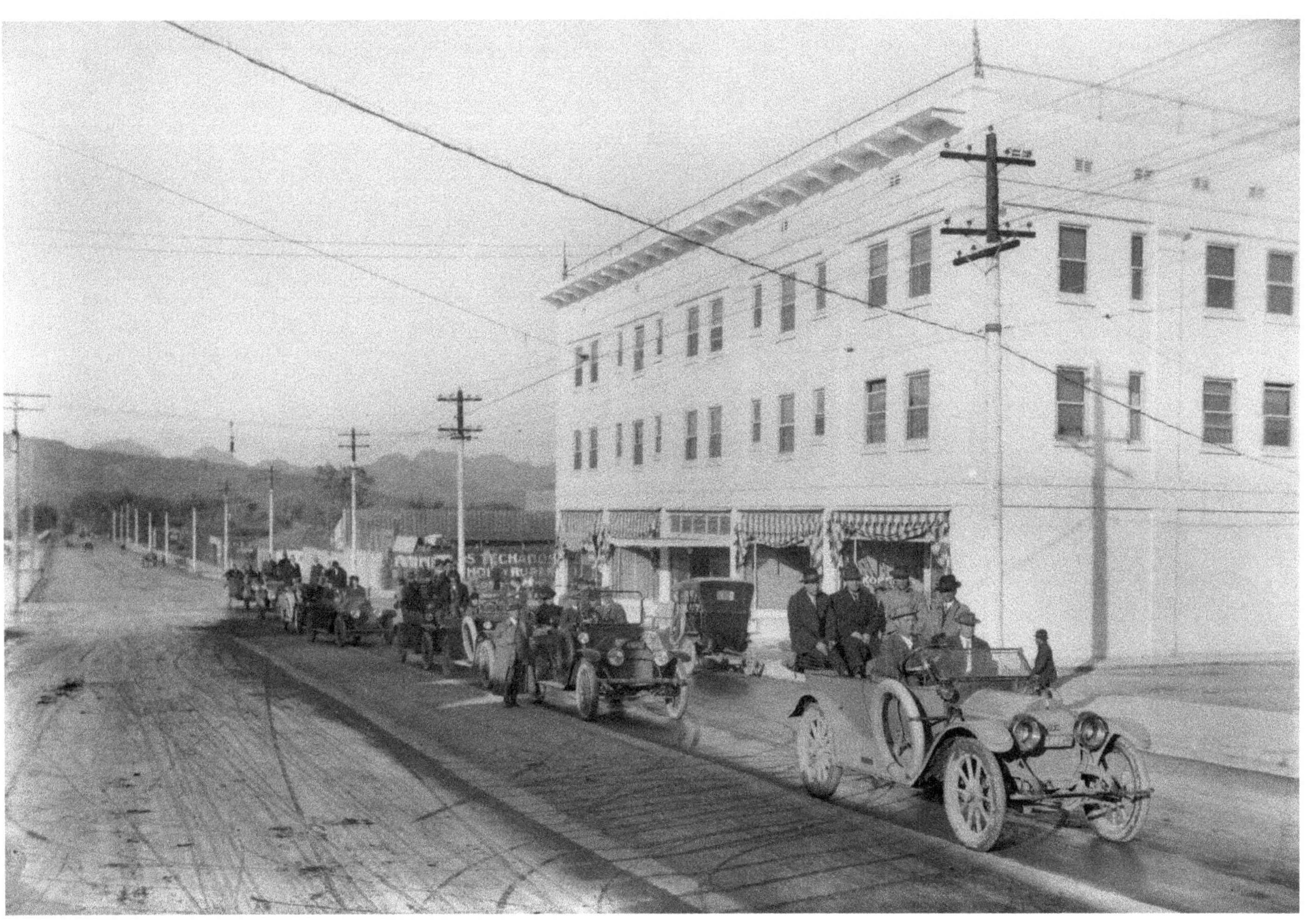

The 1915 Santa Cruz River flood, which destroyed the Congress Street Bridge.

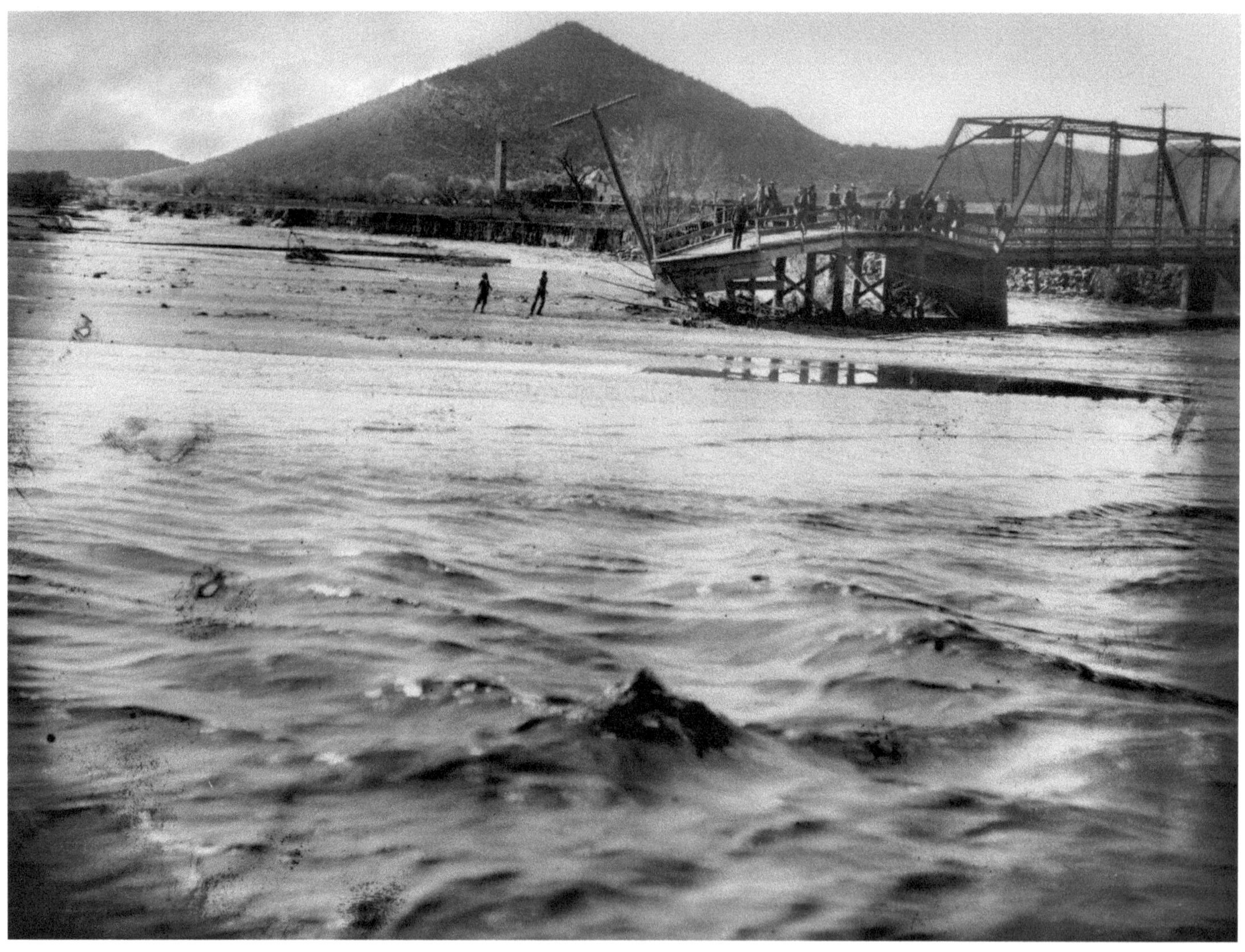

Around 1890, the Cosmopolitan Hotel was taken over by a Mrs. Orndorff who changed the name to the Hotel Orndorff. This view is around 1915.

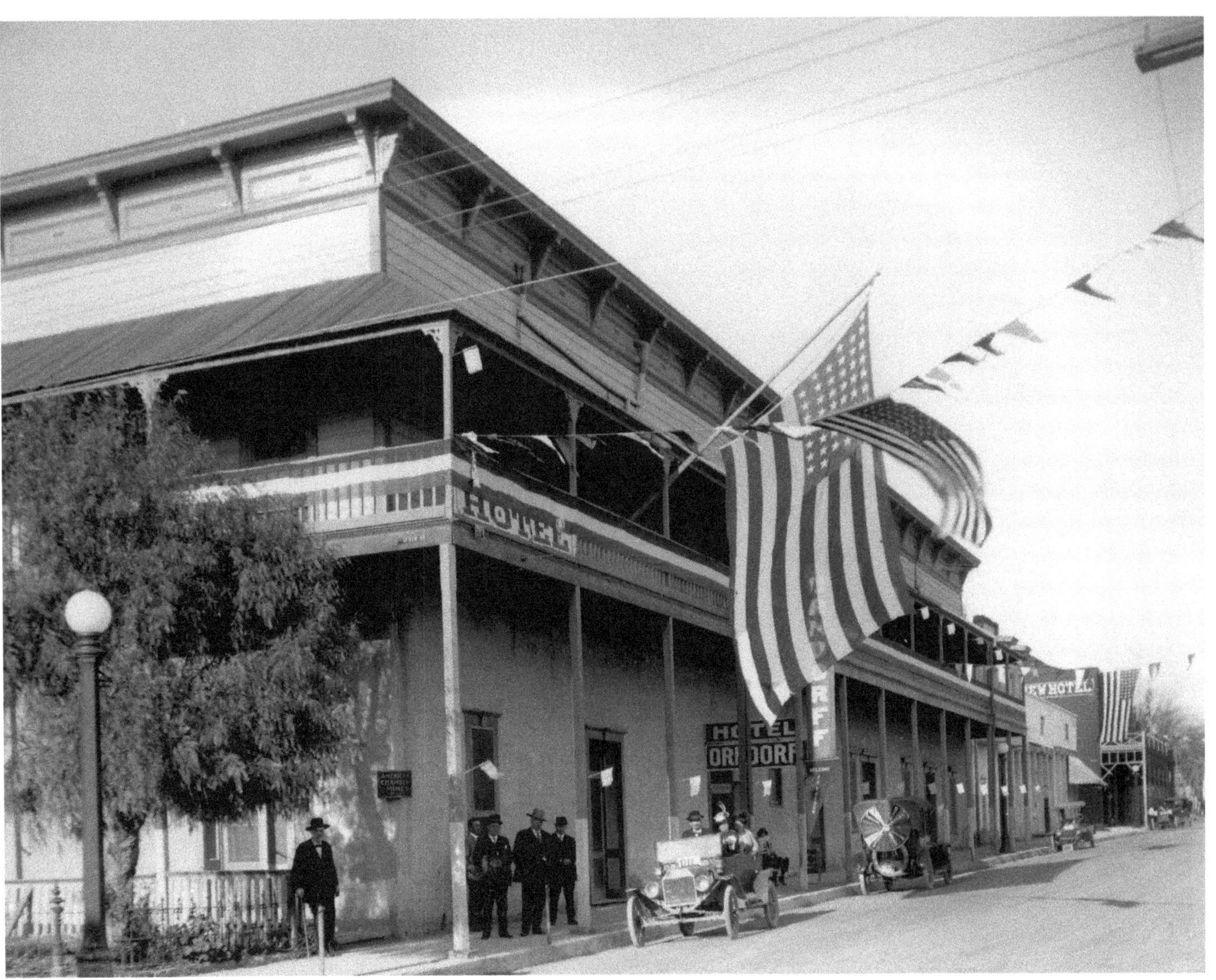

The buildings of Fort Lowell, seen here around 1915, continued to deteriorate until 1963 when Fort Lowell Park was created.

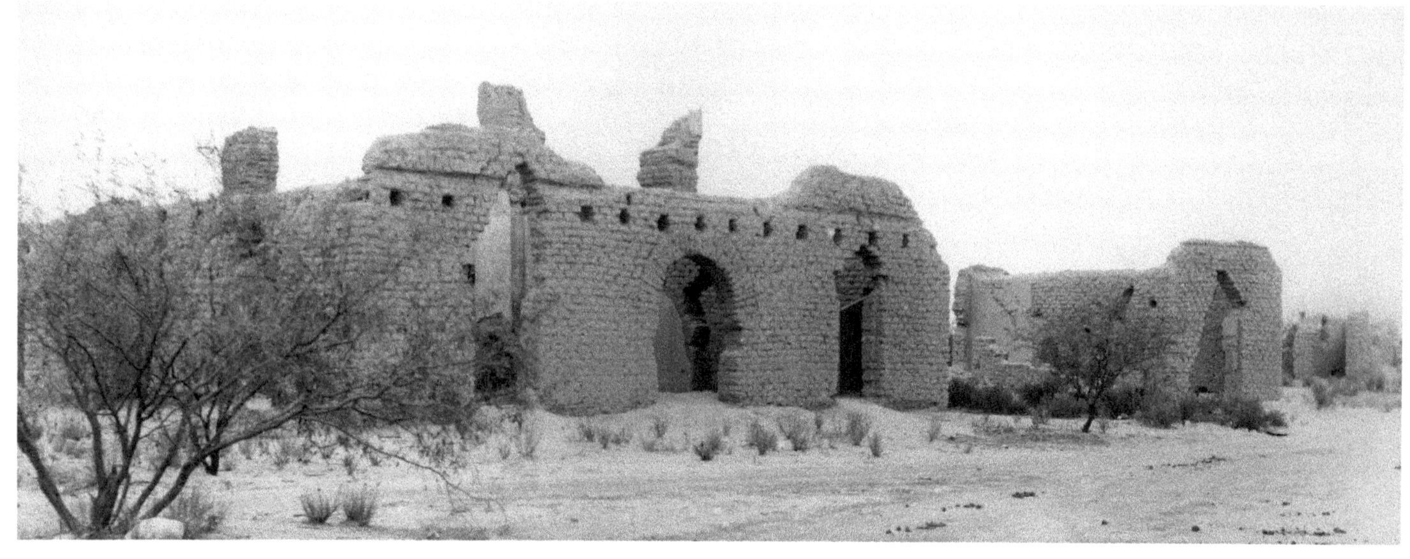

Horse racing in its many forms has long been a favorite Tucson sporting event. Harness racing attracted a crowd at the new half-mile track at the Southern Arizona Fair Grounds (ca. 1915).

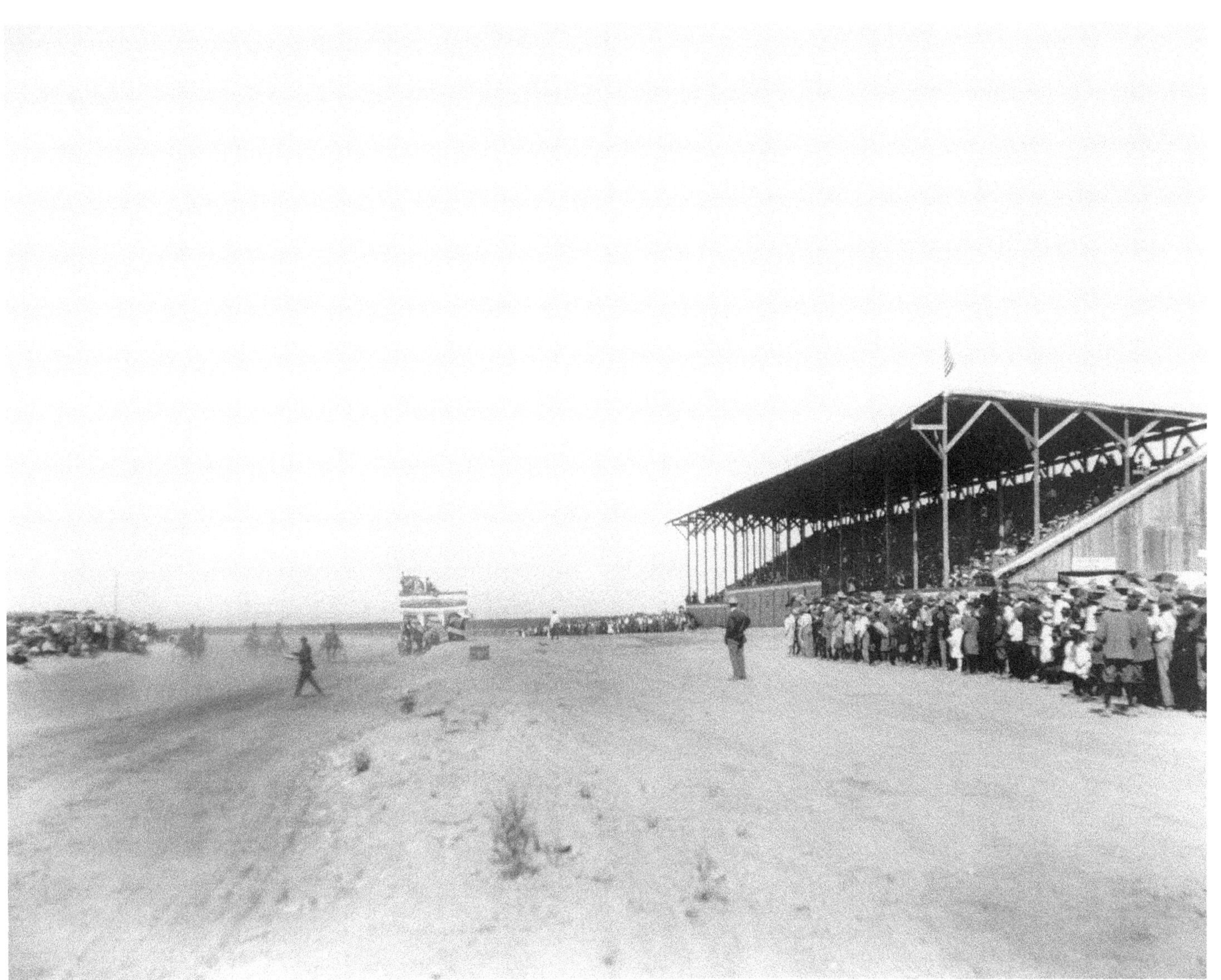

Auto racing was also an attraction at the new track (ca. 1915).

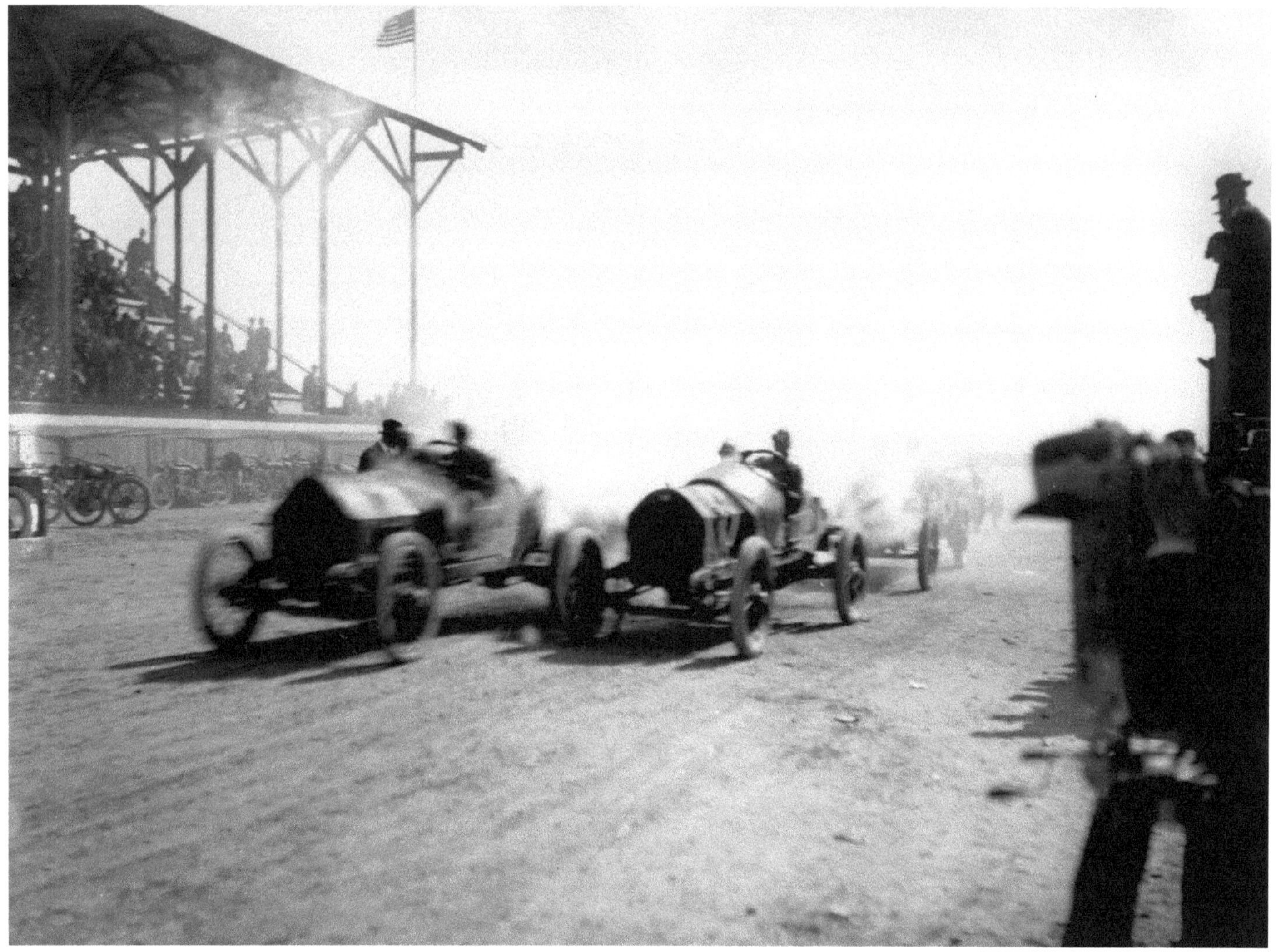

Eddie Rickenbacher was one of the competitors in a 103.152-mile auto race held March 20, 1915, at the Fair Grounds track. A few years later, he won the Medal of Honor as a World War I flying ace.

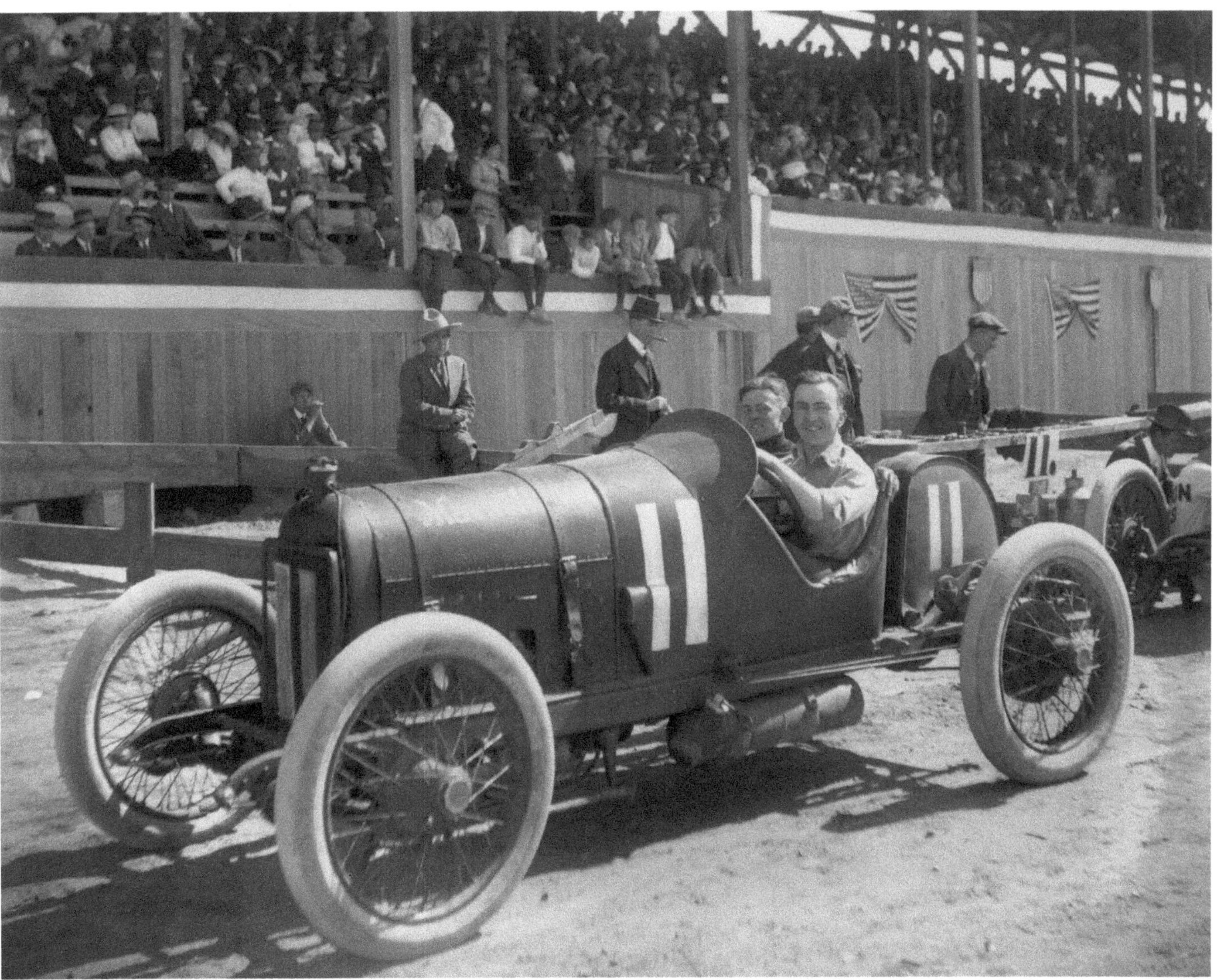

Congress Street looking east across Stone Avenue (ca. 1915). Automobiles quickly outnumbered horse-drawn wagons on Tucson's streets.

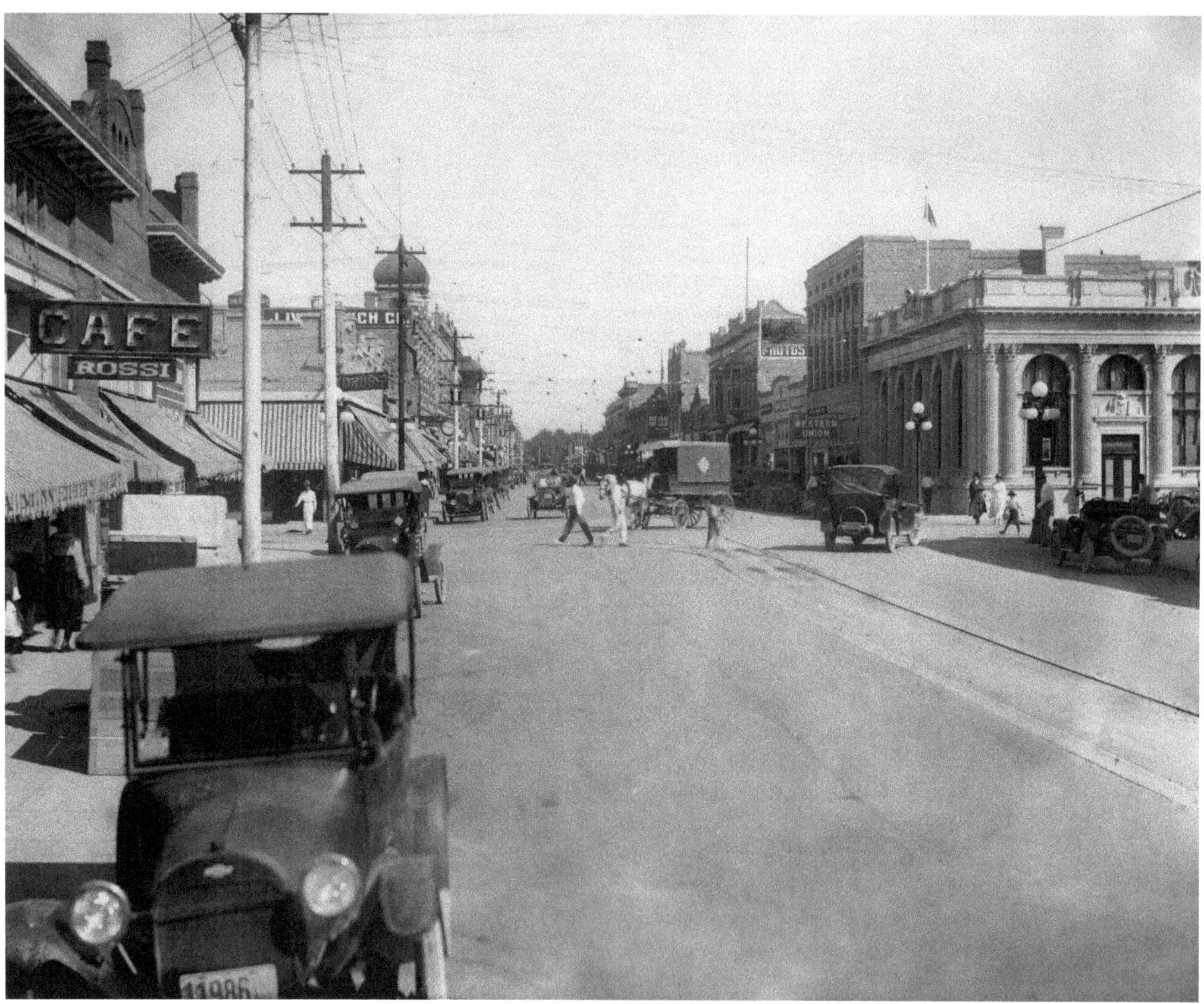

A float decorated for a convention of the Alianza Hispano Americana, a fraternal organization formed in Tucson in 1895. The banners and oars reflect its goals and standards. The girls wear sashes bearing the names of Arizona cities with chapters of the organization (ca 1916).

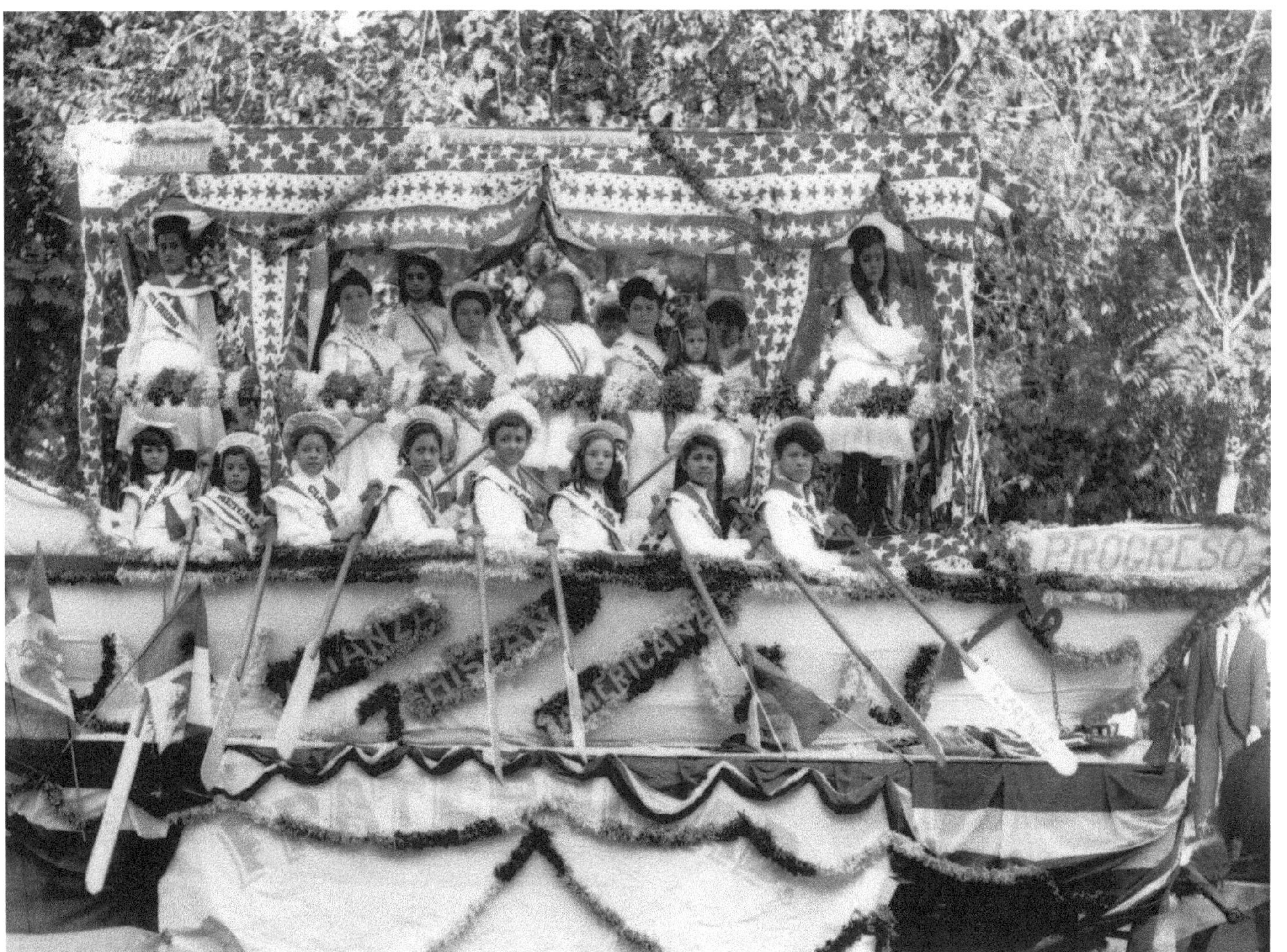

Tucson's second city hall was built in 1917 and replaced in 1972.

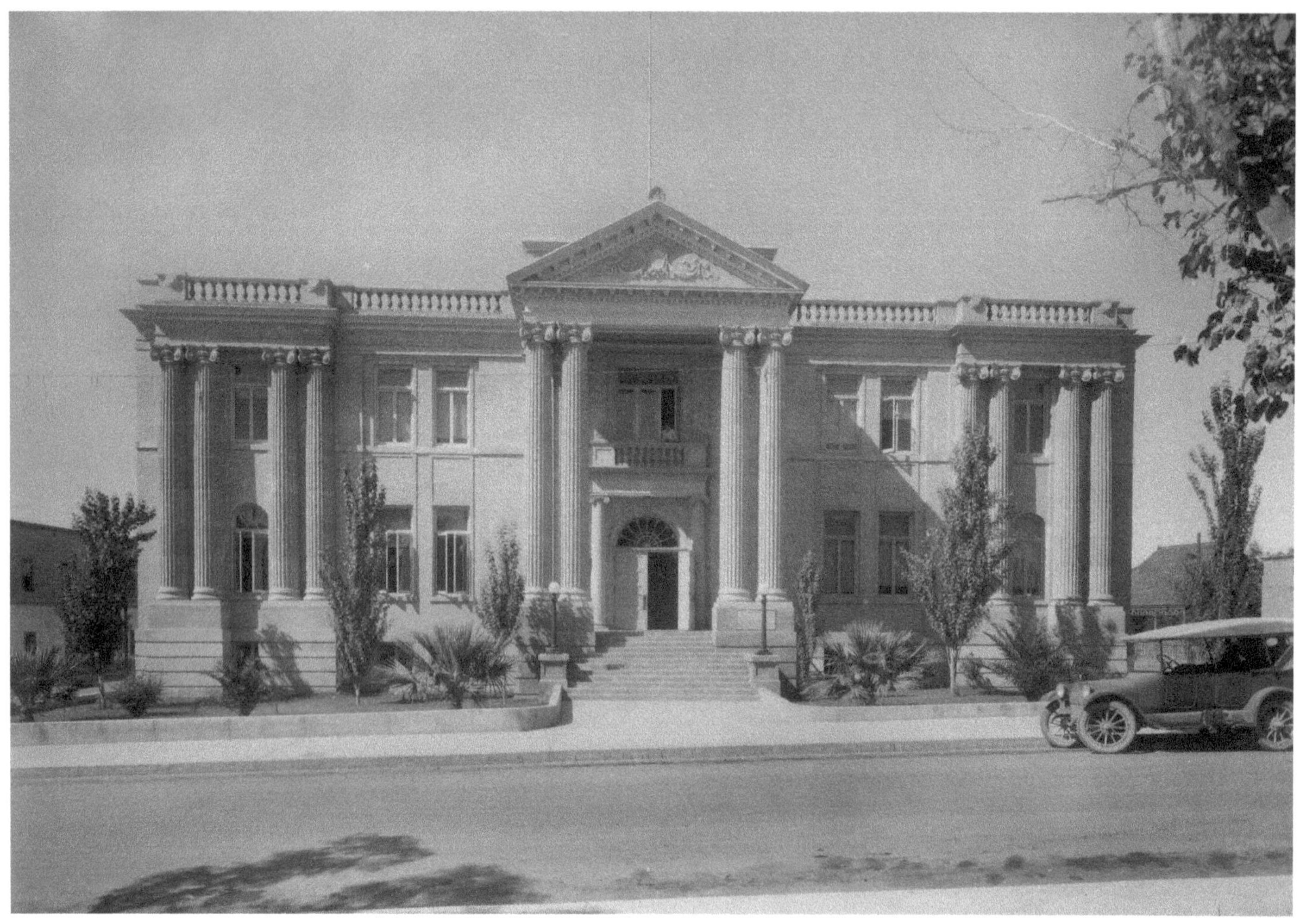

A float from a World War I parade.

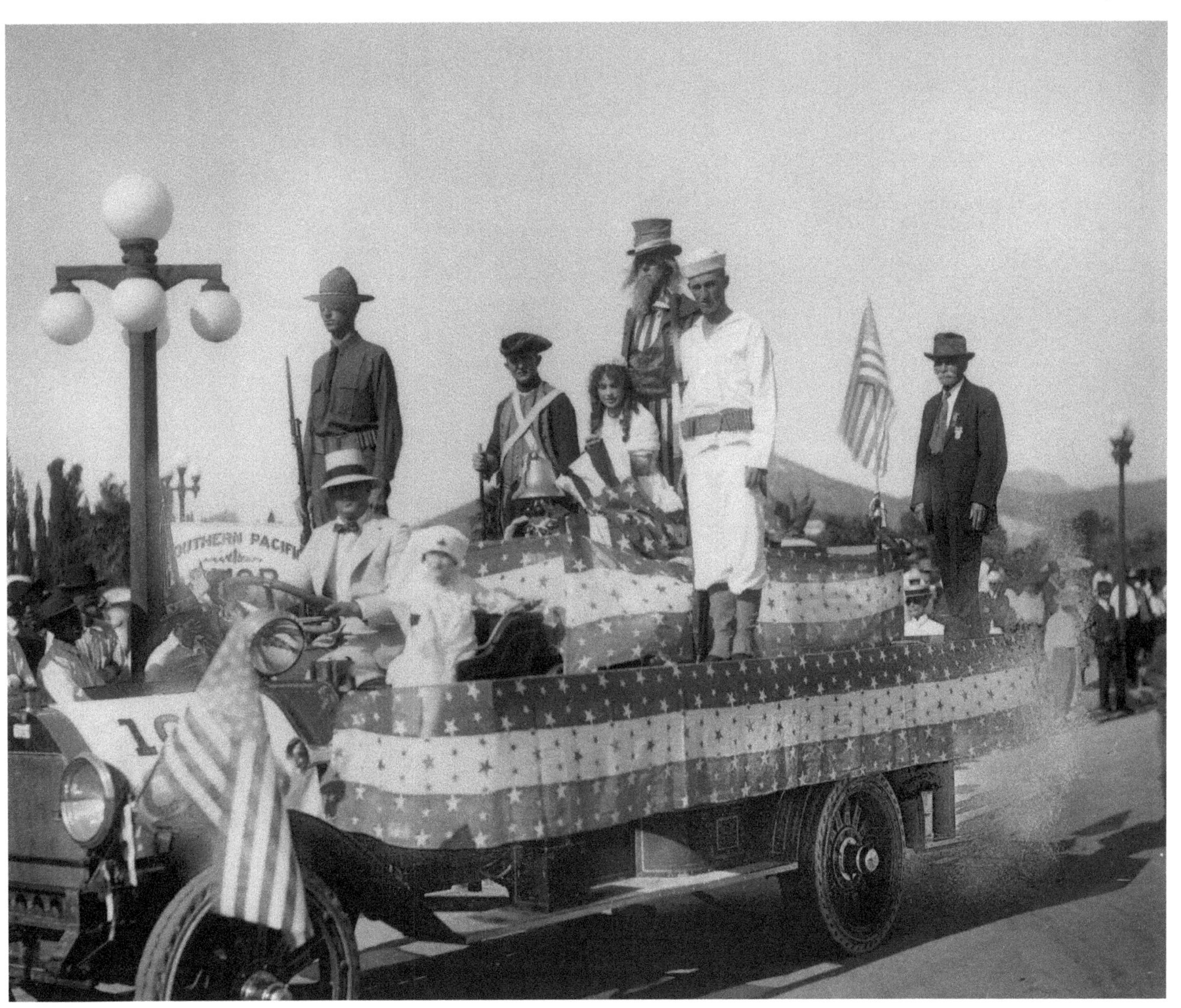

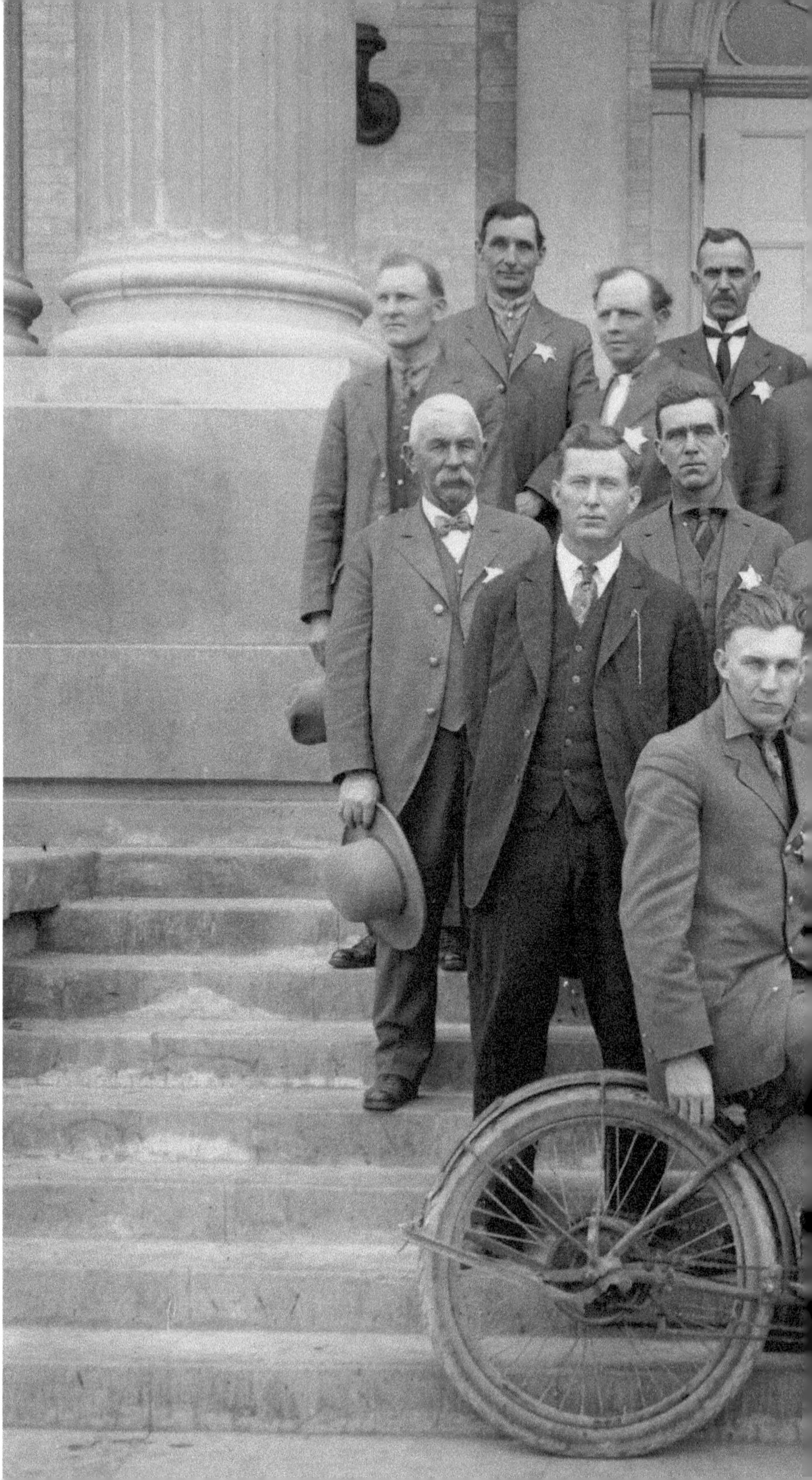

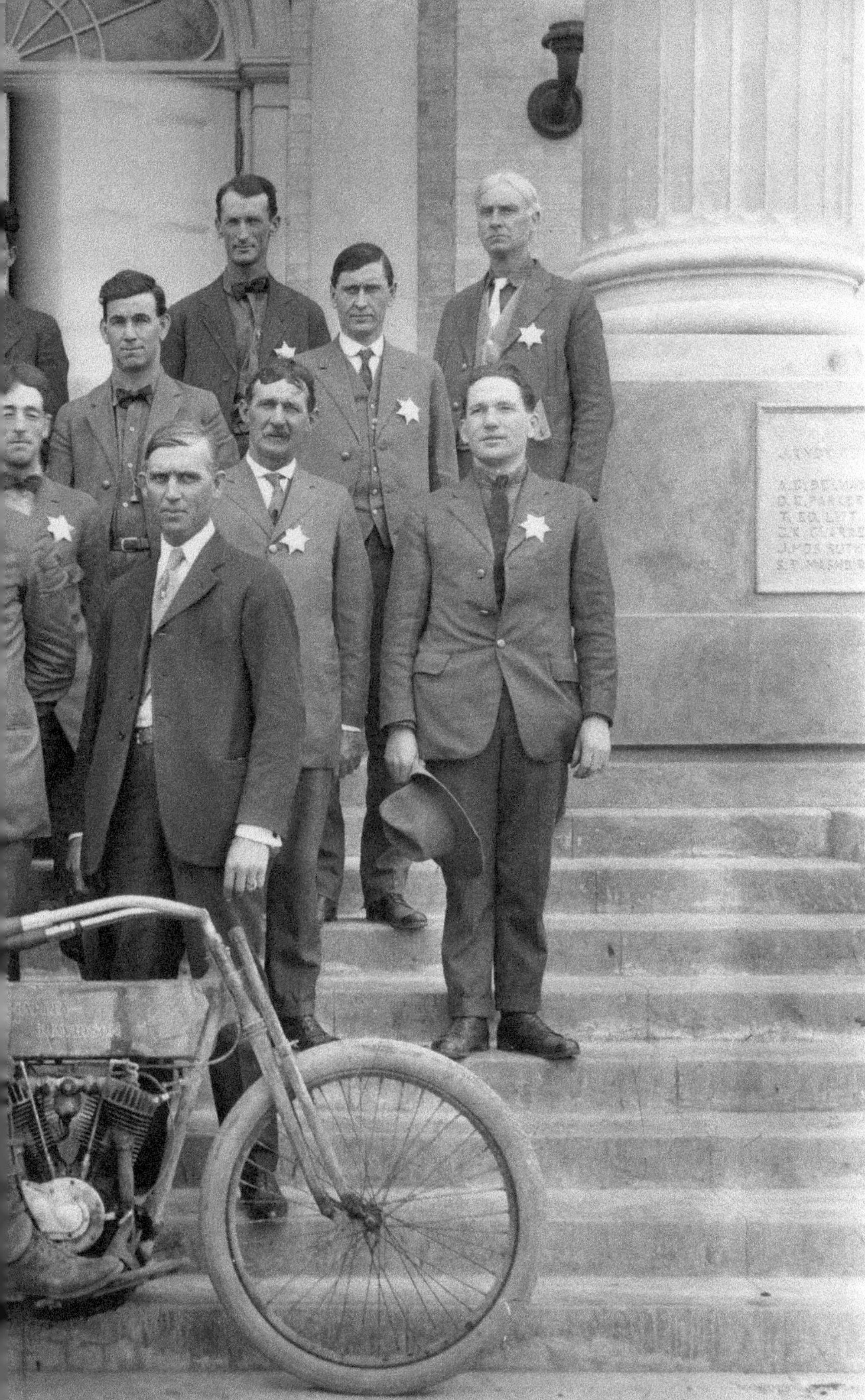

The Tucson Police Department posed on the steps of City Hall with the first police motorcycle (ca. 1917).

A Liberty Bell float waiting for a World War I parade to begin.

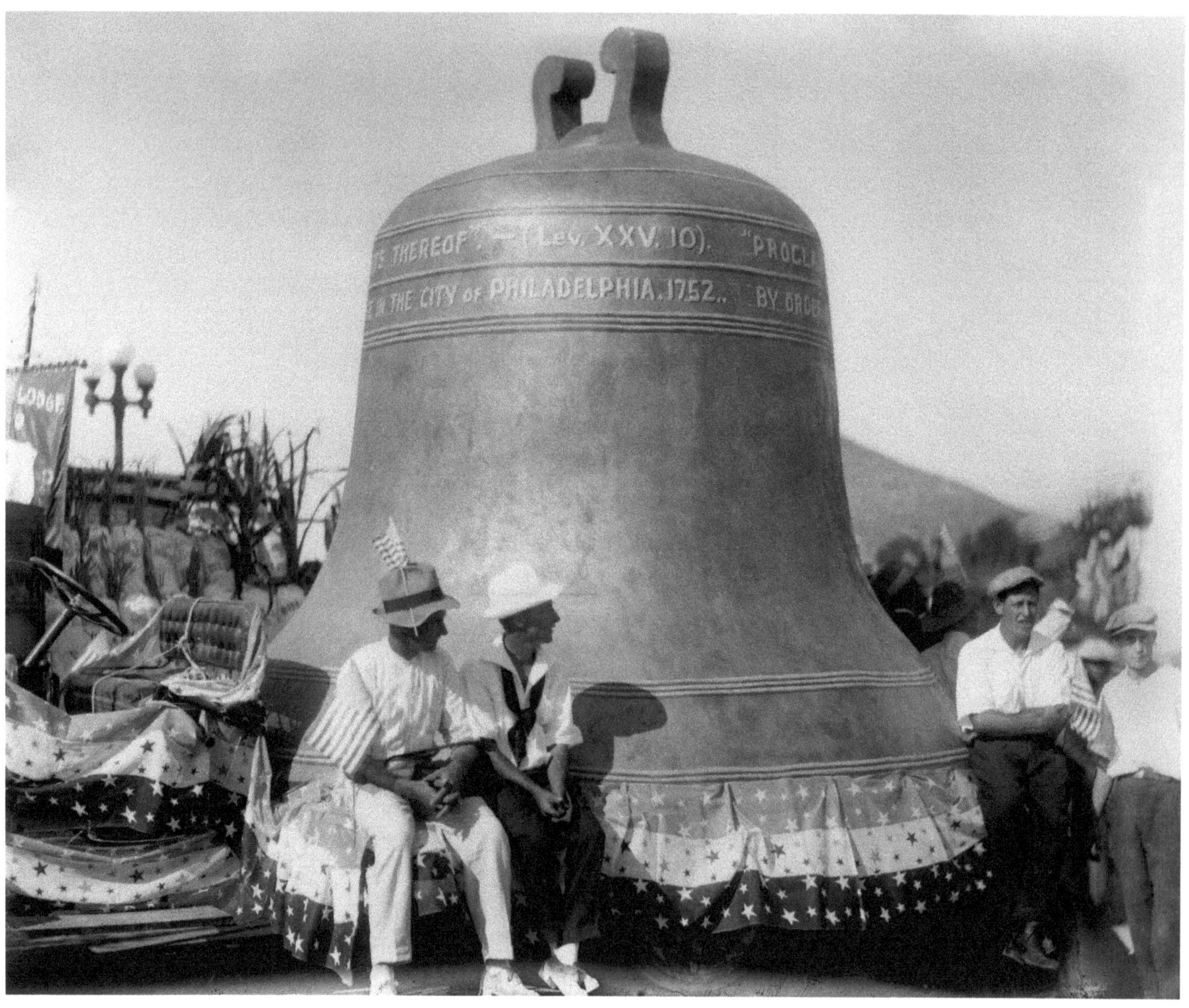

Troops marching in a World War I parade. The El Paso and Southwestern Depot is in the background.

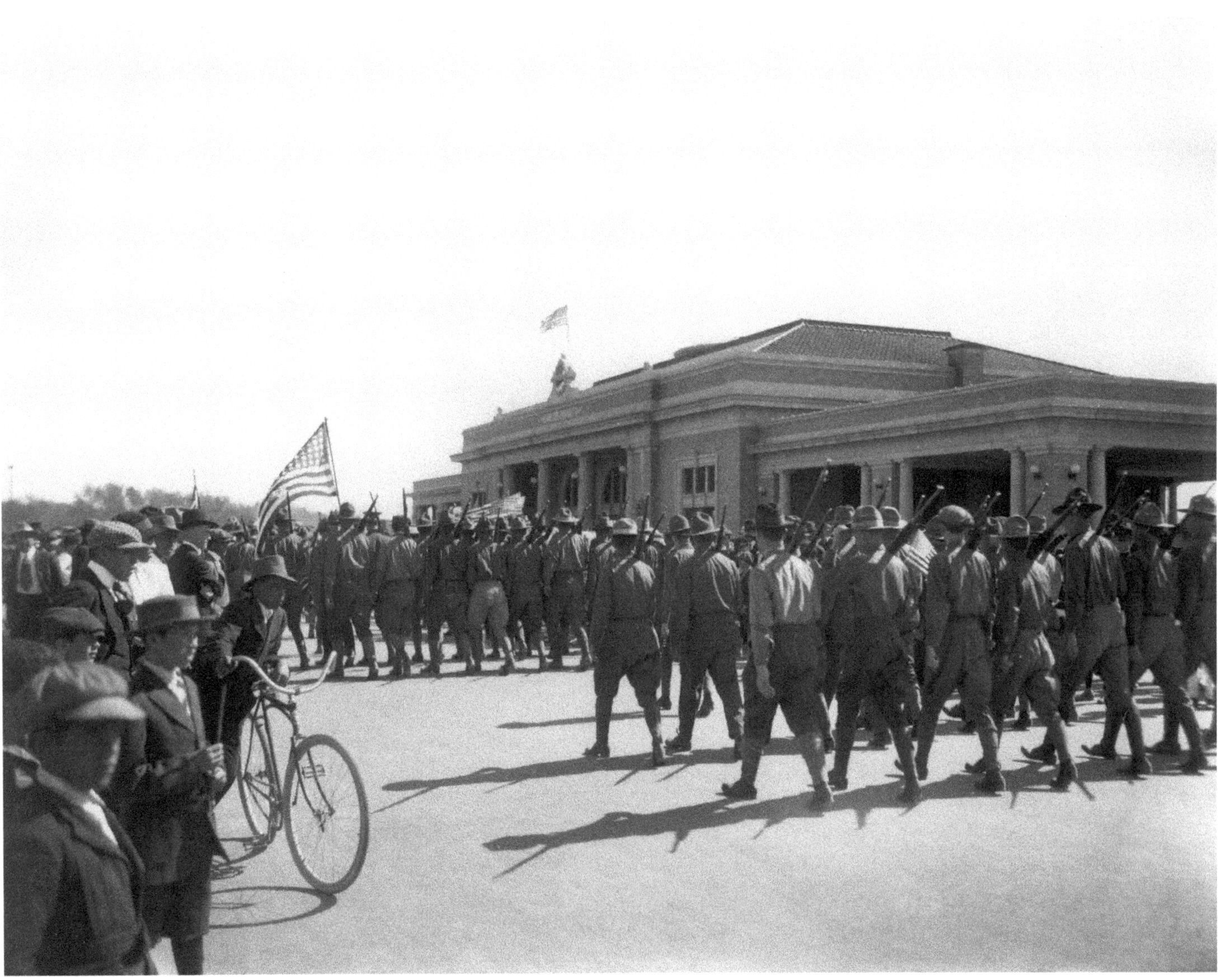

A military band in a World War I parade.

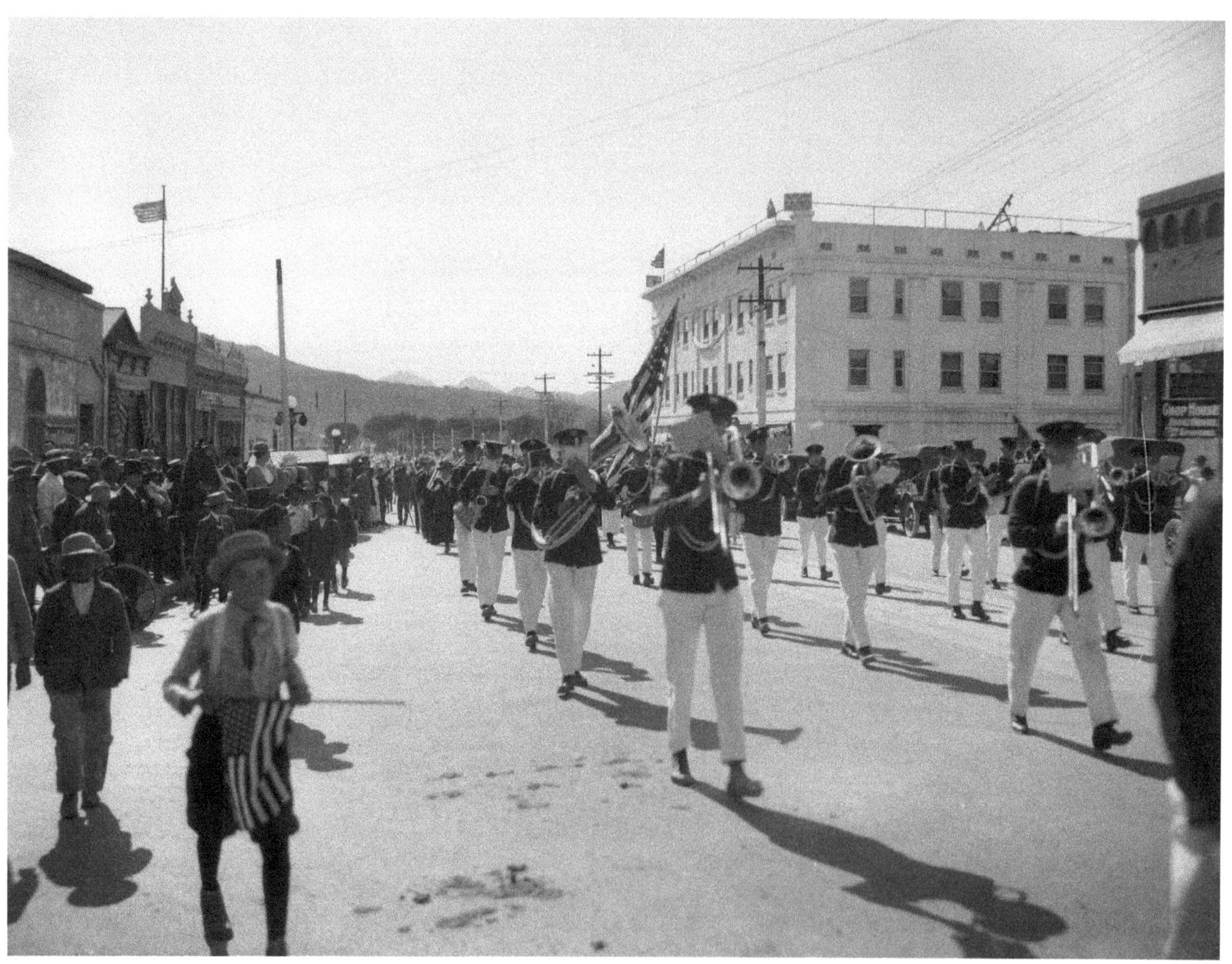

A night rally for Liberty Bonds on Congress Street around 1917.

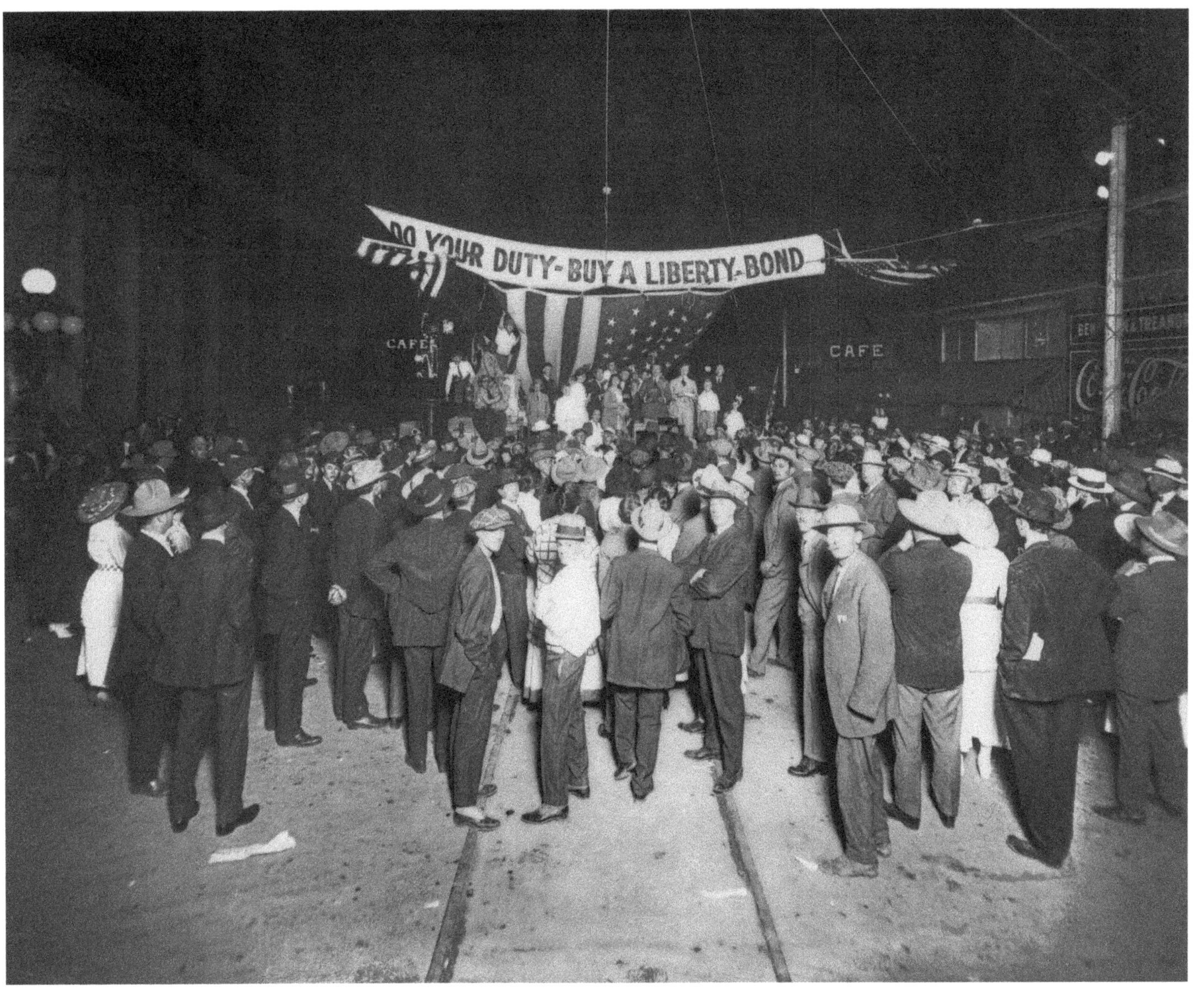

A race car driver and his crew posed in front of the Schweitzer Machine Company on South Sixth Avenue around 1917.

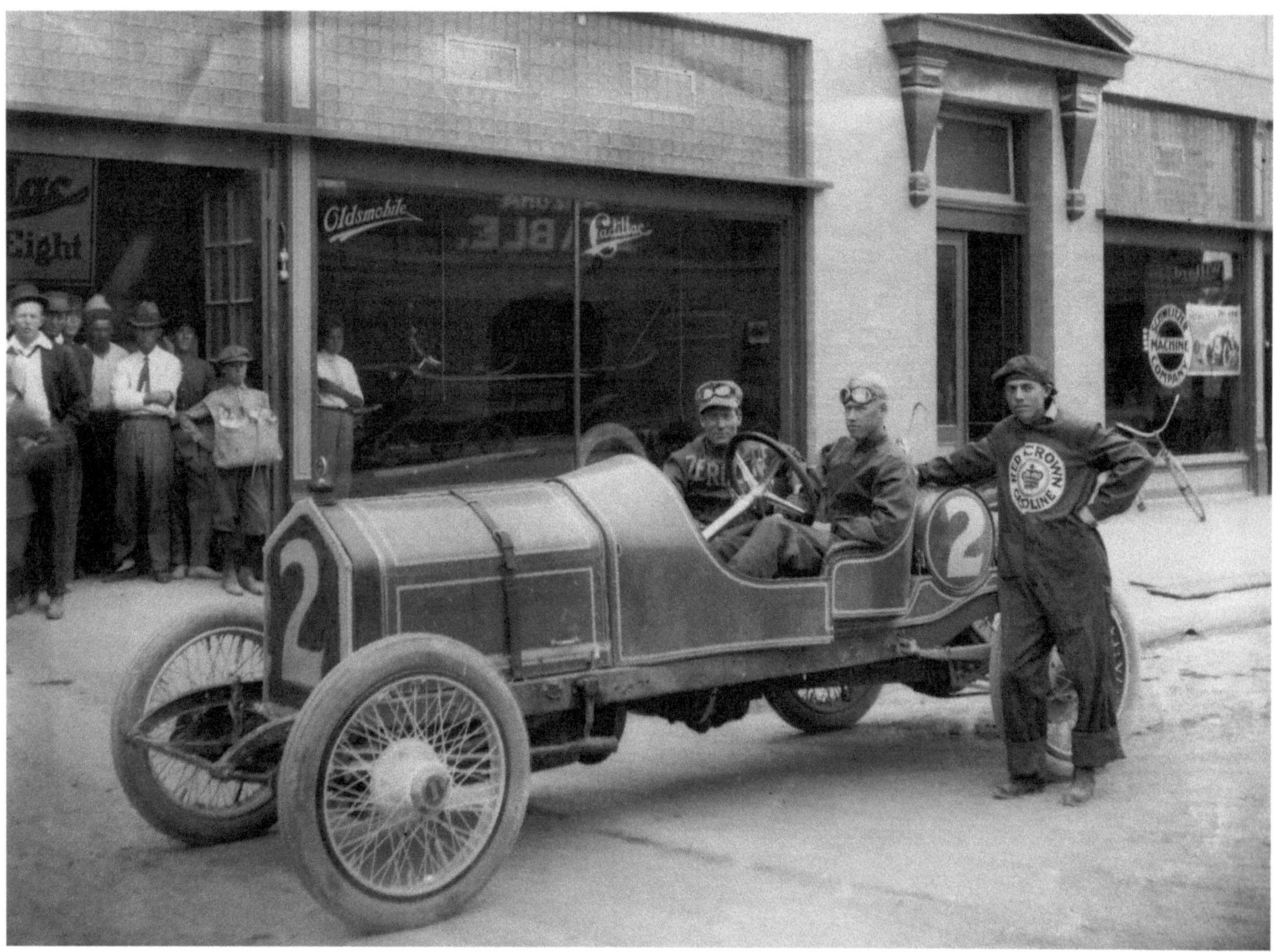

Looking west on Broadway Boulevard from Stone Avenue (ca. 1918). Broadway was still unpaved. The Broadway Rooms was formerly the Hotel Hall.

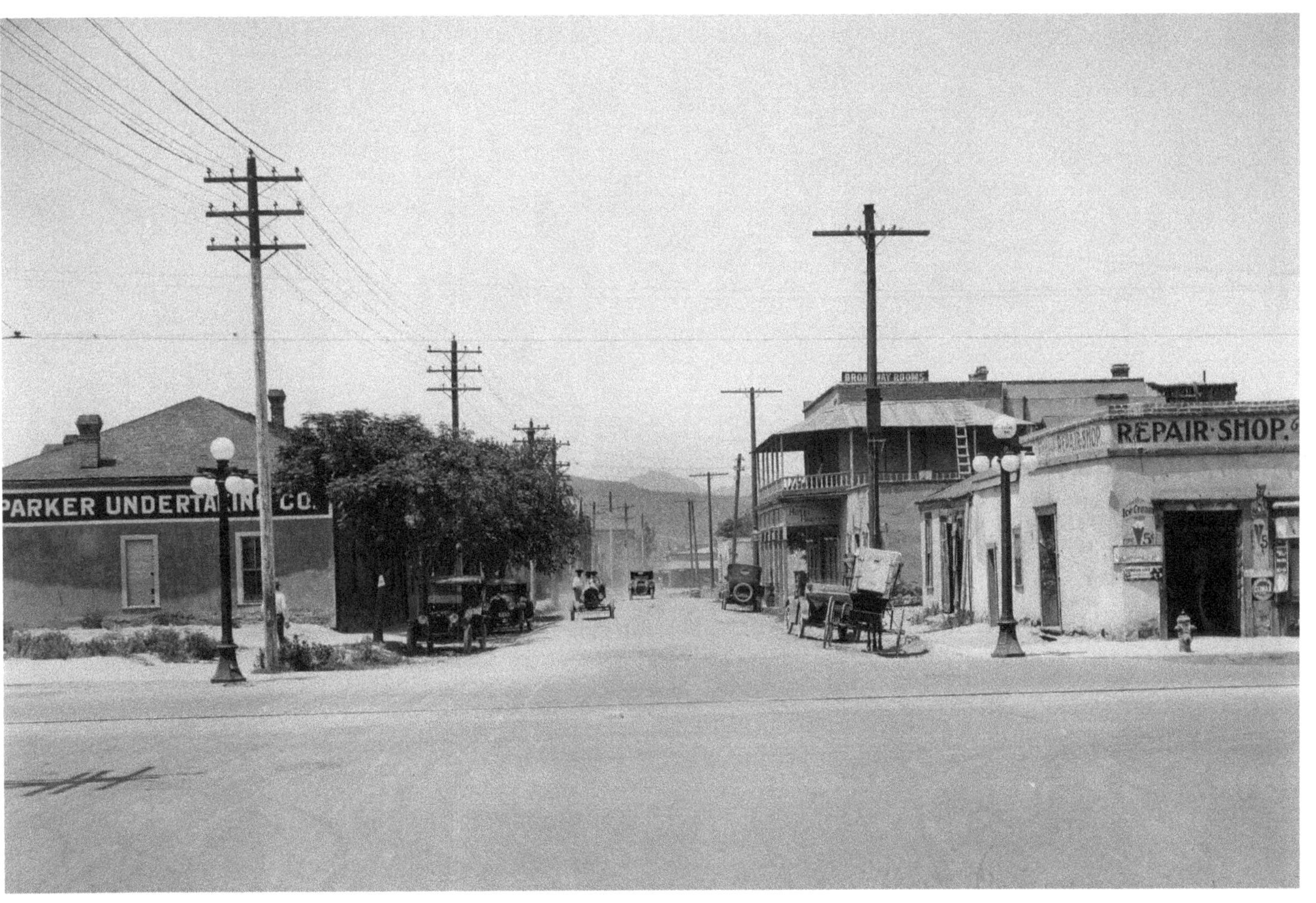

A multiracial float for a Fourth of July parade in 1918.

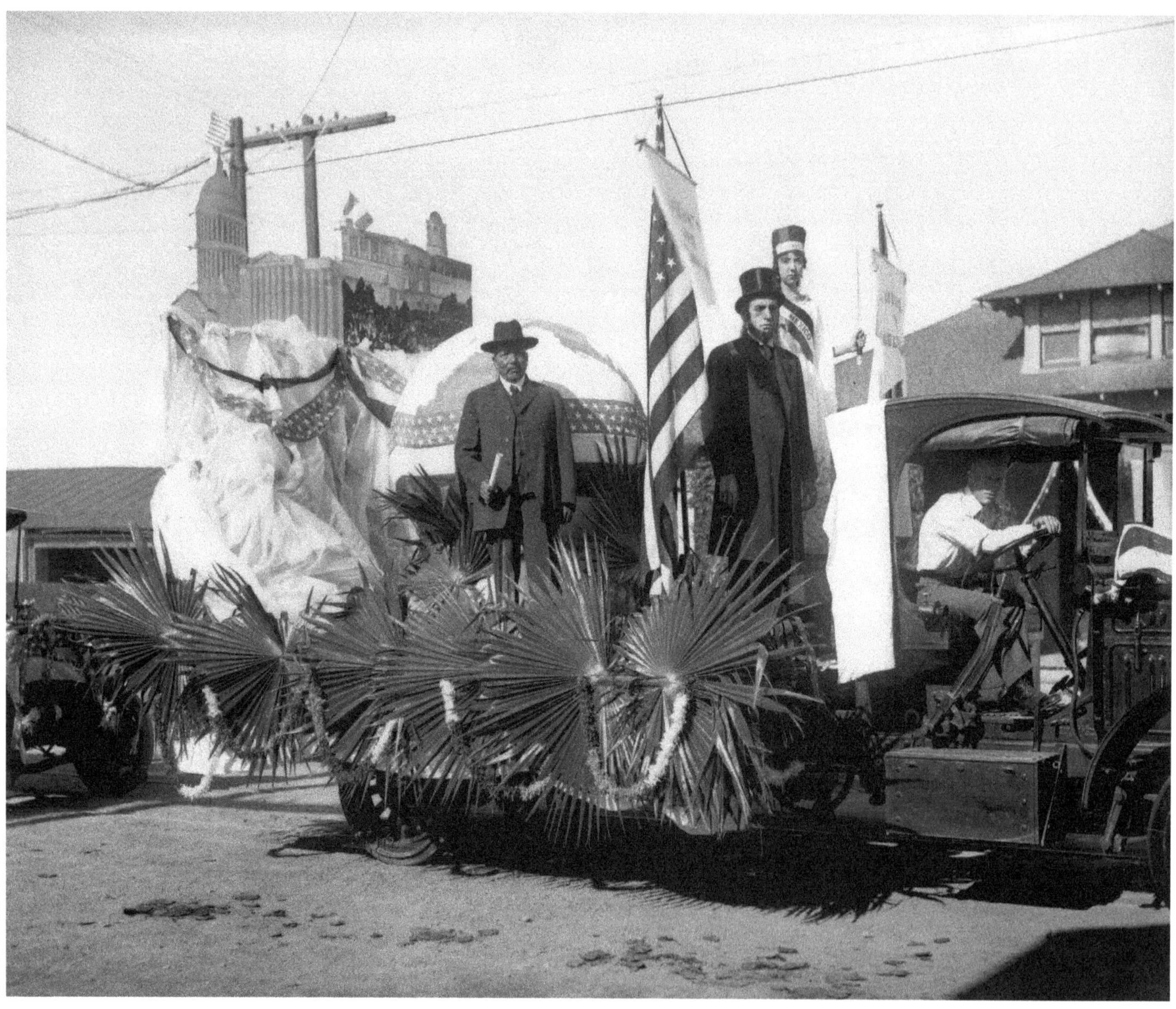

Looking south on Sixth Avenue around 1919. The SP railroad crossing is in the distance.

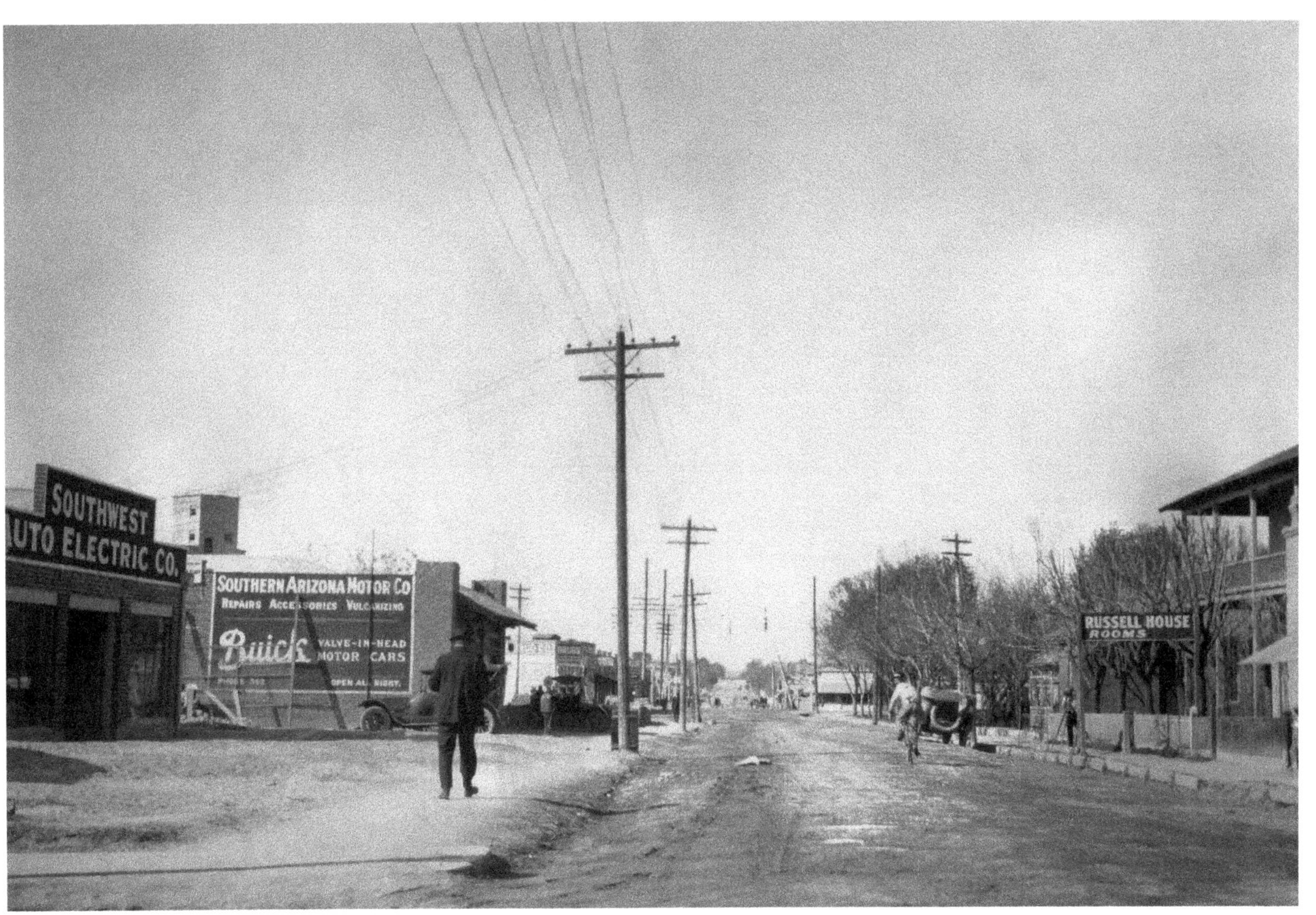

An American Legion float in a parade, perhaps for the first state caucus, which was held in Tucson in July 1919.

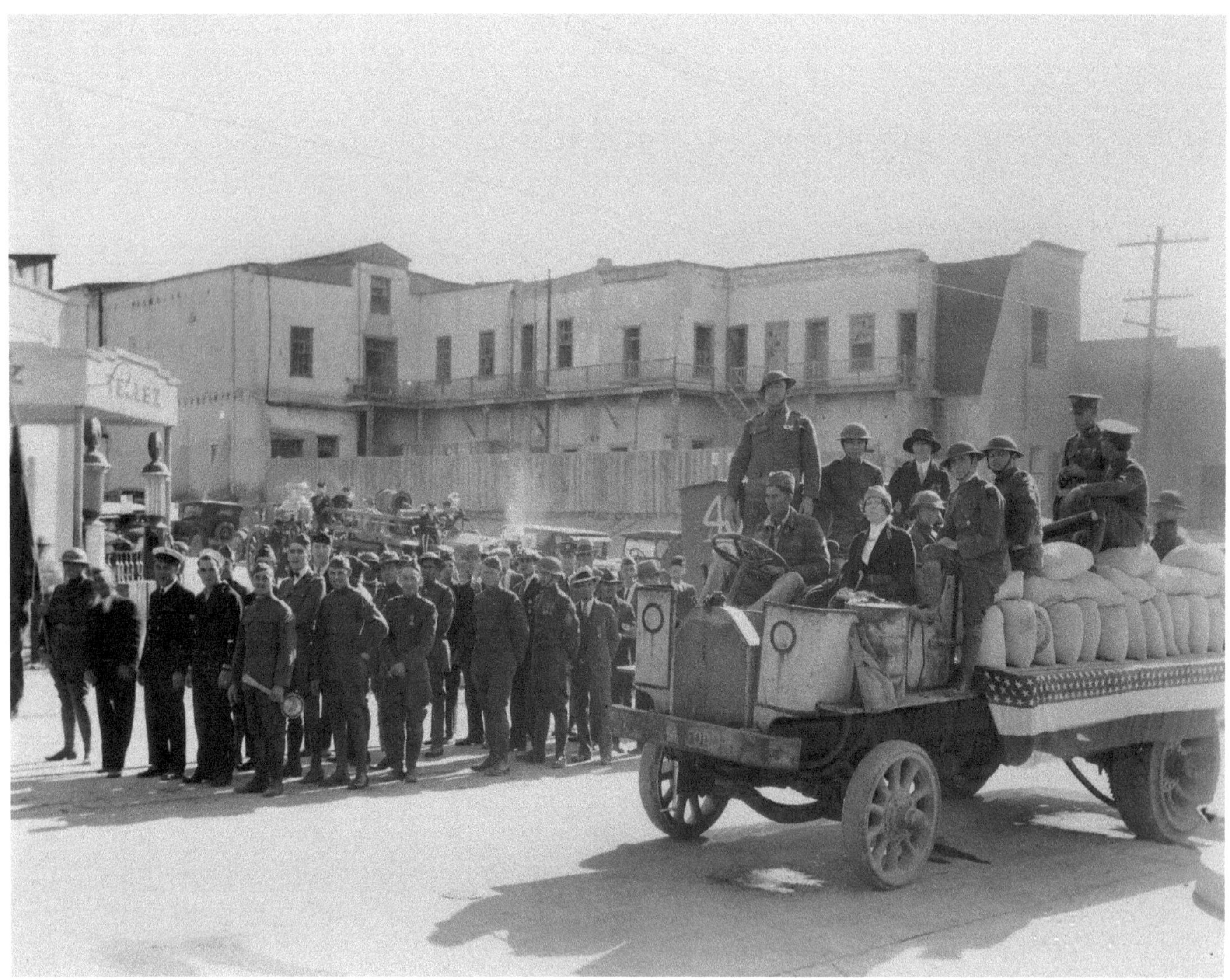

Between the Wars

(1920–1939)

In 1920, Tucson's population of 20,292 still faced shortages and hard times, but national Prohibition increased the flow of bootleg alcohol across the Mexican border; Tucson's speakeasies flourished. Serious gambling retired to private clubs, and a harassed red-light district endured. In 1922, the Tucson Sunshine Climate Club was formed to attract a different clientele by actively promoting the city as a tourist destination and gateway to the southwest. Statewide, anti-labor sentiments developed in reaction to strikes and food shortages; employers pressed for open-shop workplaces where union membership was not required.

Tucson took on the look and feel of a modern city. The first skyscrapers were built in 1929, but it would be many years before others joined them. Two makeshift landing strips were replaced in 1930 by the Greater Tucson Airport at Davis-Monthan Field, and regular flights began operation. The guest ranch concept, developed during the 1920s in response to tourists' interest in the cowboy and ranch life, provided a boon to the region. Many guest ranches were working ranches fallen on hard times and looking for a way to survive; others were created purely to simulate the experience.

With a new City Charter on May 26, 1929, Tucson seemed to be facing a bright future. A national effort in the early 1930s to repatriate those of Hispanic heritage to Mexico, voluntarily or not, did not gain much support here. The Depression took a little longer to hit here, but by the end of 1930 an unemployment bureau was helping those needing work, primarily carpenters and truck drivers. A few banks and businesses failed, but the situation began to improve after the mid-1930s as jobs in the building industry replaced government assistance. Other industries were still slow to arrive, though Columbia Studios came here to film the Western *Arizona*.

Tucson added to its cultural resources with the Temple of Music and Art in 1927 and the Fox Theater in 1930. The Tucson Symphony Orchestra began performances in 1928, and the world-famous Tucson Boys Chorus formed in 1939. Randolph Park, an eighteen-hole municipal golf course opened on October 27, 1927. In 1932, Isabella Greenway became Arizona's first Congresswoman. The summer of 1939 brought parking meters to downtown.

As the summer desert heated up and humidity thickened, Mt. Lemmon in the Santa Catalina Mountains north of Tucson provided a cool retreat. Part of the Coronado National Forest, access by automobile became possible about 1920.

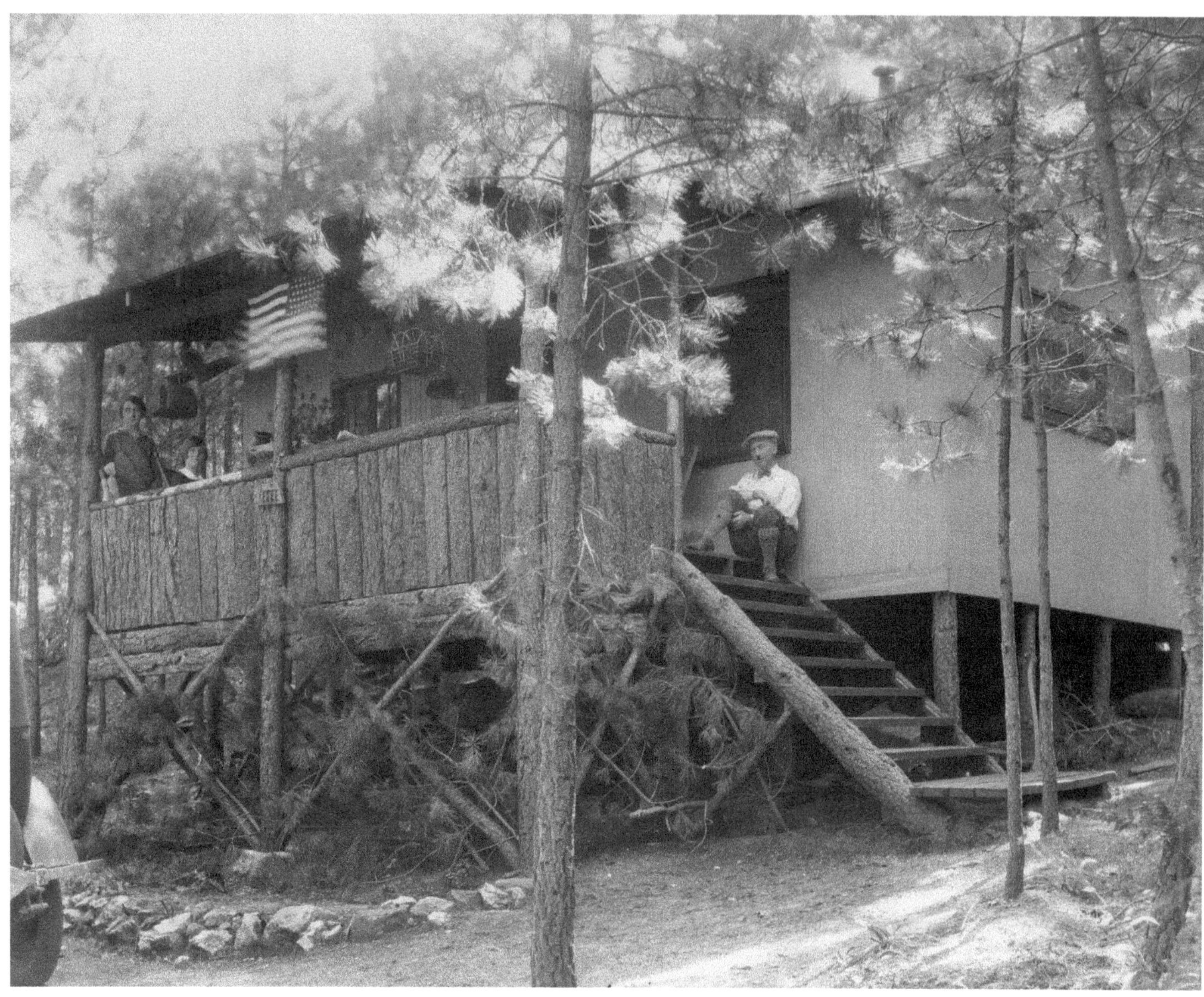

Formerly a mining claim and cattle ranch, the Flying V Ranch became a guest ranch in 1920, offering visitors a chance to experience the desert firsthand.

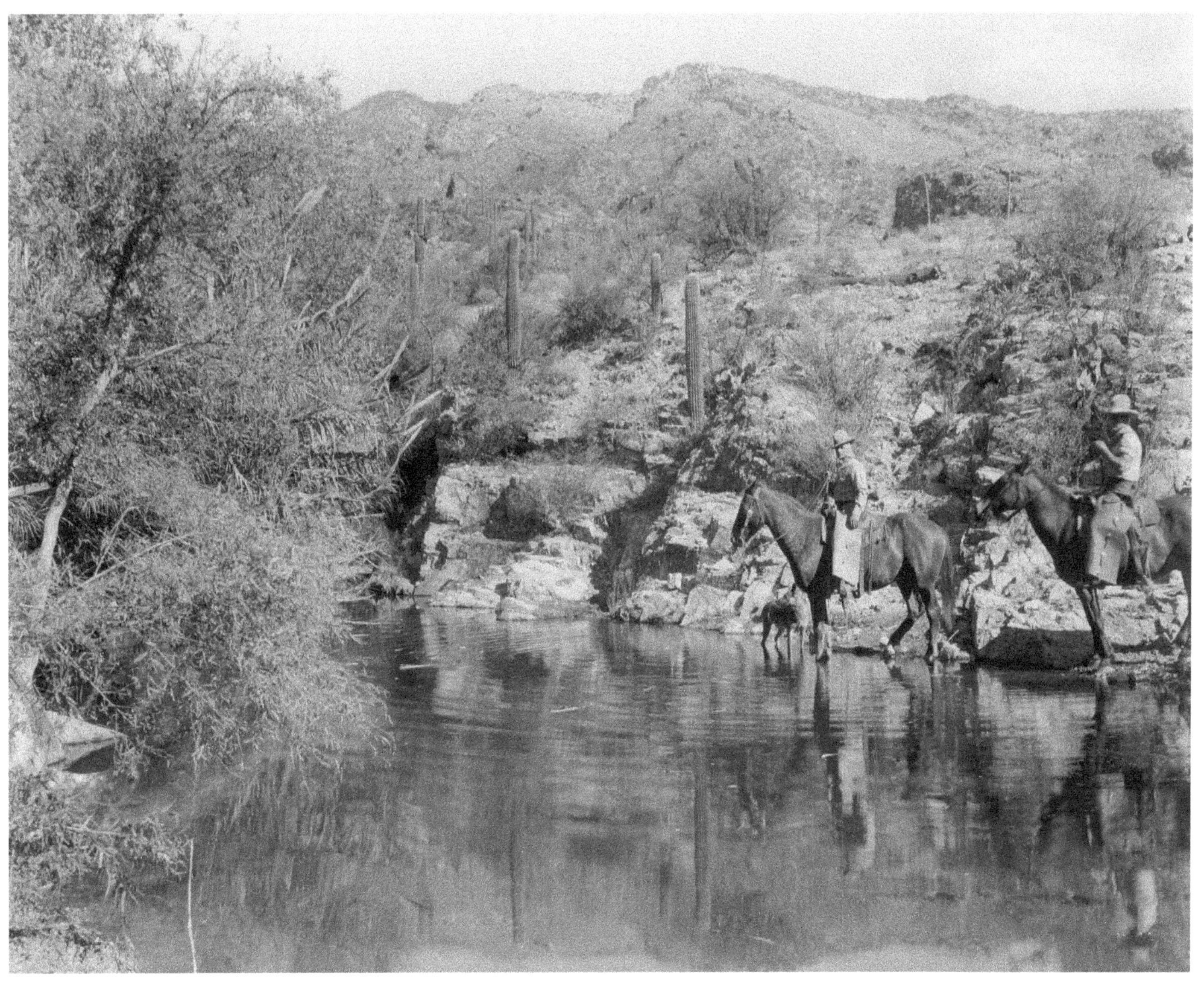

Stylish cowgirls got a taste of Southwestern life on a visit to the Flying V Guest Ranch.

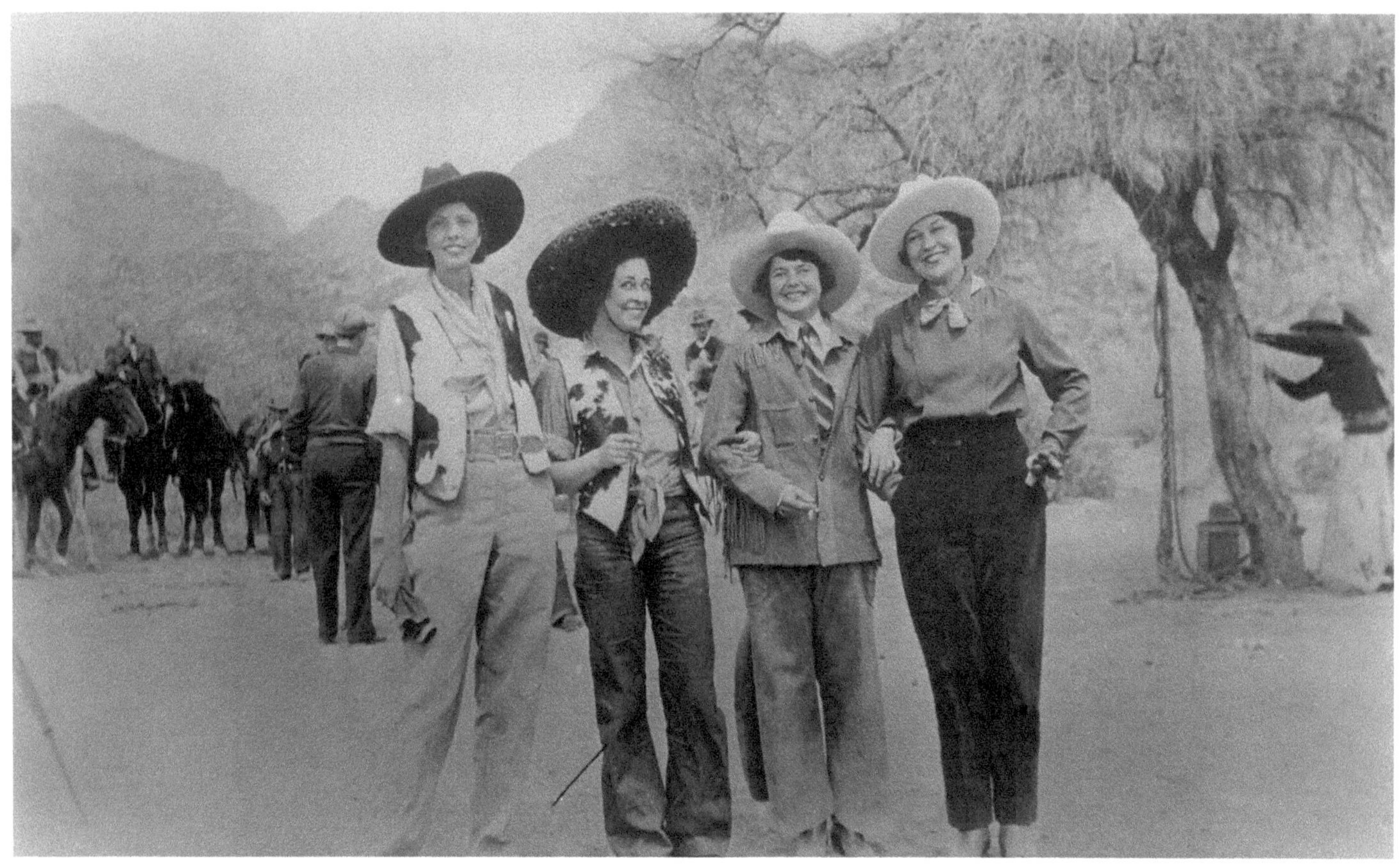

The Tucson Citizen building at Stone Avenue and Jackson Street (ca. 1920).

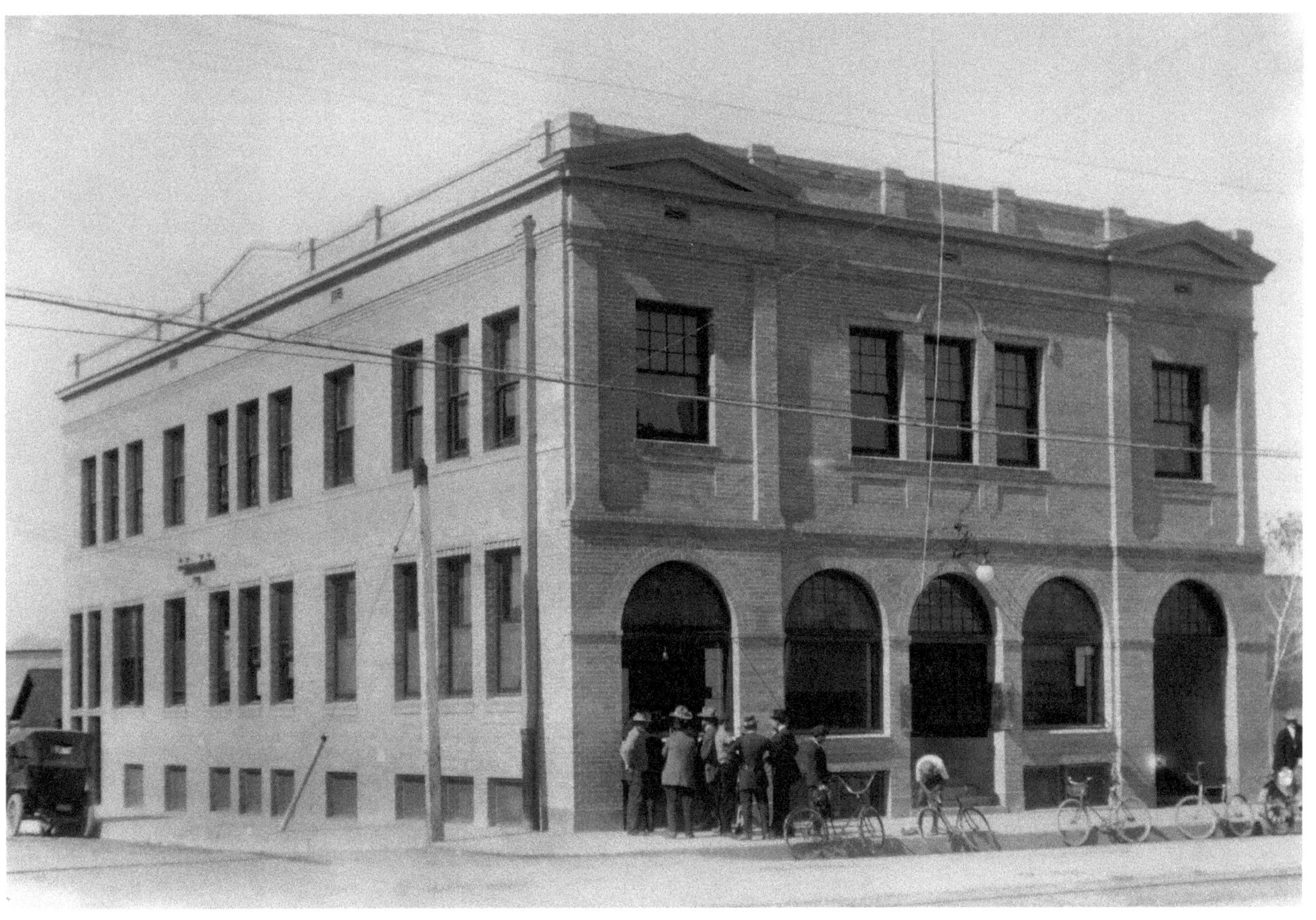

Newspaper delivery boys posed in front of the Tucson Citizen building around 1920.

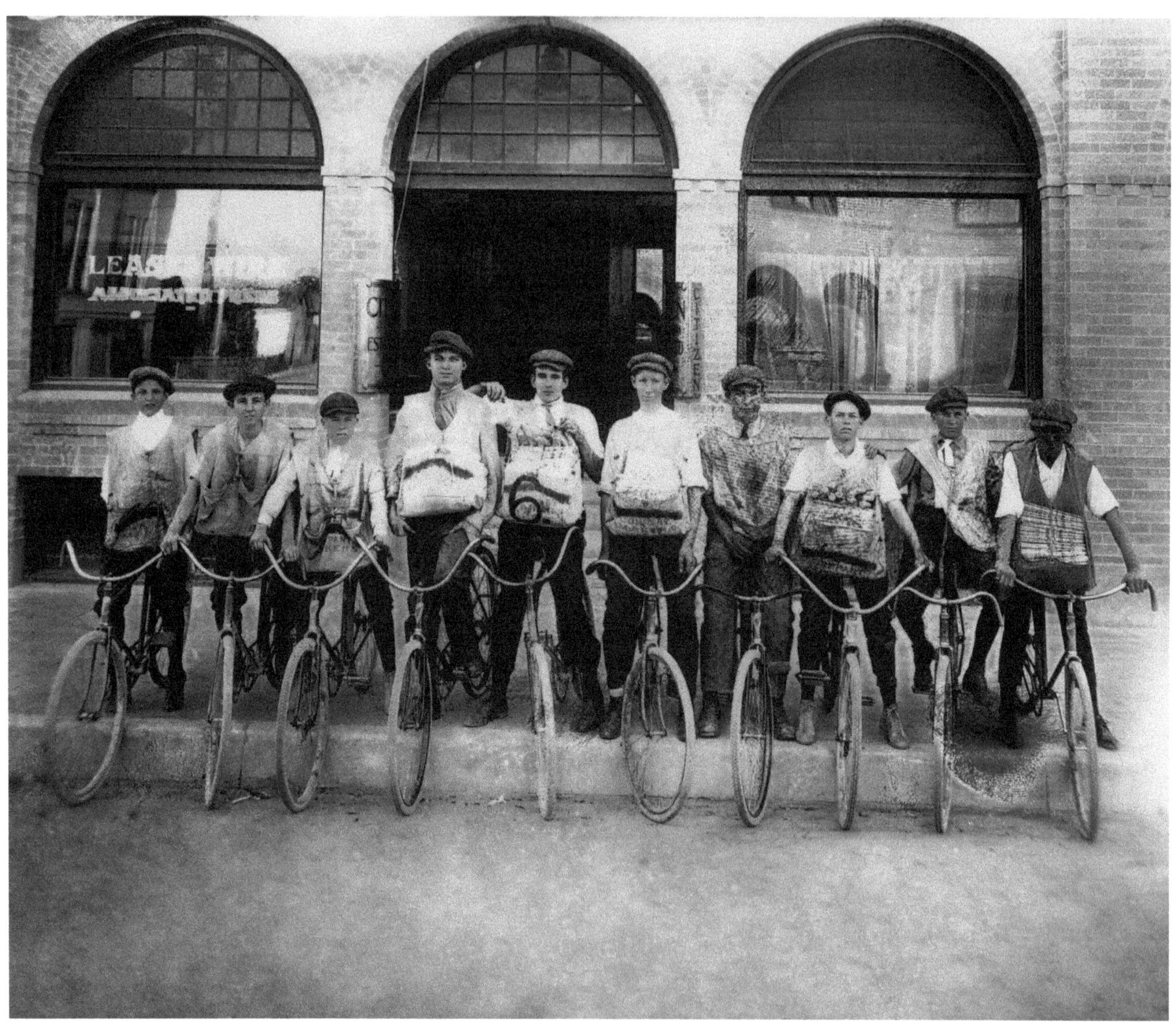

The Alianza Hispano Americana float pausing during the 1920 Rodeo Parade.

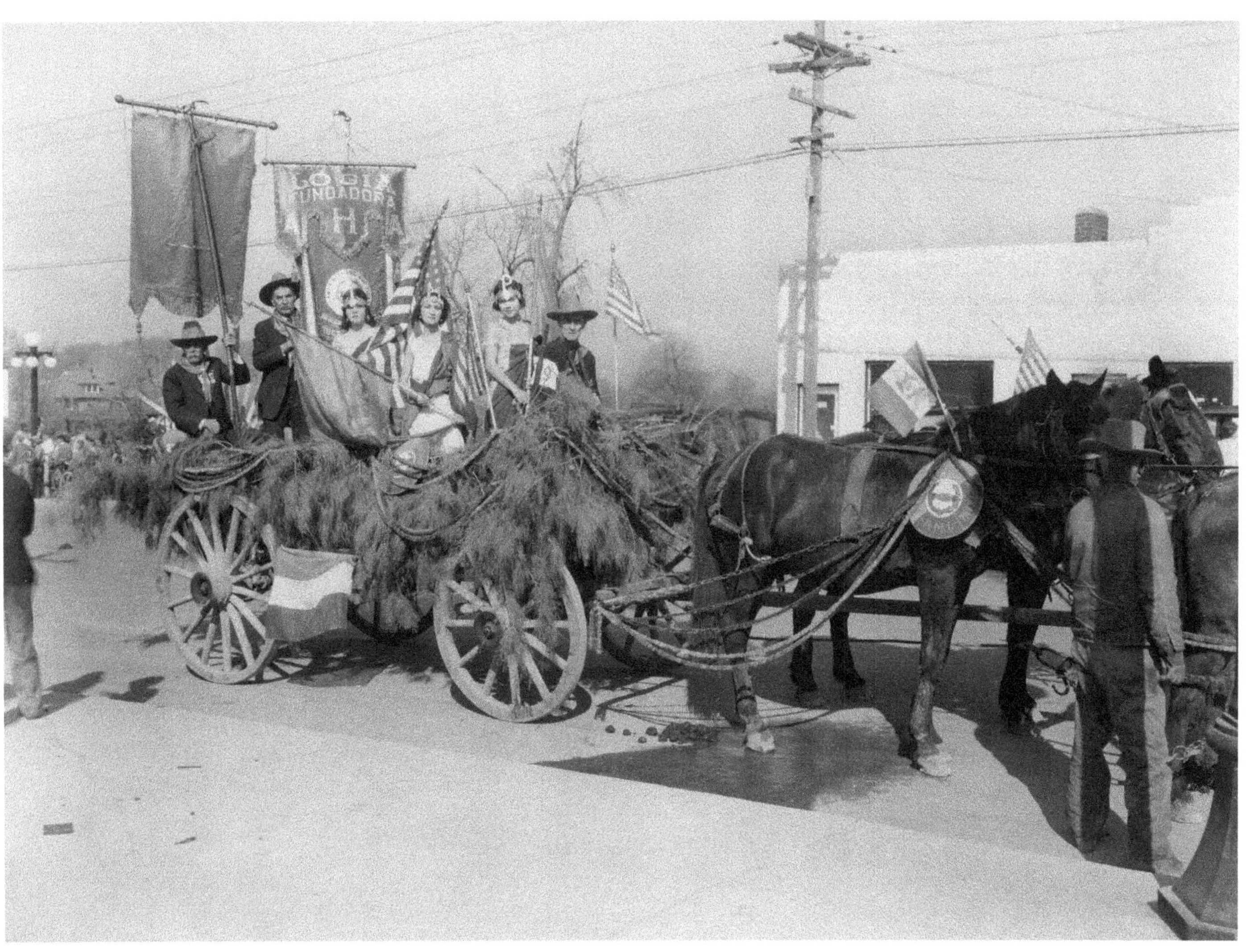

The Alianza Hispano Americana float on Congress Street during the 1920 Rodeo Parade.

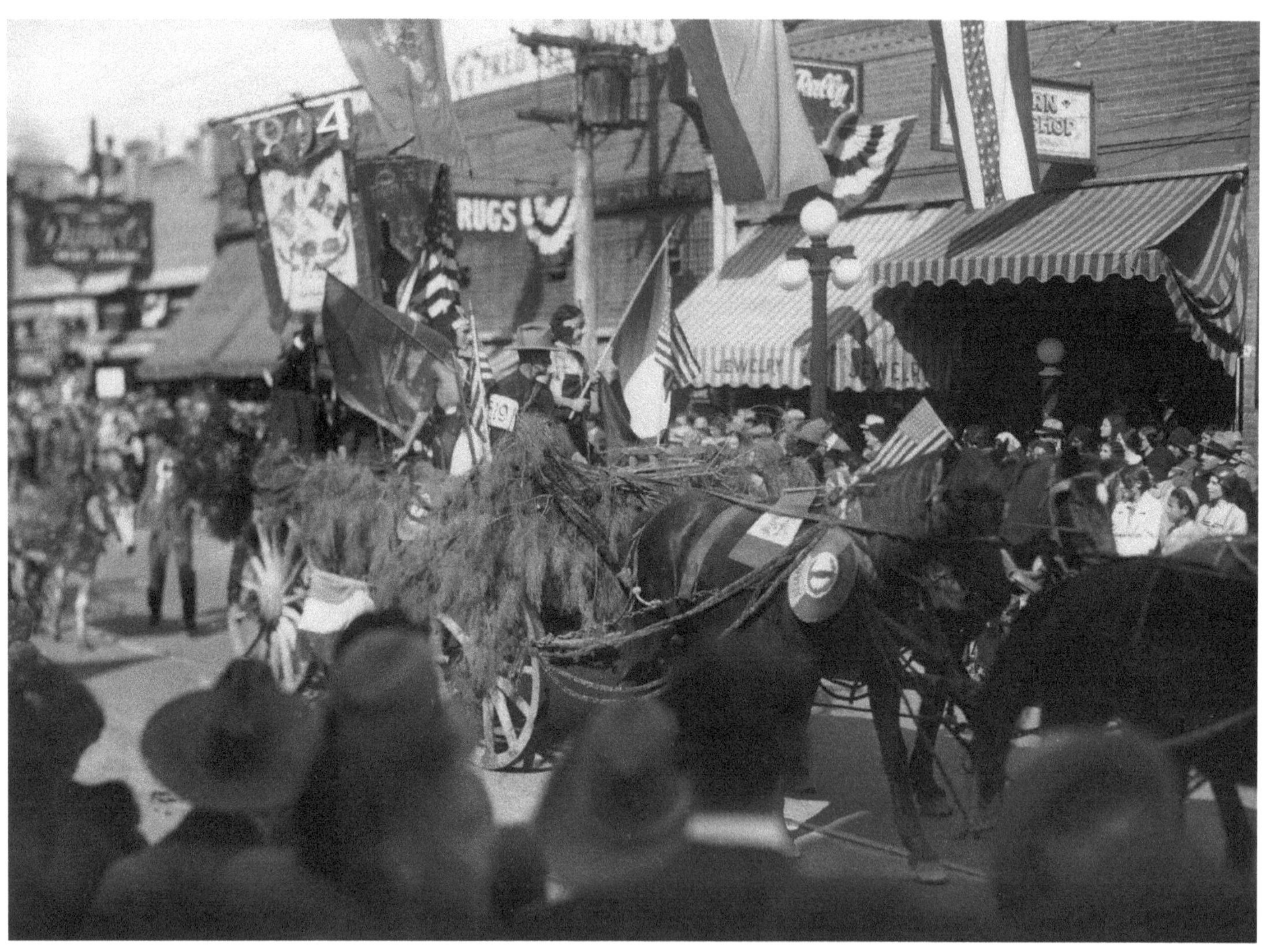

The Hotel Arizona was constructed at 35 N. Sixth Avenue in 1917 and remained in business until 1986. Designed by Tucson architect Henry Jaastad, this is a view of the hotel around 1921.

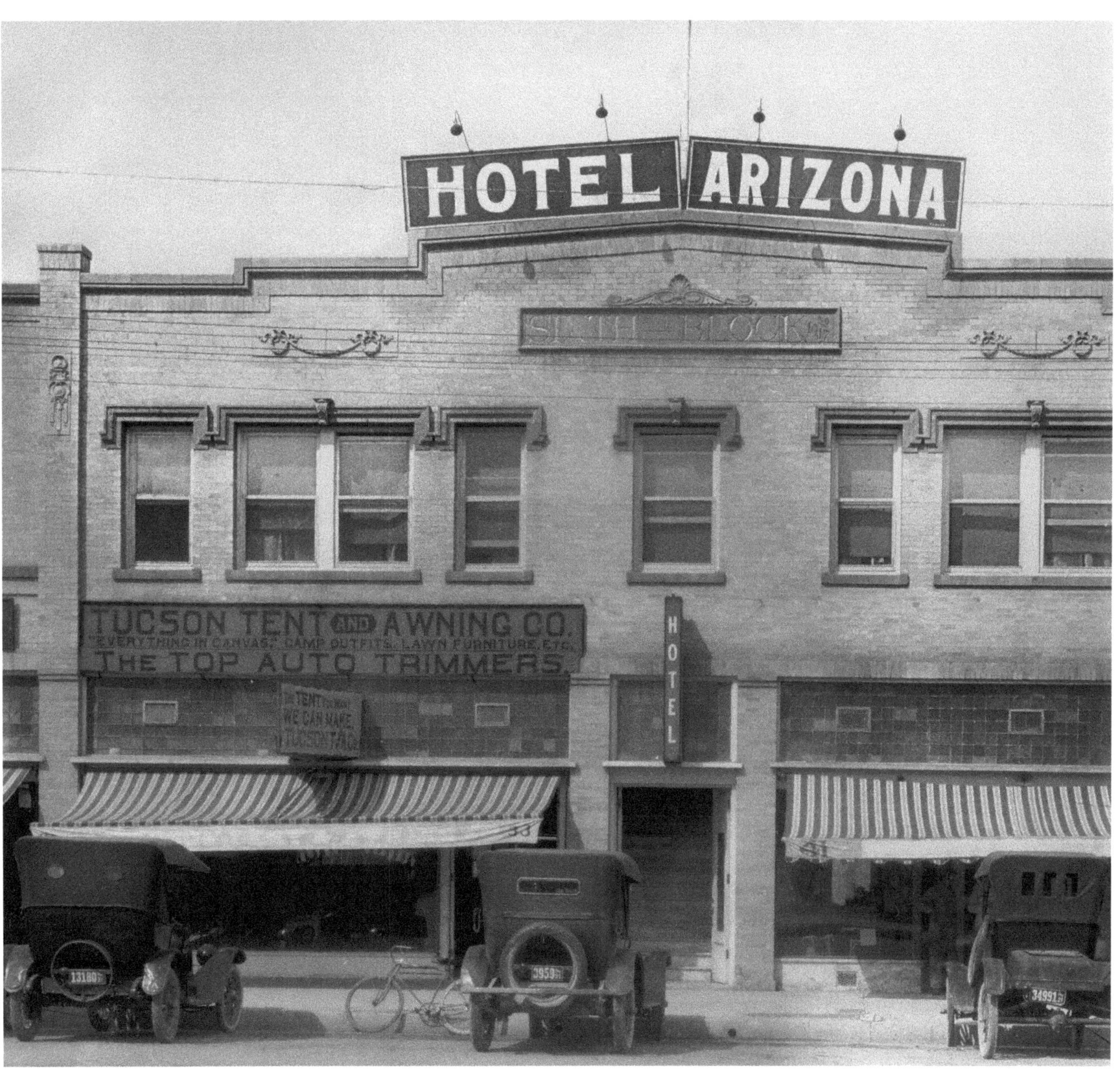

Harold Bell Wright, a popular early twentieth-century novelist, built a home on 160 acres at Speedway Boulevard and Wilmot in 1922. Following his example, other wealthy Tucsonans bought similar large tracts, spurring Tucson's growth into the desert to the east.

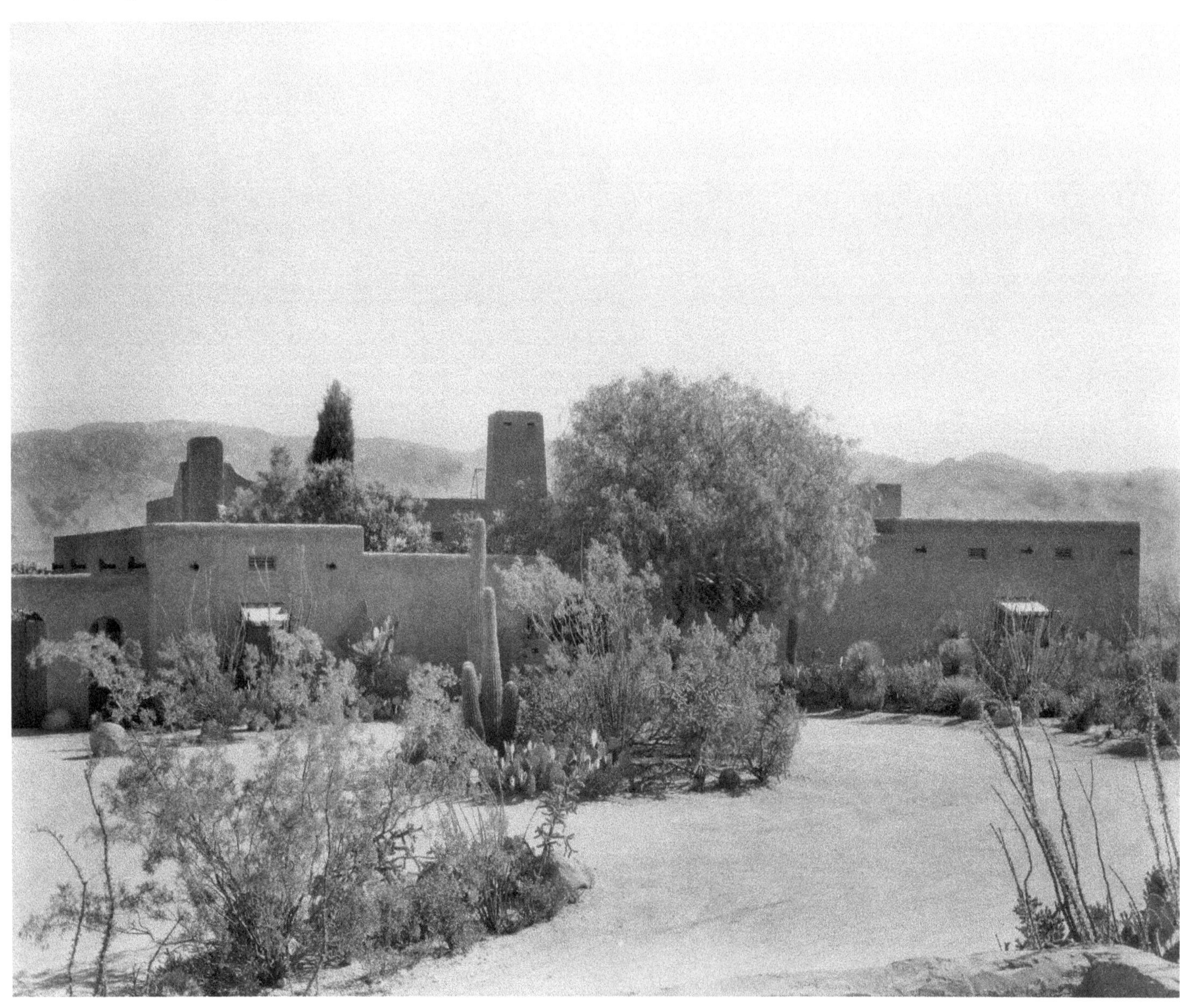

Harold Bell Wright in front of his home.

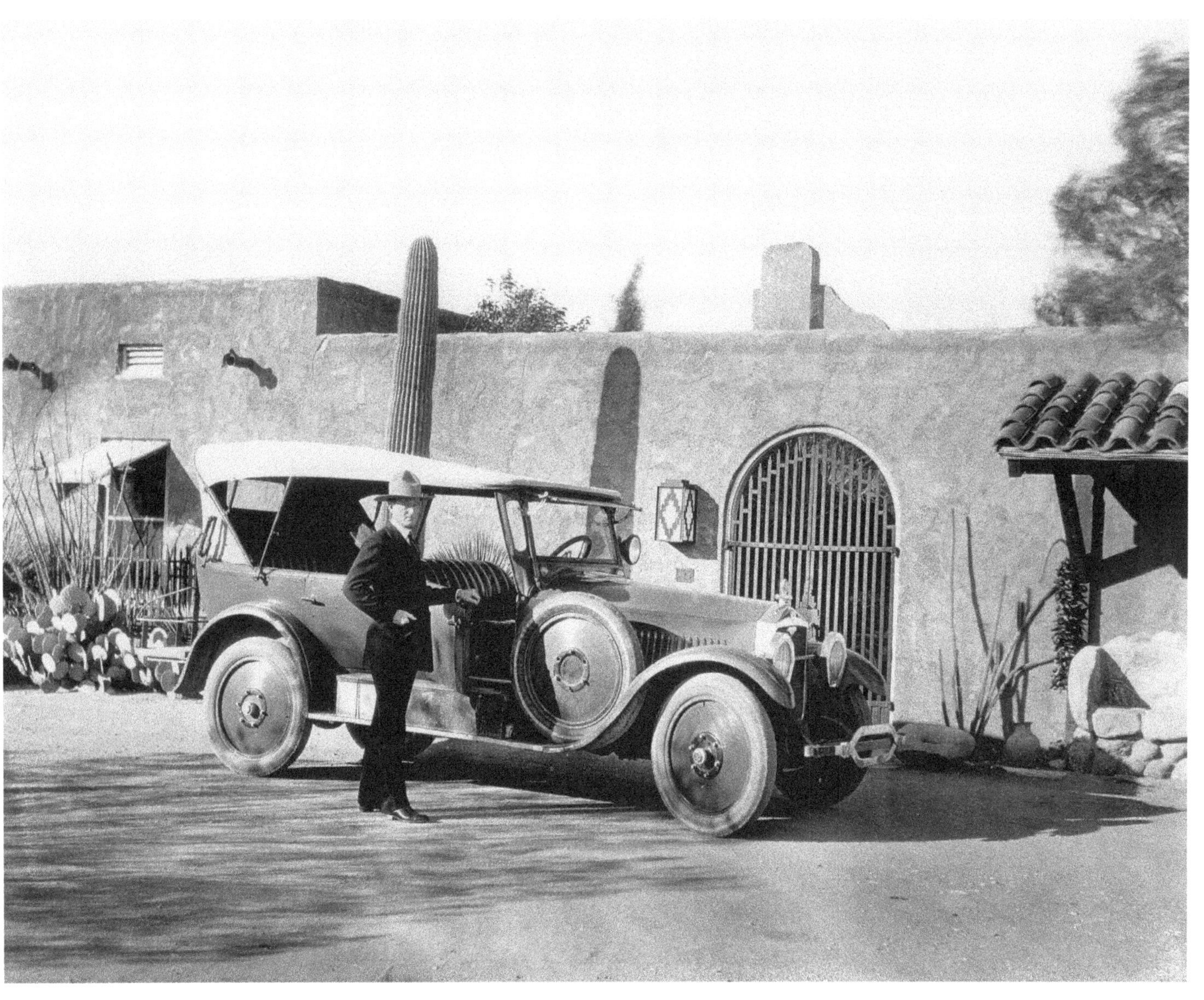

Looking west on Congress Street from Stone Avenue around 1923. On the right, the Palace of Sweets offers homemade "Cactus Candy," a desert specialty.

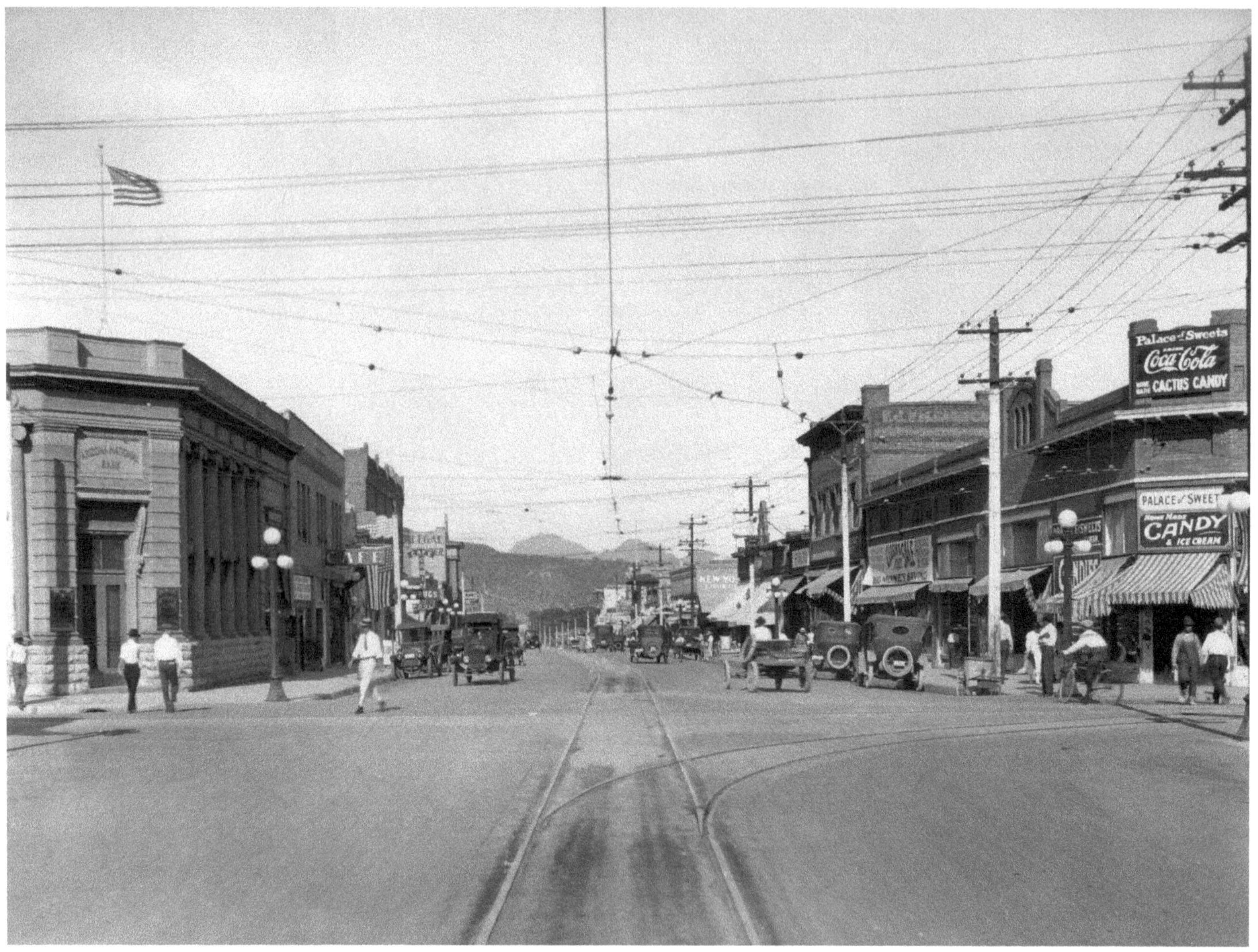

A group of Rotarians from Prescott, Arizona, posed before San Xavier del Bac in the early 1920s.

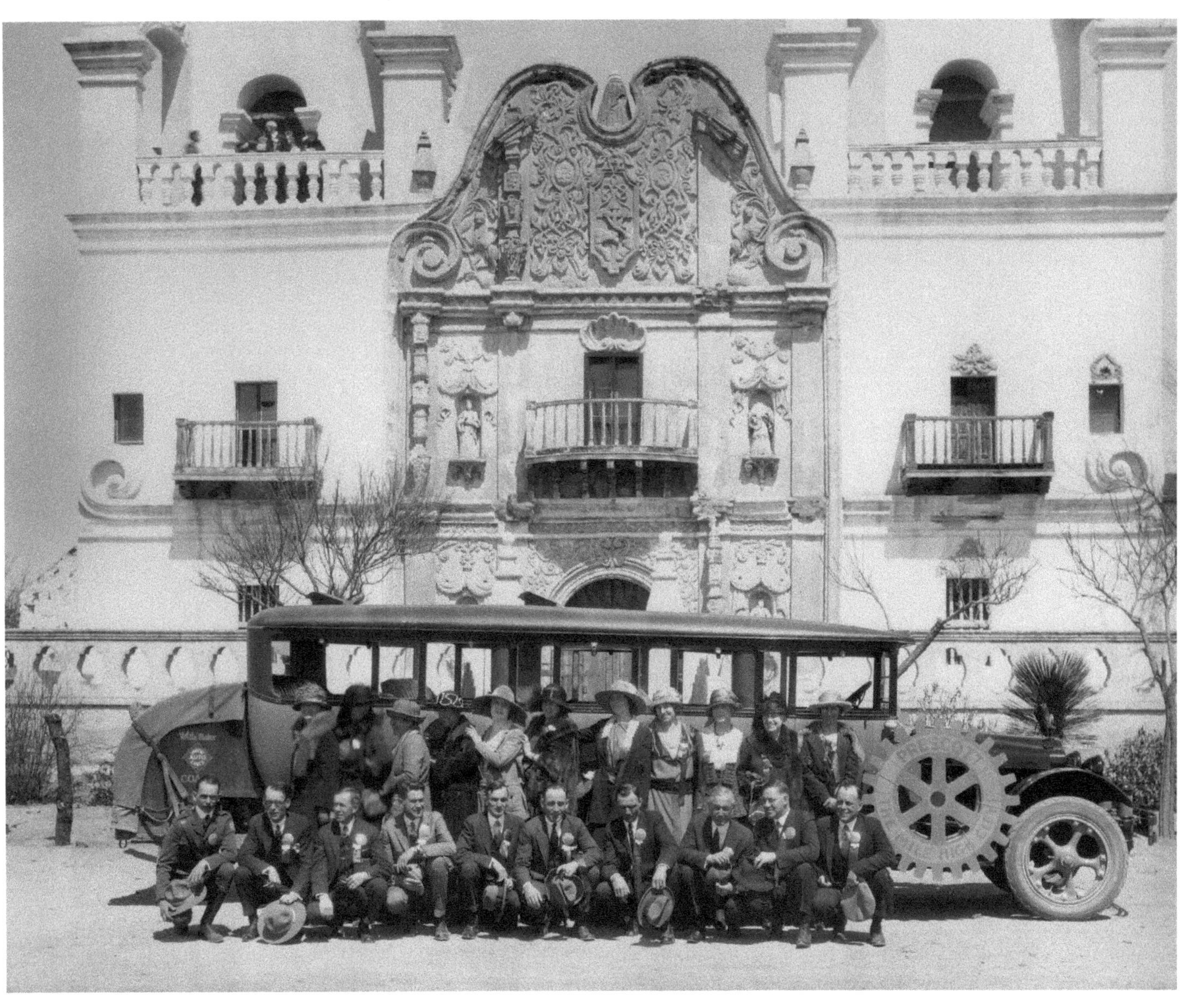

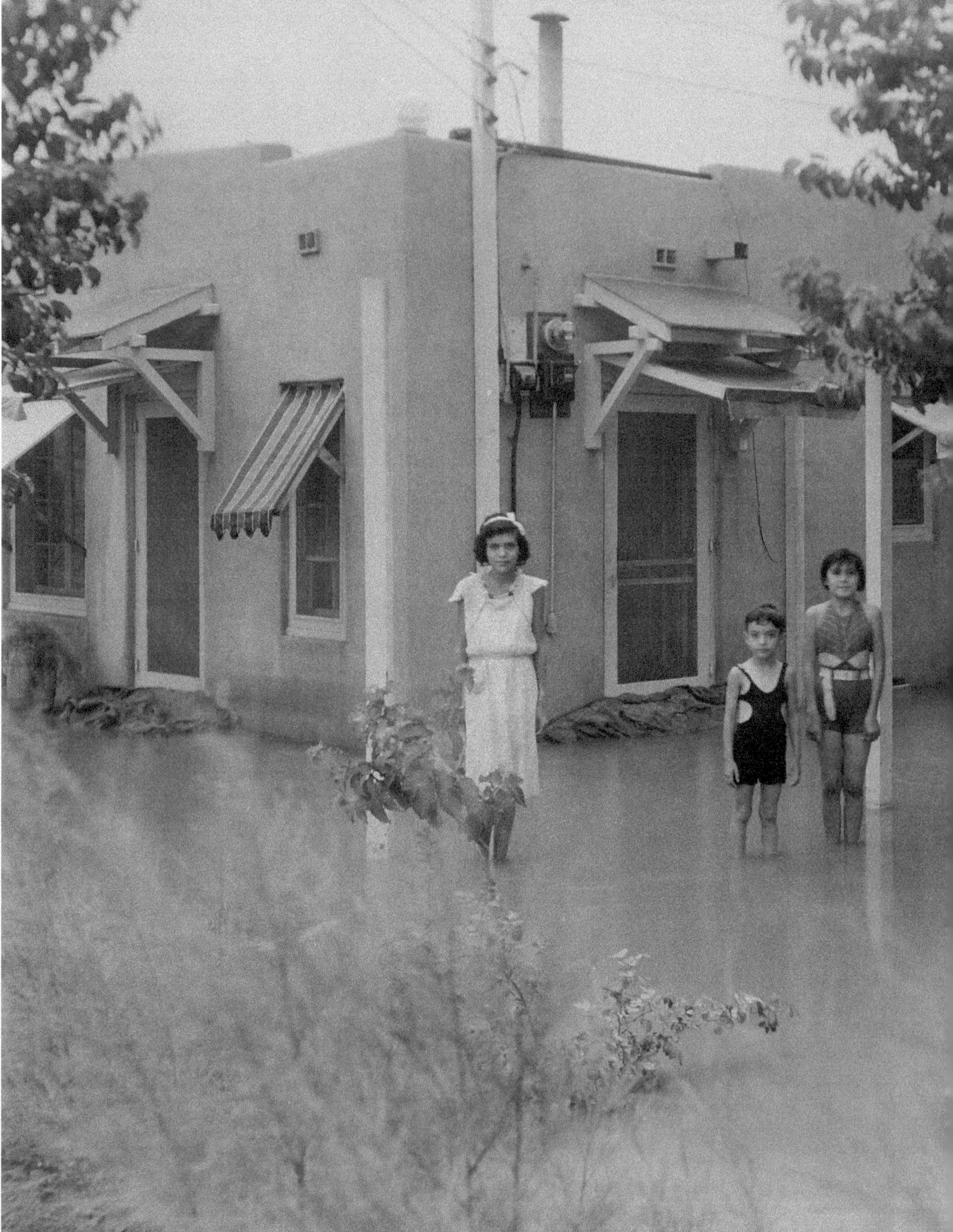

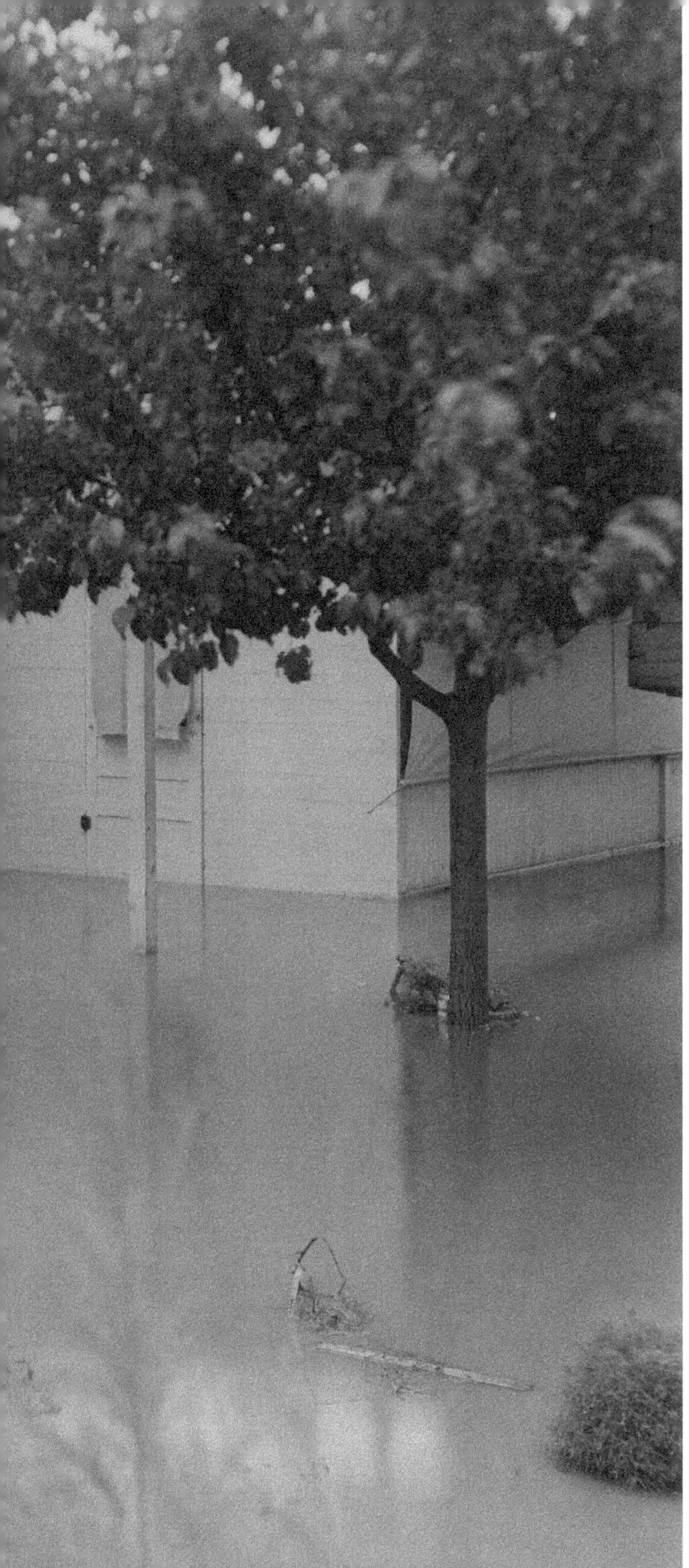

Children pose in their flooded front yard as the Santa Cruz River overflowed its banks once again (ca.1925).

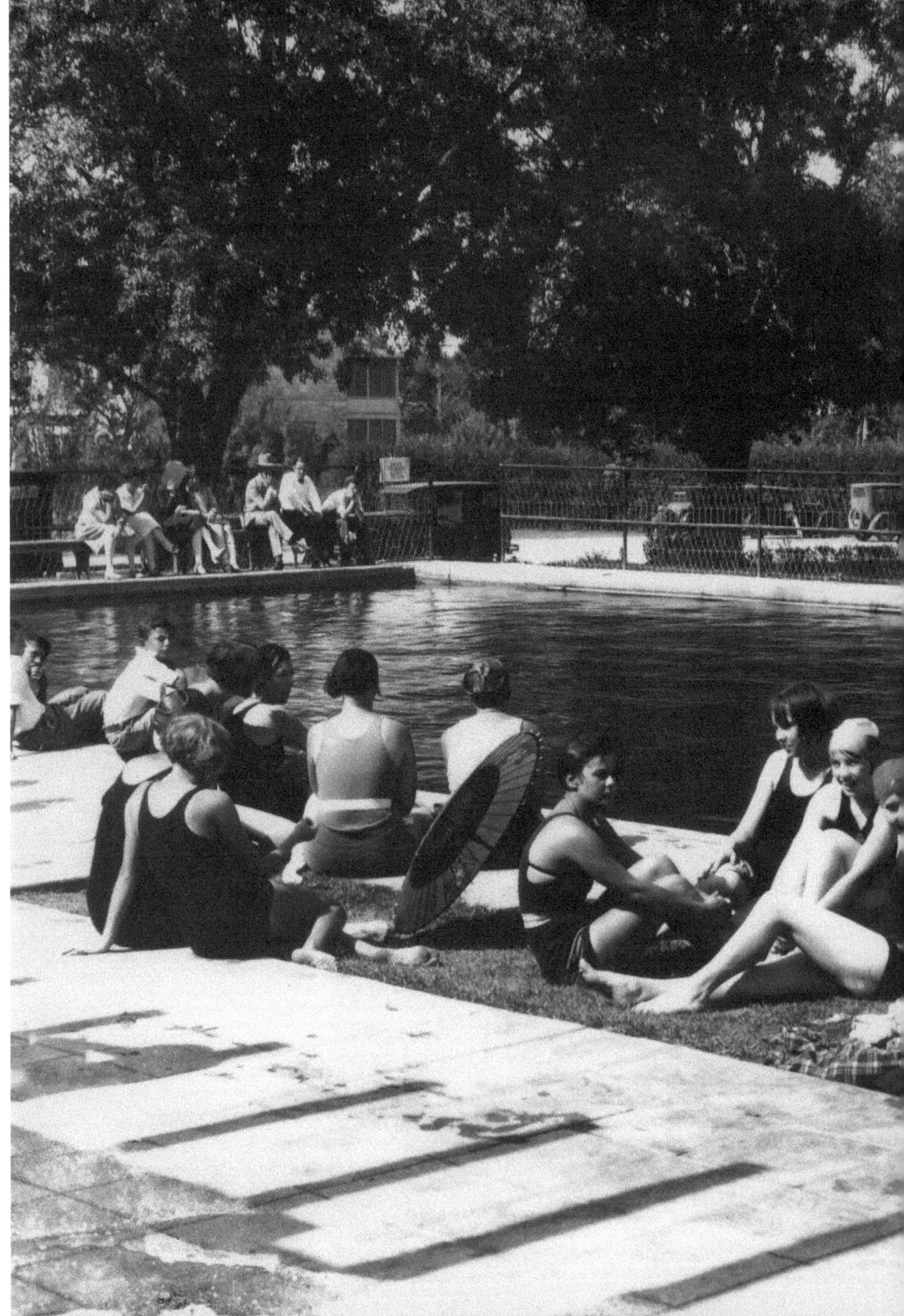

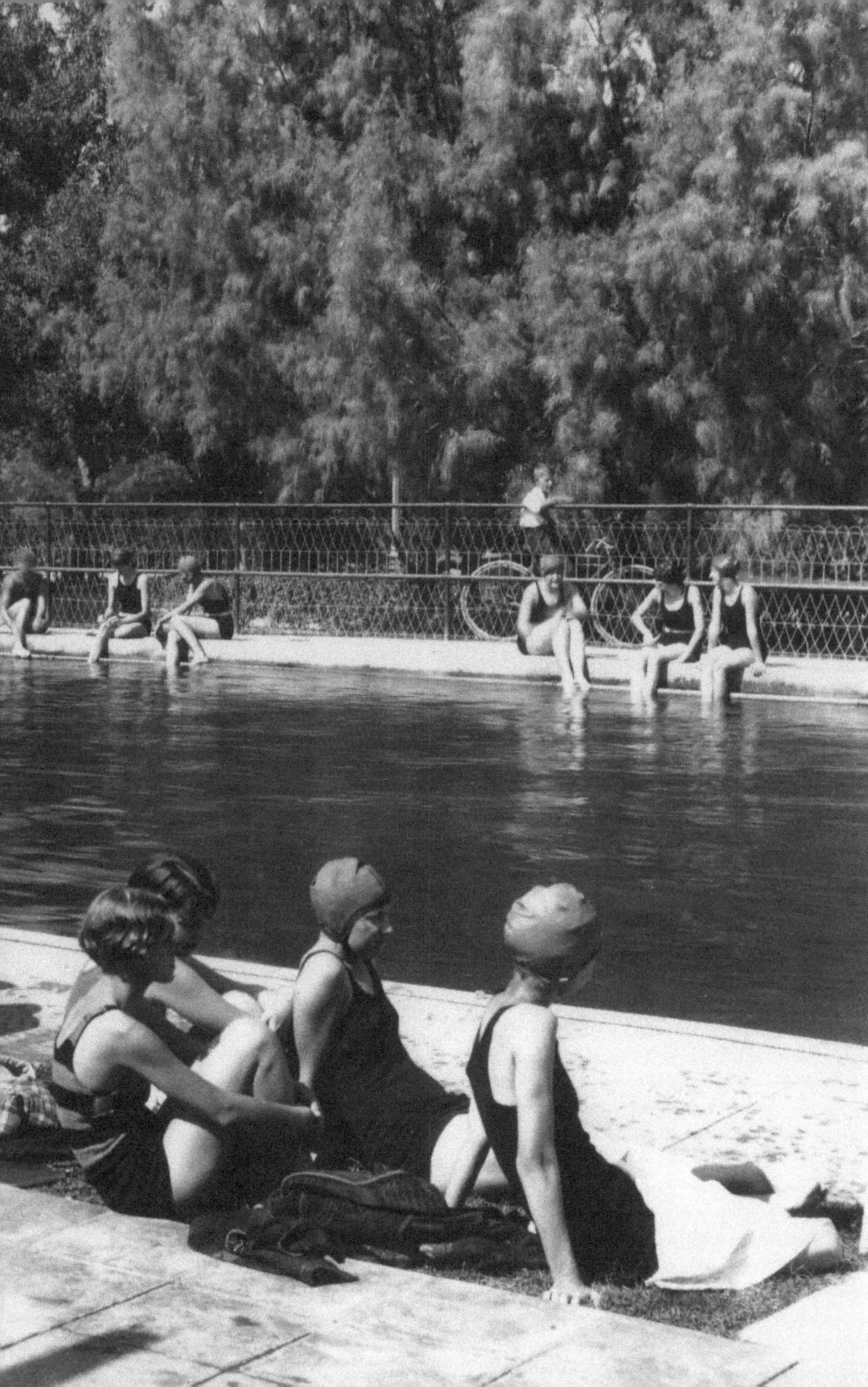

The University of Arizona swimming pool (ca. 1925).

By 1926, downtown traffic had become heavy enough at Congress Street and Sixth Avenue to require a traffic officer to direct vehicles. In May 1927, he would be replaced by the first traffic light.

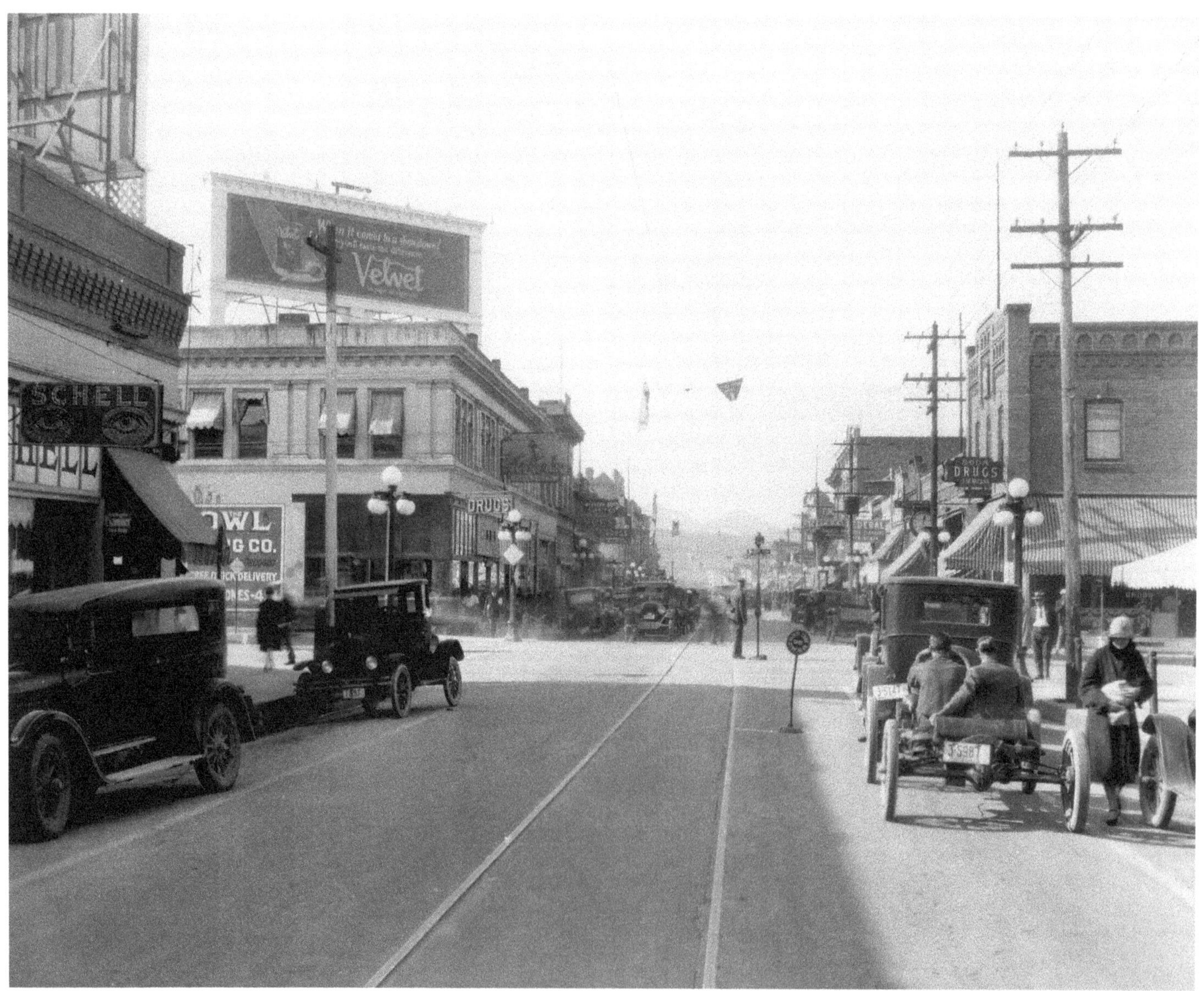

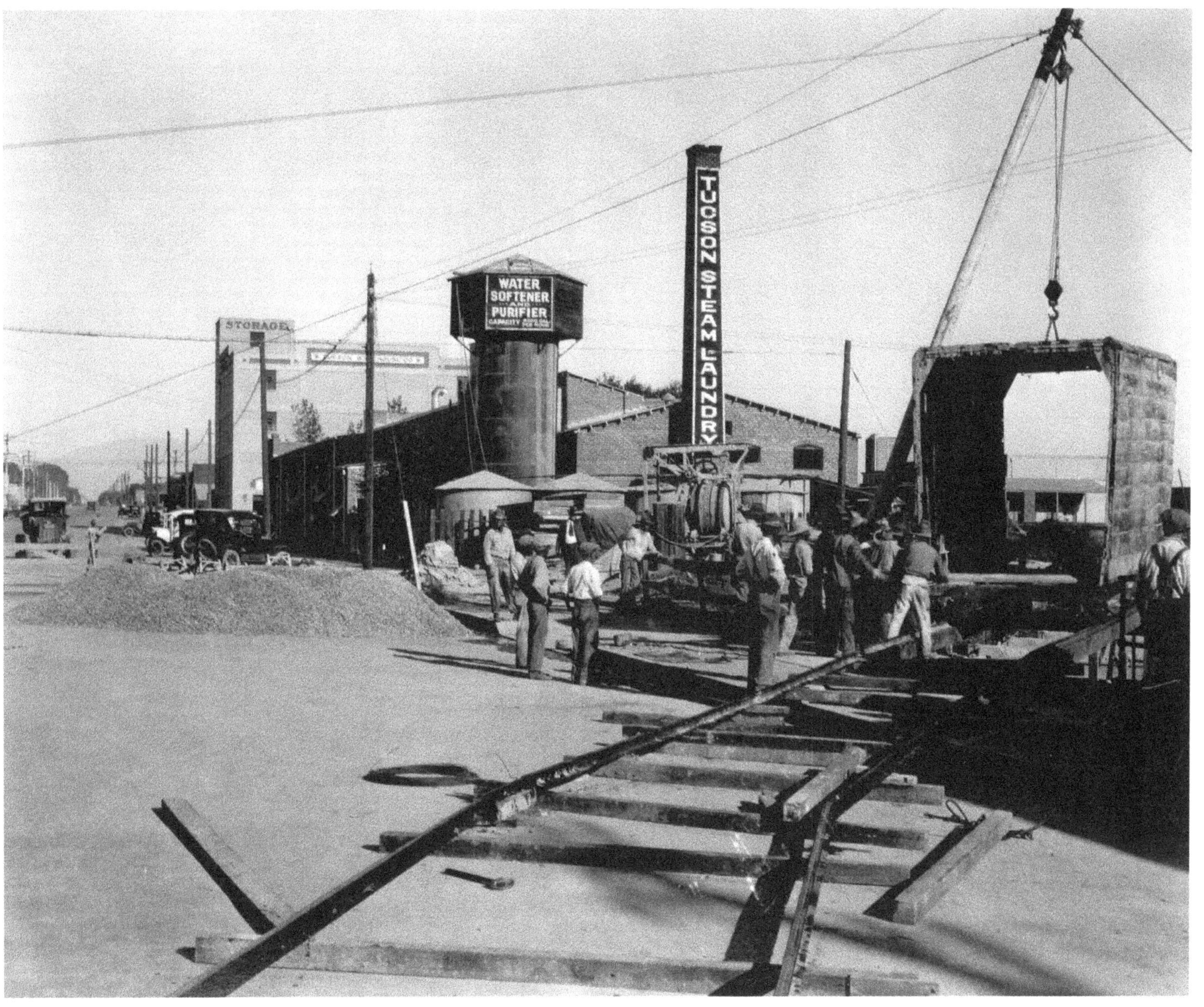

Workers refurbishing the Southern Pacific Railroad tracks just west of the intersection of Sixth Street and Stone Avenue in the 1920s.

The Rodeo Parade making its way along Congress Street. The parade continues to the present day, though it no longer passes through the downtown area.

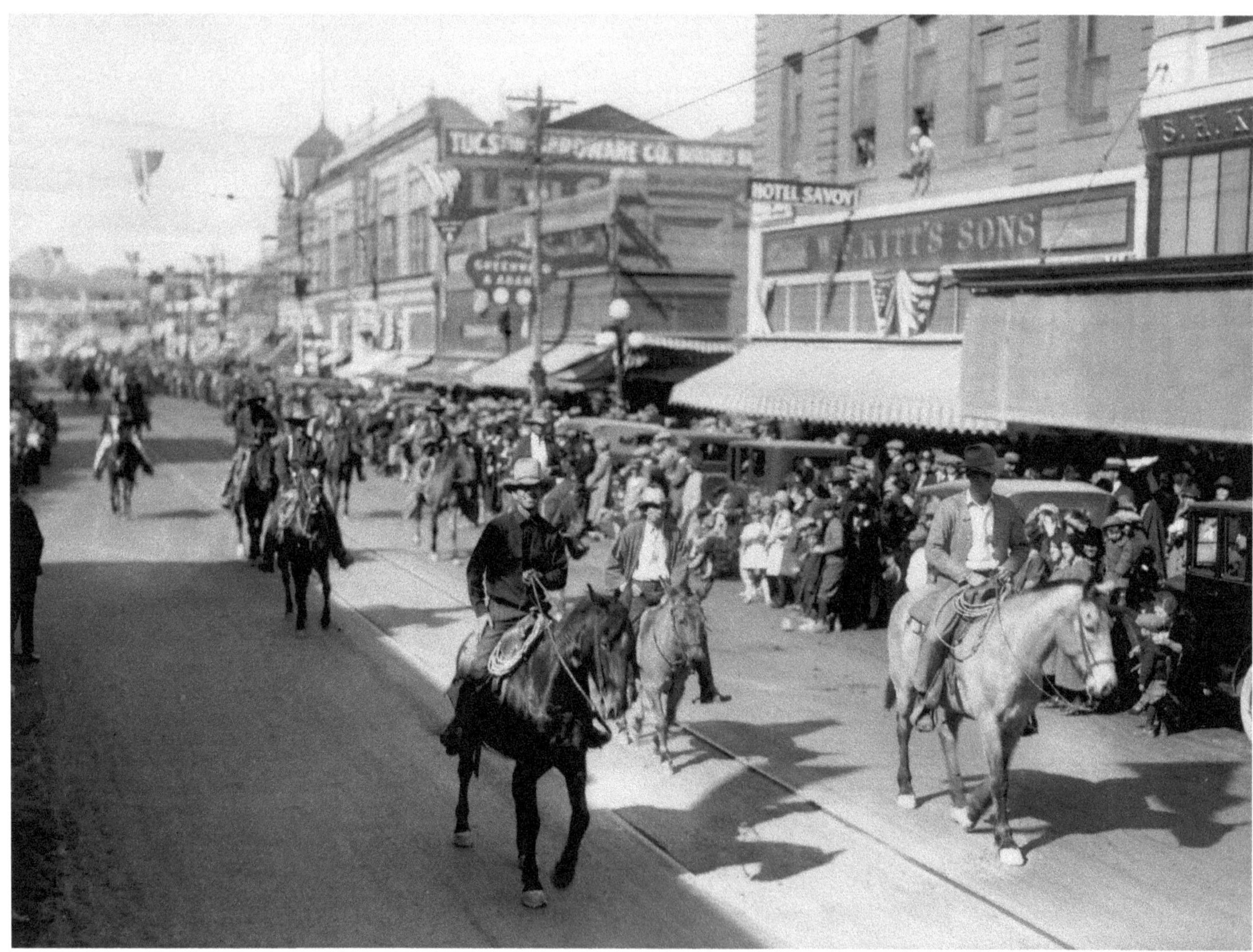

The southeast corner of Congress Street and Sixth Avenue. The building housed the optometric office of Schell & Schell for many years.

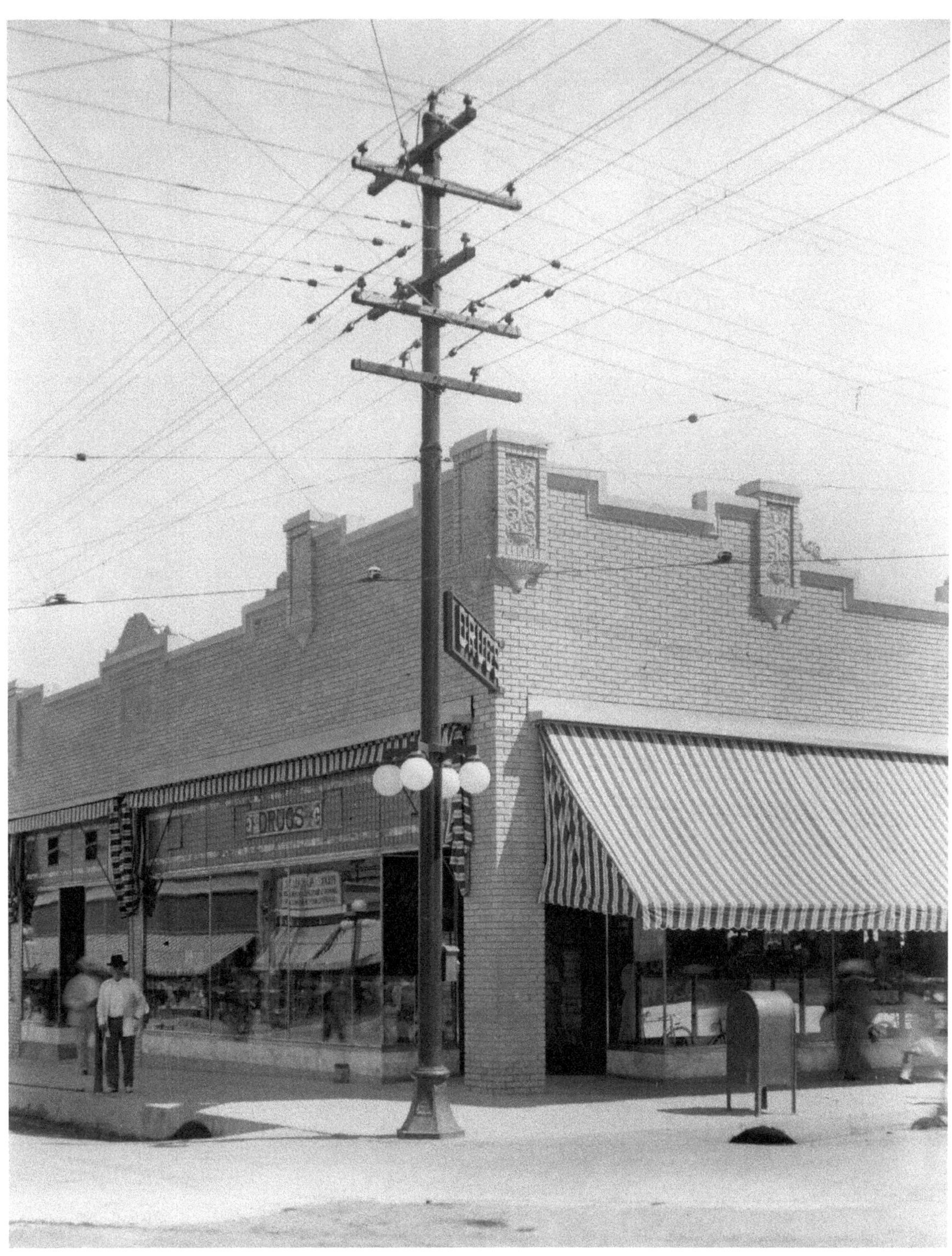

An interior view of Lazaro Romero's Barbaría Nacional at 166 W. Broadway around 1926. The helpers were Lazaro's sons.

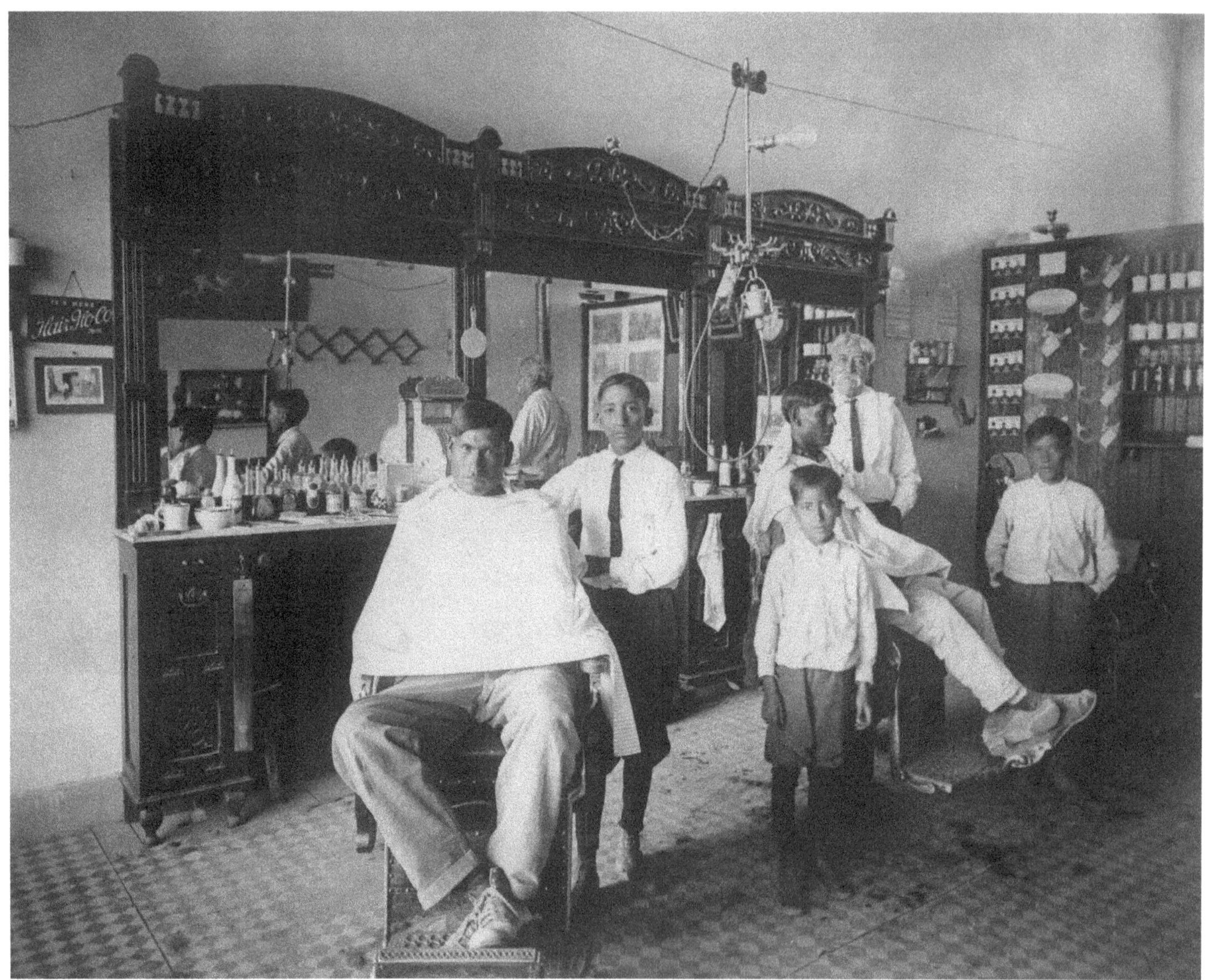

A crowd greeted a special Christmas Train at the Southern Pacific Depot in December 1926.

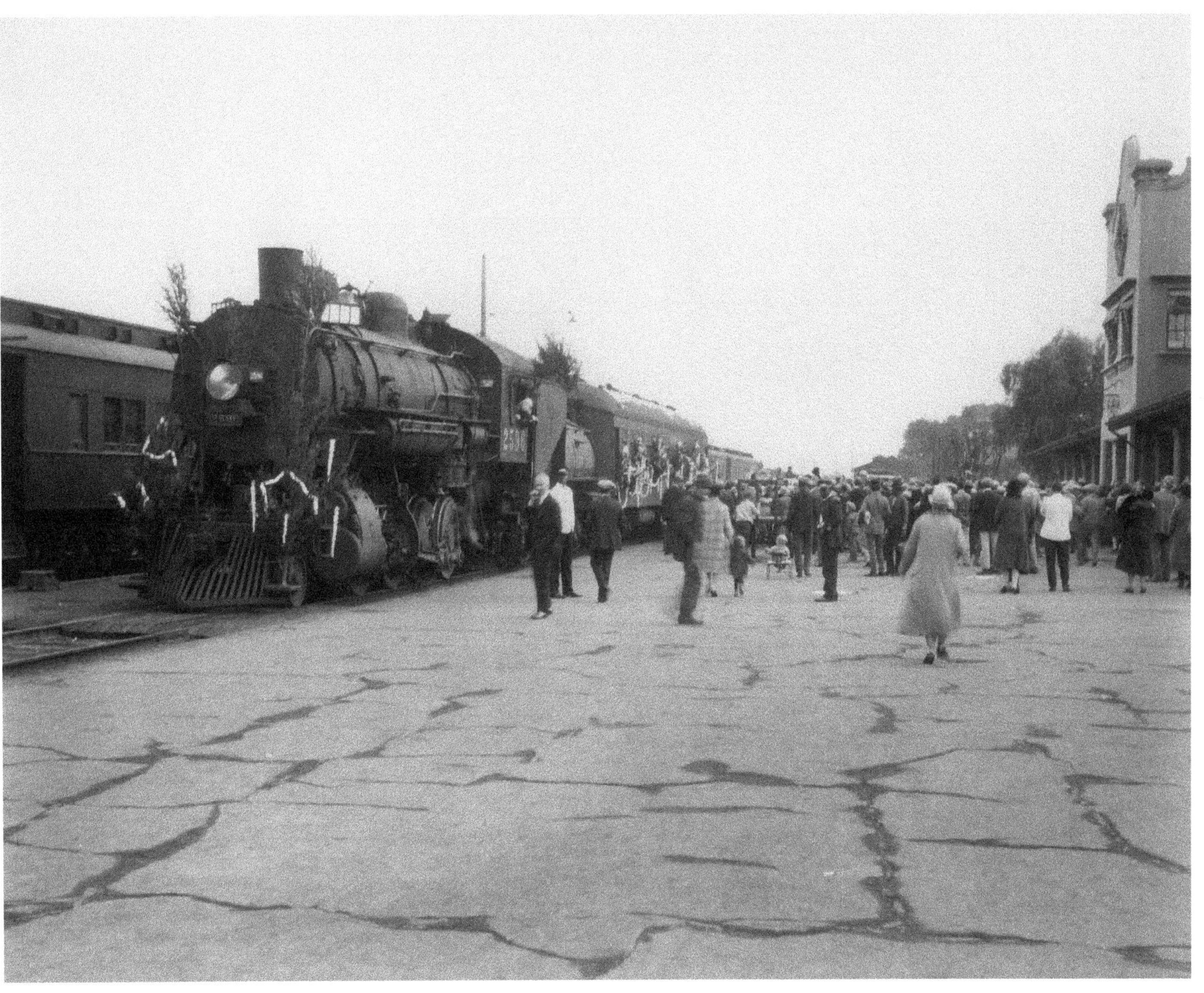

Santa Claus posed for a picture after arrival on the Christmas Train. Albert Steinfeld, who sponsored the event, stands on the right next to the car. For many years he was president of the Consolidated National Bank.

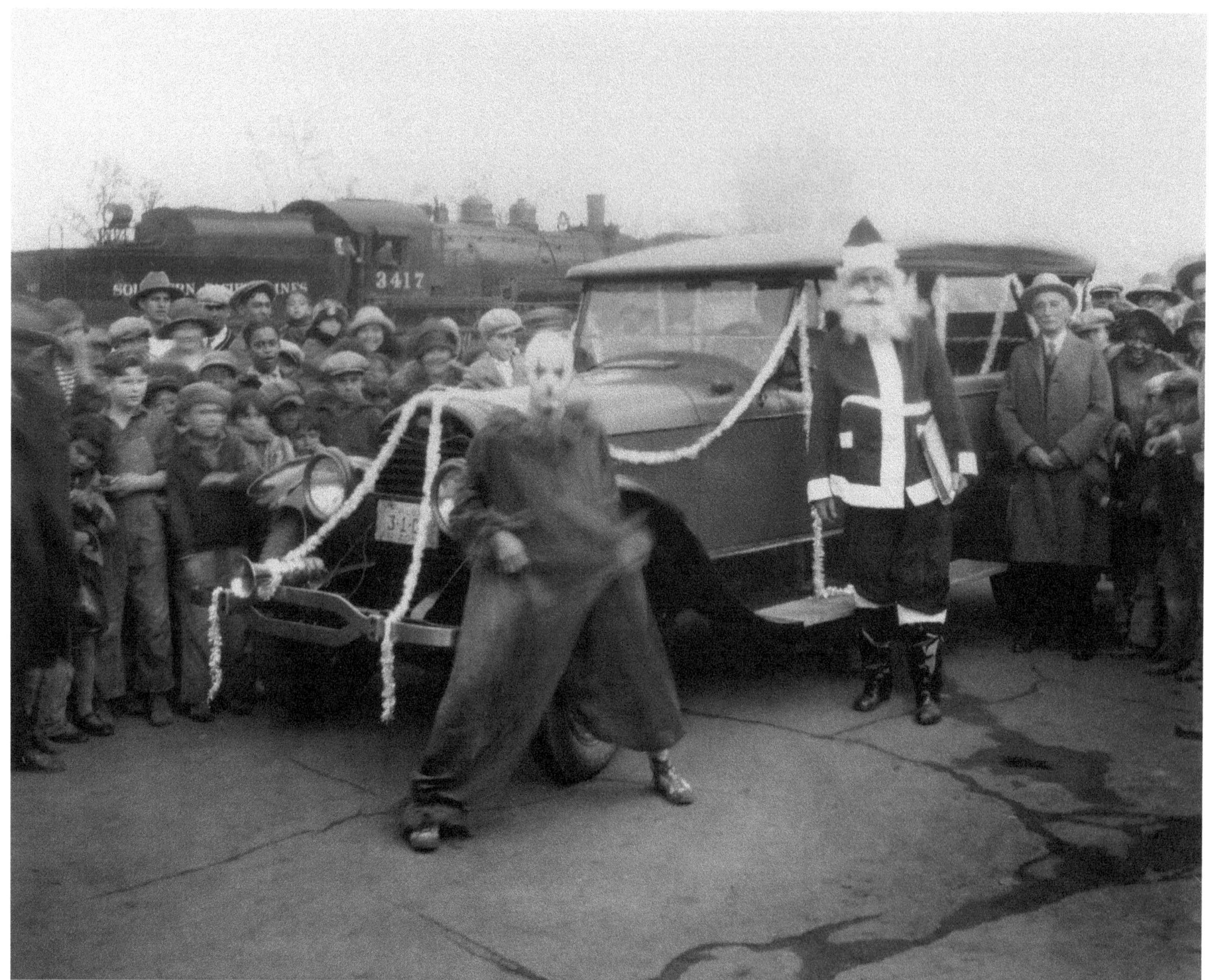

The Southern Pacific Company Band preparing for a parade around 1927. This popular local band gave many outdoor concerts and was a staple in parades.

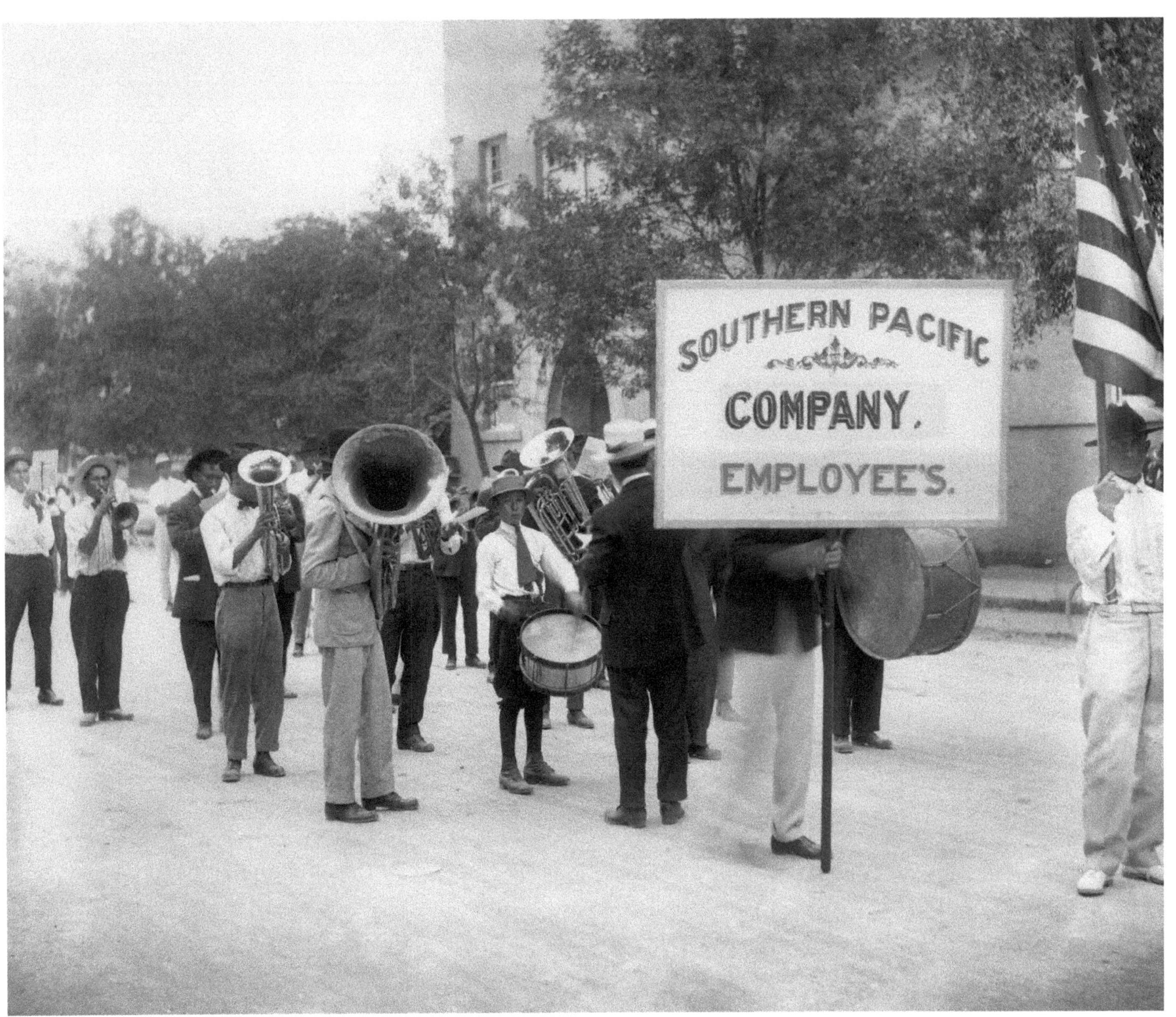

Looking south on Stone Avenue from Pennington Street around 1927. Electric trolleys, called "Izzers" because of their unique sound, ran on Tucson's streets from 1906 through the end of 1930.

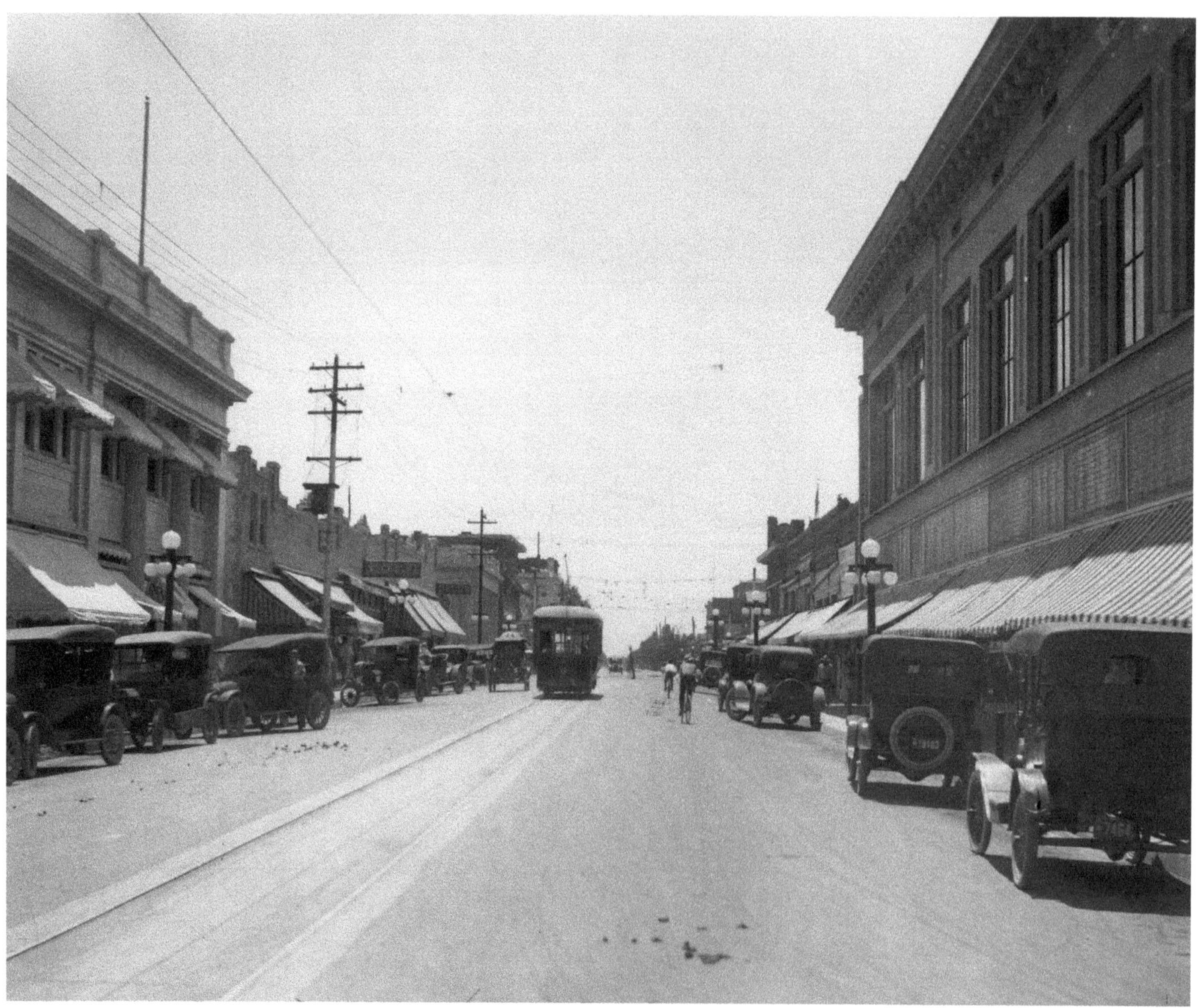

Aviator Charles Lindbergh was honored with a parade in Tucson during his 1927 trip around the country following his record-setting crossing of the Atlantic Ocean.

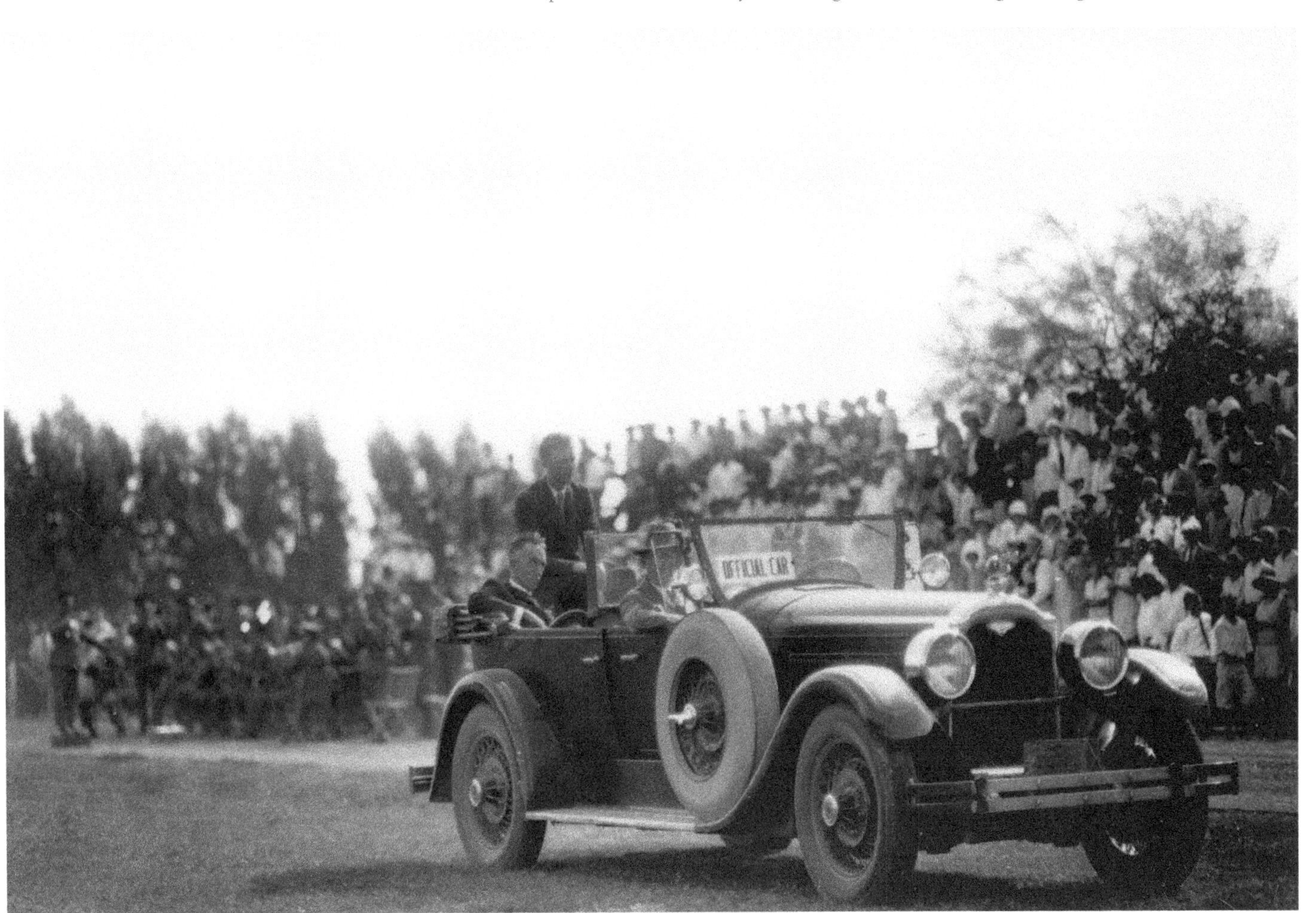

Lindbergh's *Spirit of St. Louis* at the new Davis-Monthan Field in Tucson, September 23, 1927. He had come to help mark the opening of the airfield.

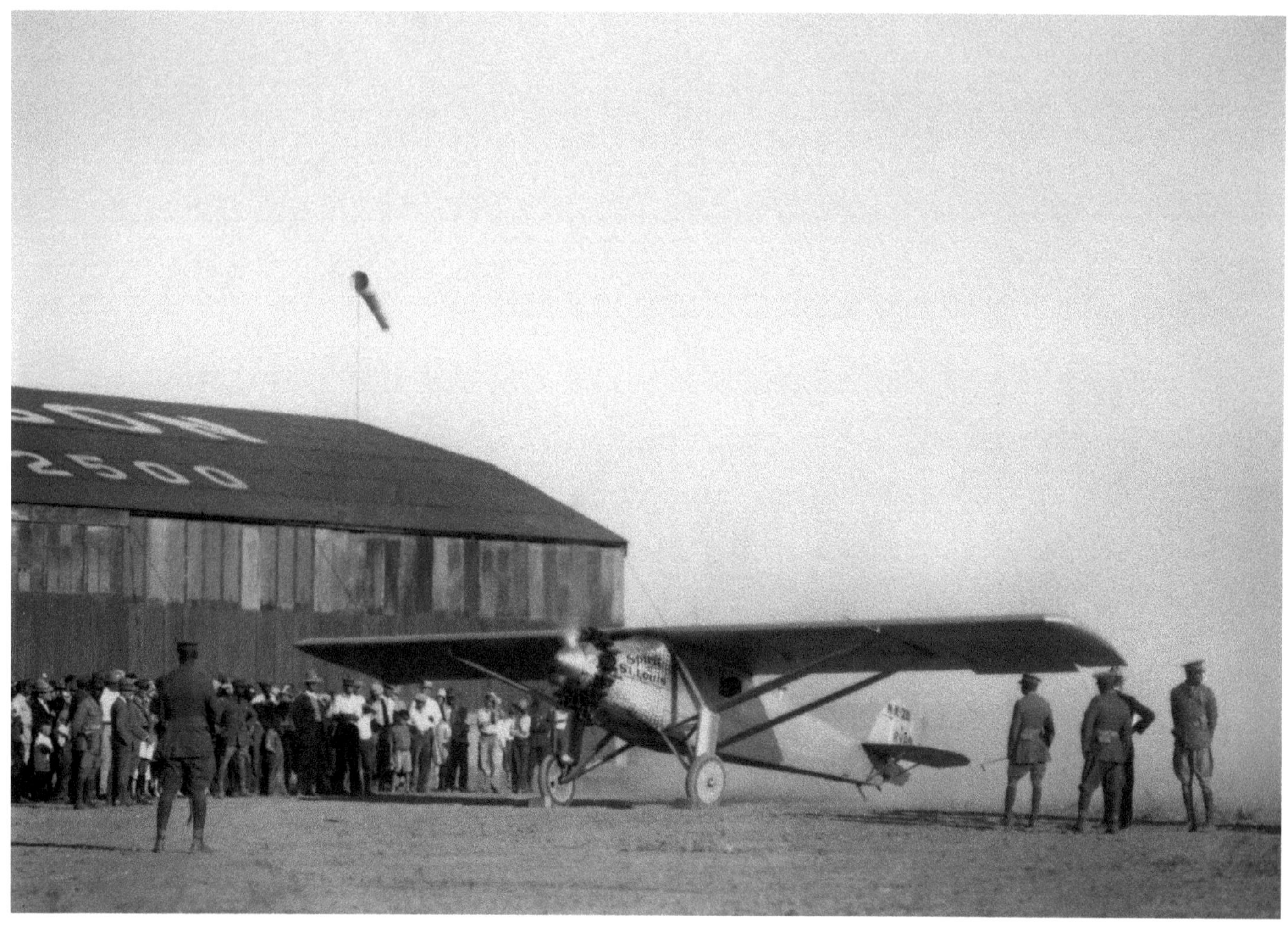

Standard Airlines made the first commercial flight to Tucson from Los Angeles, going by way of Phoenix, on November 28, 1927. Jack Frye, the president and chief pilot of the airline, is pictured with his wife.

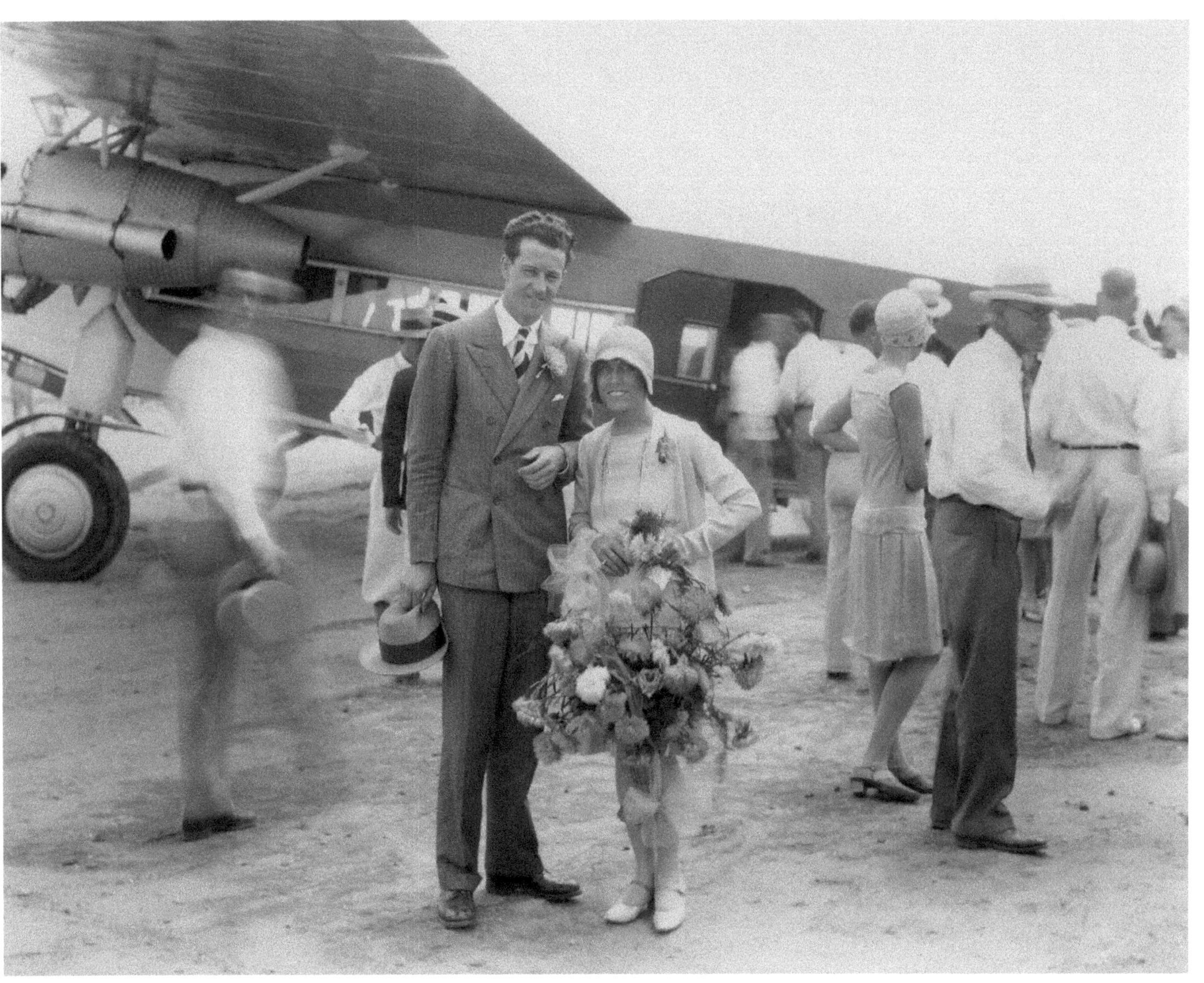

A crowd gathered around a Fokker F-VIIb airplane at the Davis-Monthan Airfield in the late 1920s. This eight- to twelve-passenger aircraft was the most popular passenger plane of its time.

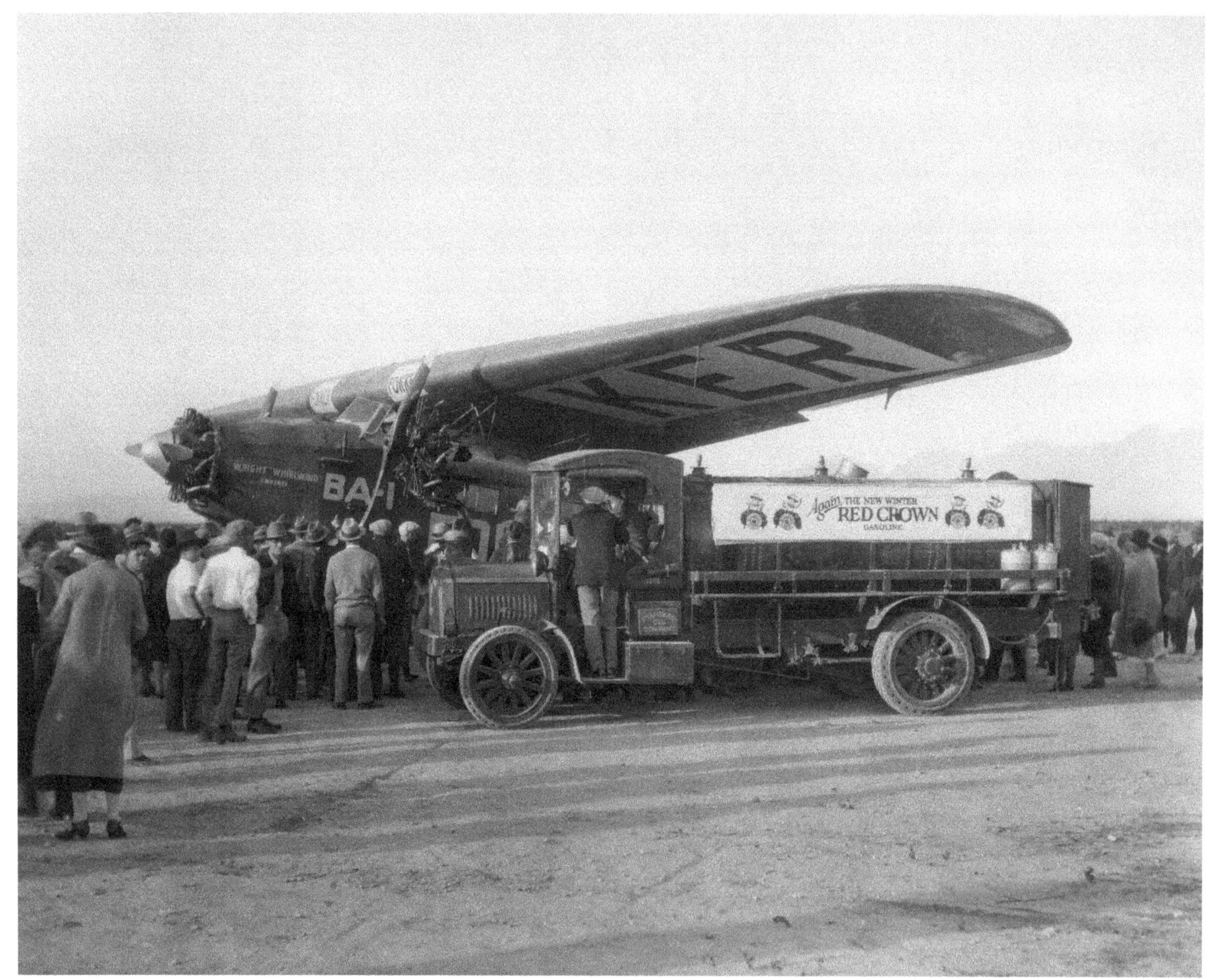

Small commuter airlines came and went in the early days of aviation. A group of airplane passengers posed with a mechanic.

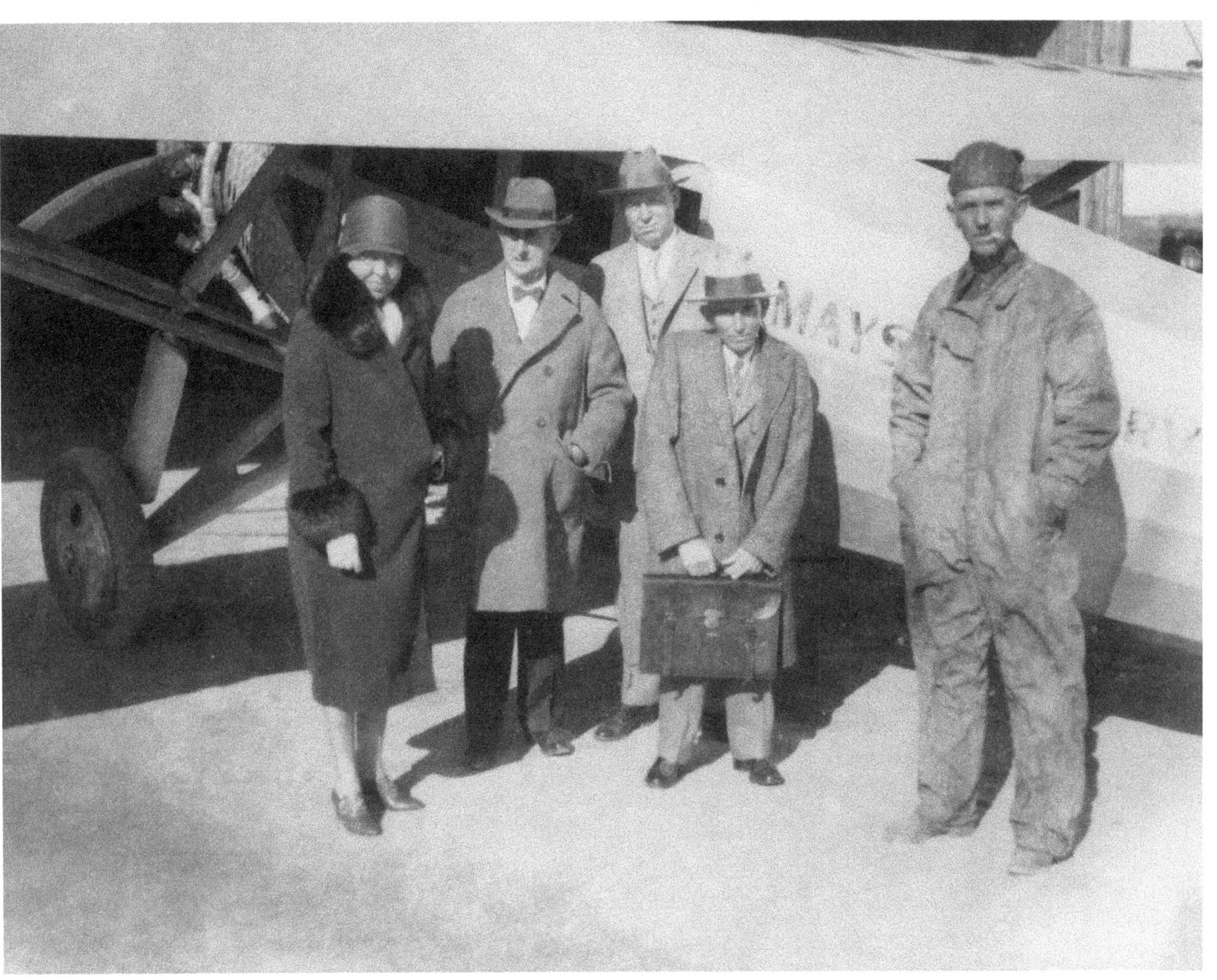

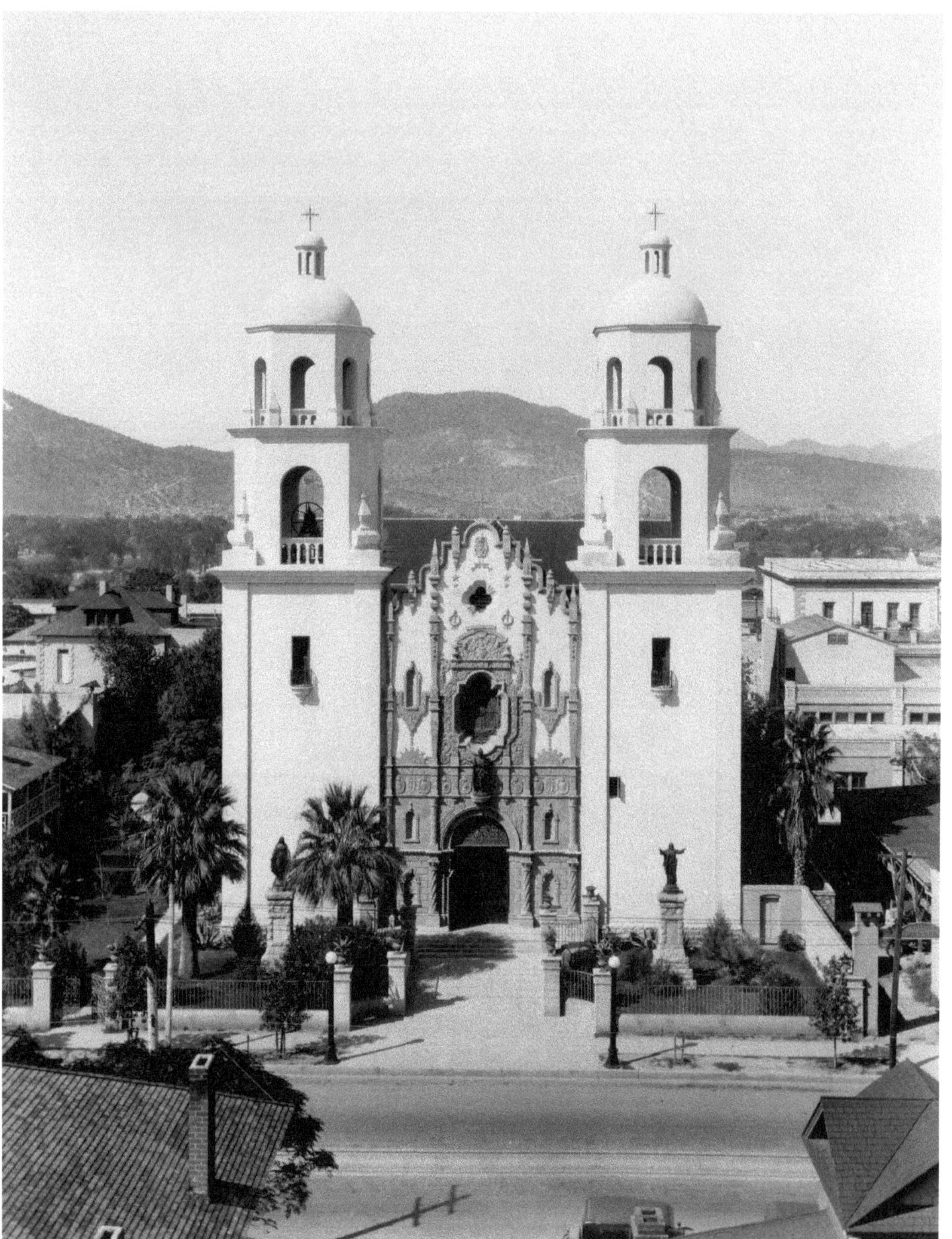

The front of the San Augustine Cathedral on South Stone Avenue, after two towers and a southwestern-style façade had been added to the original brick building in 1928.

When the luxurious, 150-room El Conquistador Hotel was built in 1928, it was still far outside the city limits. This is a picture taken not long after its opening.

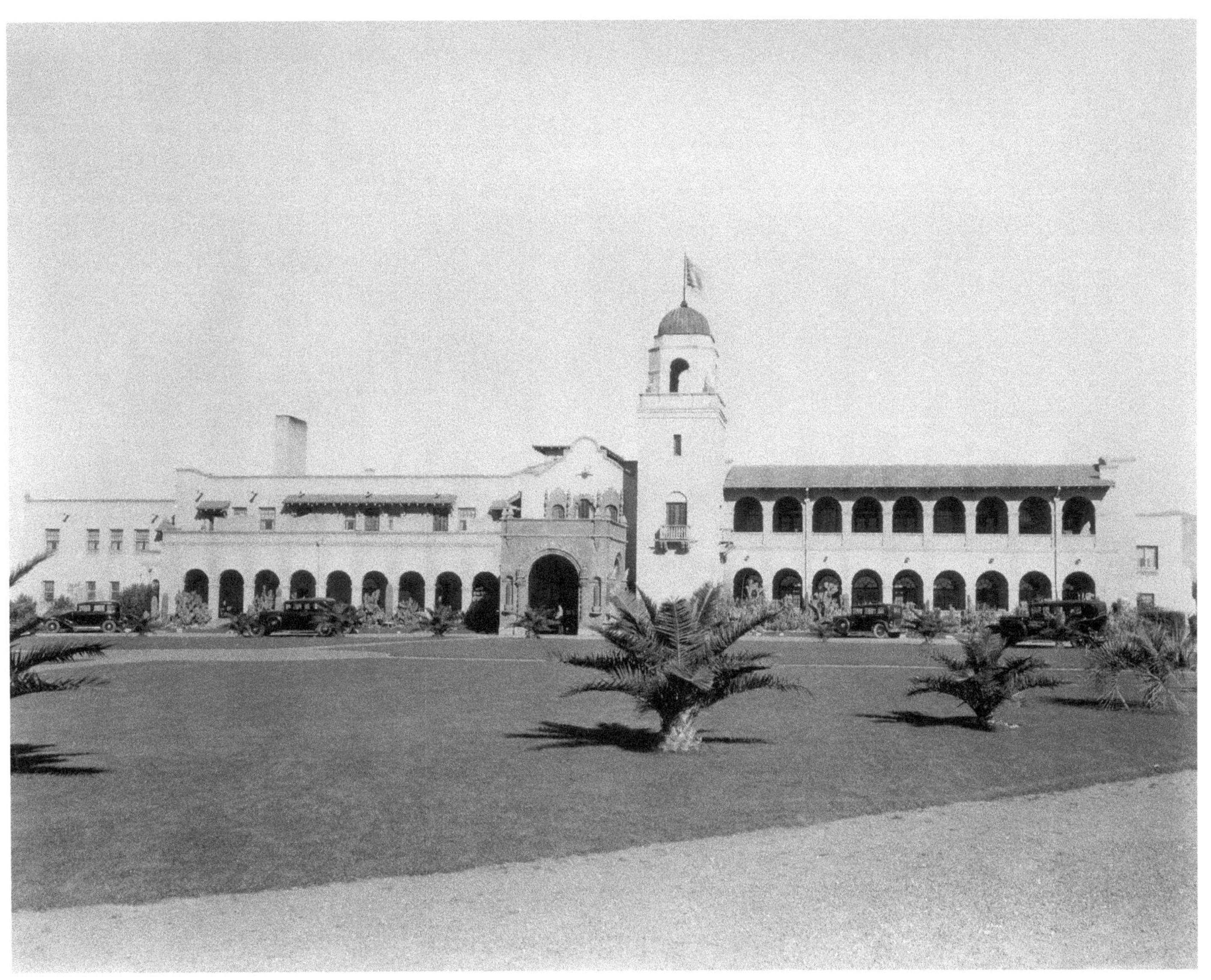

The corral at the El Conquistador Hotel (ca. 1928).

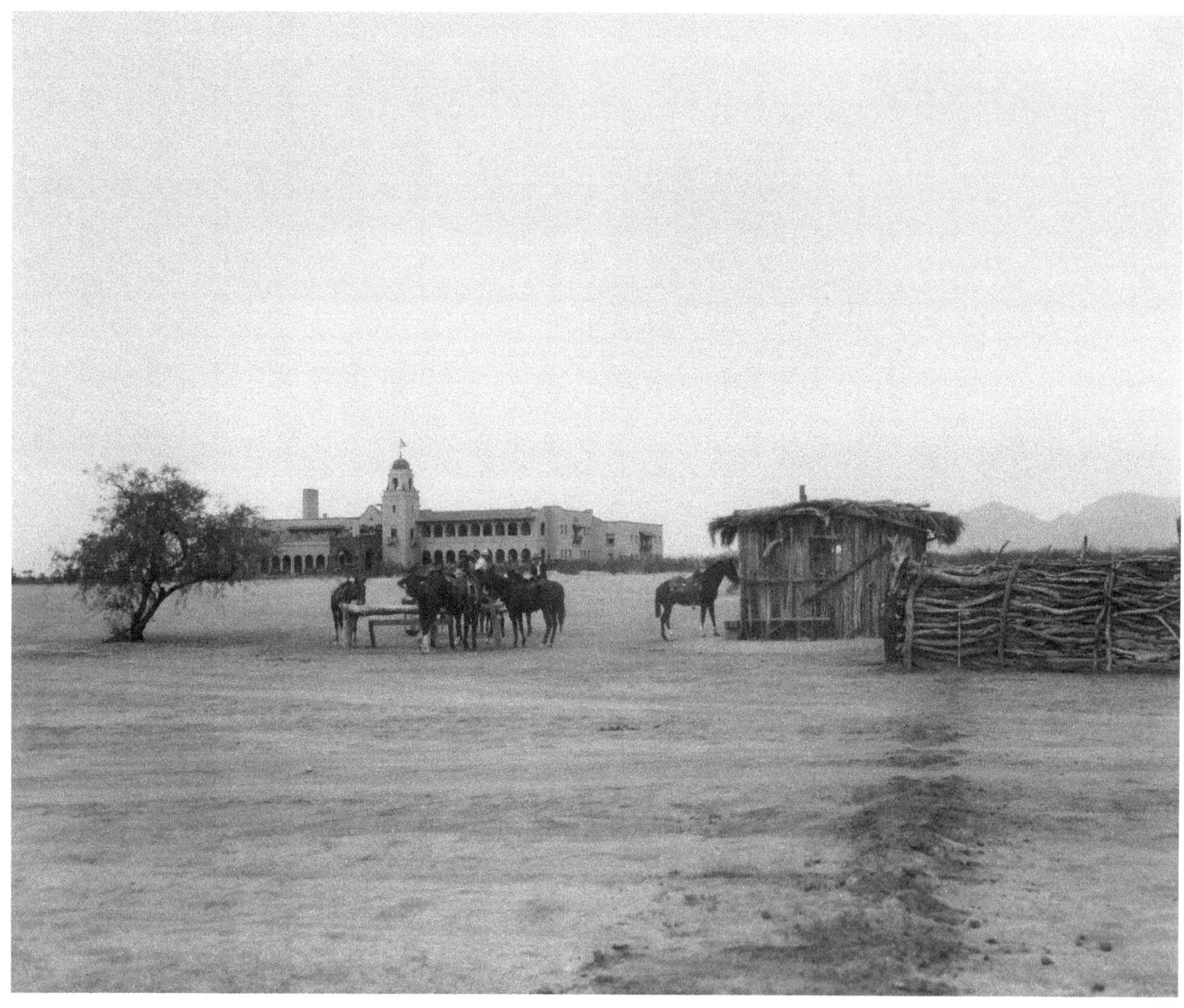

Guests gather in front of El Conquistador Hotel prior to a ride.

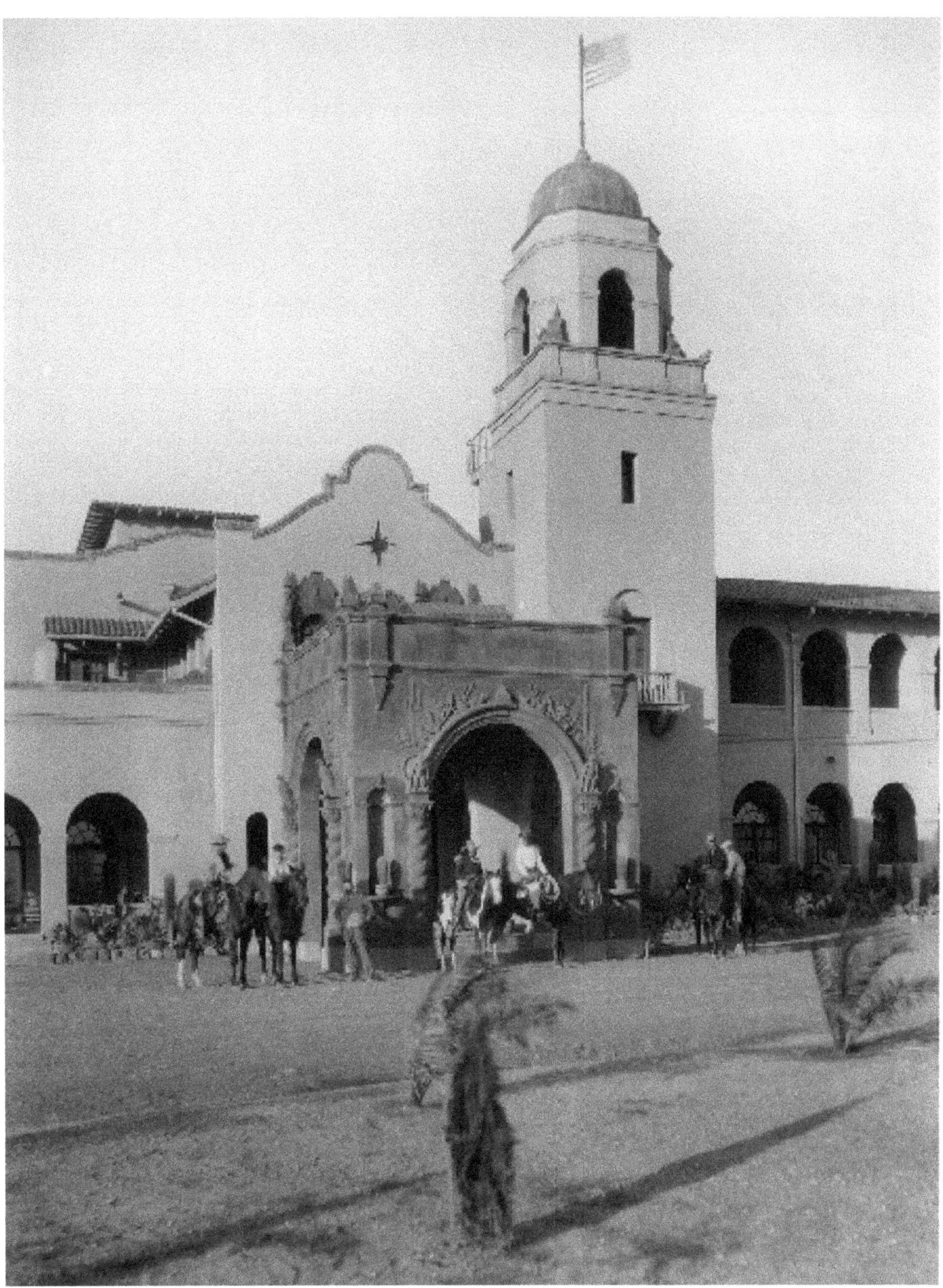

Riders in the Rodeo Parade proceed along Stone Avenue (ca. 1928).

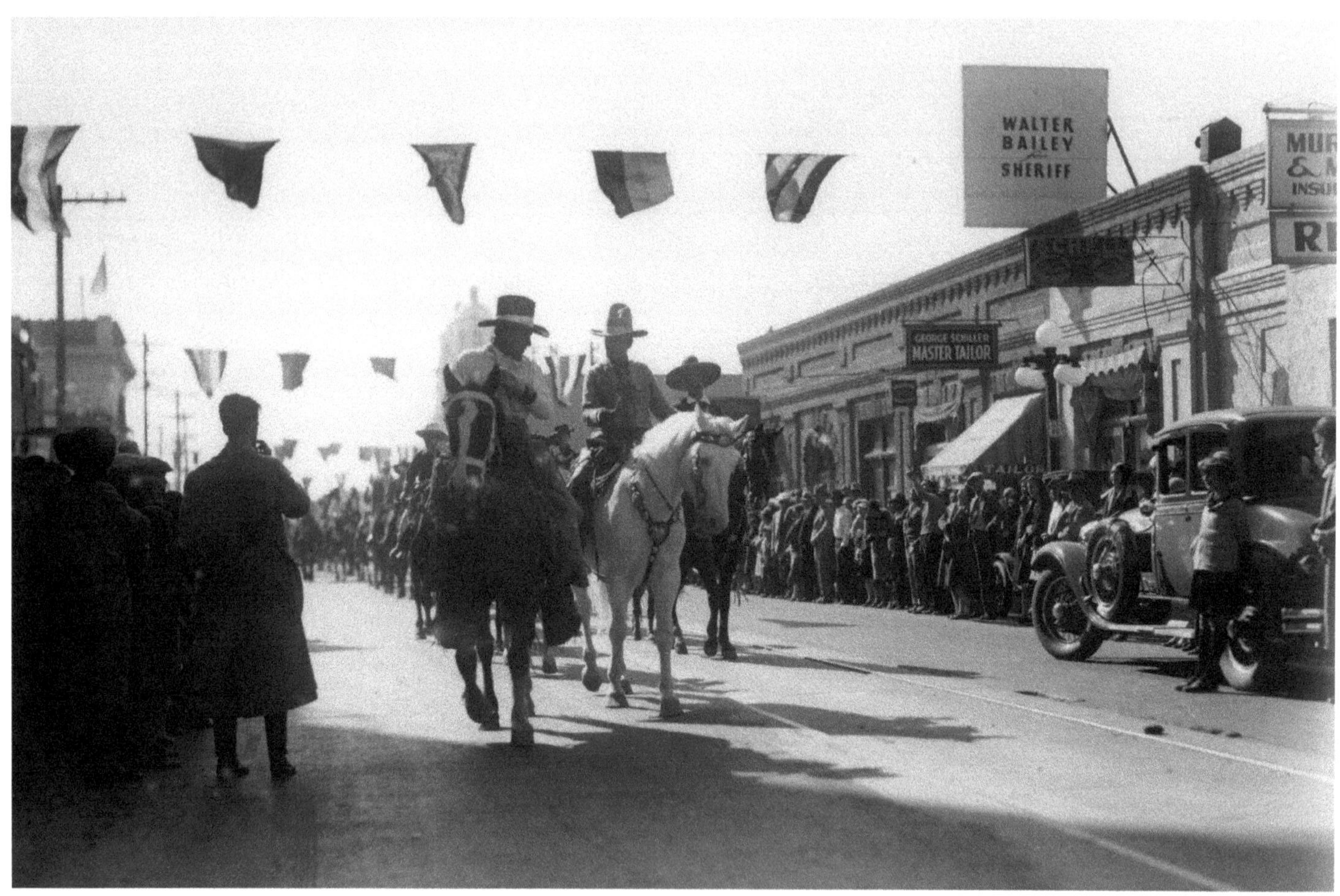

The Firestone Company airplane at the Tucson airfield around 1929.

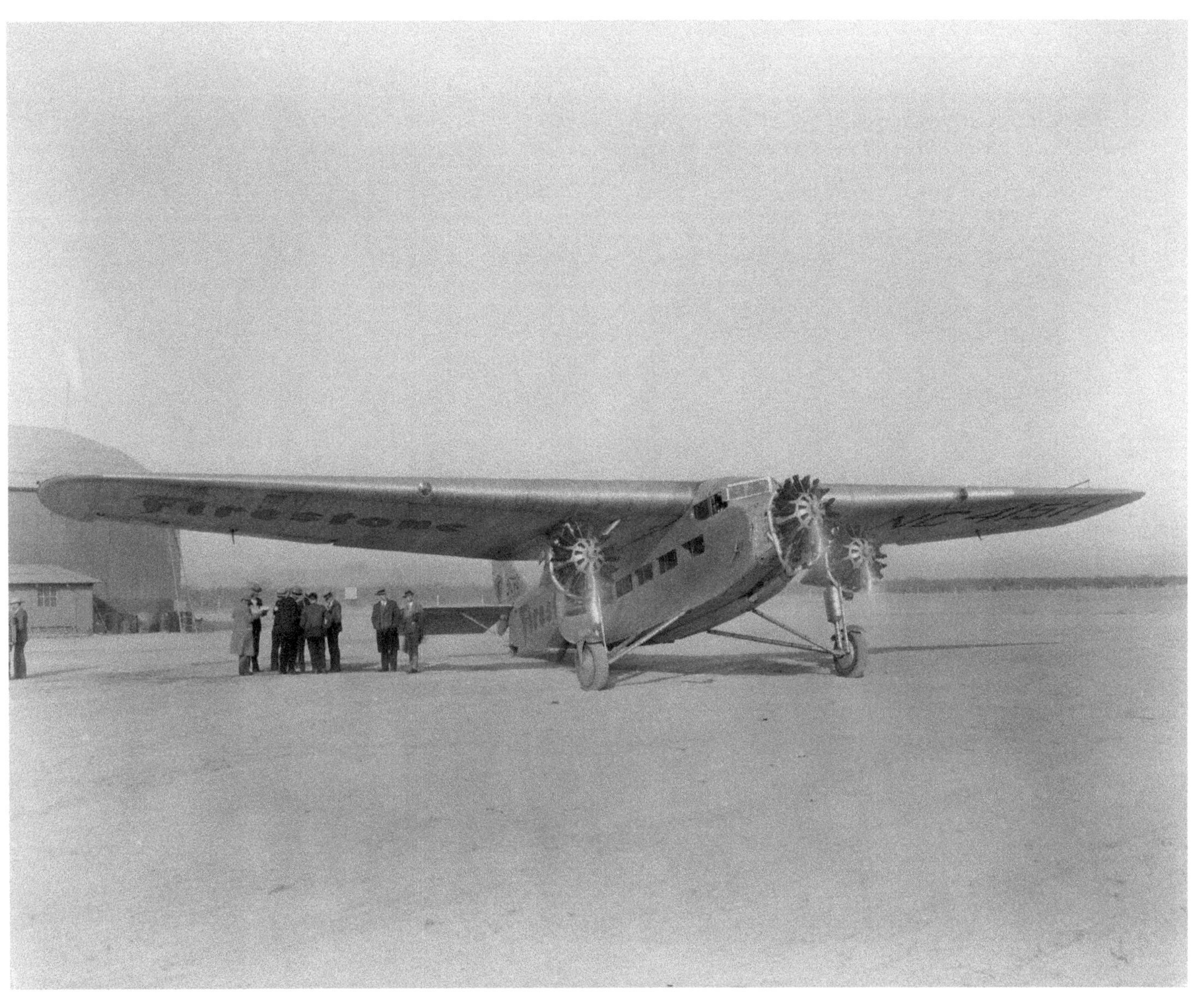

Some motorized floats made an appearance in the early days of the Rodeo Parade, such as this Alianza Hispano Americana float in 1929.

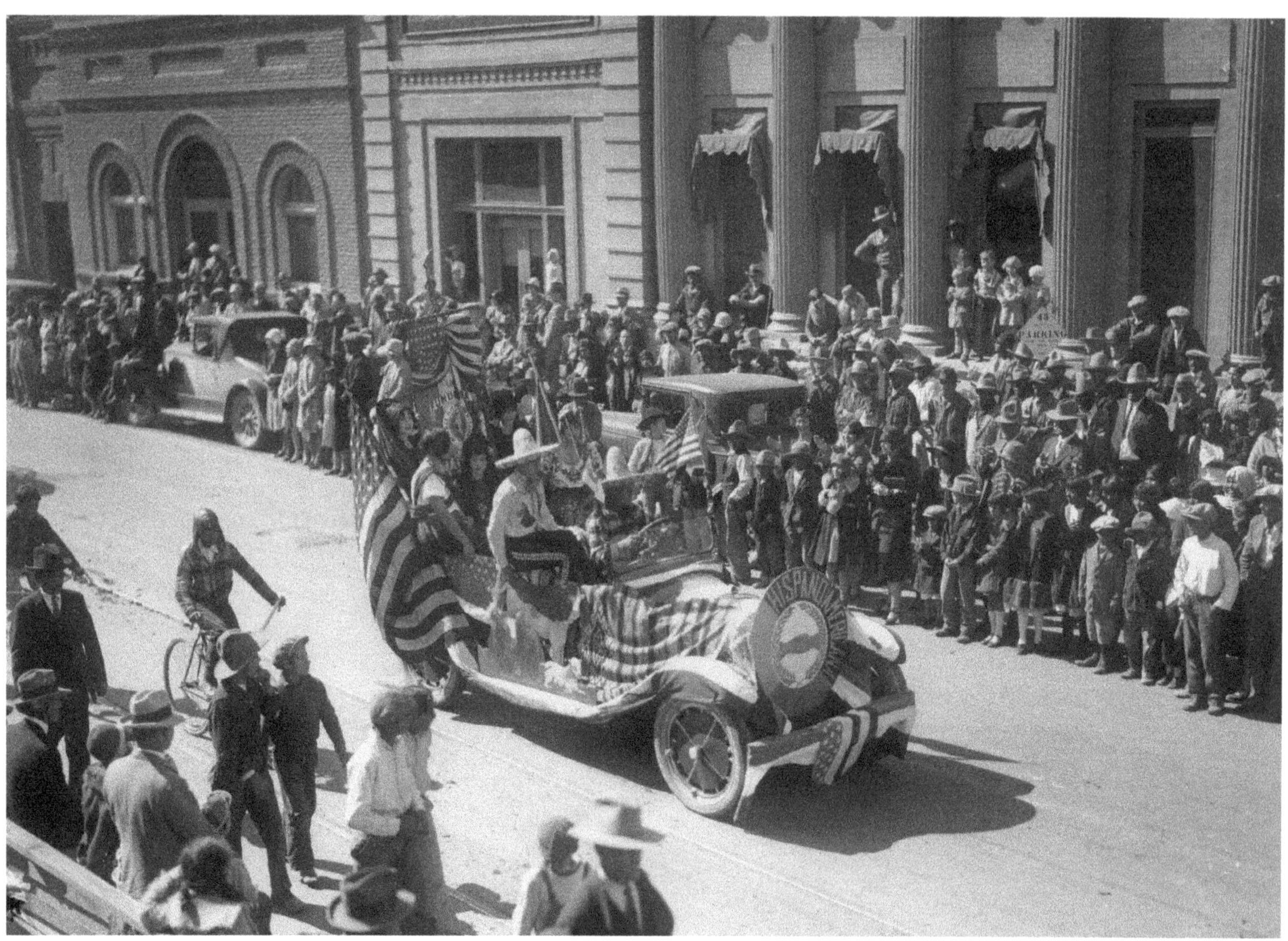

A new building for the Consolidated National Bank was constructed on the site of the original at the southeast corner of Stone Avenue and Congress Street, beginning in February 1929. Tucson's first skyscraper, the building was eleven stories and still stands downtown.

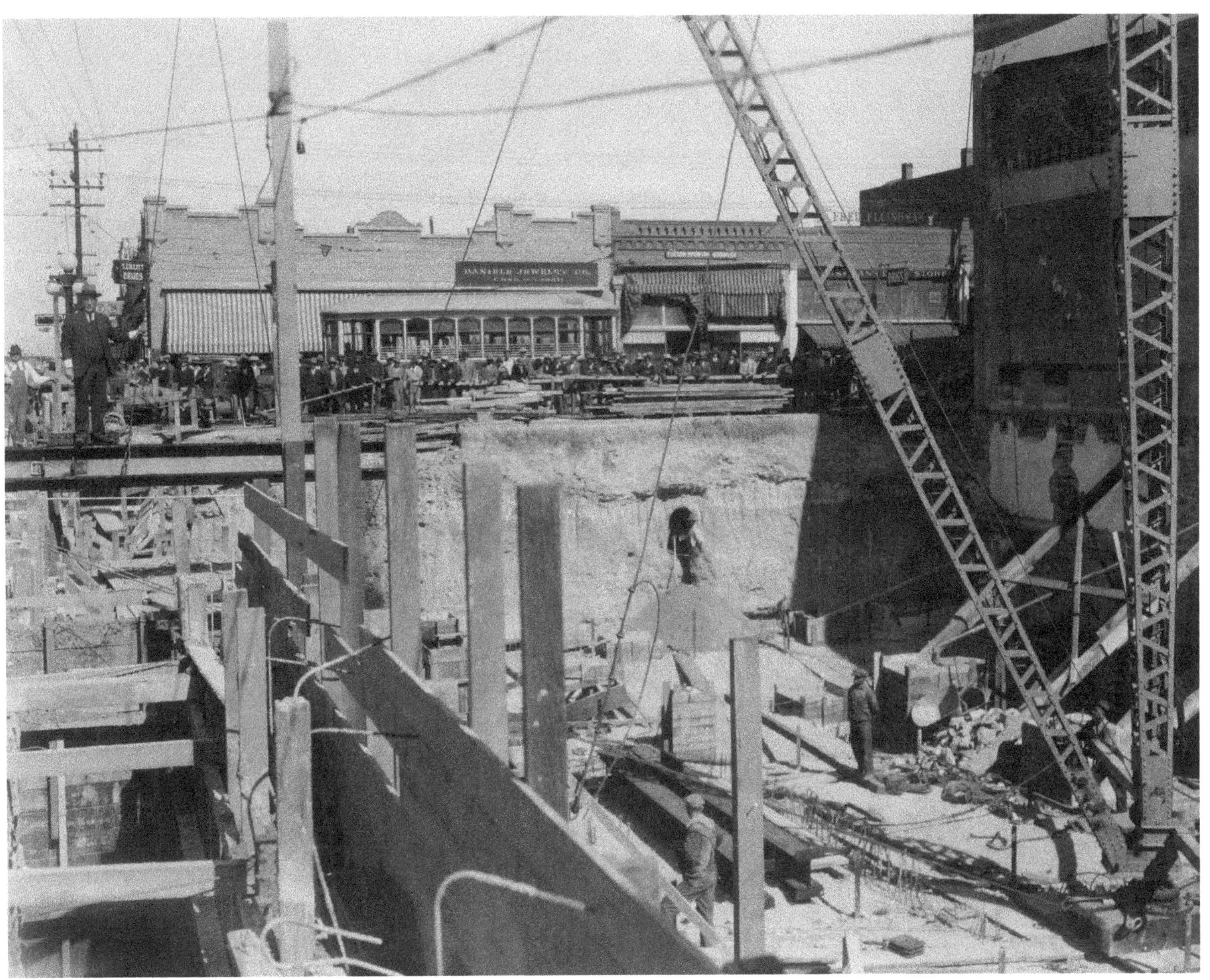

A float pulled by a tractor in the 1930 Rodeo Parade on Congress Street. In the background, the Fox Theater marquee is under construction.

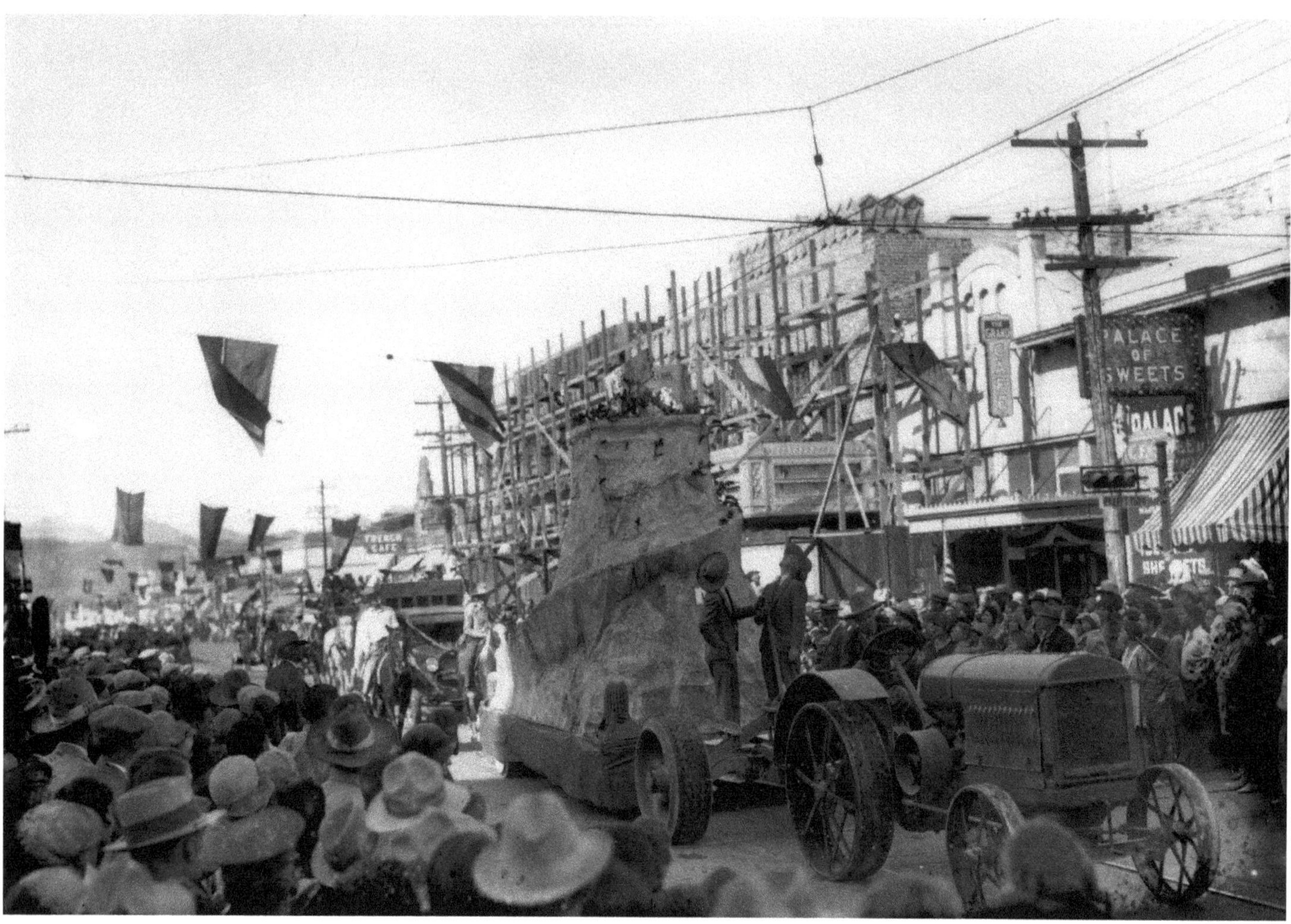

Hollywood movies provided a needed distraction at the beginning of the Depression. In 1930, people line up to see *The Big Trail*, John Wayne's first starring role. The newly opened Fox Theater was Tucson's largest theater at the time.

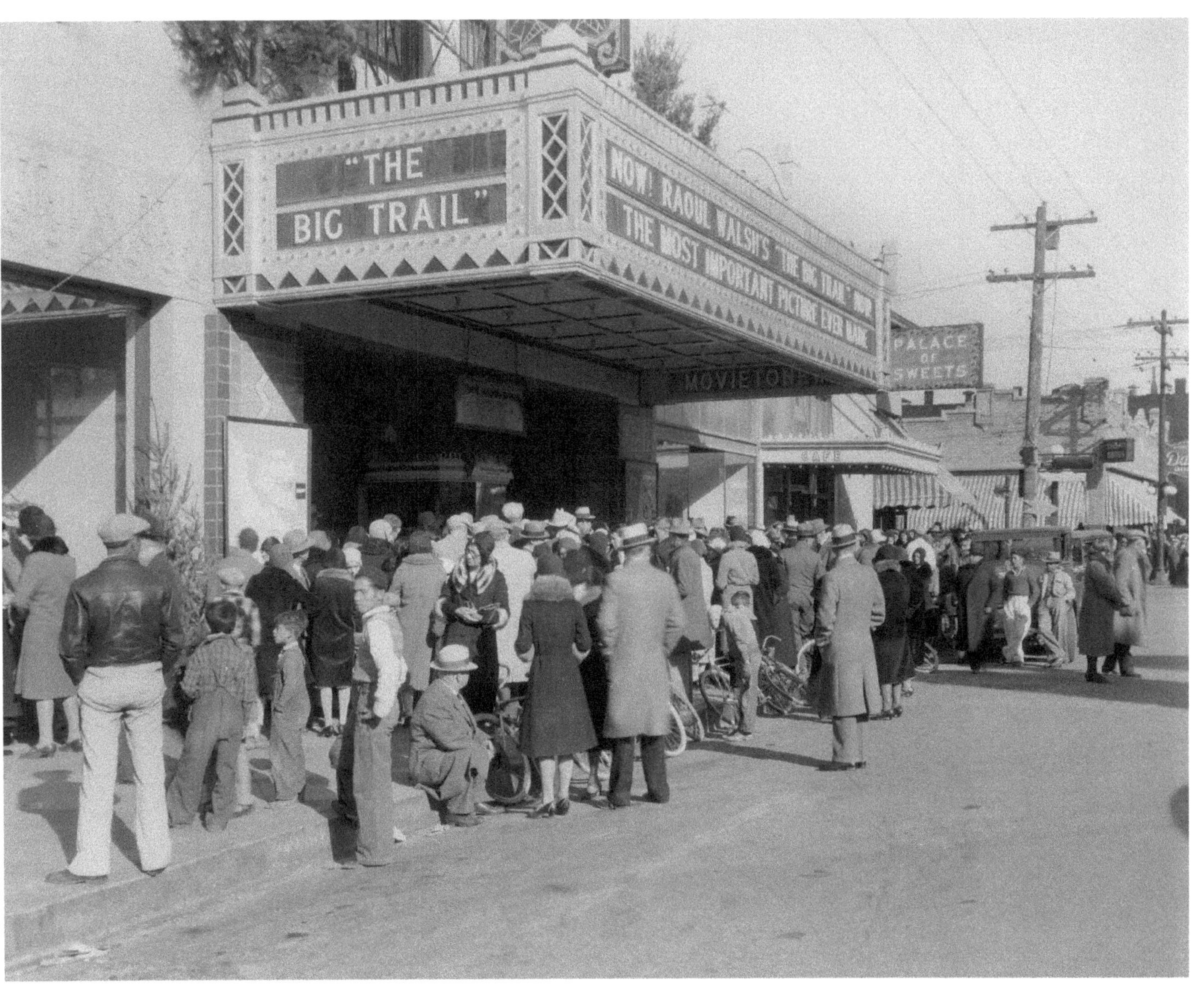

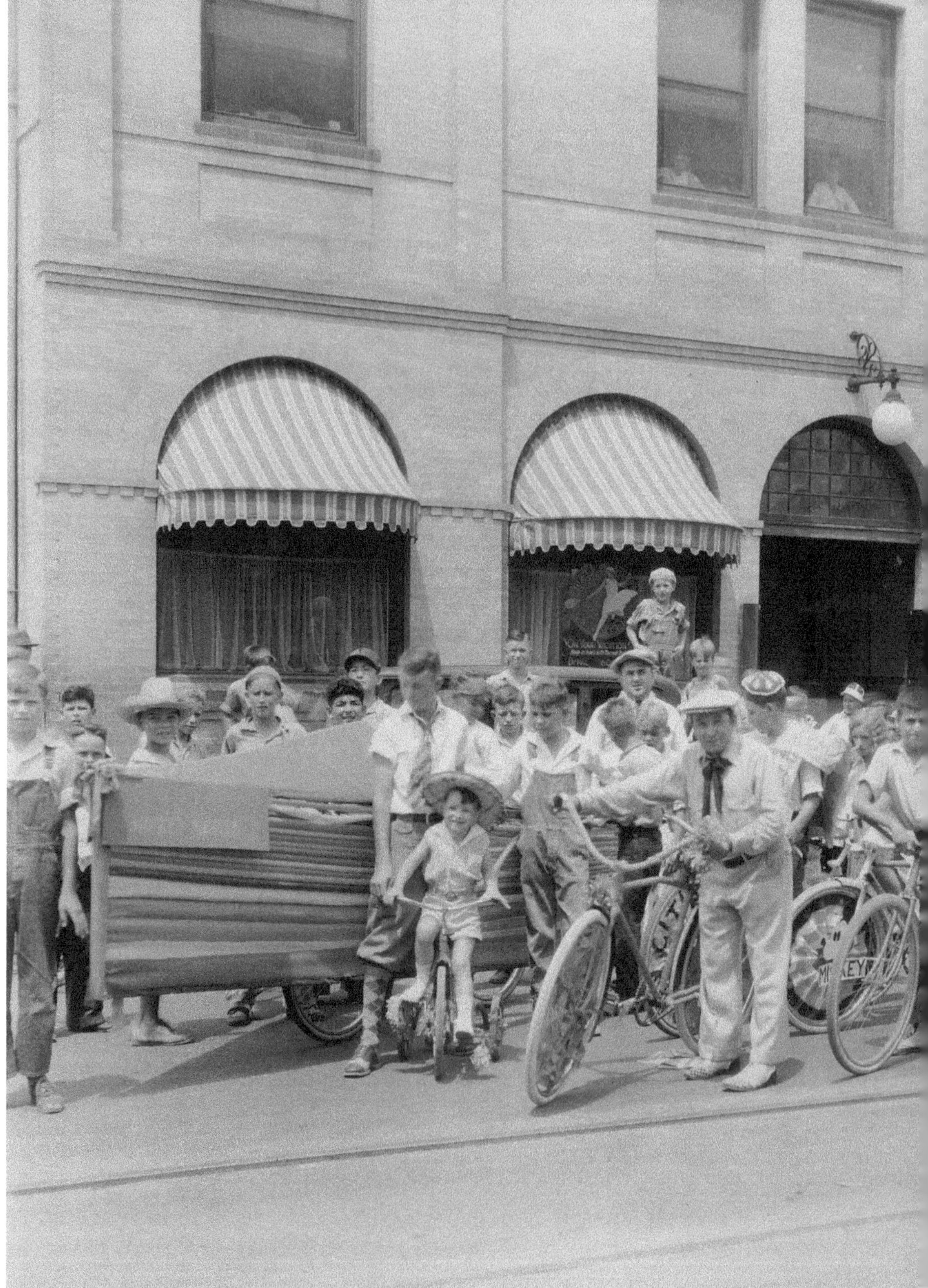

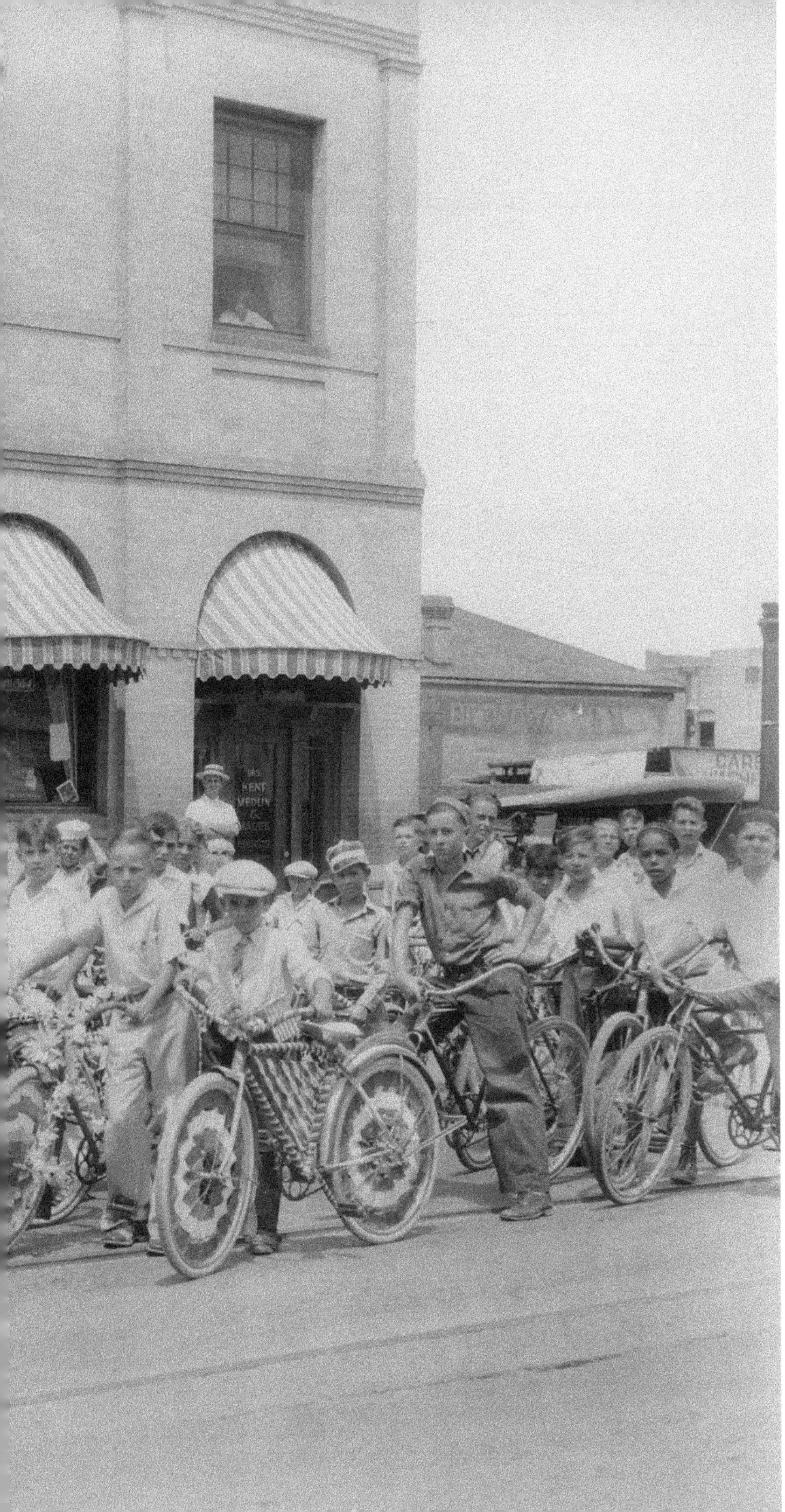

New members gather in front of the Tucson Citizen building to mark the forming of a local chapter of the Mickey Mouse Club, sponsored by the *Citizen* and the Fox Theater, in July 1930. Walt Disney started Mickey Mouse clubs the previous year.

The Santa Rita Hotel and a view to the southeast (ca. 1930).

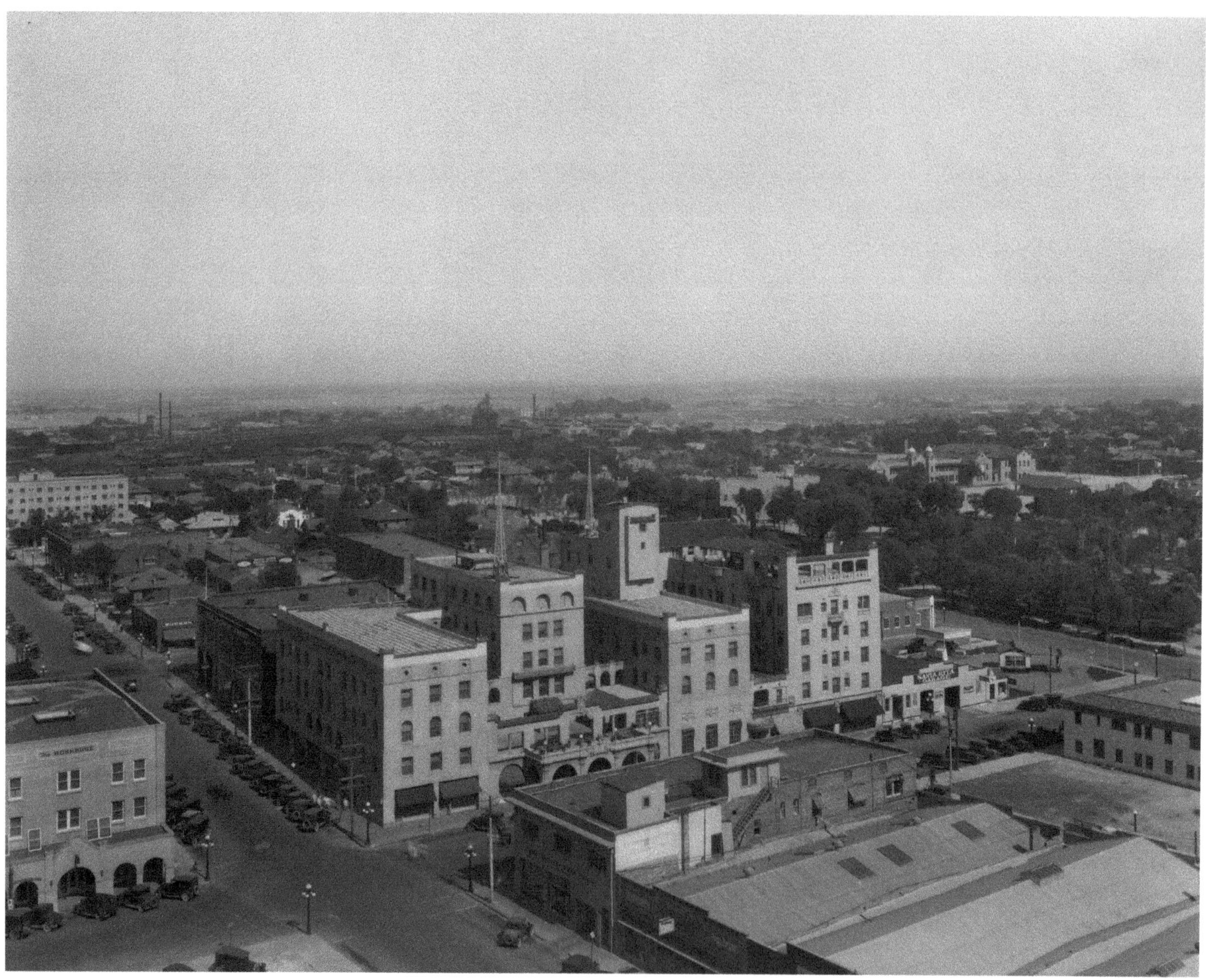

A man hung upside down to write on a blackboard posted over the entrance to the Arizona Daily Star offices at 33 W. Congress around 1930. The blackboard was used primarily for headlines and advertising.

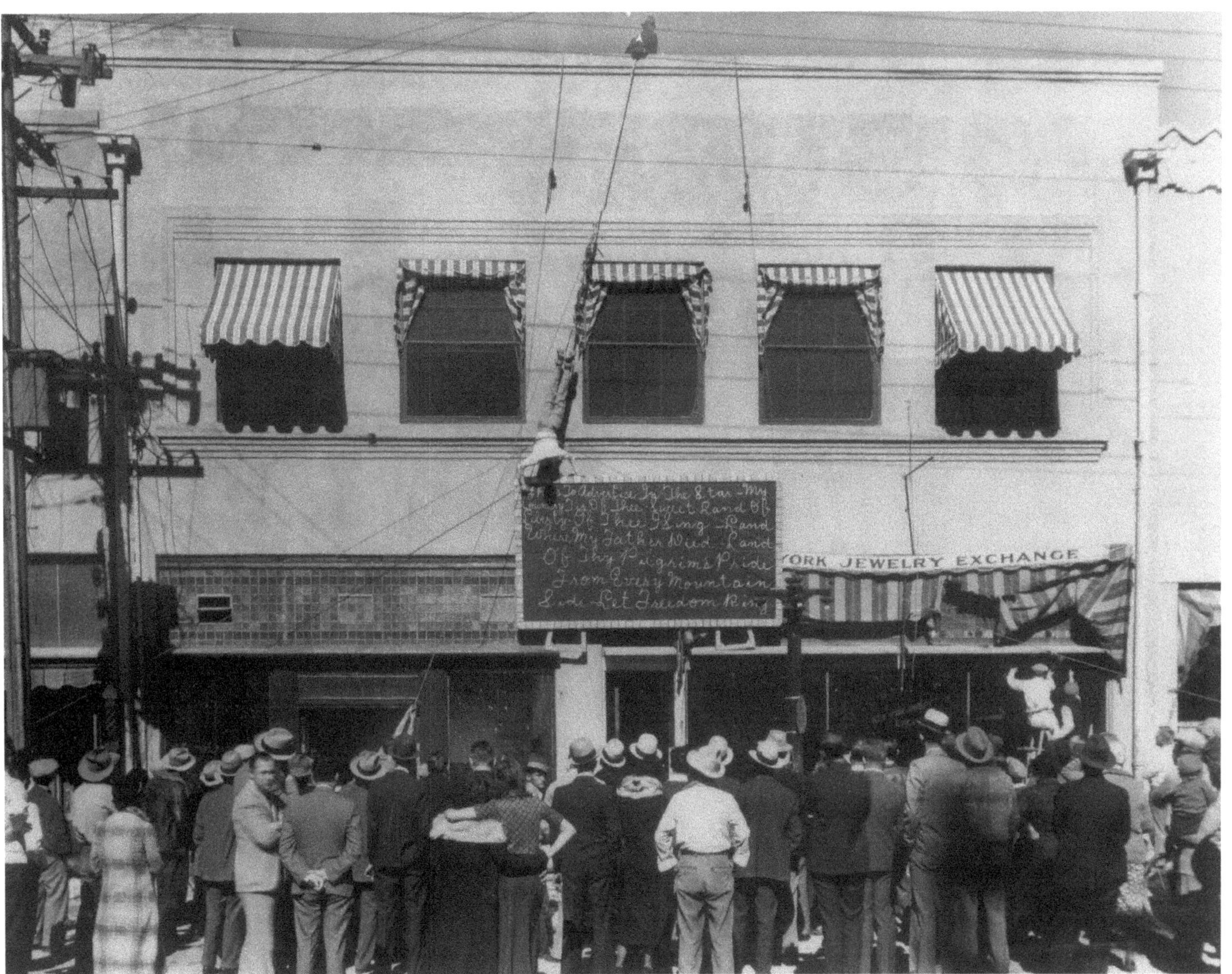

Future Congresswoman Isabella Greenway built the Arizona Inn in 1930, when it was two miles outside of town, offering elegant, stylish accommodations. Guests play a game of croquet on its lawn in the 1930s.

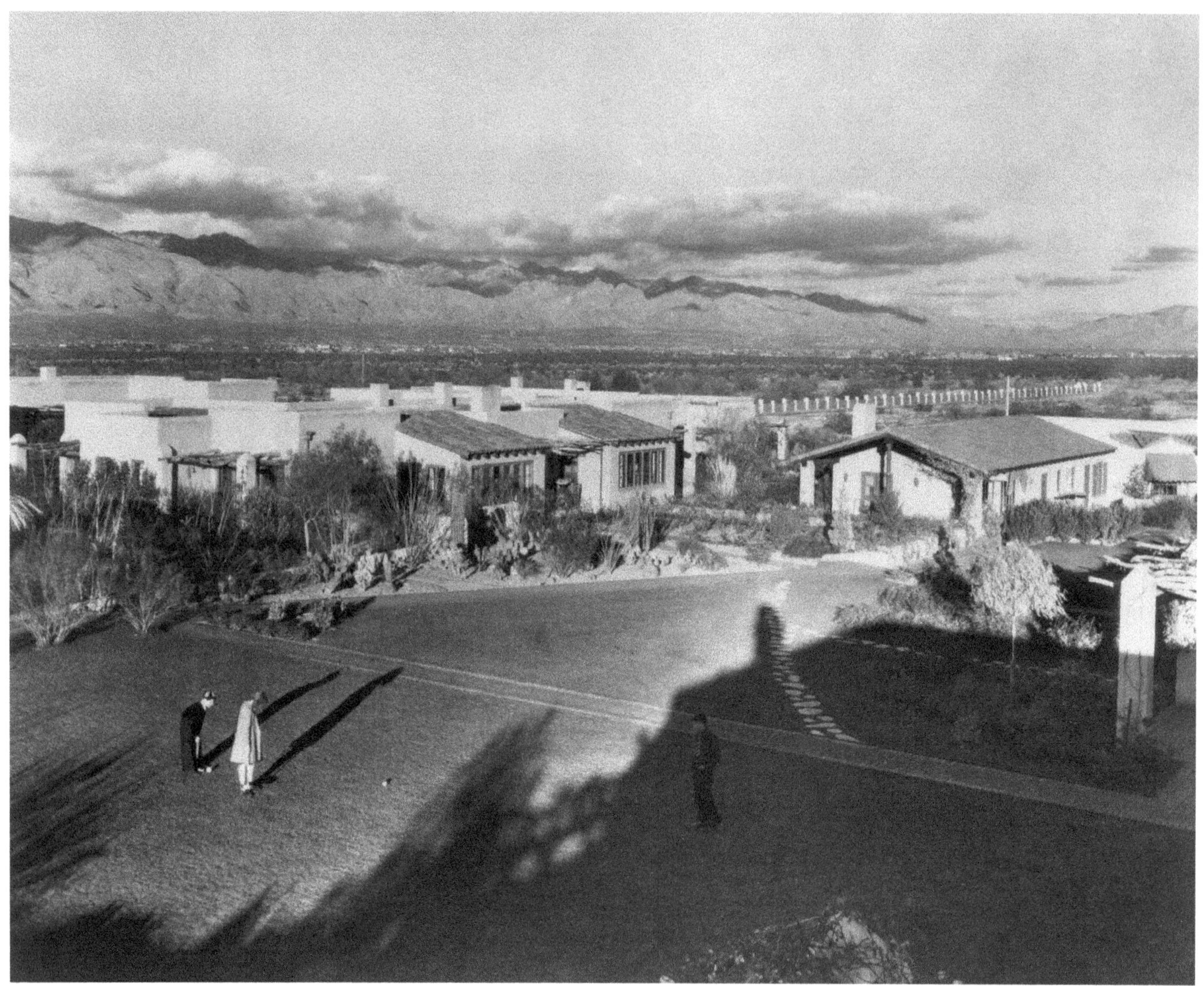

Built in 1909 and remodeled in 1928, the Central Station of the Tucson Fire Department stood at 142 S. Sixth Avenue for many years.

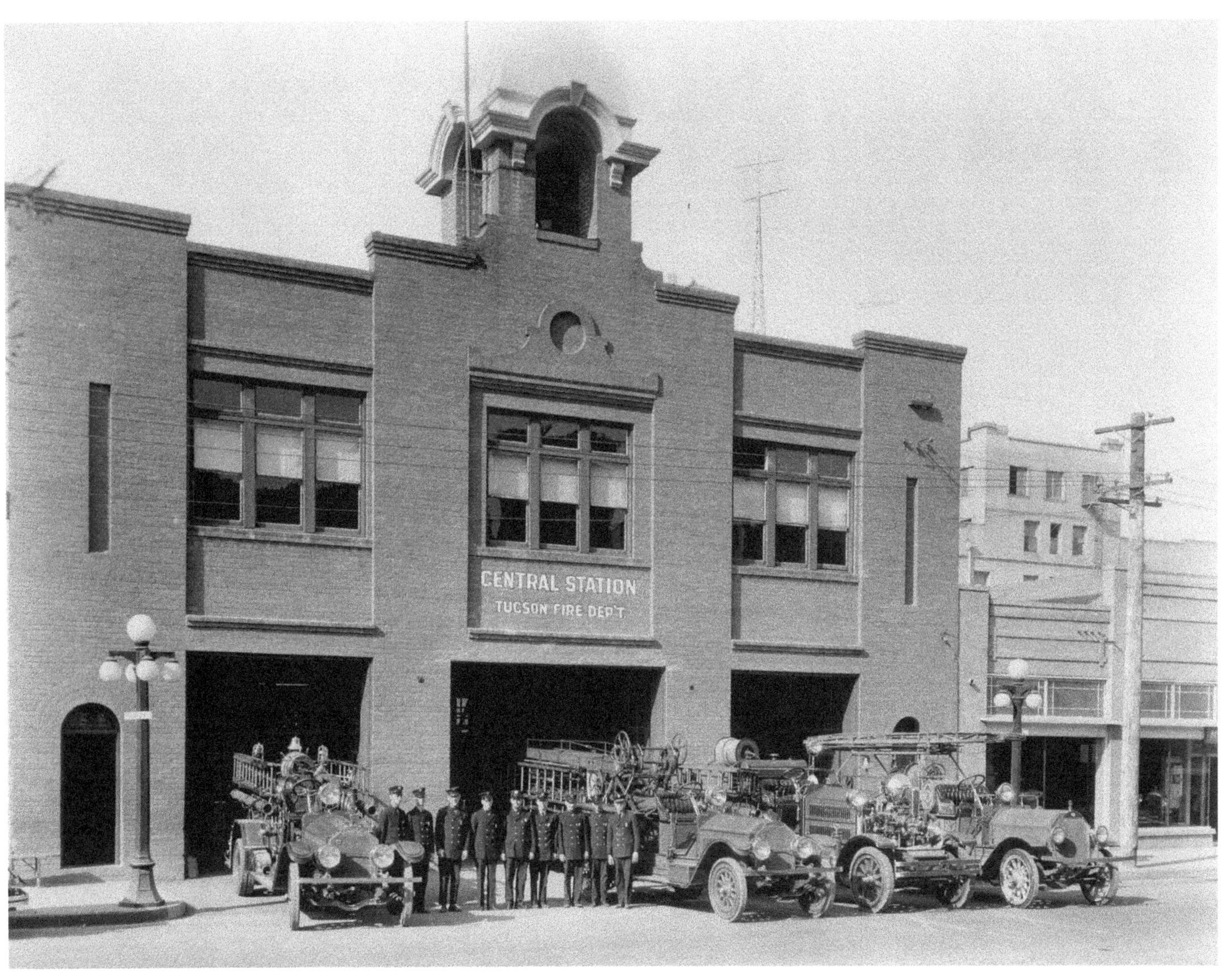

Another view of the Central Station of the Tucson Fire Department.

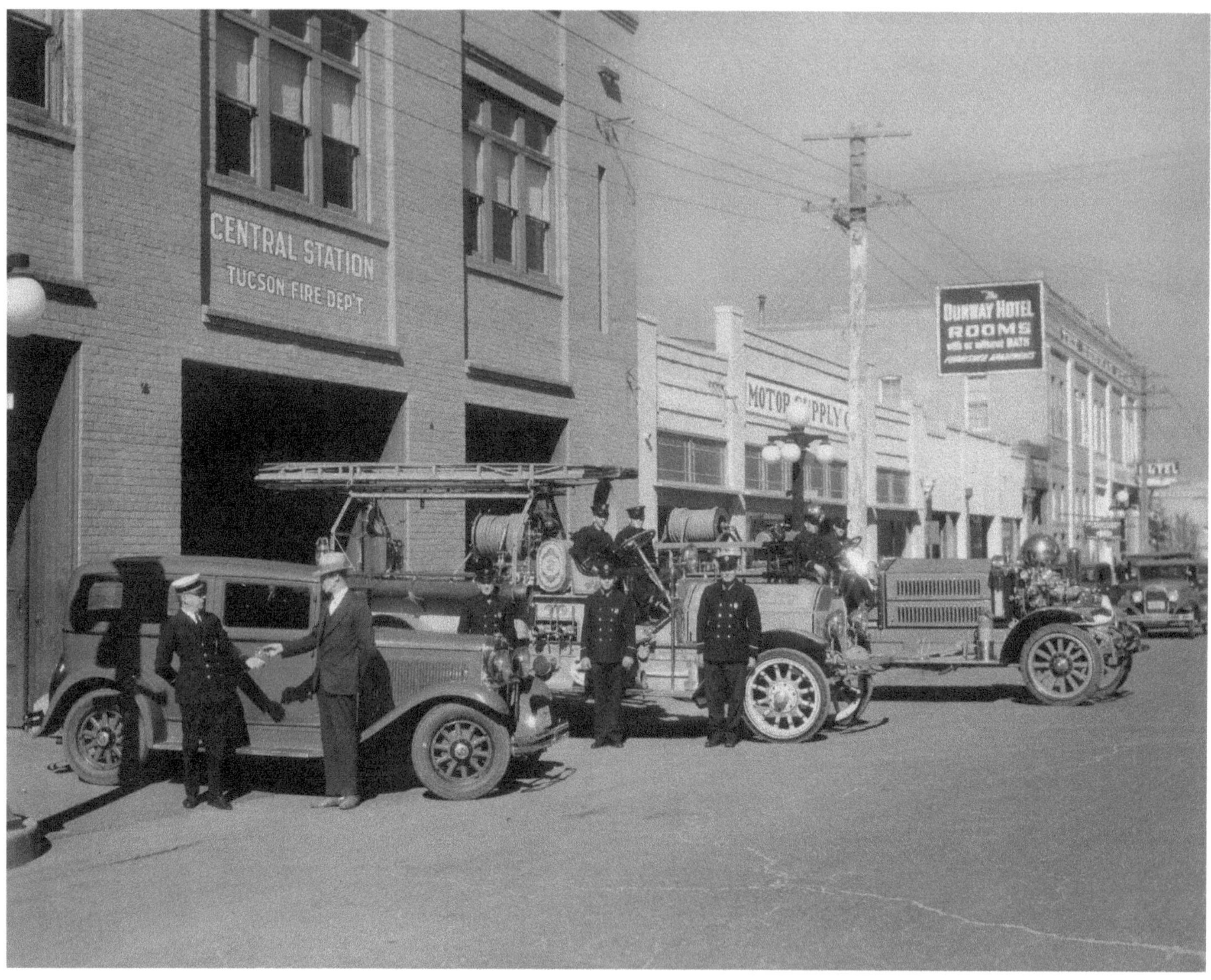

The Bowen-Sime Motor Co. sold Studebakers and Pierce Arrows at the corner of Broadway Boulevard and Fifth Avenue (ca. 1930).

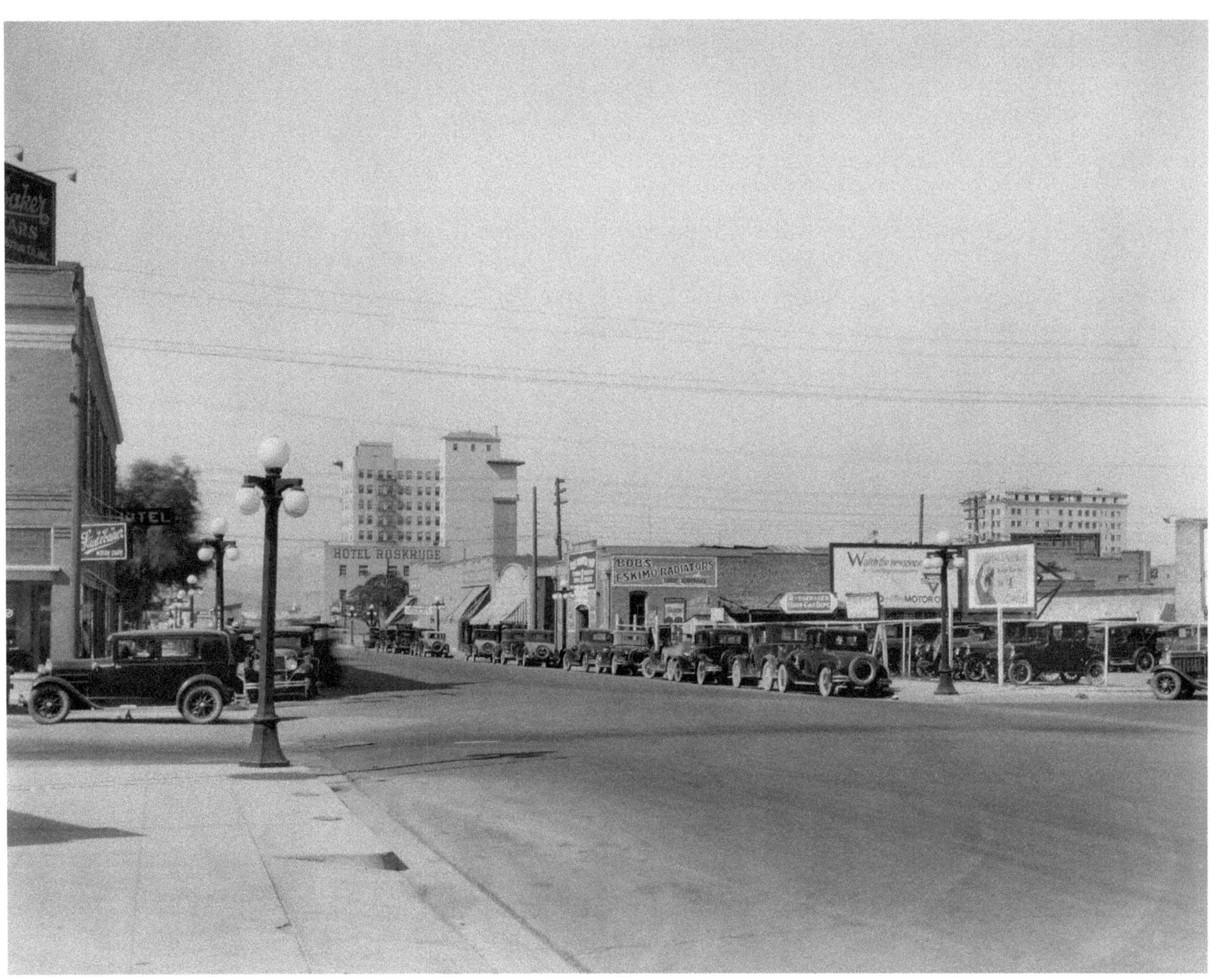

A view of Tucson looking northeast across the valley from Sentinel Peak (ca. 1930).

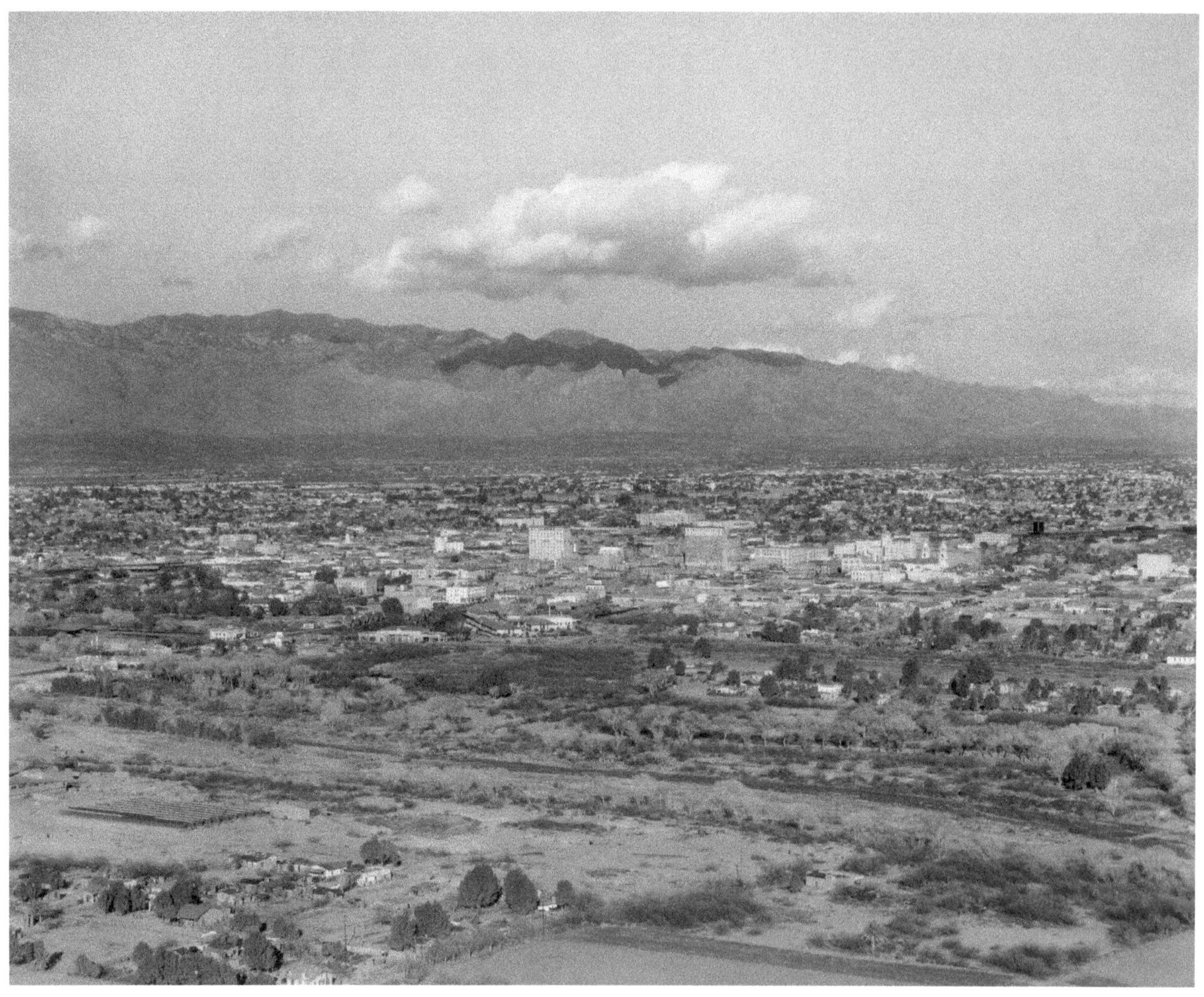

An art class taught by Edith Kitt uses San Xavier as a subject (ca. 1930). The church has long attracted the interest of artists and photographers.

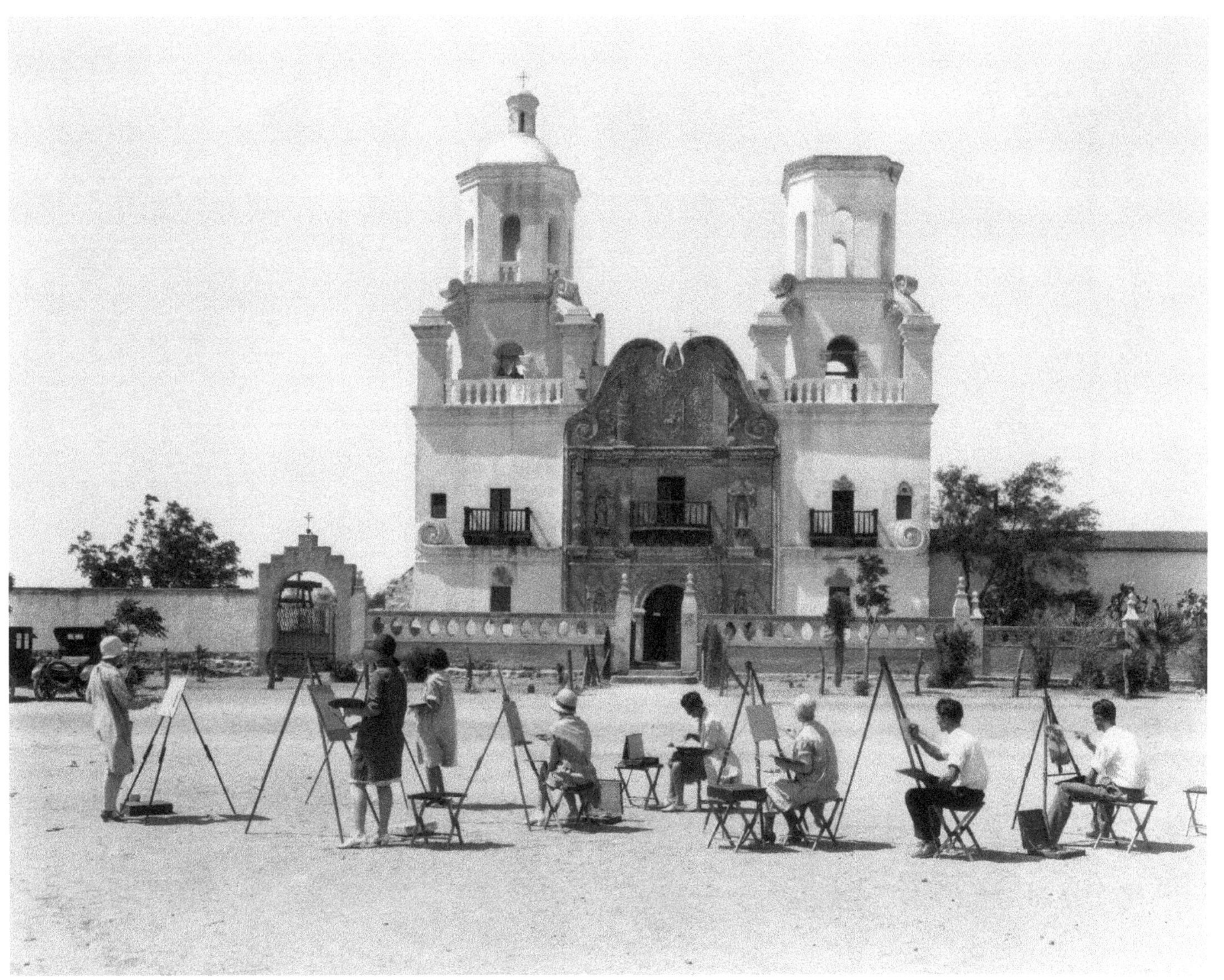

A diamondback rattlesnake caught at Harold Bell Wright's camp at the foot of the Santa Catalina Mountains., near Ventana Canyon.

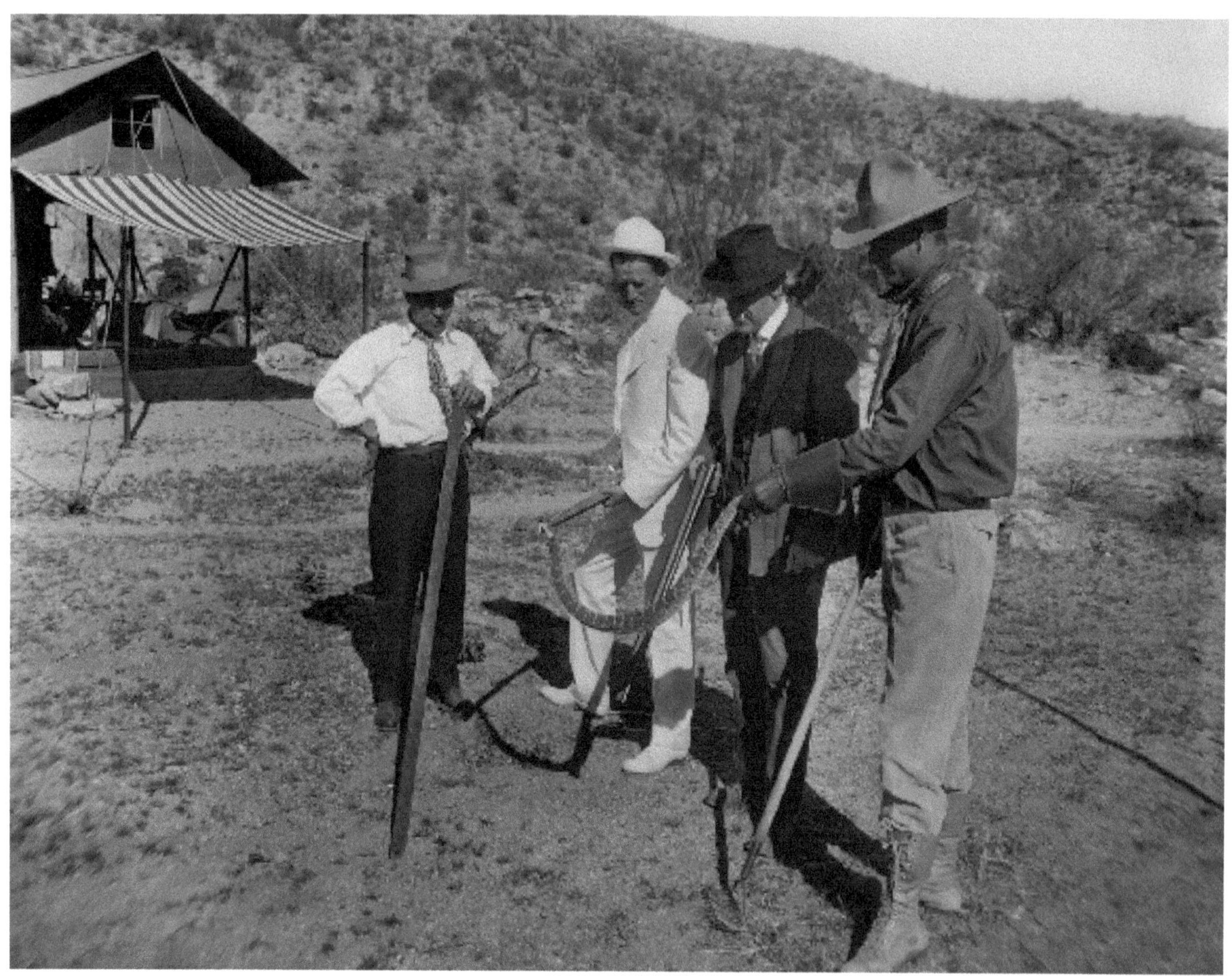

Looking north on Scott Street to Jacome's department store in the distance at Congress Street (ca. 1930). The wheel cover on the car by the lamppost in the foreground displays the Tucson Senior High School Badgers' football schedule.

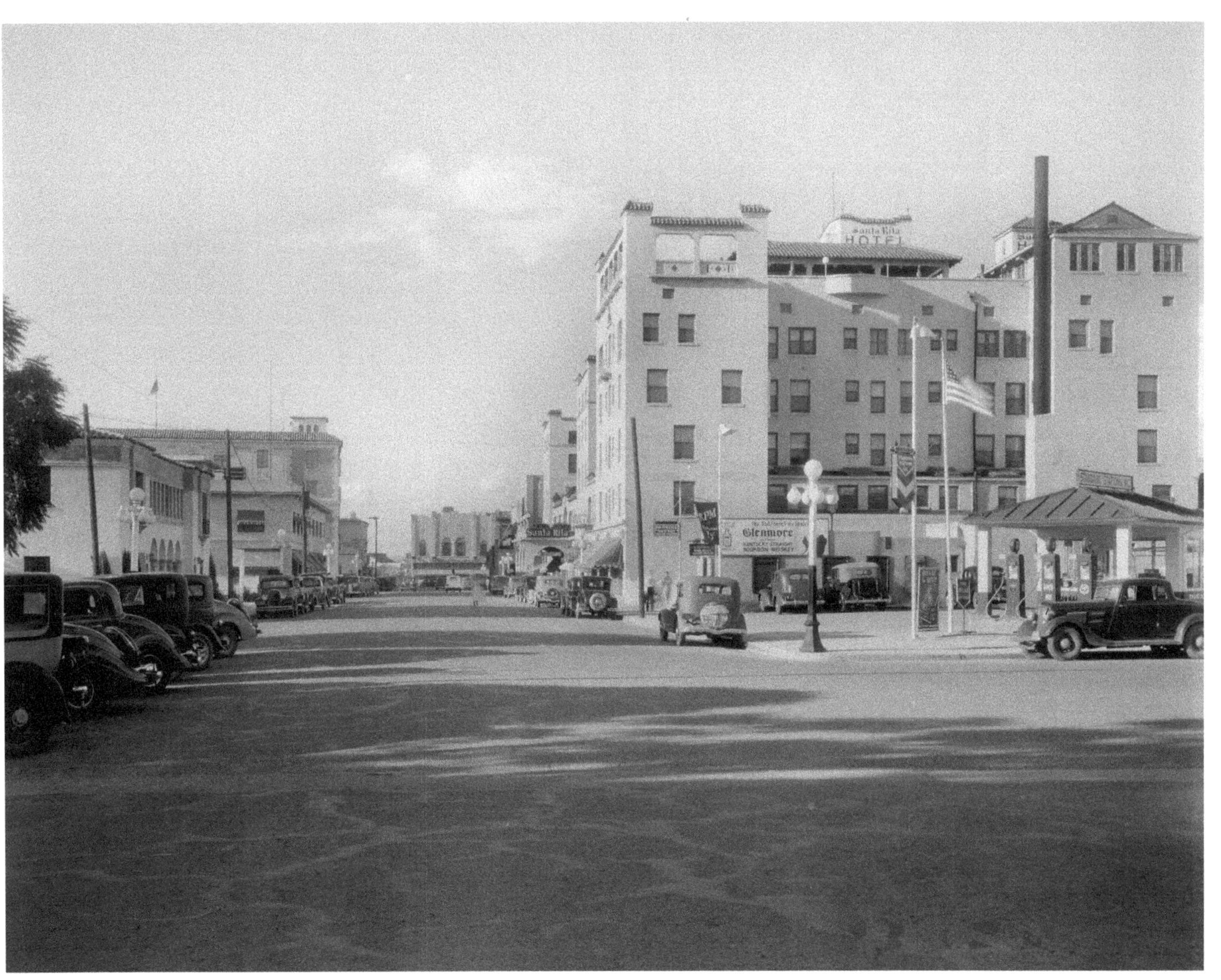

As Tucson's population grew, so did the number of newspaper delivery boys needed by the *Citizen* (ca. 1930). Four motorcyclists took the papers to delivery points further away. Across the street was Louis May's Kosher Restaurant at Stone Avenue and Jackson Street.

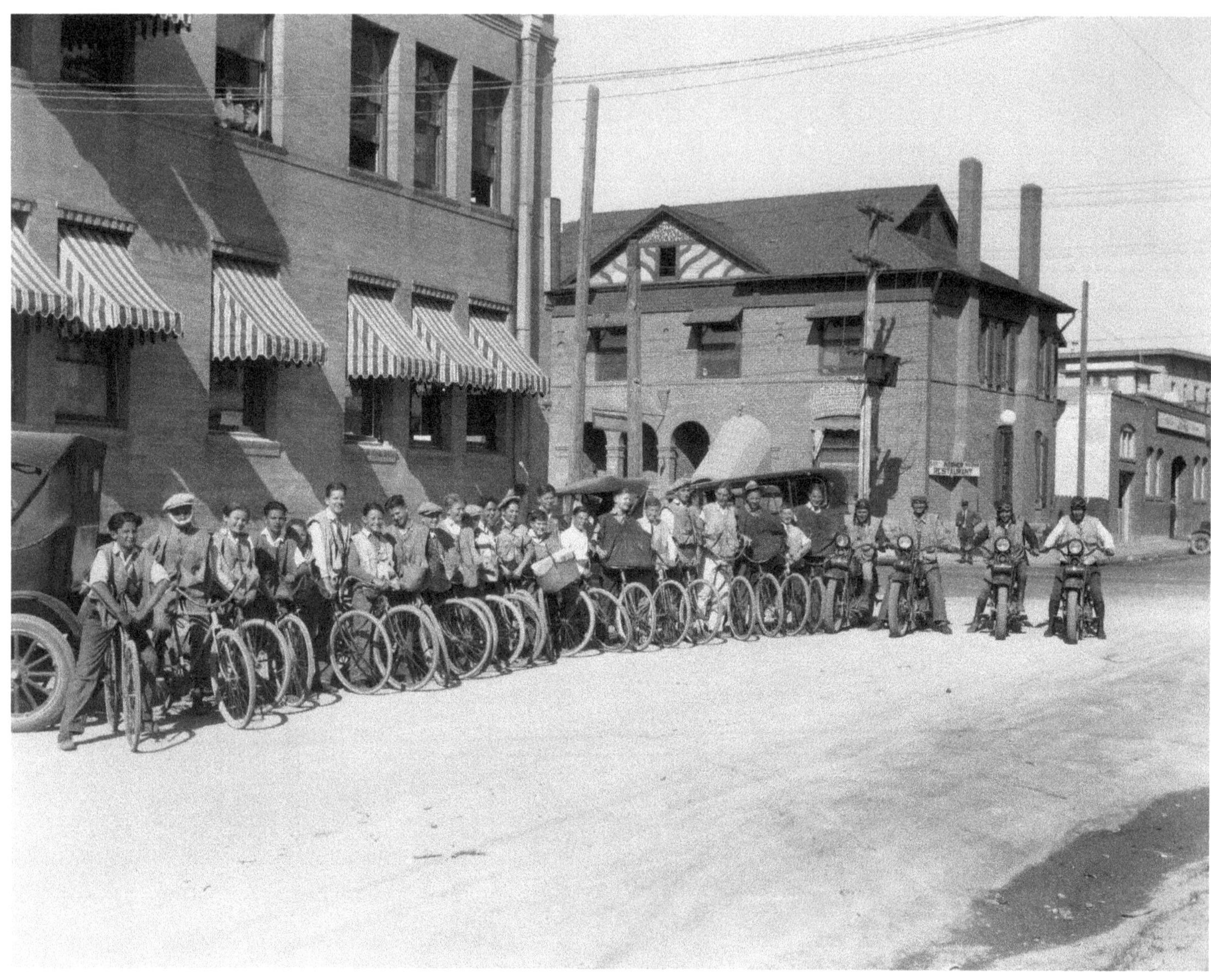

At twelve stories with 220 rooms, Harold Steinfeld's Pioneer Hotel, at Stone Avenue and Pennington Street, became Tucson's second and tallest skyscraper of 1929. This view was taken around 1930. The Consolidated National Bank Building is in the background.

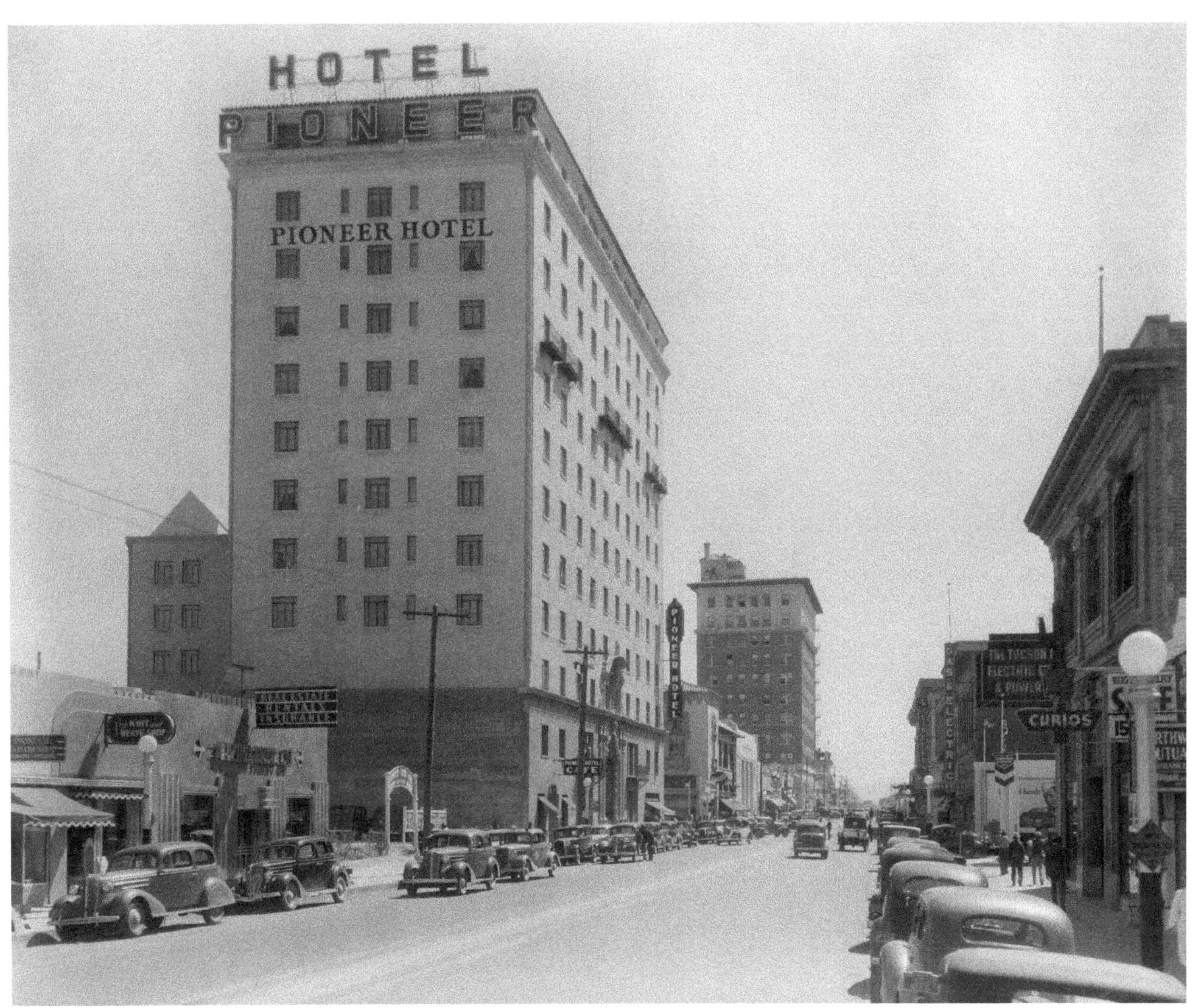

Karston the Magician headlines one of many Saturday afternoon stage shows, mixing live performances with movies, for Tucson children during the 1930s.

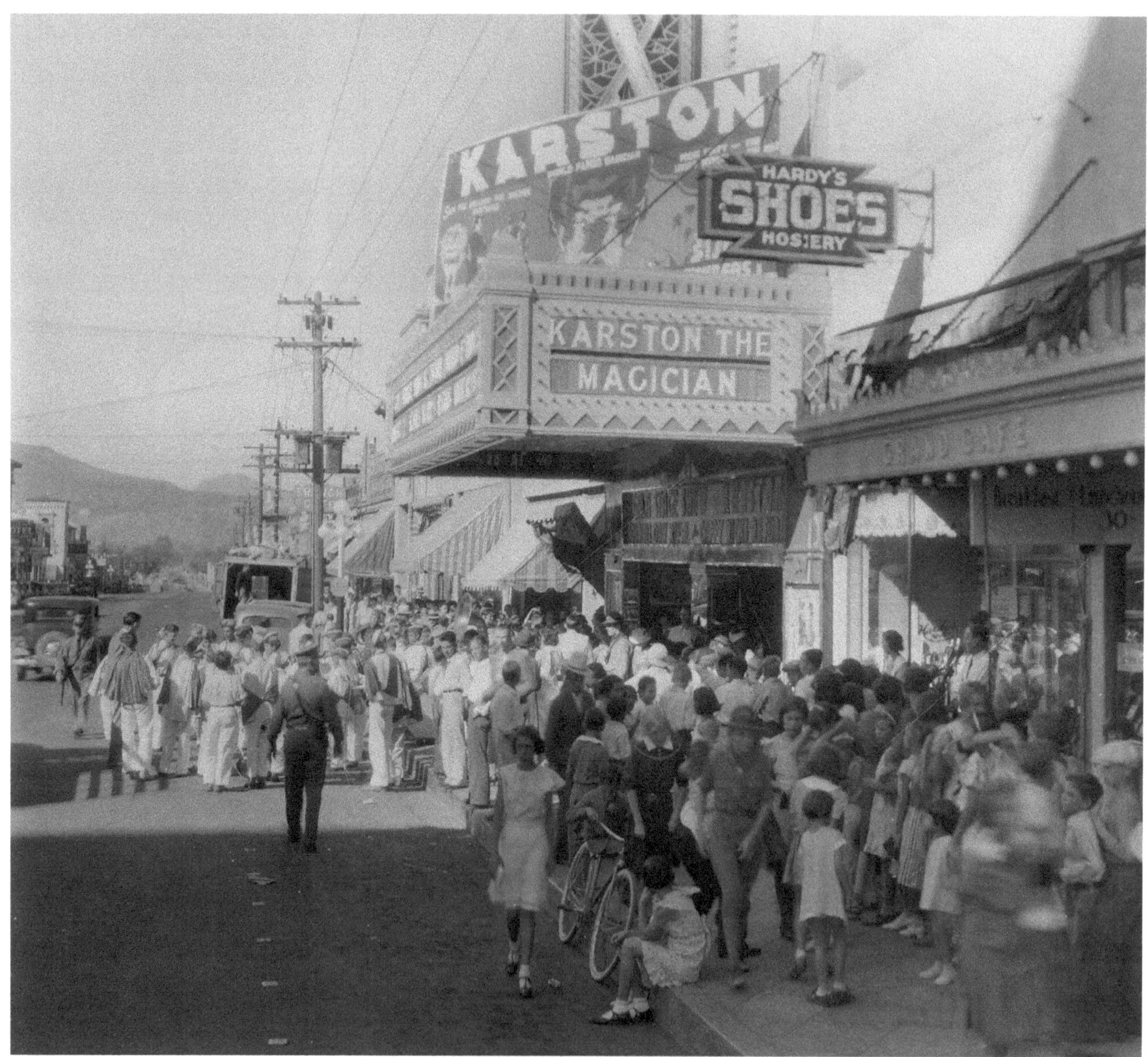

Dooley Bookman, owner of the Varsity Shop, won the gratitude of Tucson's children for the Halloween Mardi Gras parties he staged between 1924 and 1932. Stone Avenue was closed and decorated for the event.

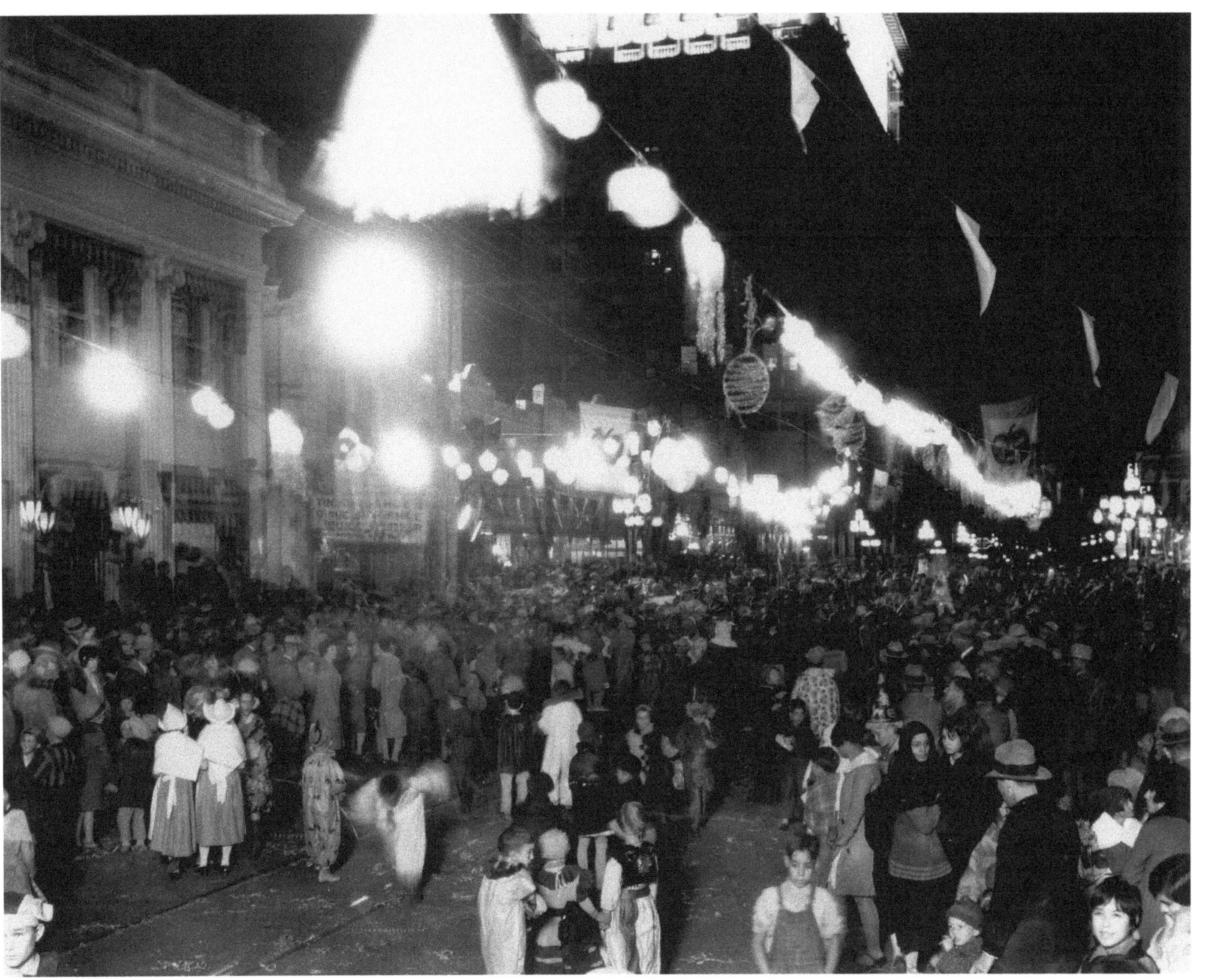

A view from the roof of the Consolidated National Bank at Congress and Stone streets, showing Tucson's expansion to the south in the early 1930s. The San Augustine Cathedral is in the foreground.

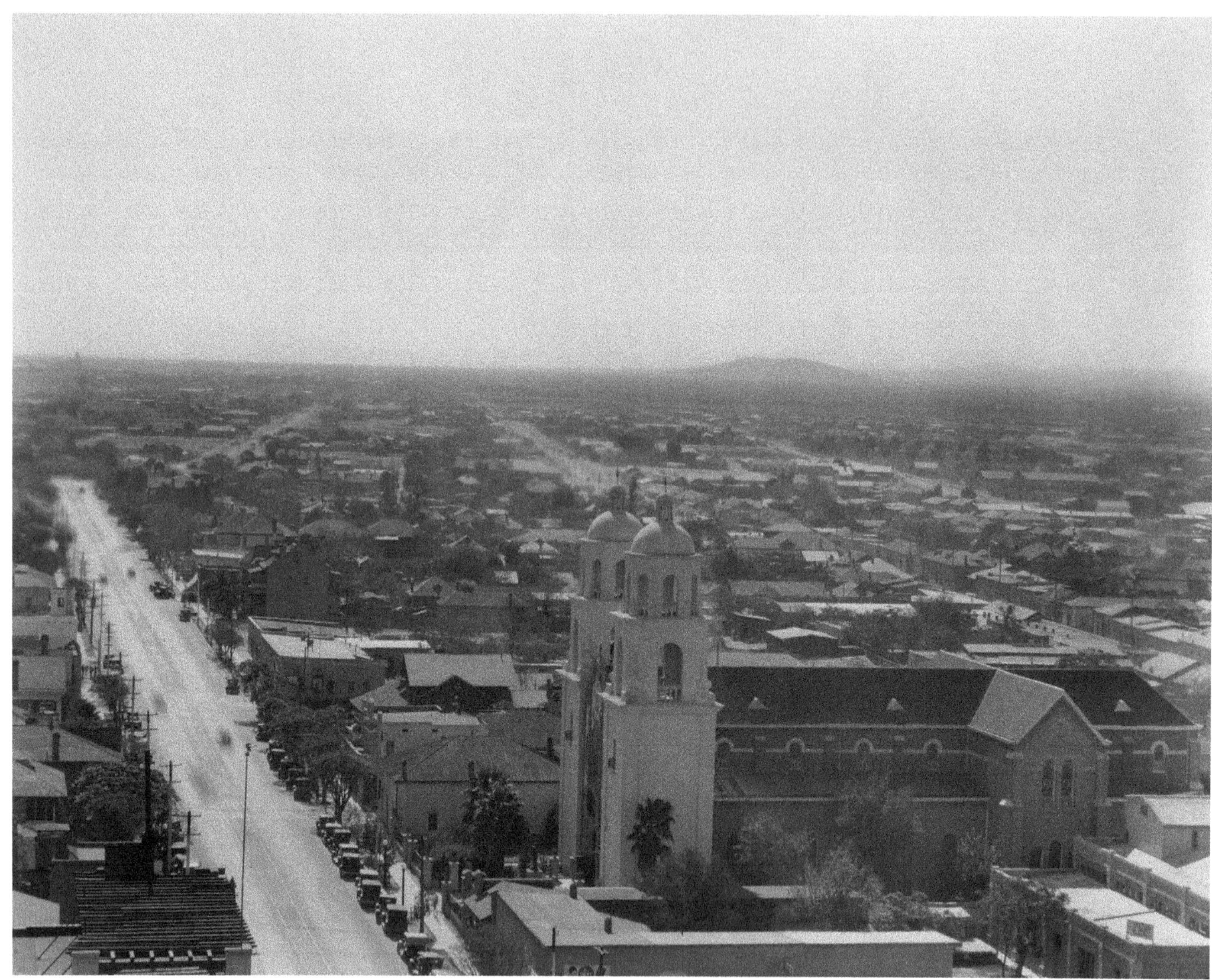

Archery was one of many sports the University of Arizona offered its students (ca. 1930).

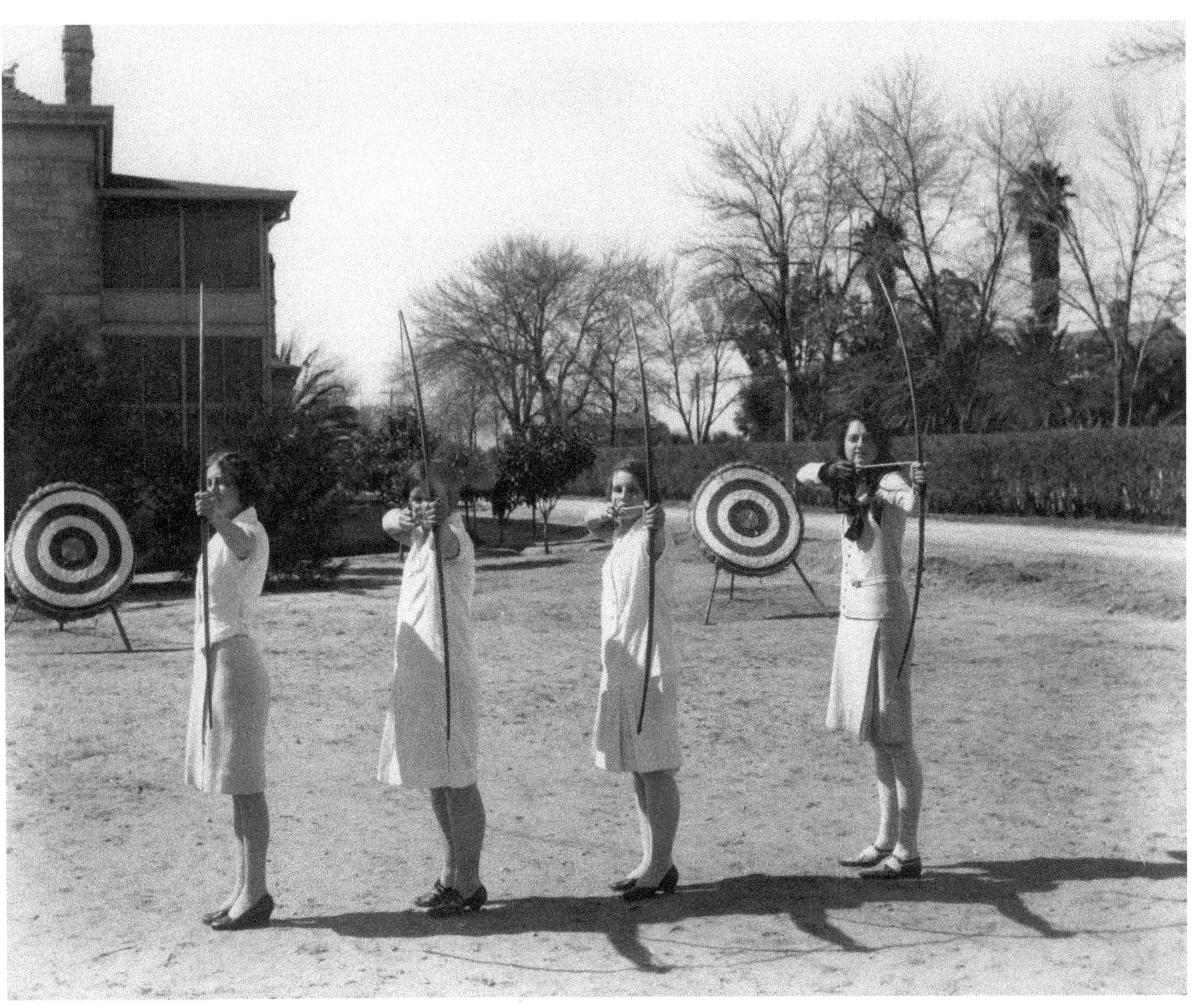

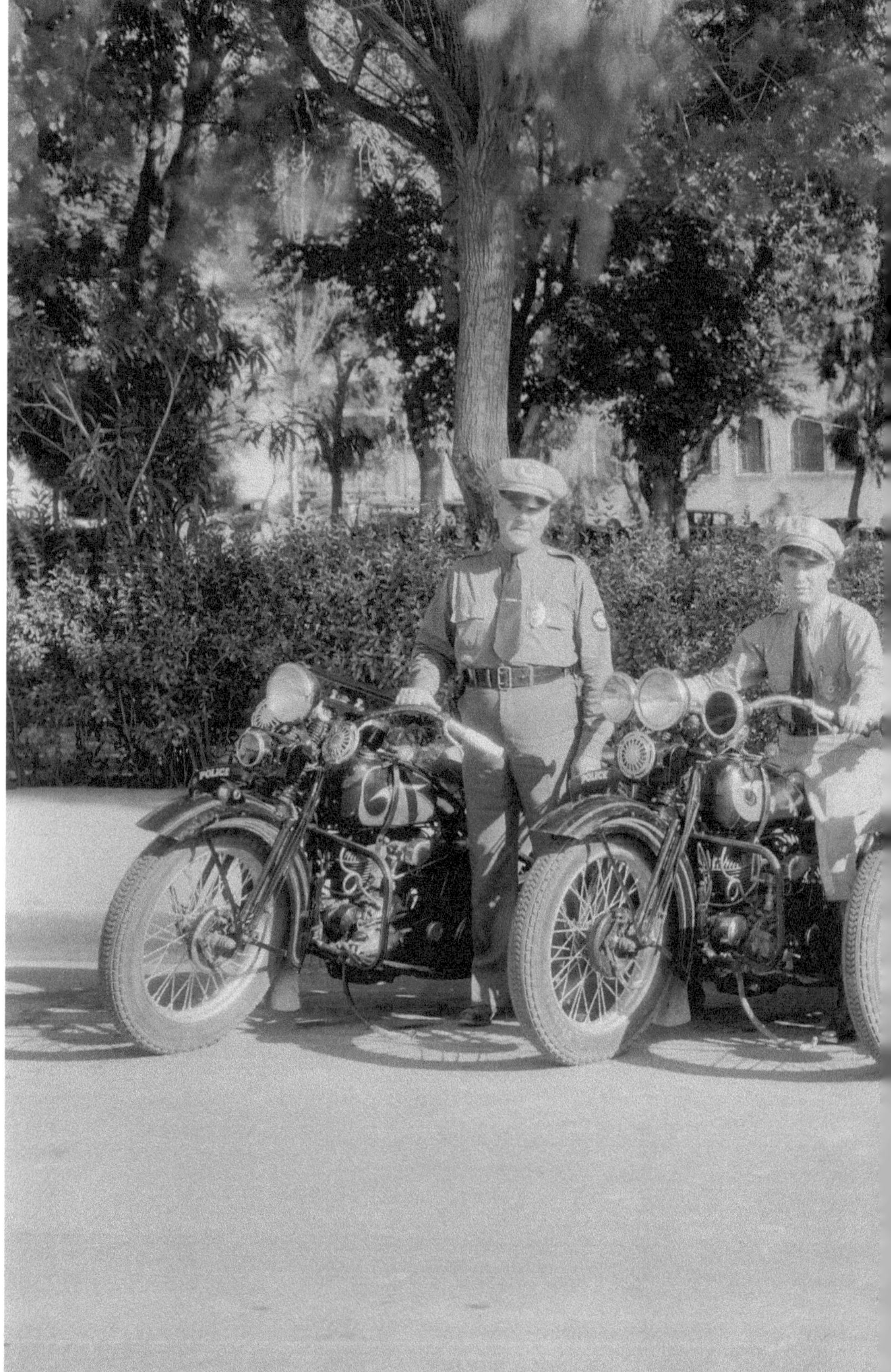
POLICE
POLICE

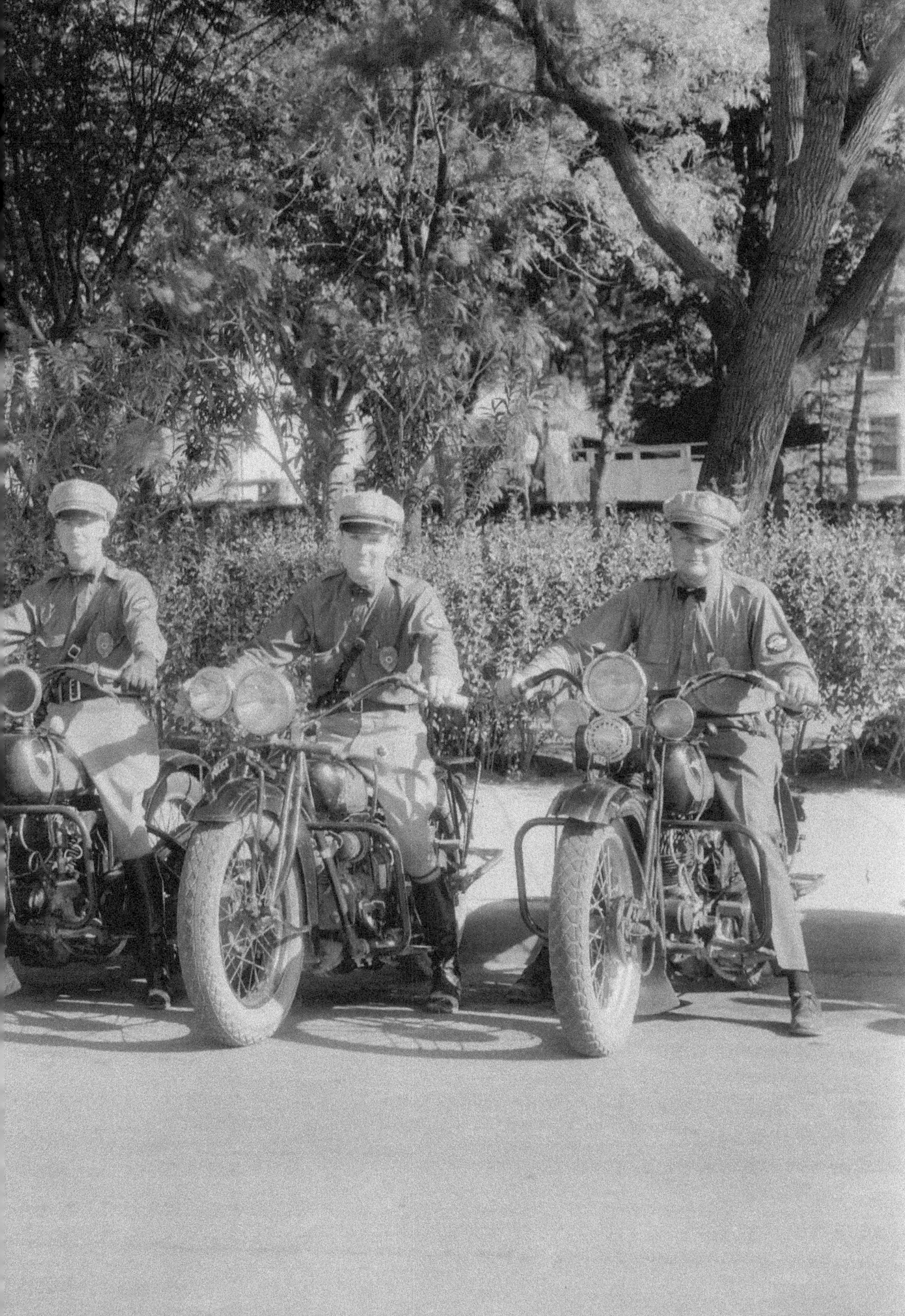

As cars became faster, the Tucson Police used a squad of motorcycle police to help enforce the speed limit (ca. 1930). Tucson's first speed limit for automobiles, 7 mph, was set in 1903. The first speeding tickets were issued in 1920.

The Montgomery Ward & Co. building at Stone Avenue and Broadway Boulevard (ca. 1931).

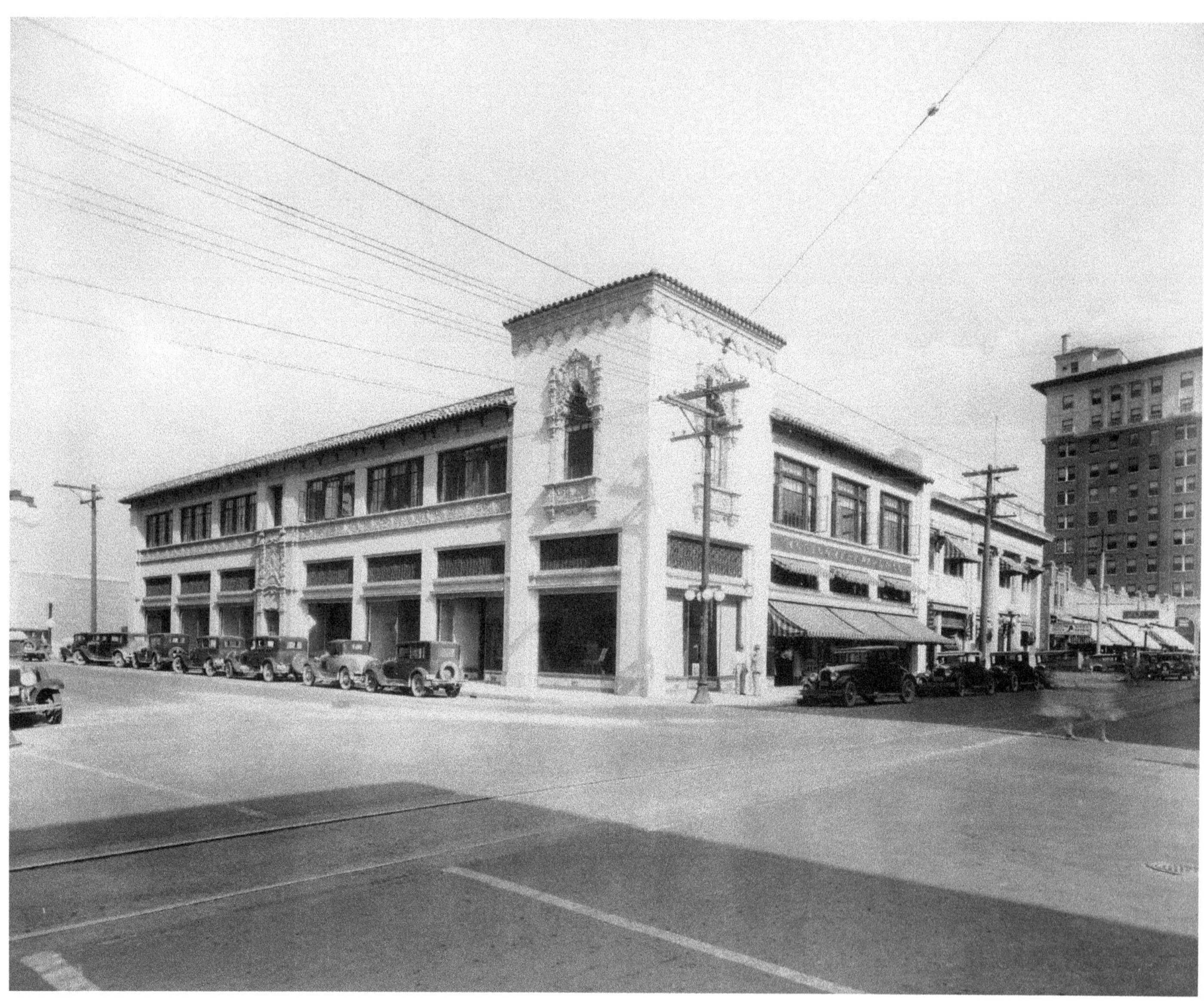

Women who lost sons or husbands in World War I ride in the Armistice Day parade of 1932.

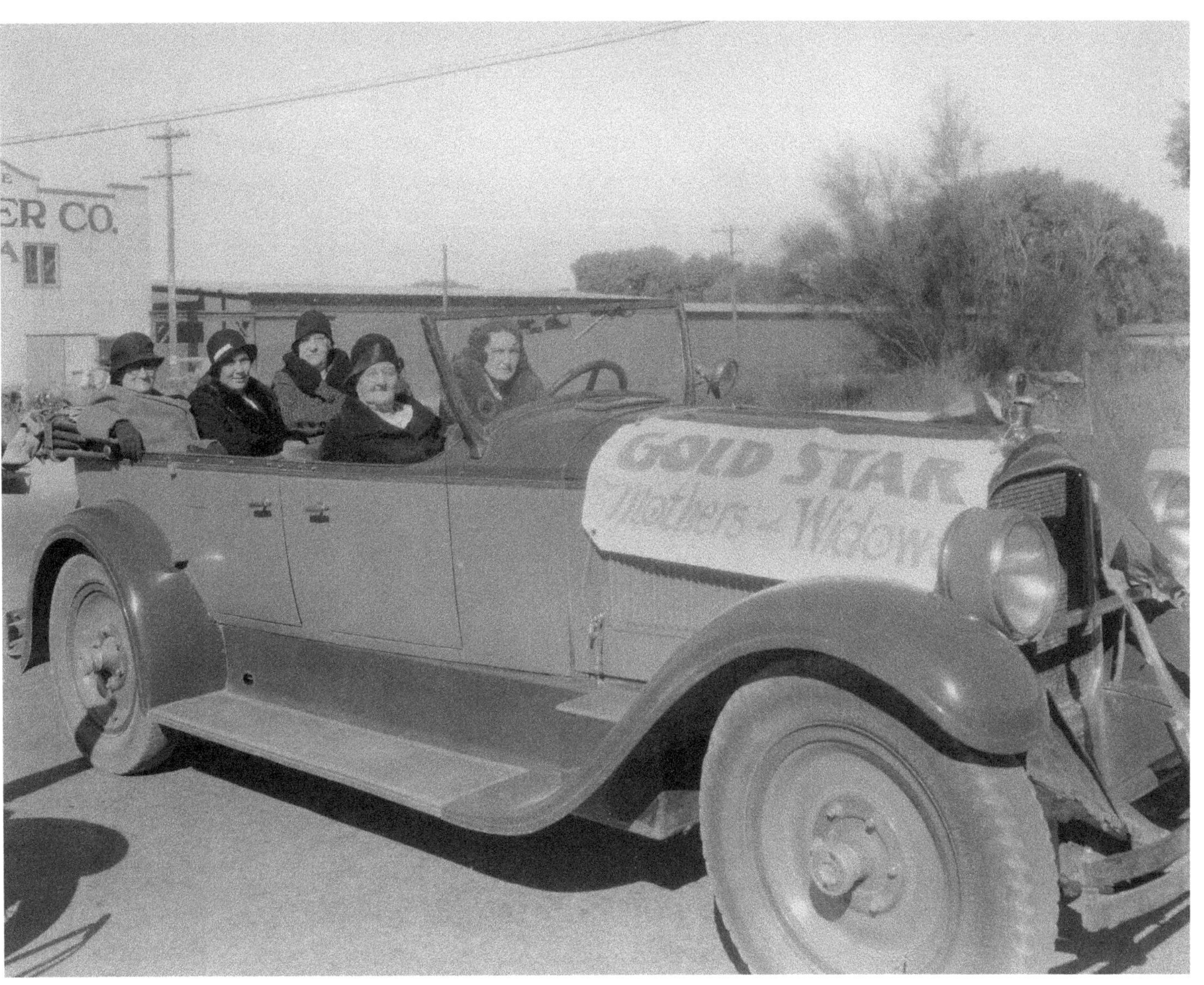

A touring Country and Western band from the Signal Oil Company radio show *Carefree Carnival*, during the early 1930s.

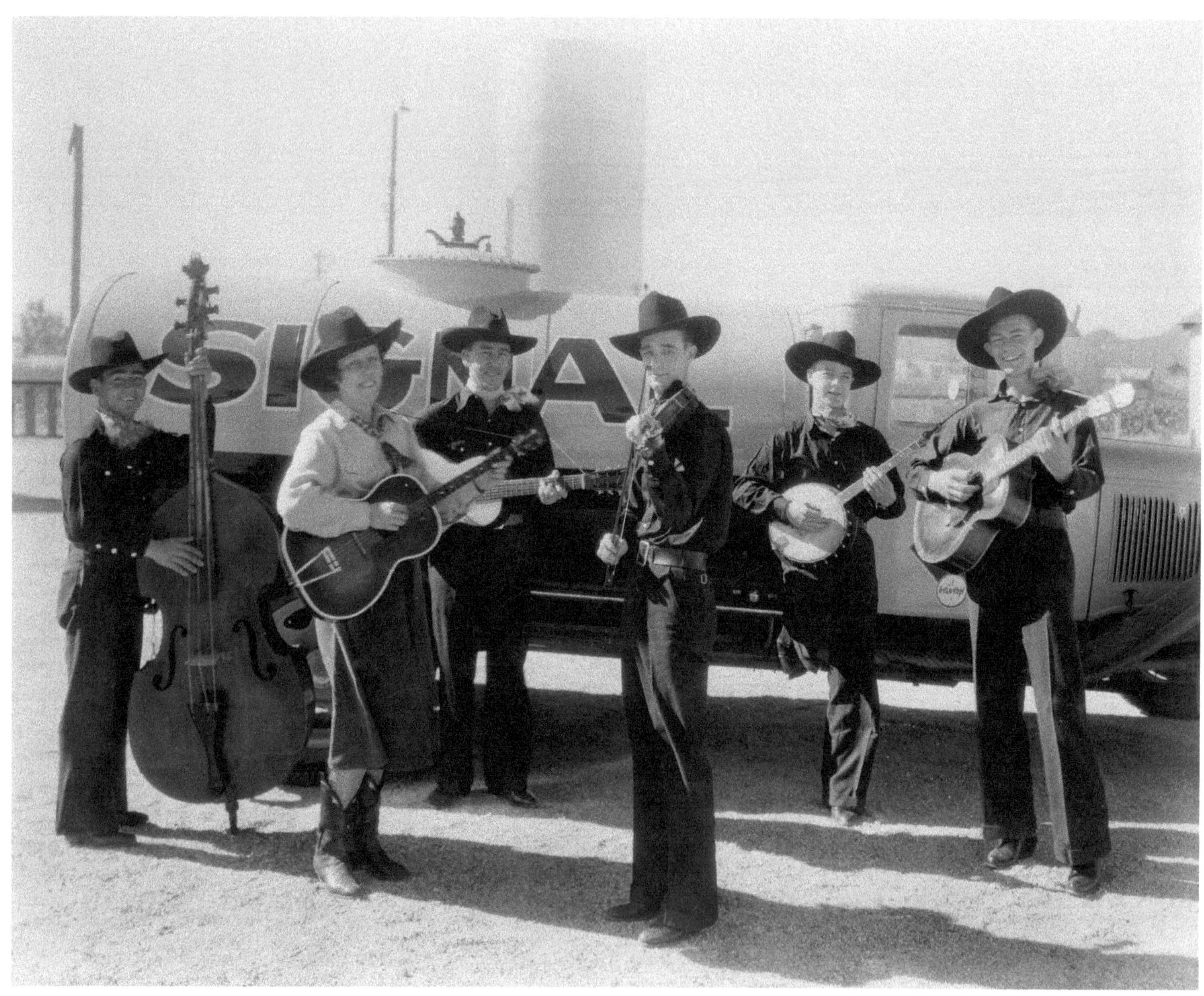

The Fox Theater decorated to promote the documentary feature *Bring 'Em Back Alive*, starring Frank Buck, in 1932. Ushers wore pith helmets and shorts.

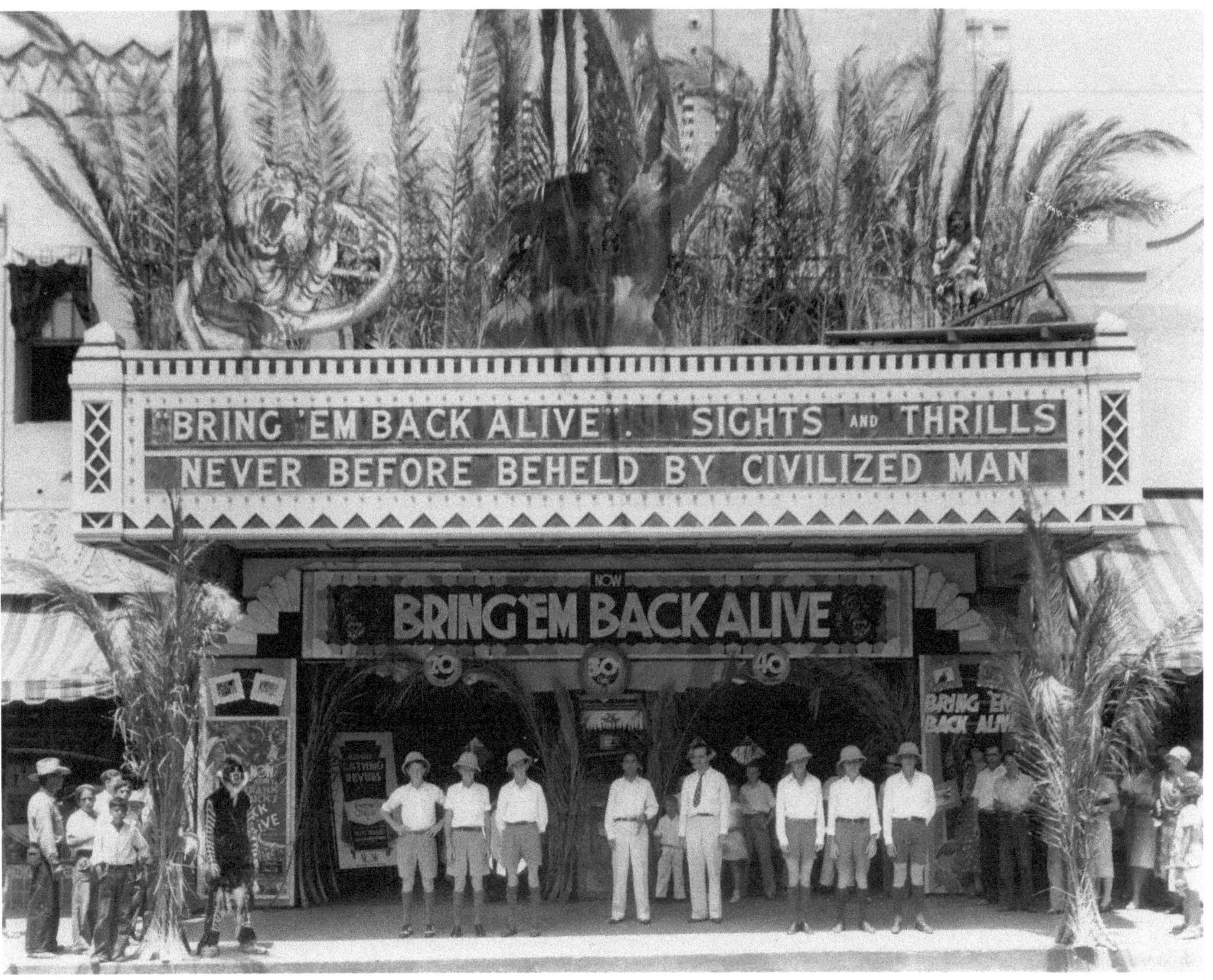

A parade held to promote the movie *Cavalcade* playing at the Fox Theater in February 1933.

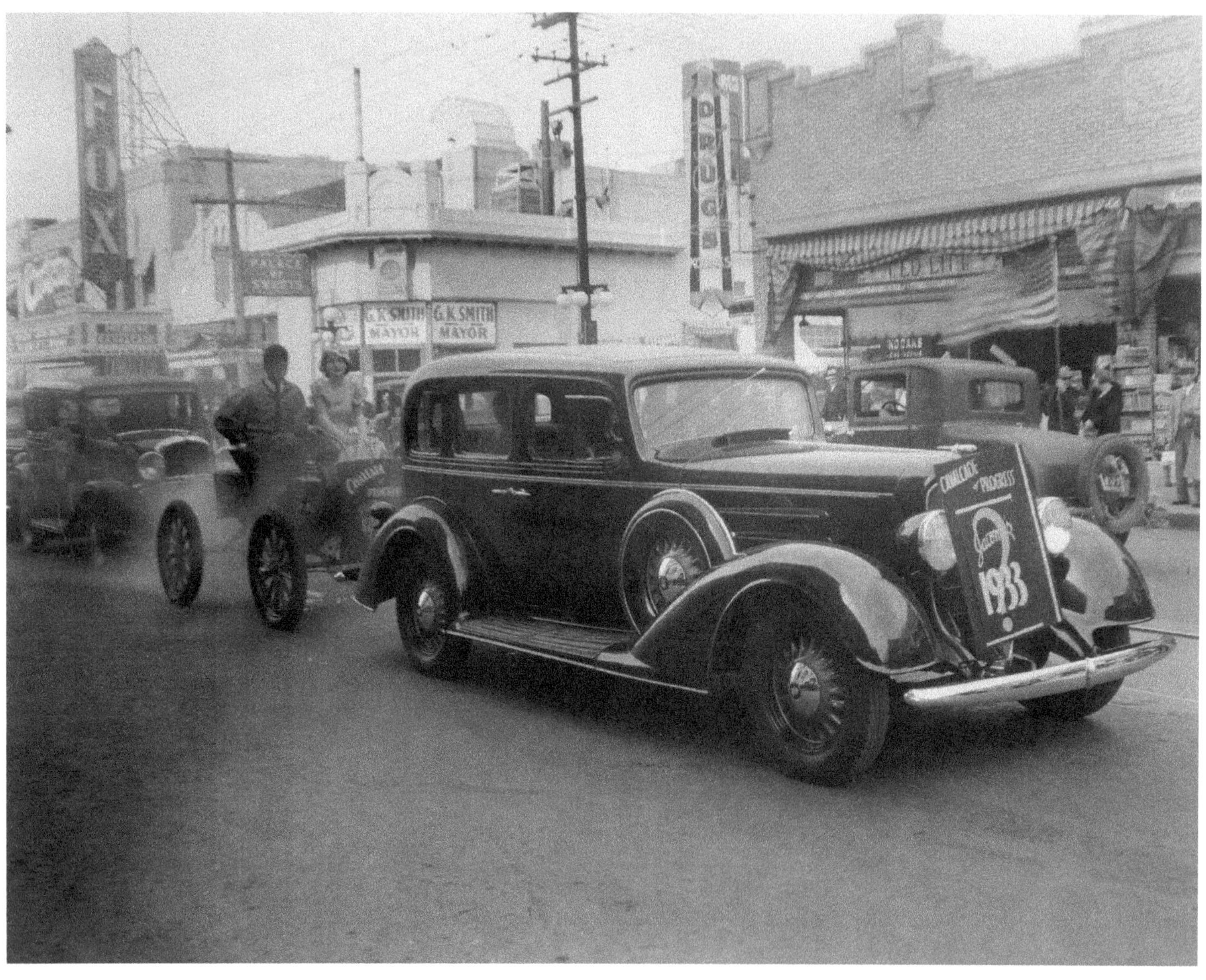

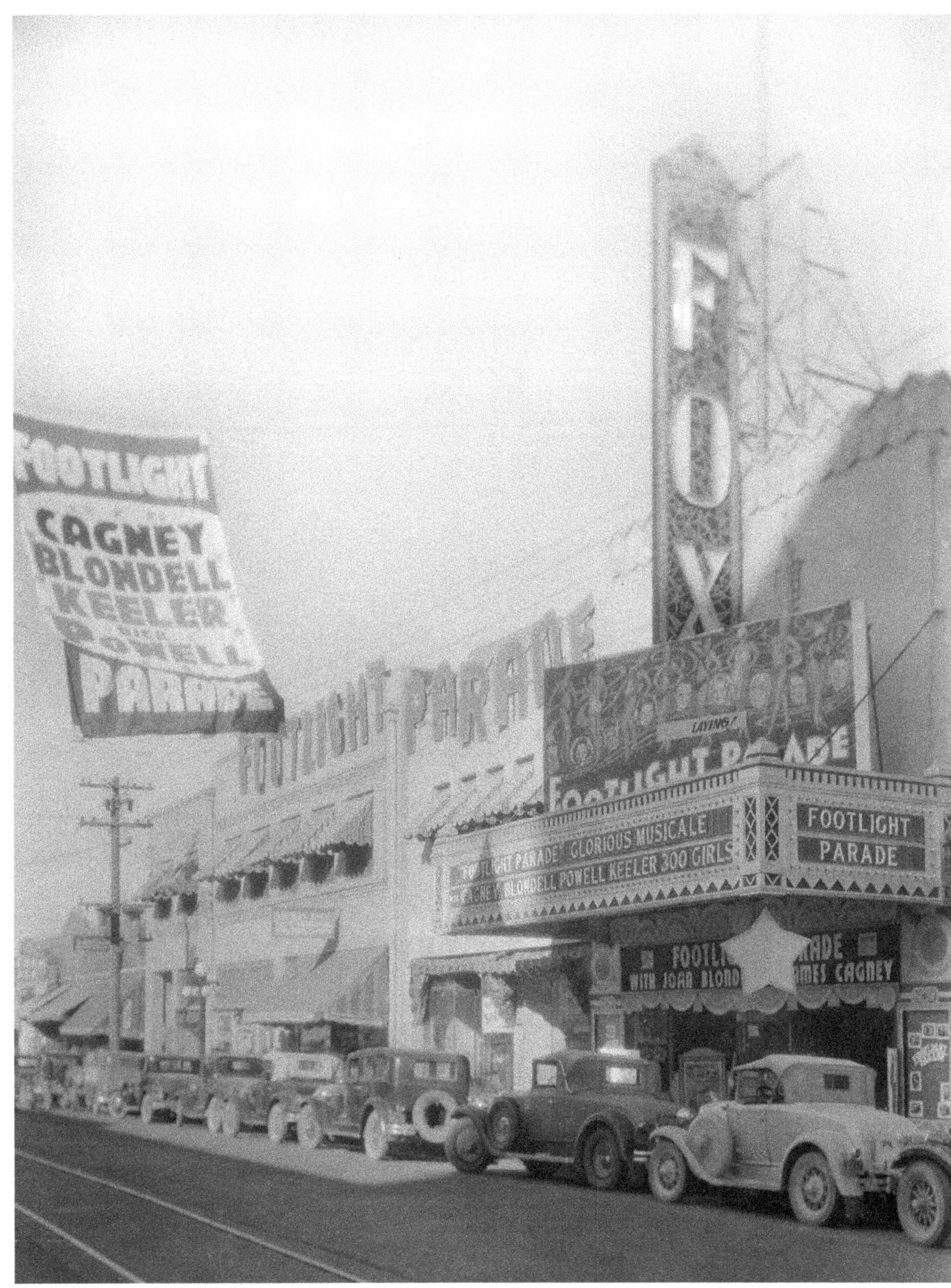

The musical *Footlight Parade* played the Fox in 1933. Beside the theater, a Depression-era merchant's sign proclaims "We buy, sell and exchange everything of value."

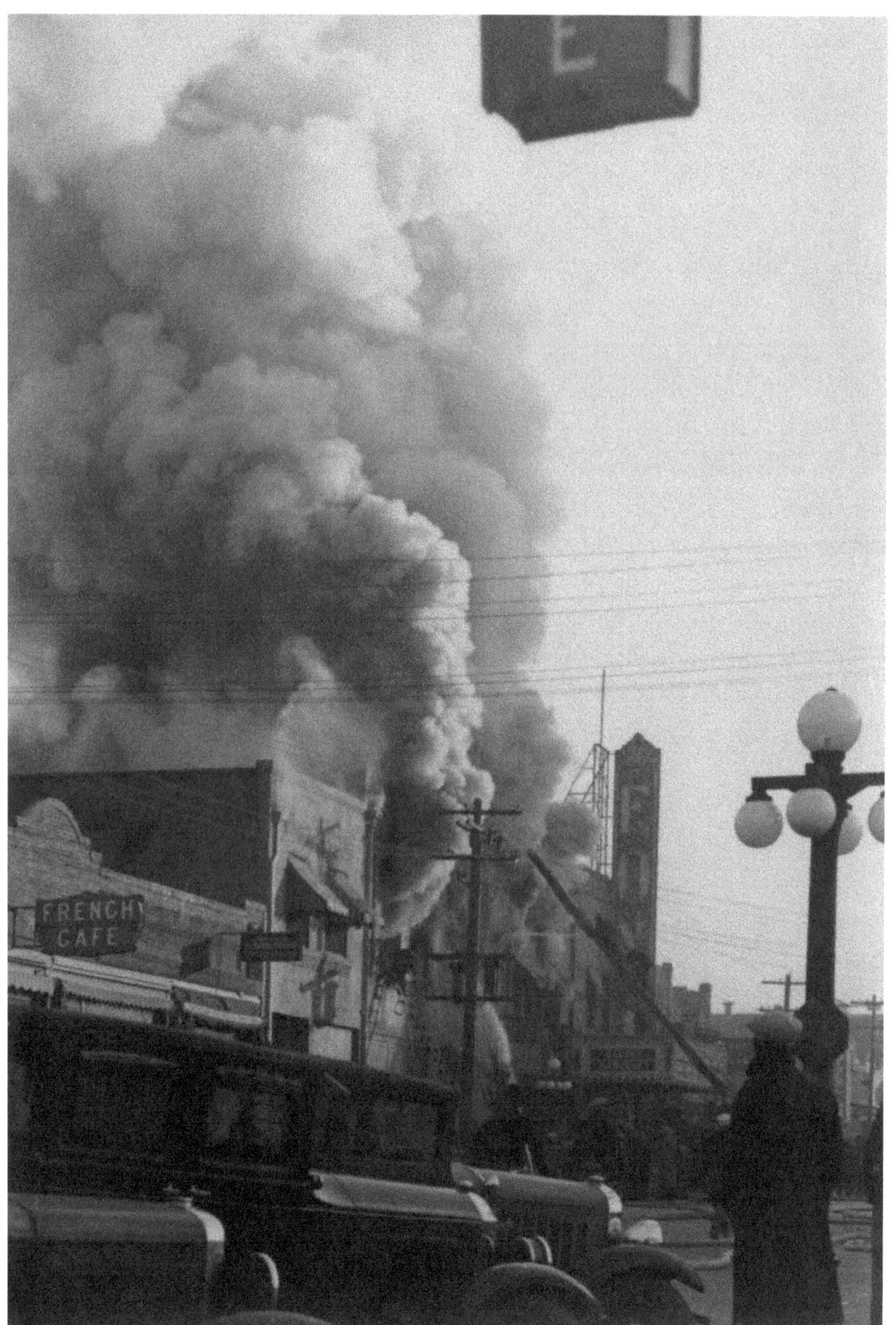

Fire struck the Arizona Daily Star building on December 18, 1933. The building, at 33 W. Congress, was rebuilt after the fire. Both the Daily Star and the Citizen suffered previous fires in their adobe and wood buildings.

Film comedian and character actor Roscoe Ates posed in N. Porter's Saddle and Harness Shop on Congress Street to promote his appearance in a movie in 1933.

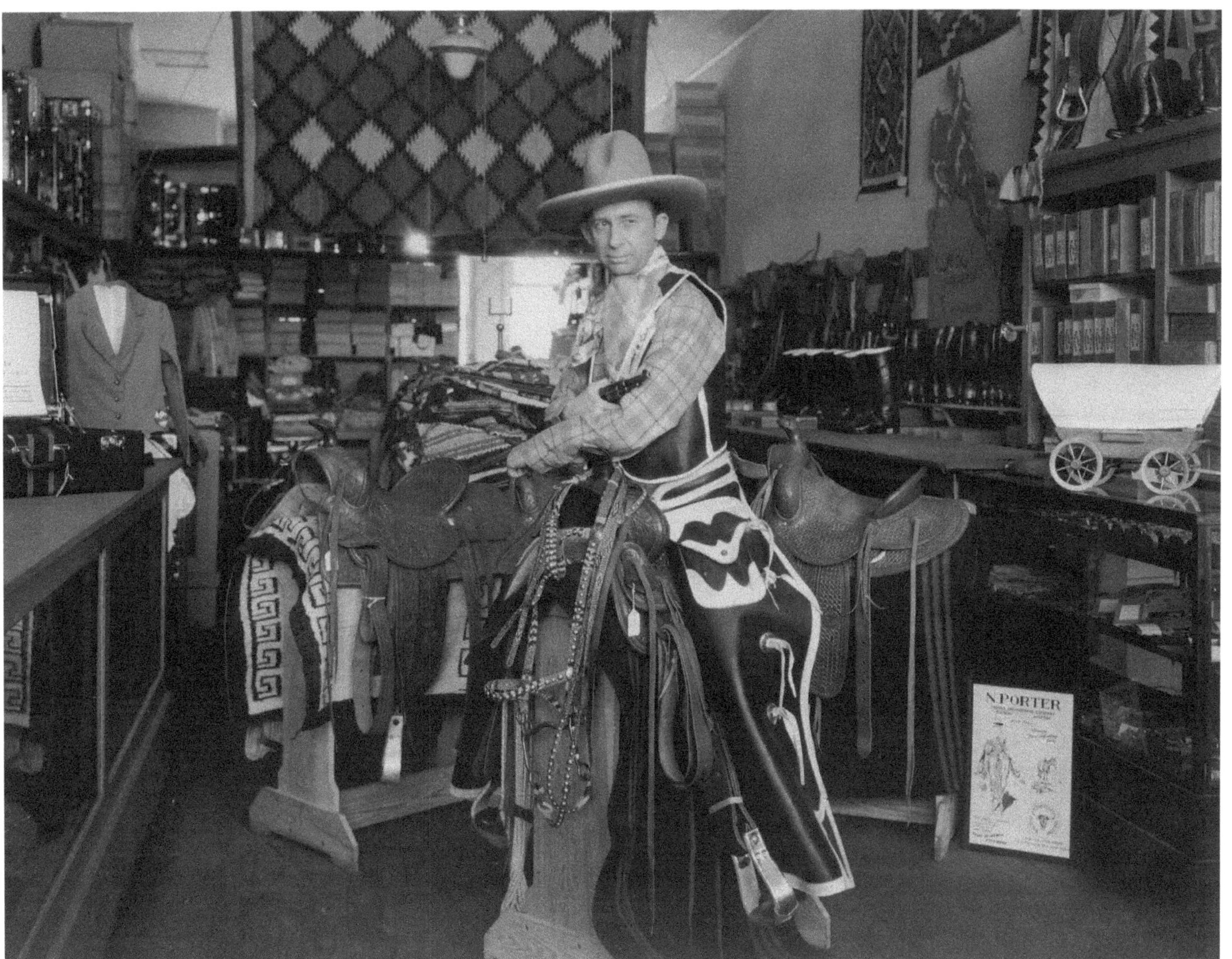

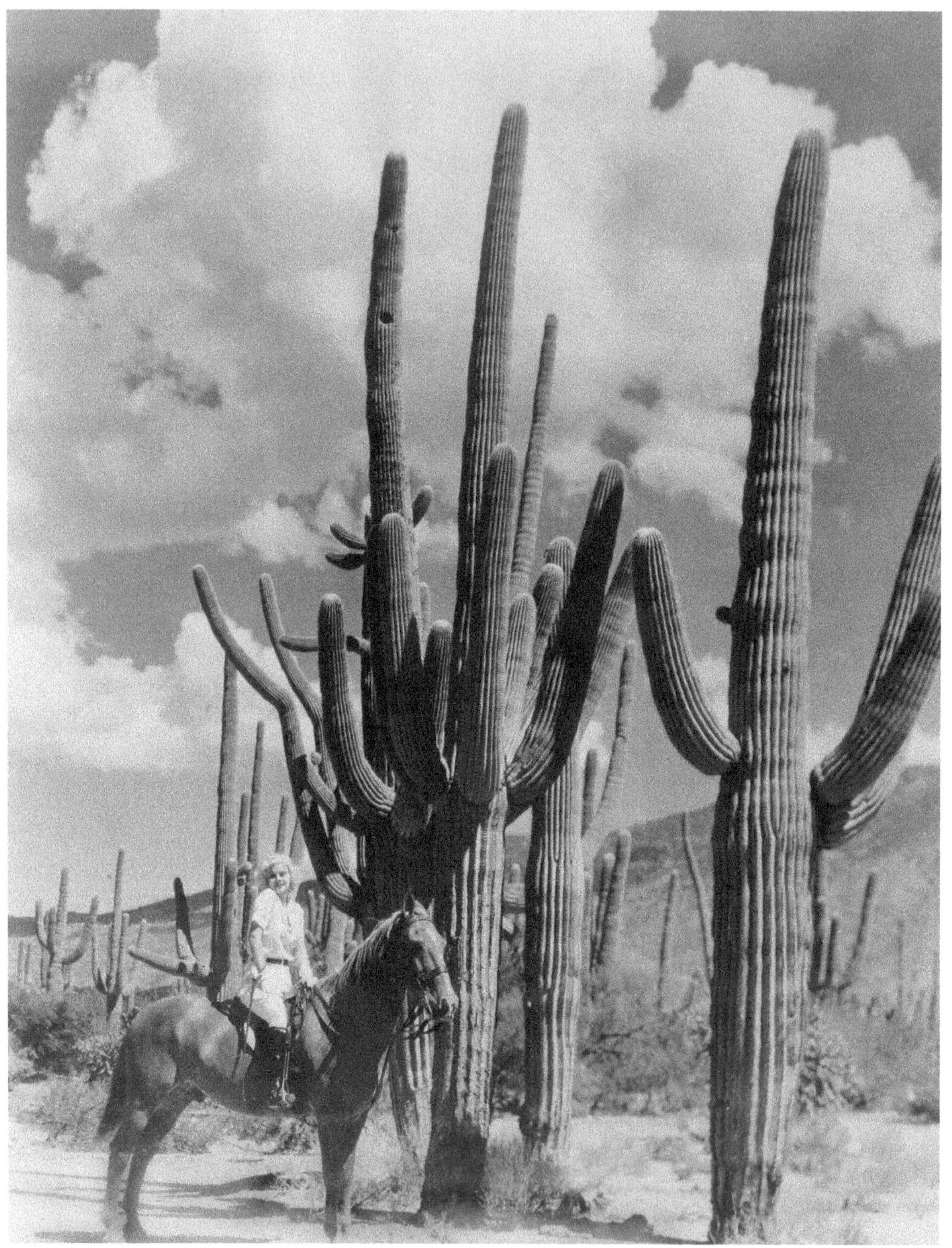

Actress Jean Harlow posed before a stand of saguaro cactus while filming the movie *Bombshell* in Tucson in 1933. She was one of many Hollywood stars who found Tucson's climate and resorts inviting.

The participants in a men's bicycle contest gathered in front of the Fox Theater in 1933.

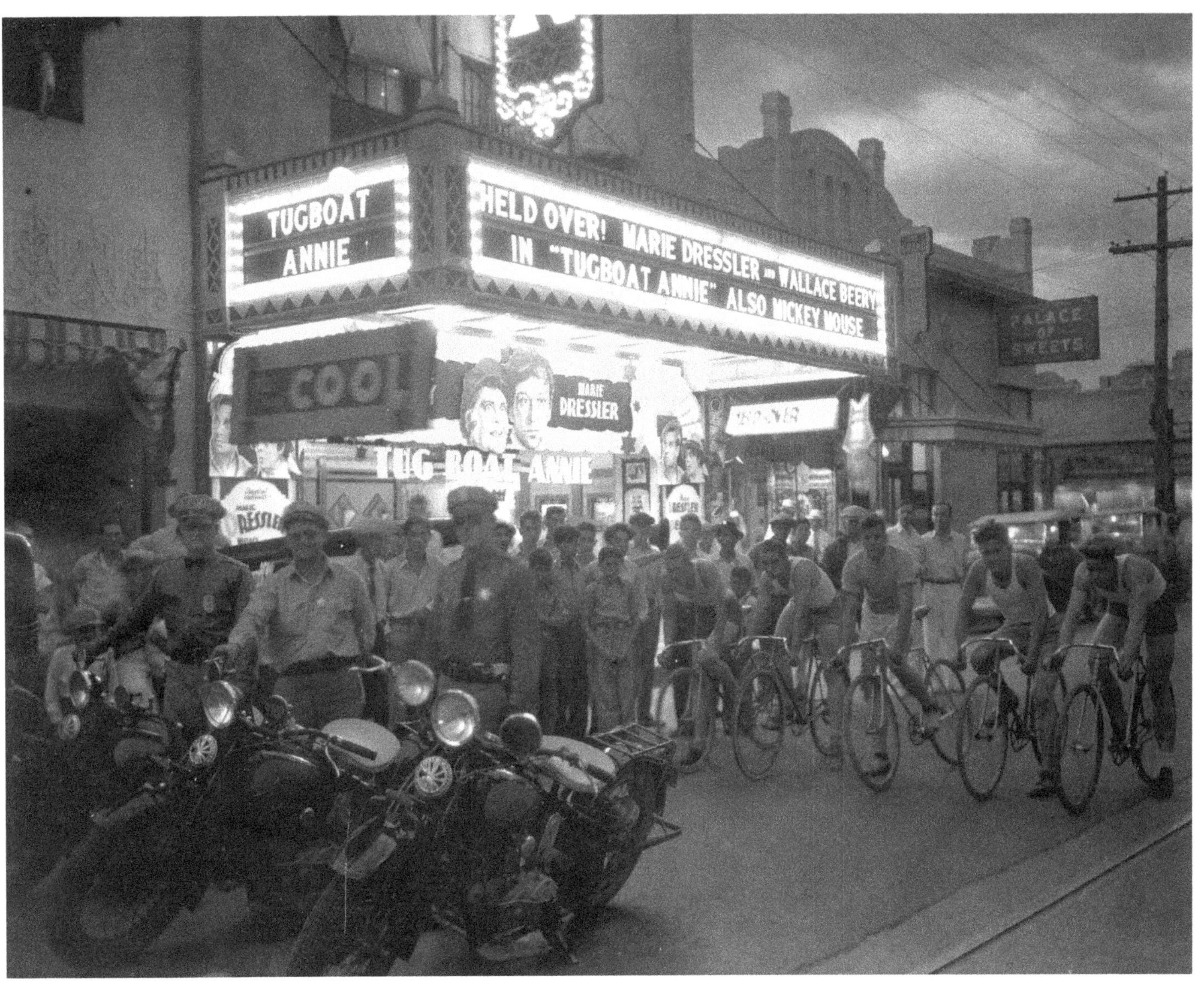

Women came into their own as pilots with the first Women's Air Derby in 1929. During the 1930s, air derbies became extremely popular around the country. Gladys O'Donnell, a well-known pilot, posed during a stop in Tucson.

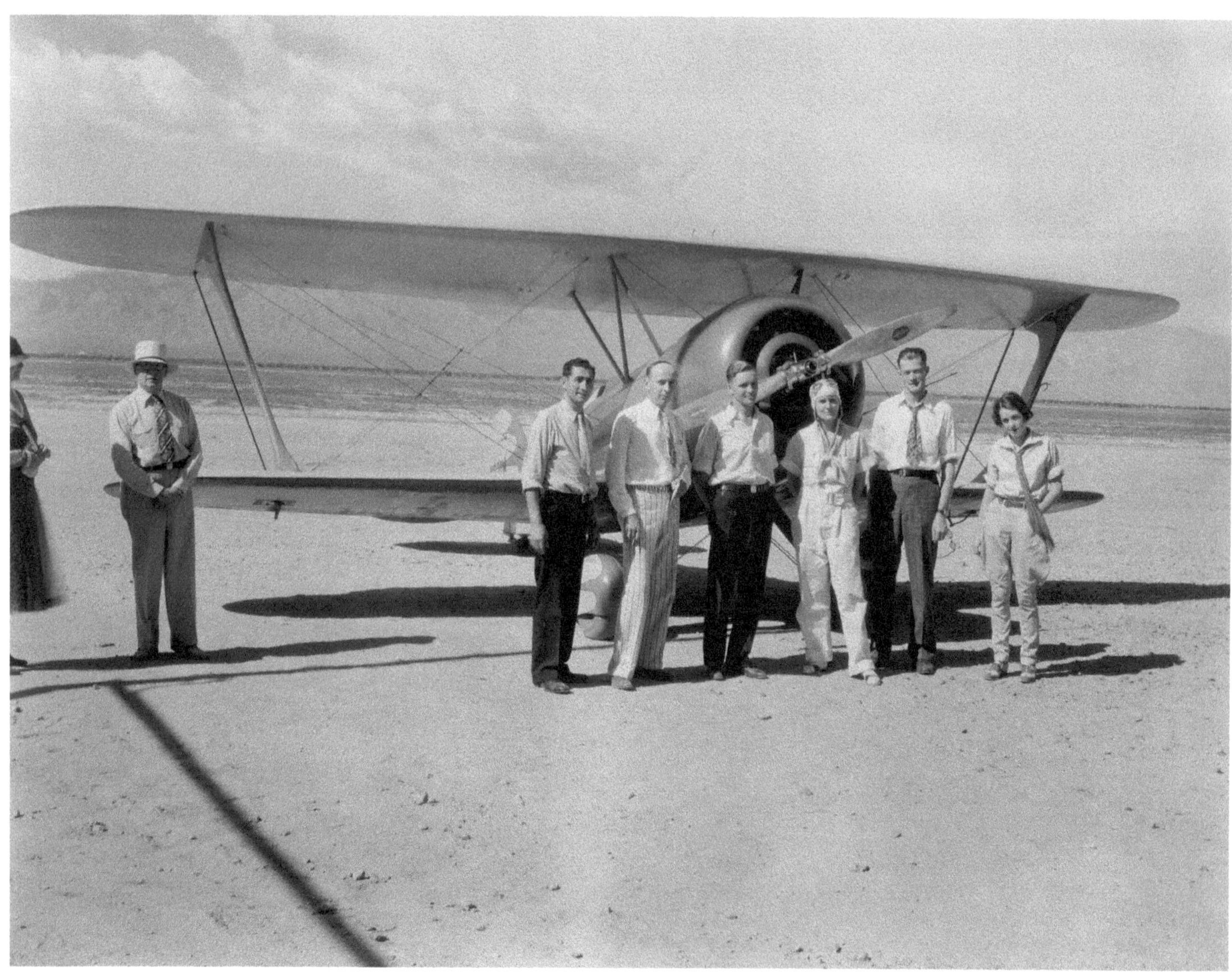

Firemen work to extinguish a fire at the Hotel Congress on January 23, 1934. As a result of this fire, a Tucson firemen and police recognized members of the John Dillinger Gang, which led to the arrest of the entire gang within days of their arrival in Tucson.

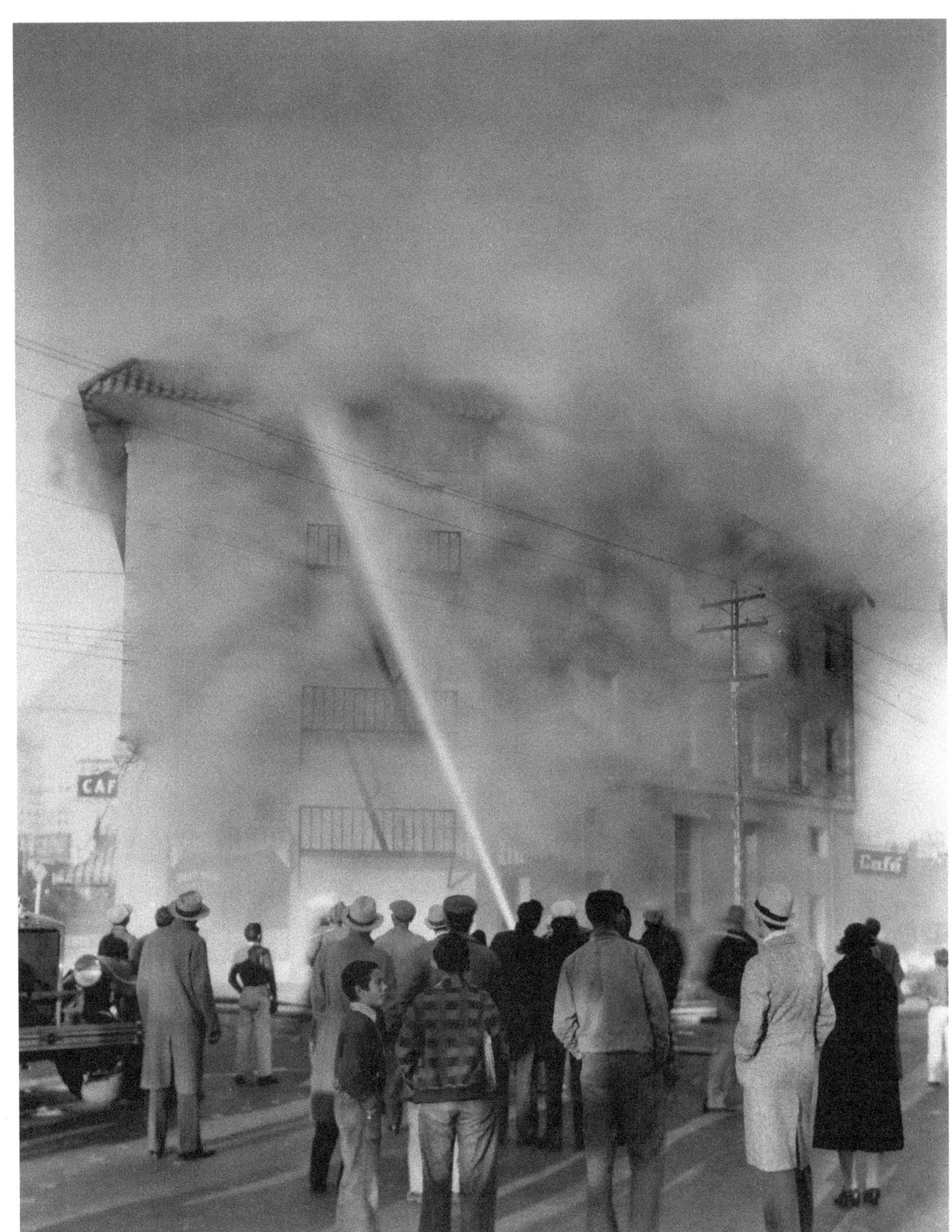

The John Dillinger Gang made a court appearance after their capture on January 25, 1934.

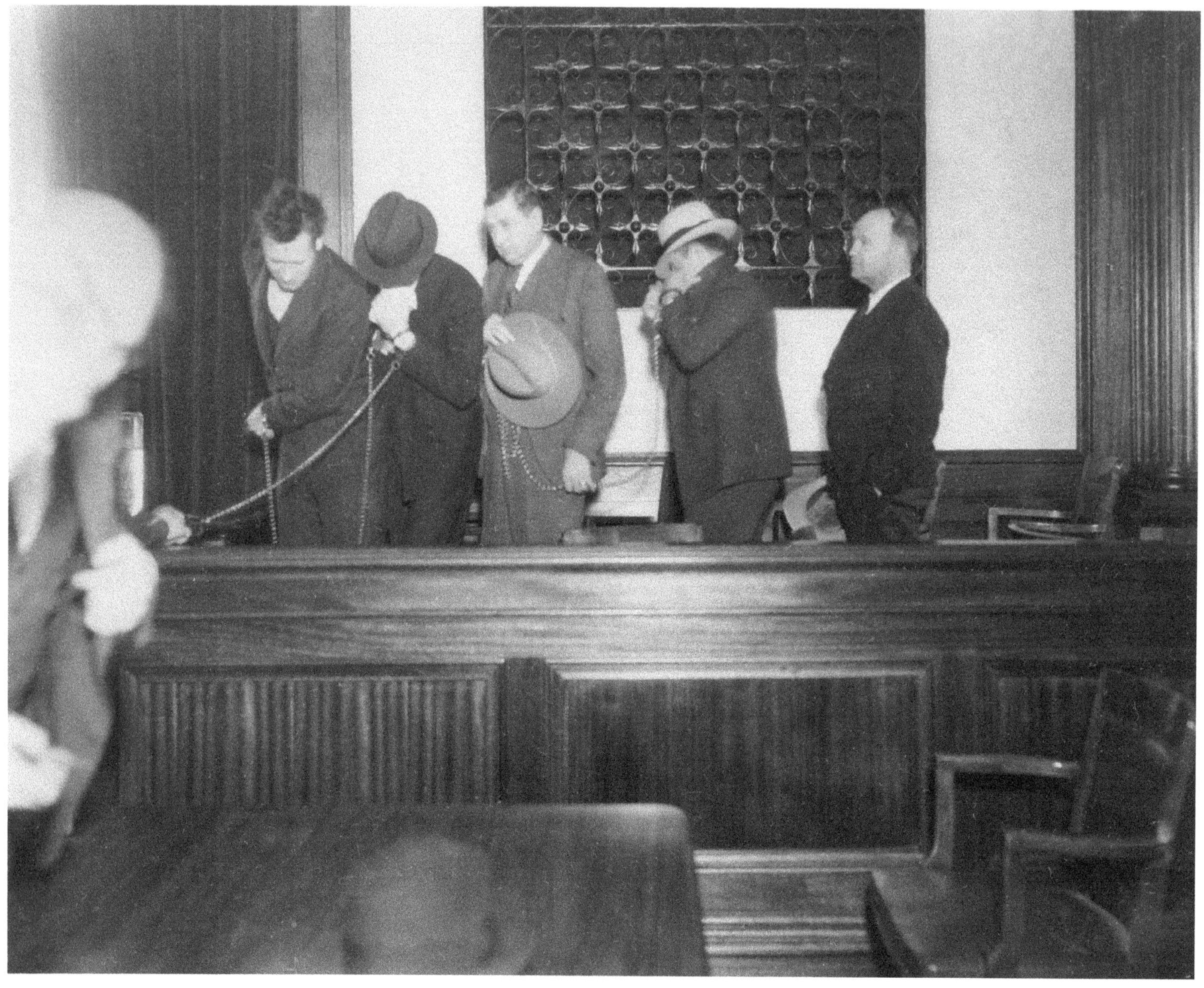

A reluctant Harry Pierpoint, the member of Dillinger's gang who had suggested Tucson for a hideout, was forced to pose for photographers.

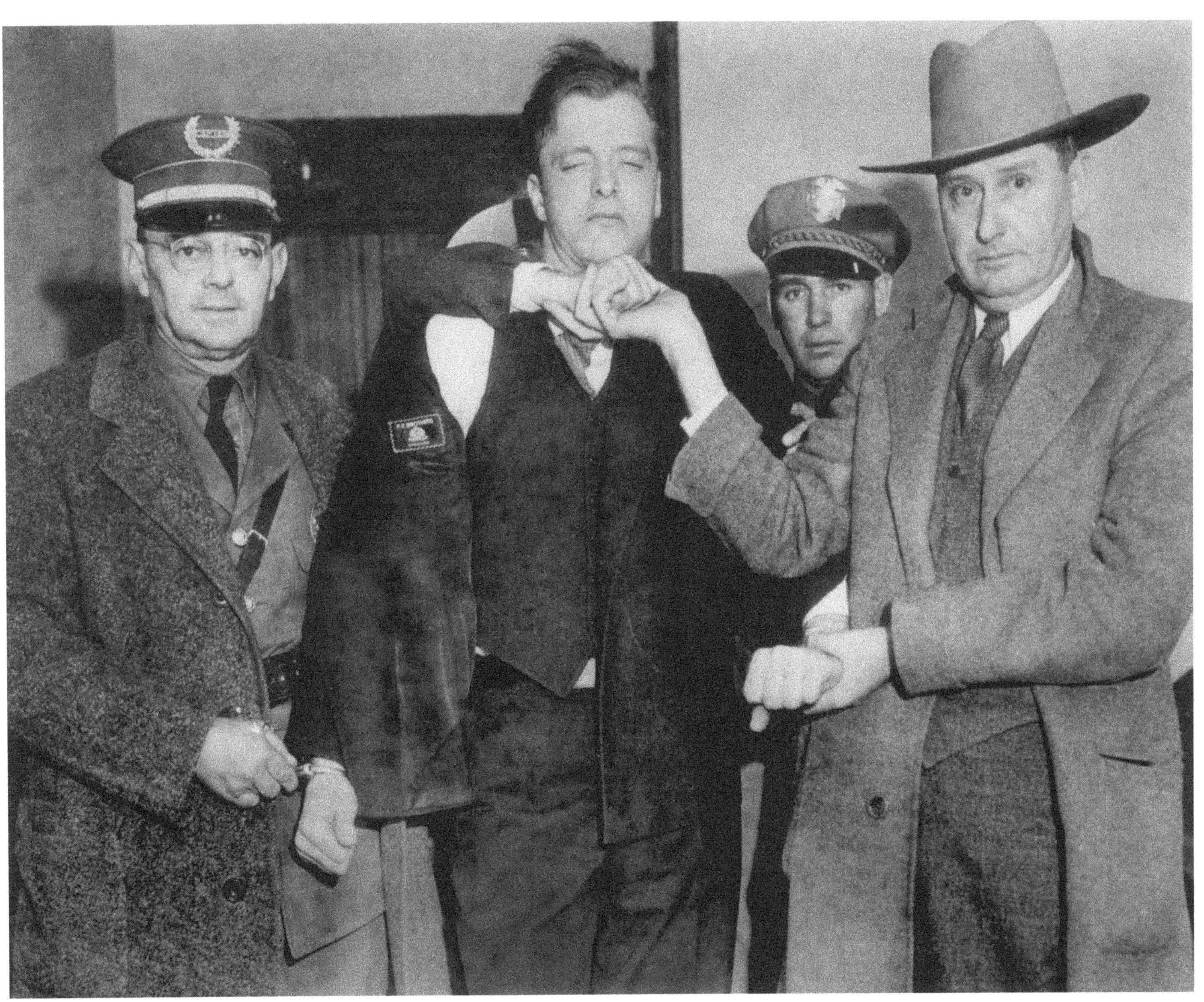

Though Dillinger himself had already been returned to Indiana by plane, a crowd gathered to watch the rest of his gang board the train to be extradited back to Ohio.

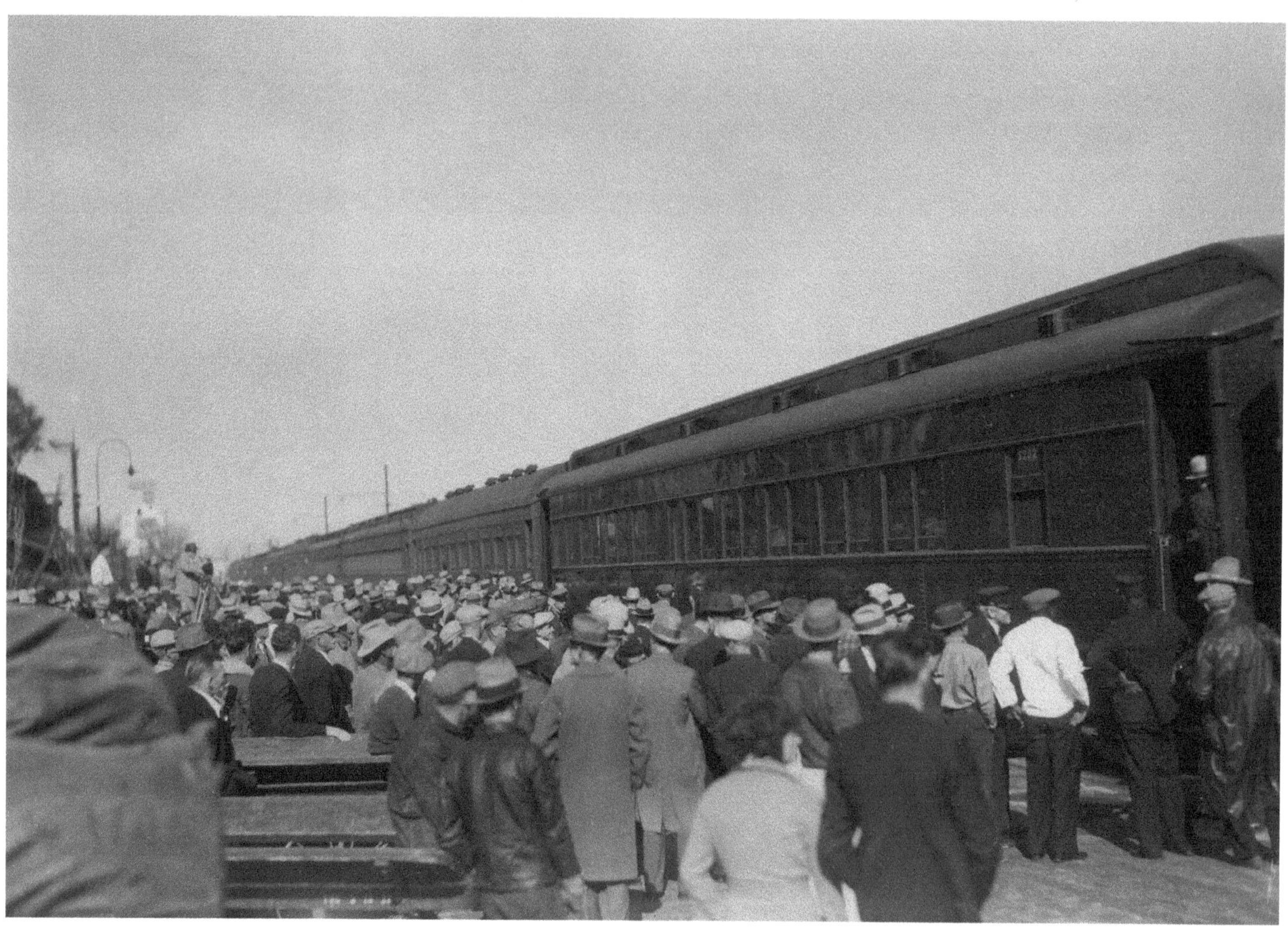

The third Pima County Courthouse built in 1929, seen here in 1934. The dome is made of glazed tile.

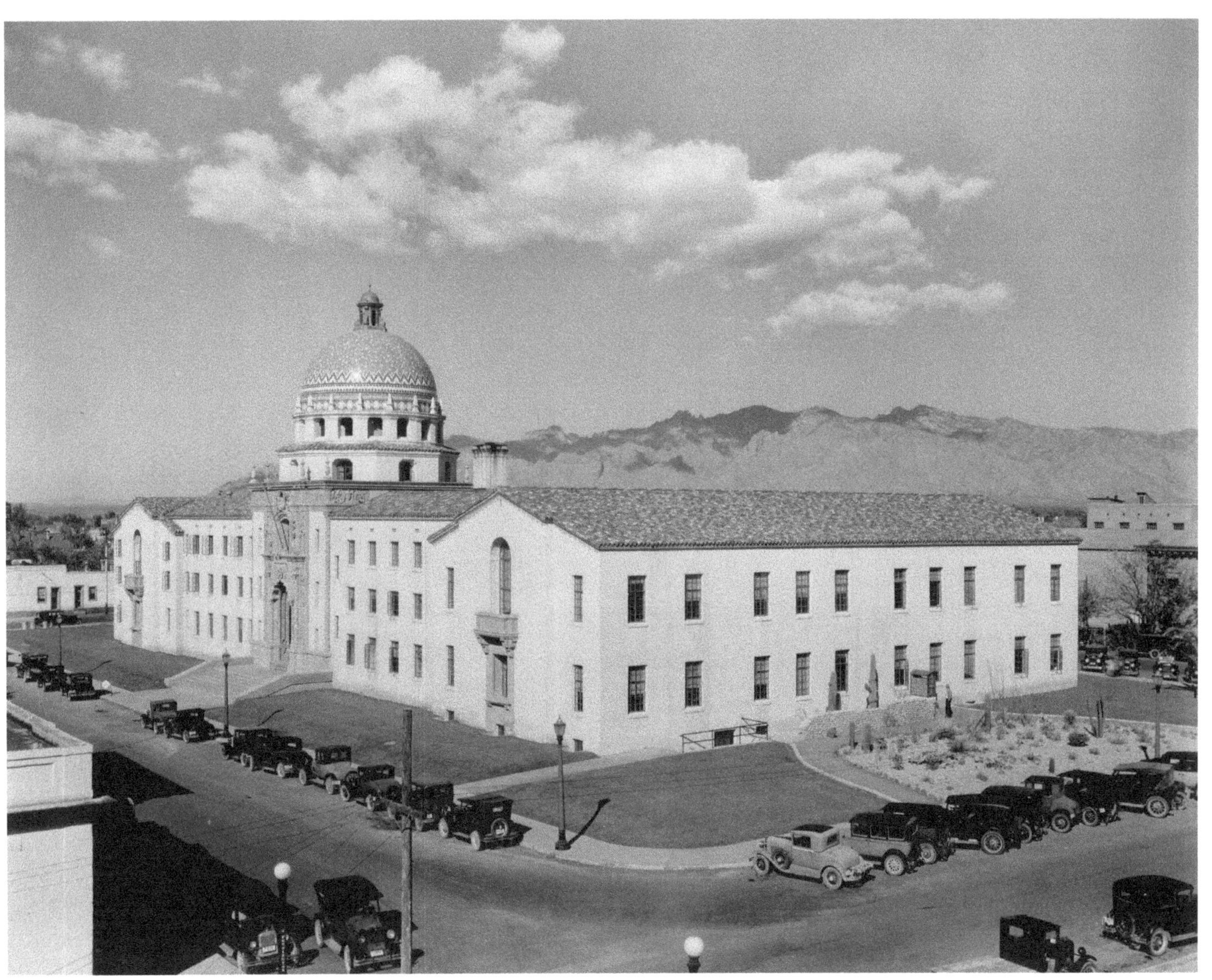

Frederick Maish and Thomas Driscoll built the Palace Hotel in 1875, luxurious by the standards of its day. Renamed the Occidental Hotel in 1894, this Tucson institution was torn down in 1935.

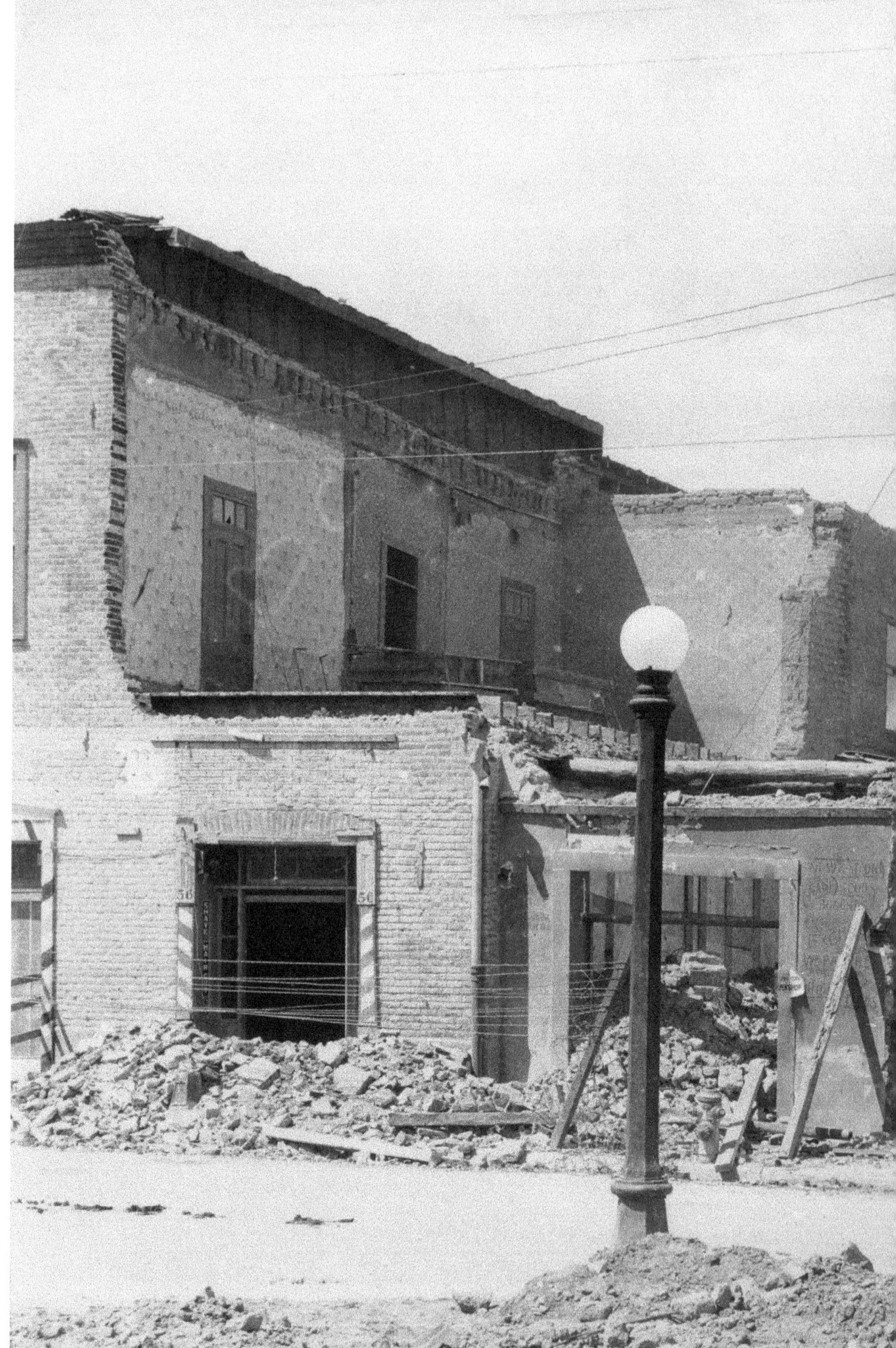

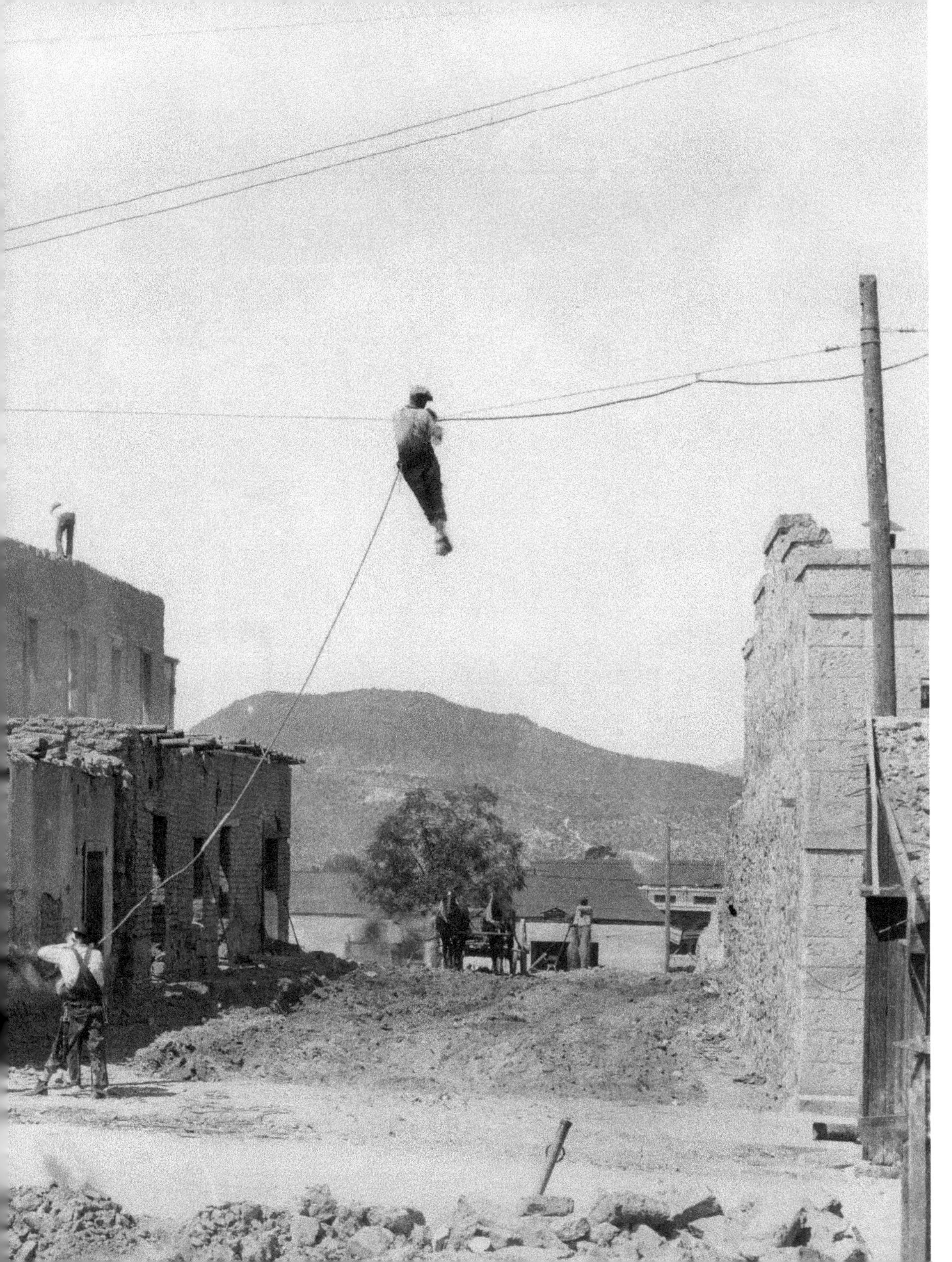

The intersection of North Fourth Avenue and Eighth Street around 1935.

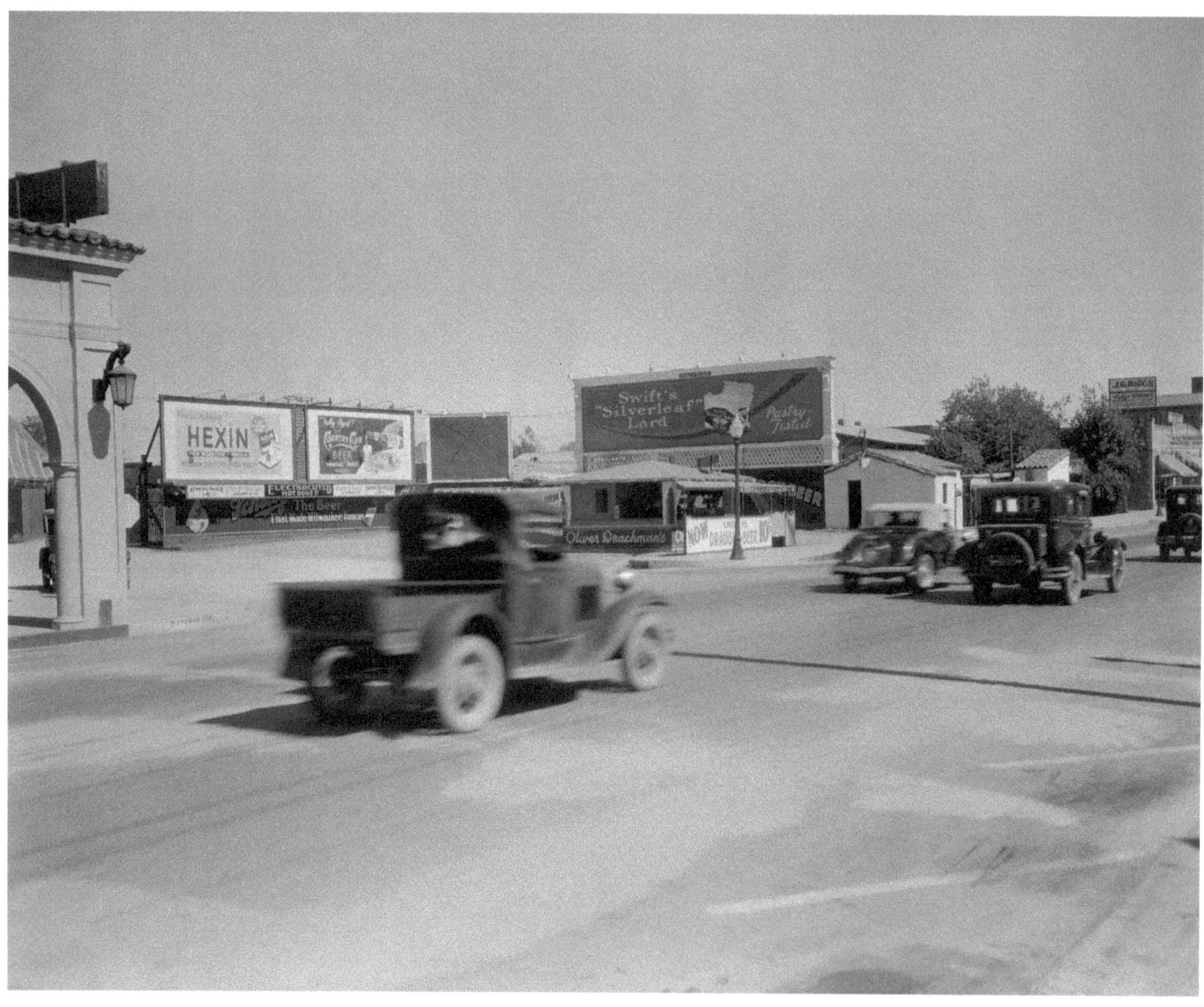

Tucson's usually mild winters made it a favorite on the horse racing circuit in the mid-1930s.

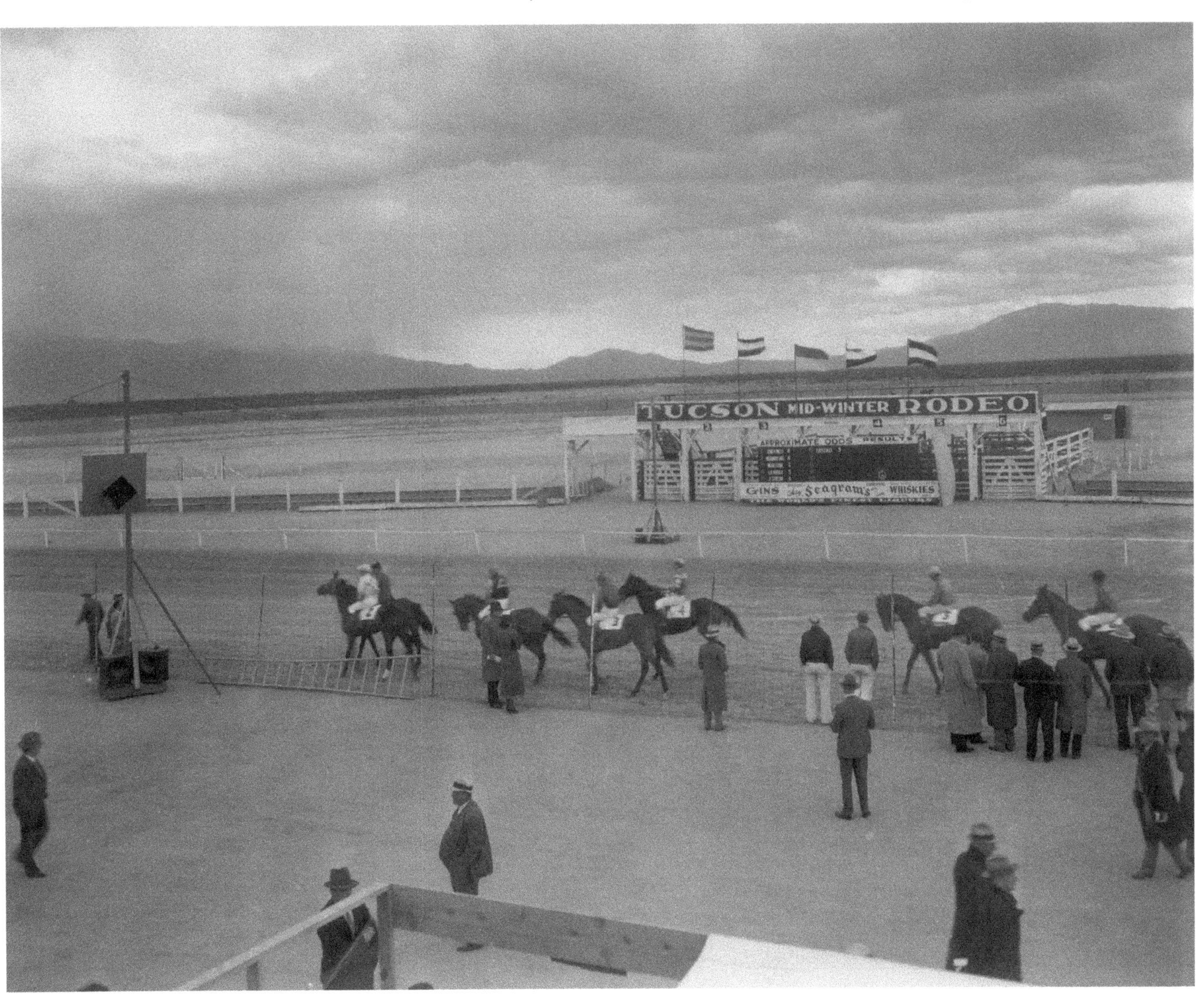

An American Legion float for a parade during the 1930s.

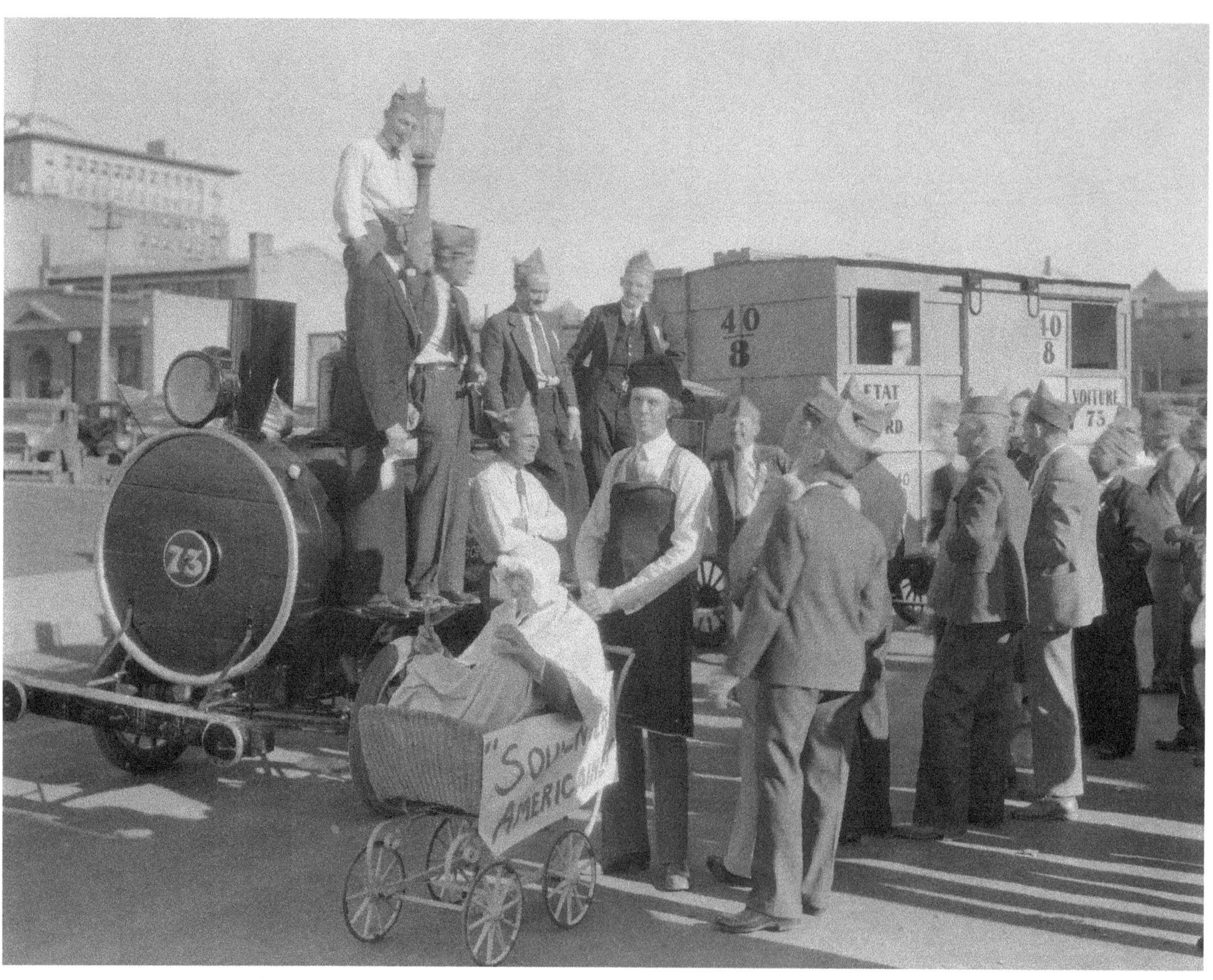

A view of the Santa Rita Hotel in the late 1930s.

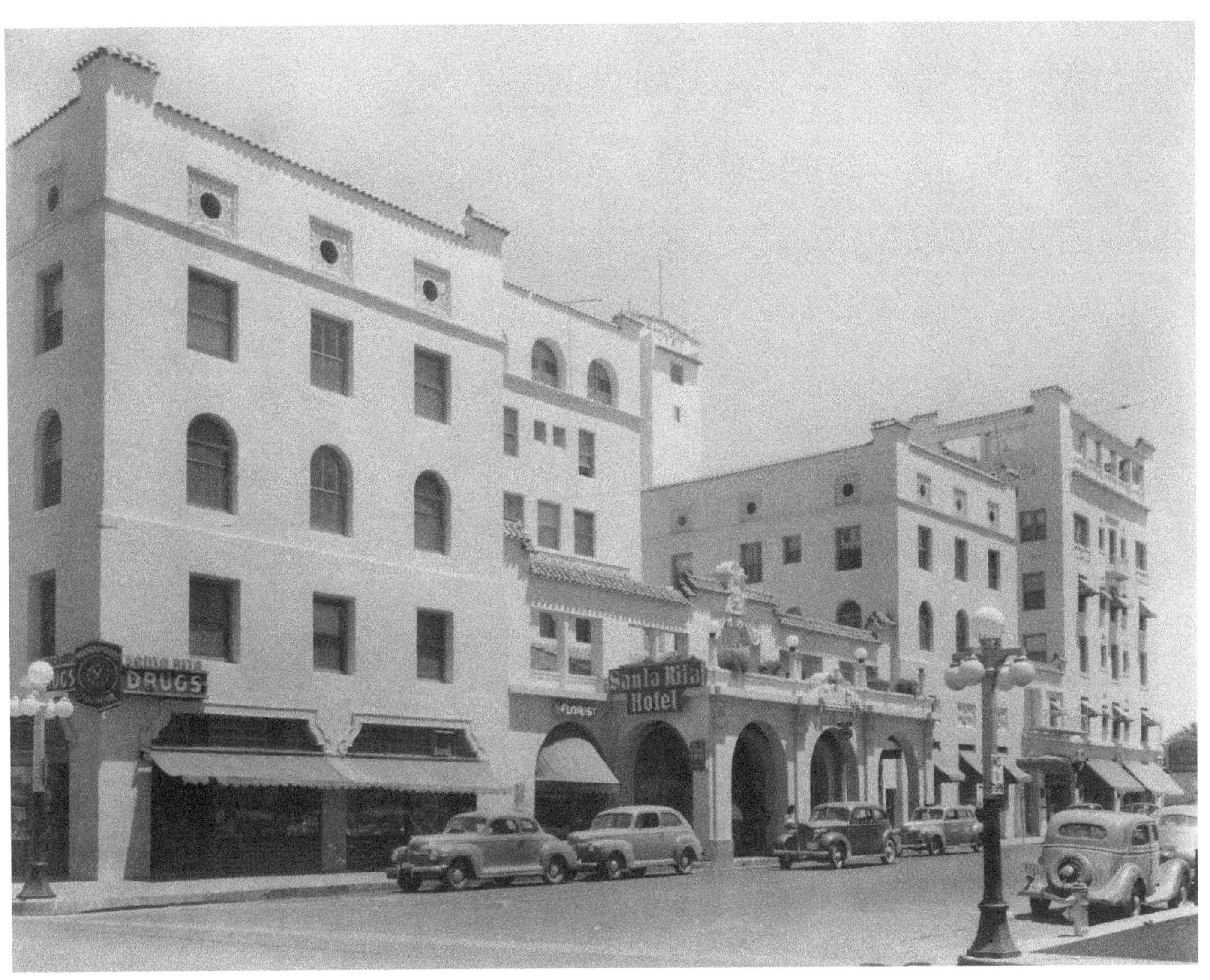

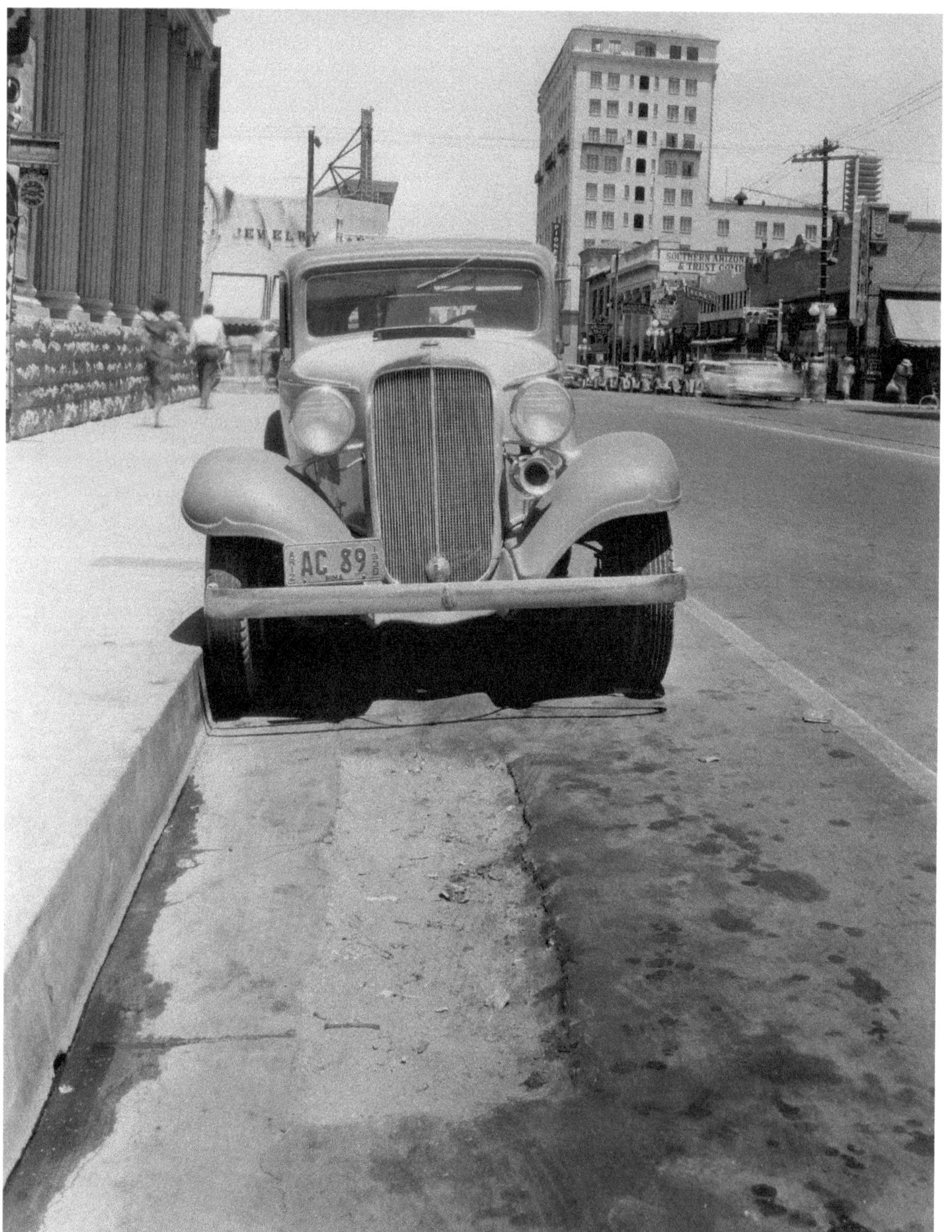

An unavoidable consequence of paved streets, the pothole. This one was on Stone Avenue in 1936.

A group of boys uses the pool of the Arizona Inn for swimming and gymnastics (ca. 1938).

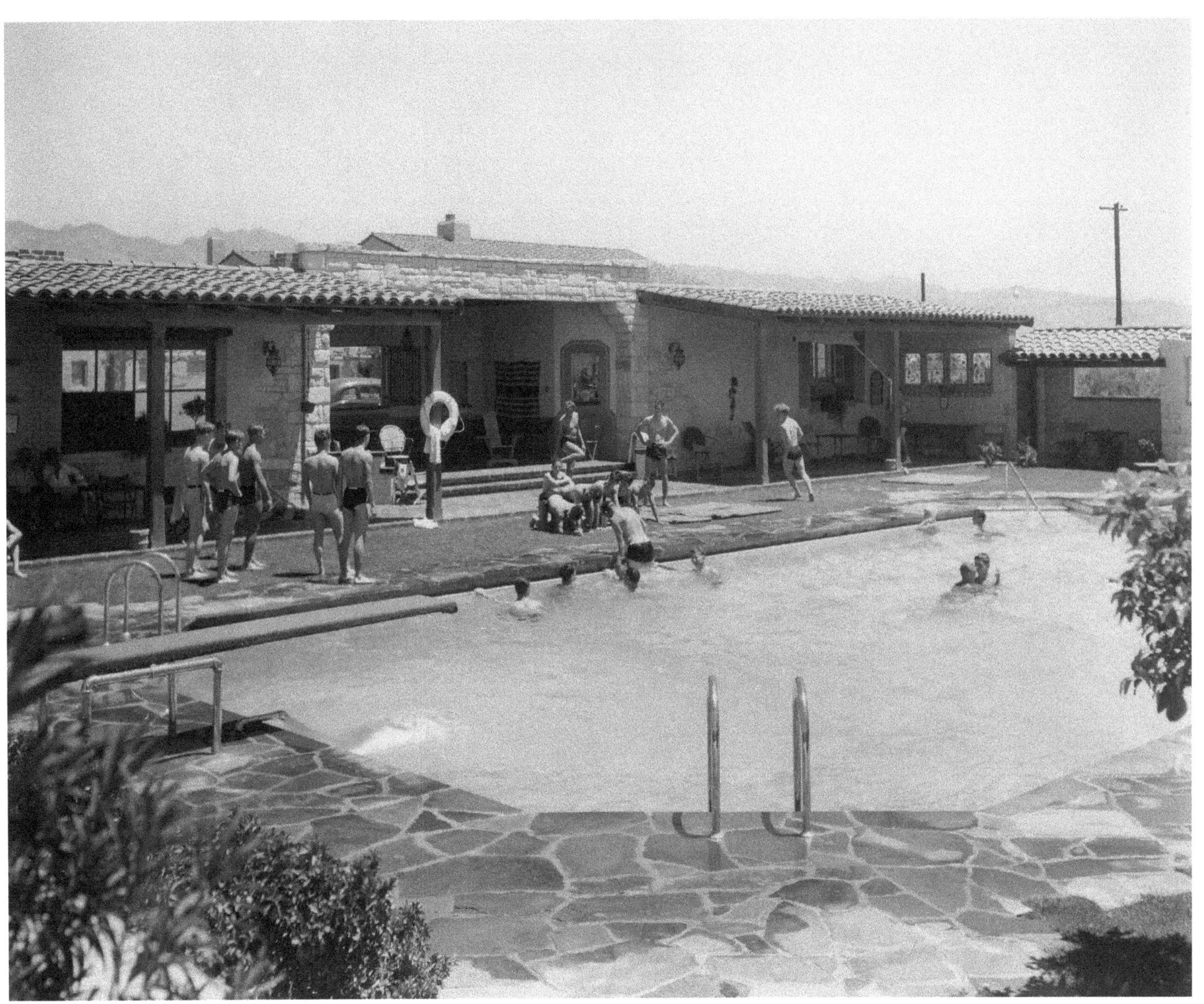

In 1939, Columbia Studios built an outdoor movie set west of Tucson for the movie *Arizona*. Old Tucson would become an important set where many of Hollywood's most famous westerns were filmed after 1945.

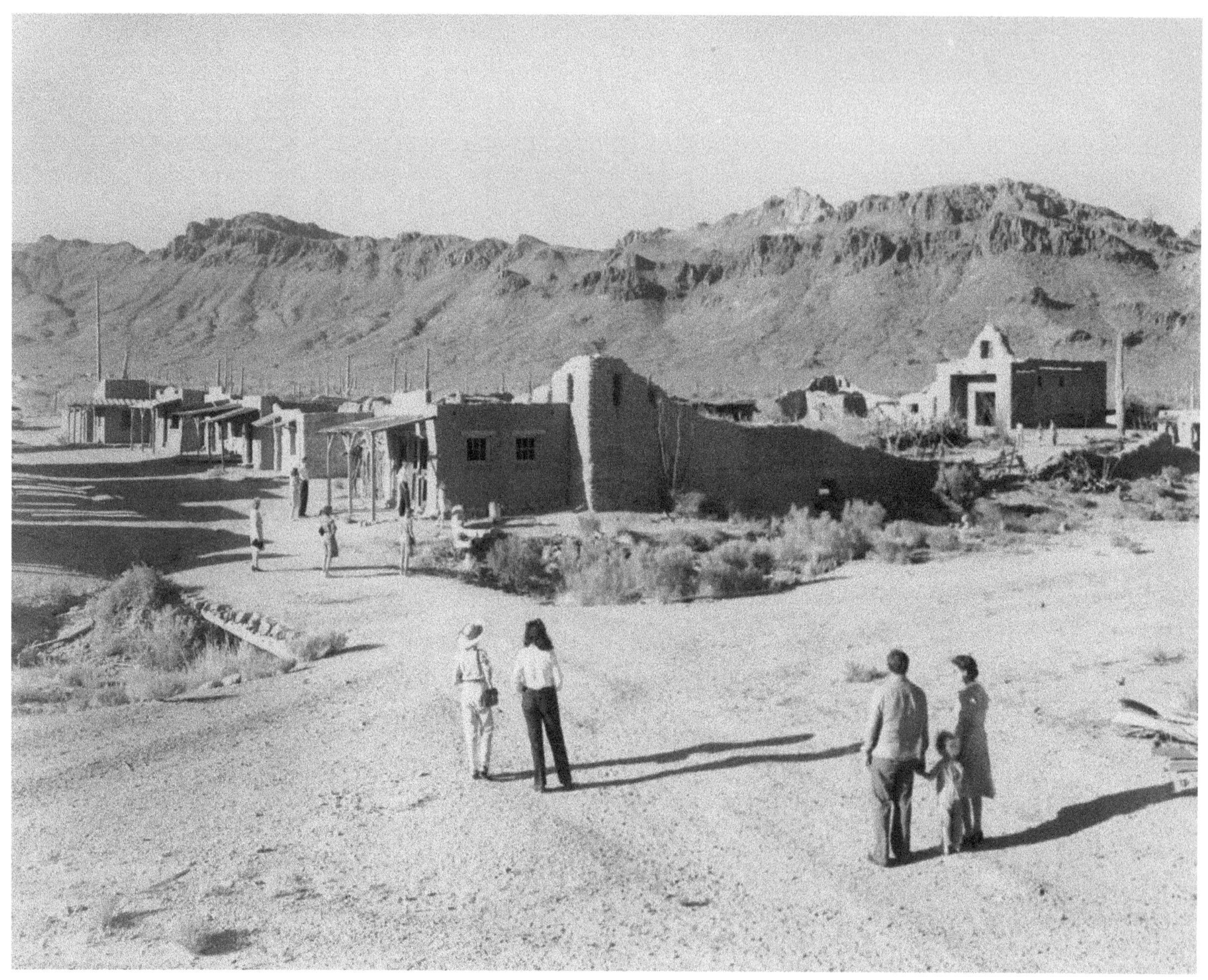

A scene from the movie *Arizona*. Many historical Tucson figures were portrayed in the film.

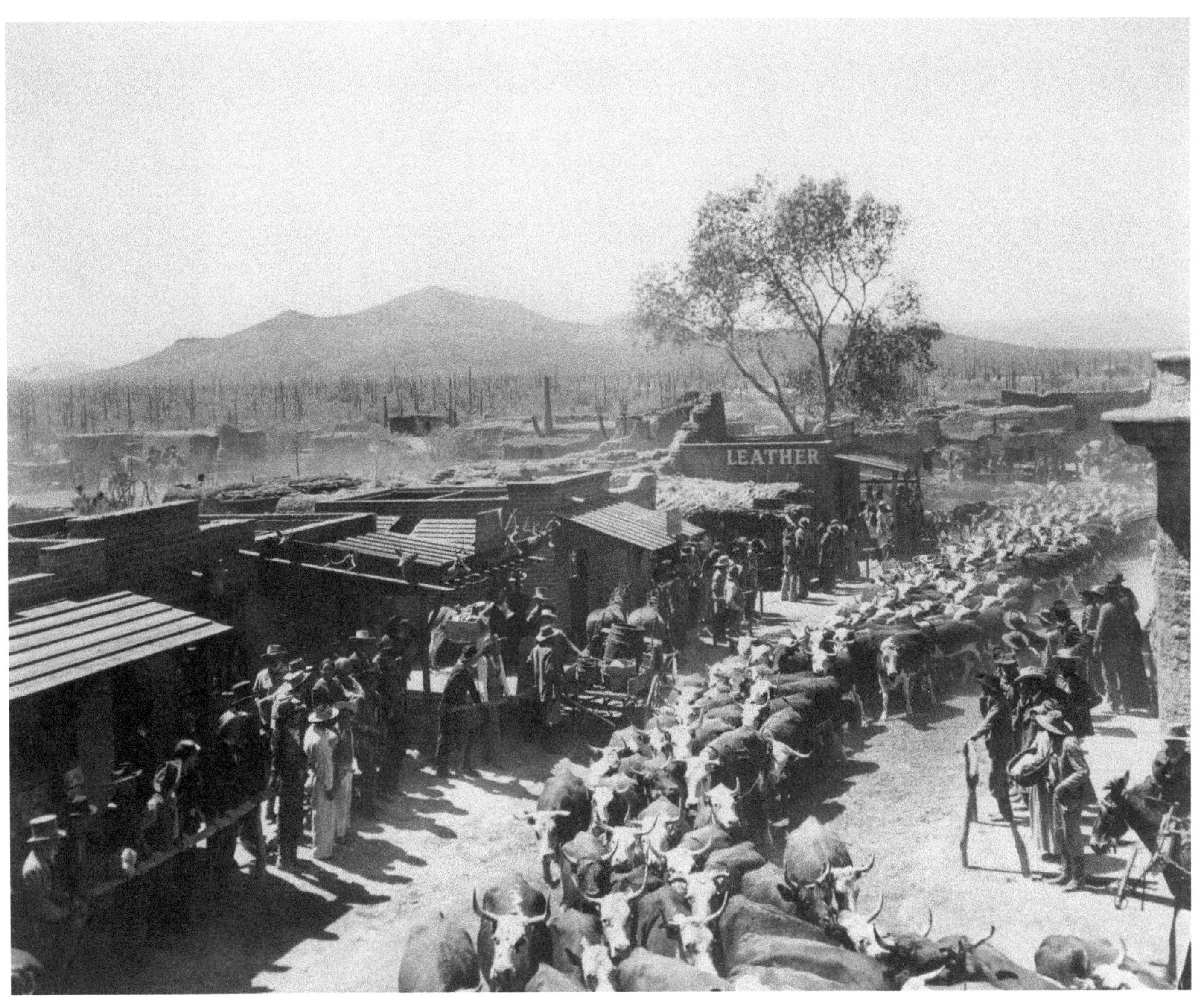

In 1933, the Fox Theater became the first building in Tucson to be cooled by air conditioning. The cooling tower, weighing eighty tons, can be seen on the roof to the left of the Fox sign. The Fox would occasionally host world premieres, such as this one in 1939.

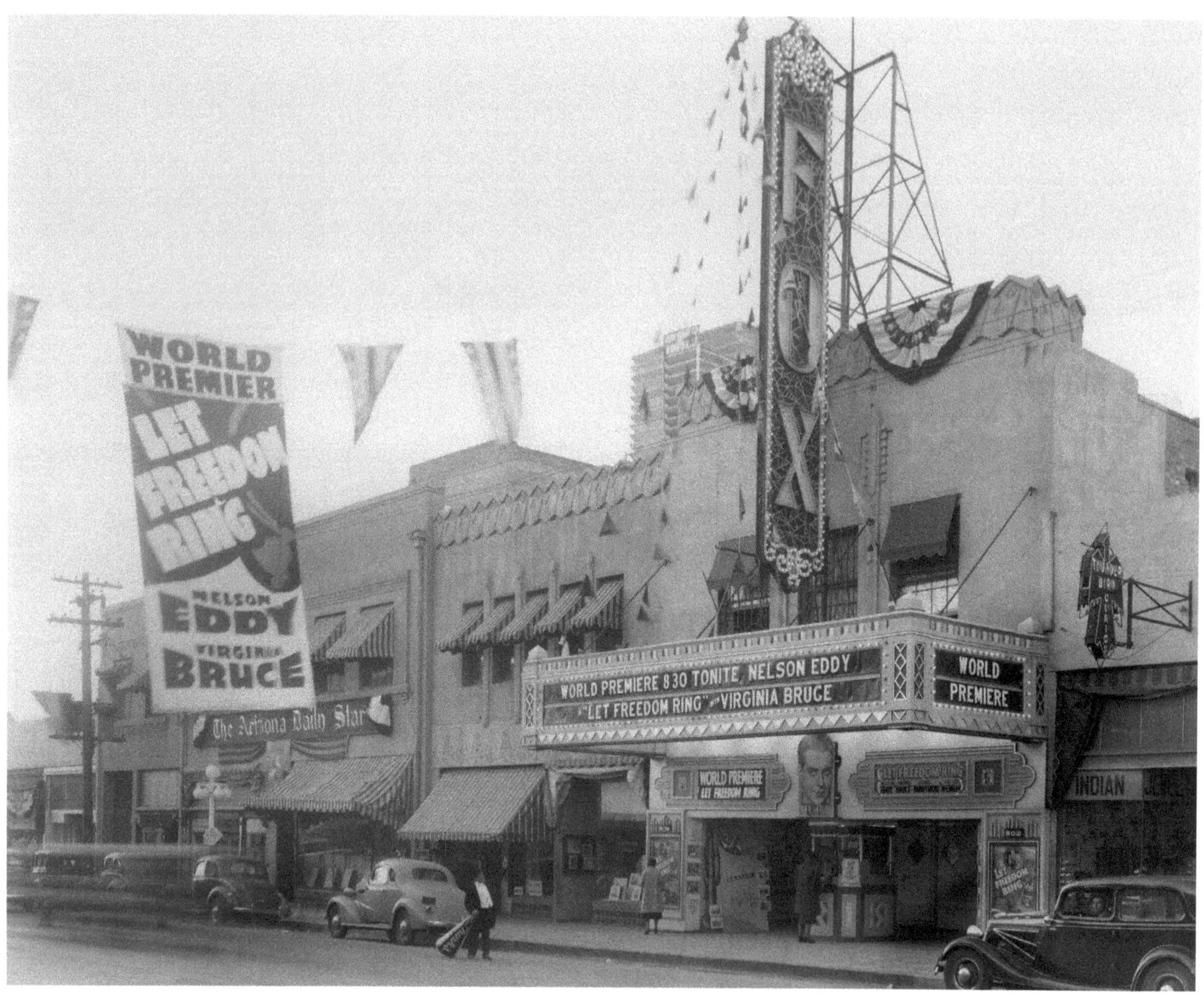

World War II and Beyond

(1940–1970)

World War II and its aftermath would change everything about the desert town. The Army Air Force requisitioned Davis-Monthan Field and two other smaller local airfields for war training and refueling stops. Though suffering from war shortages and rationing like the rest of the country, Tucson's economy benefited from the presence of the air base, a benefit that increased over time. A new international airport west of Davis-Monthan opened in 1948.

A cement plant was built along the Rillito in 1944 and Howard Hughes's Hughes Aircraft company arrived in 1951 with its many government contracts, but large factories were still rare. Construction was a mainstay of the economy. As after the Civil War, many World War II veterans who had served in Arizona returned here to take up their civilian lives. One thousand new homes rose in 1946 and five thousand in 1948. Subdivisions were built and annexed quickly as the city limits spread, ten in 1953 alone. The University of Arizona saw its student body expand as veterans used the G.I. Bill to better their education.

In 1954, the first of several large shopping centers was built to serve the expanding, more dispersed population outside the downtown core. A shrinking downtown population base caused businesses to fail or move closer to their suburban customers. Tucson's population in 1940 was 36,818. In 1950 it stood at 45,454, and by 1960 it had swelled to 212,892, but more and more buildings and storefronts stood empty downtown, reflecting a nationwide trend.

Tucson's multicultural heritage was reflected in the Tucson Festival, which began in 1951. The Arizona-Sonoran Desert Museum was formed in 1952 to help educate the public about the desert environment. On a mountaintop southwest of Tucson, the Kitt Peak National Observatory began watching the skies in 1963.

Urban renewal eliminated many old downtown buildings and even entire neighborhoods, as with the construction of the Tucson Convention Center and La Placita shopping center over a major portion of Barrio Veijo and the Old Church Plaza. Tucson continues to wrestle with the question of how to combine its past with a desire and need for change.

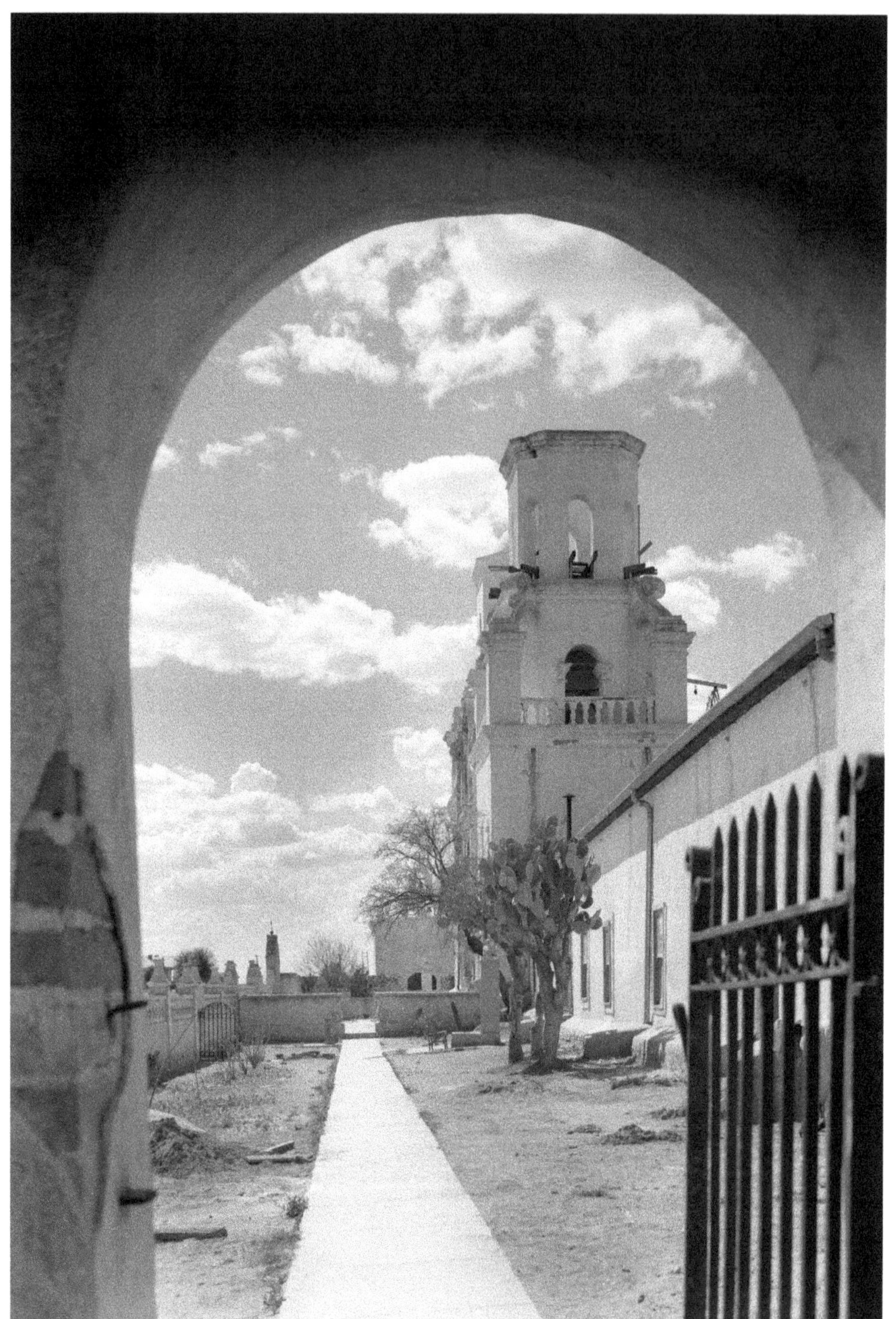

A view of the unfinished east tower of San Xavier del Bac, April 10, 1940.

Dillon Ford, manager of the Hotel Congress, stands beside a Lincoln Zephyr (ca. 1940).

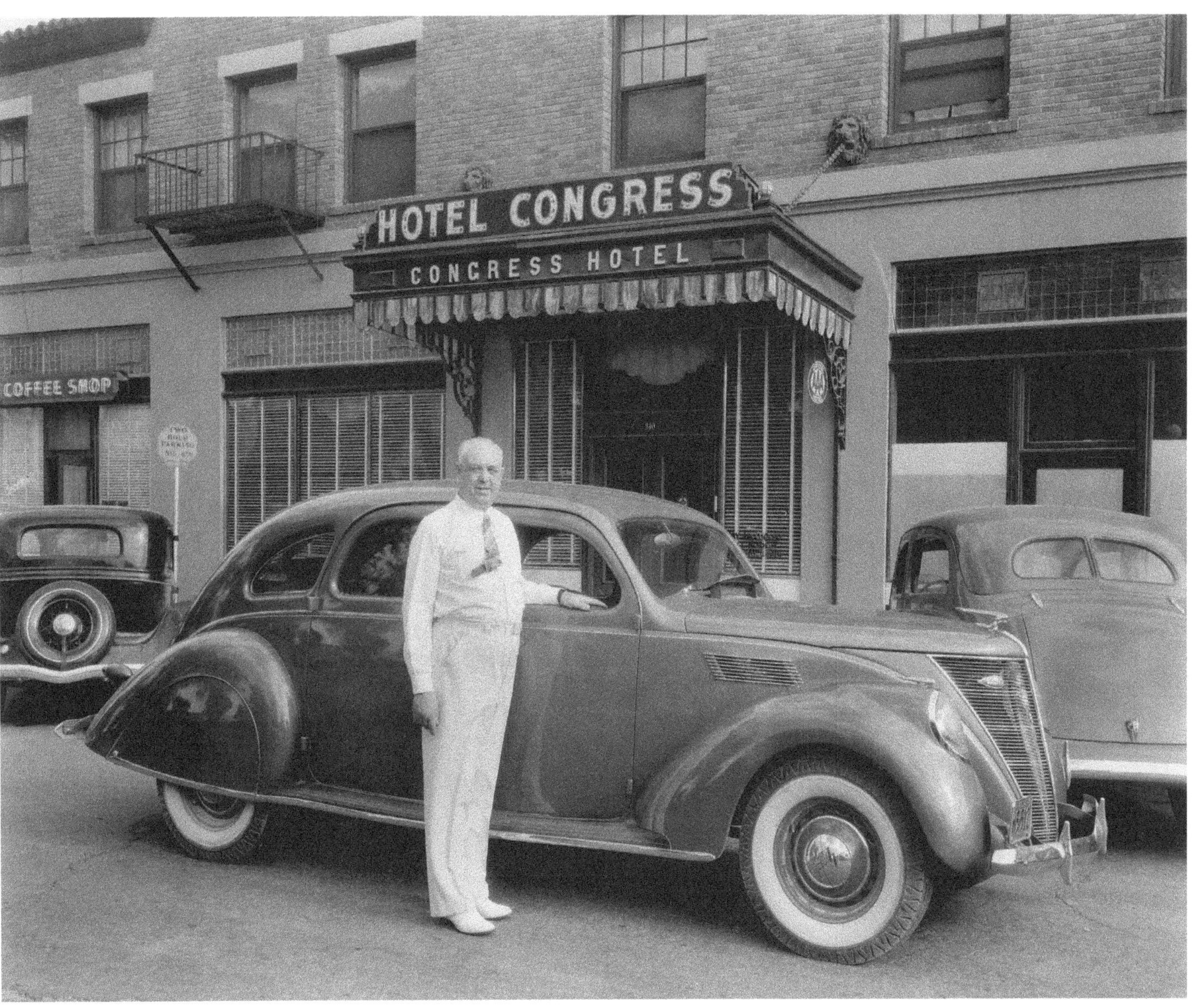

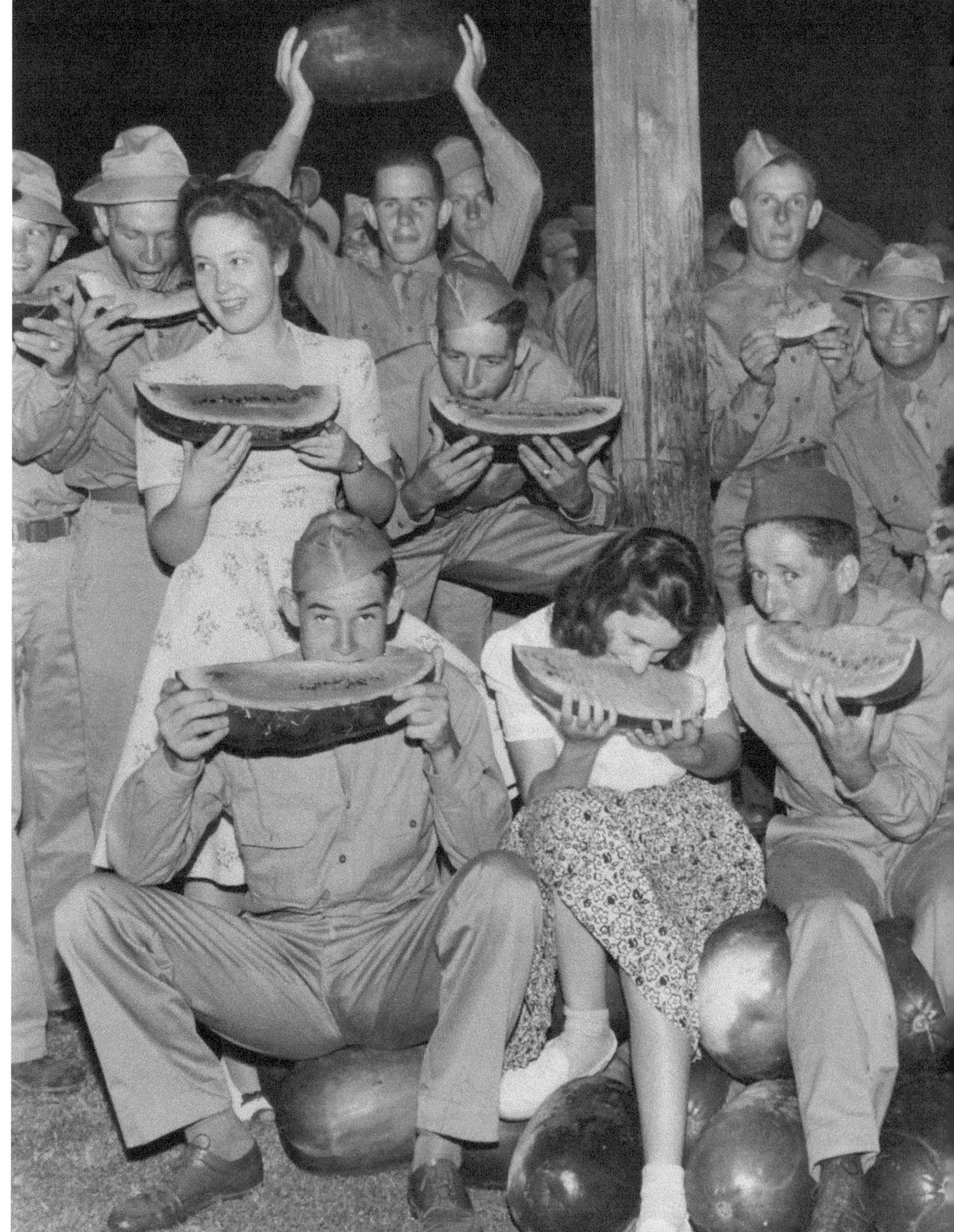

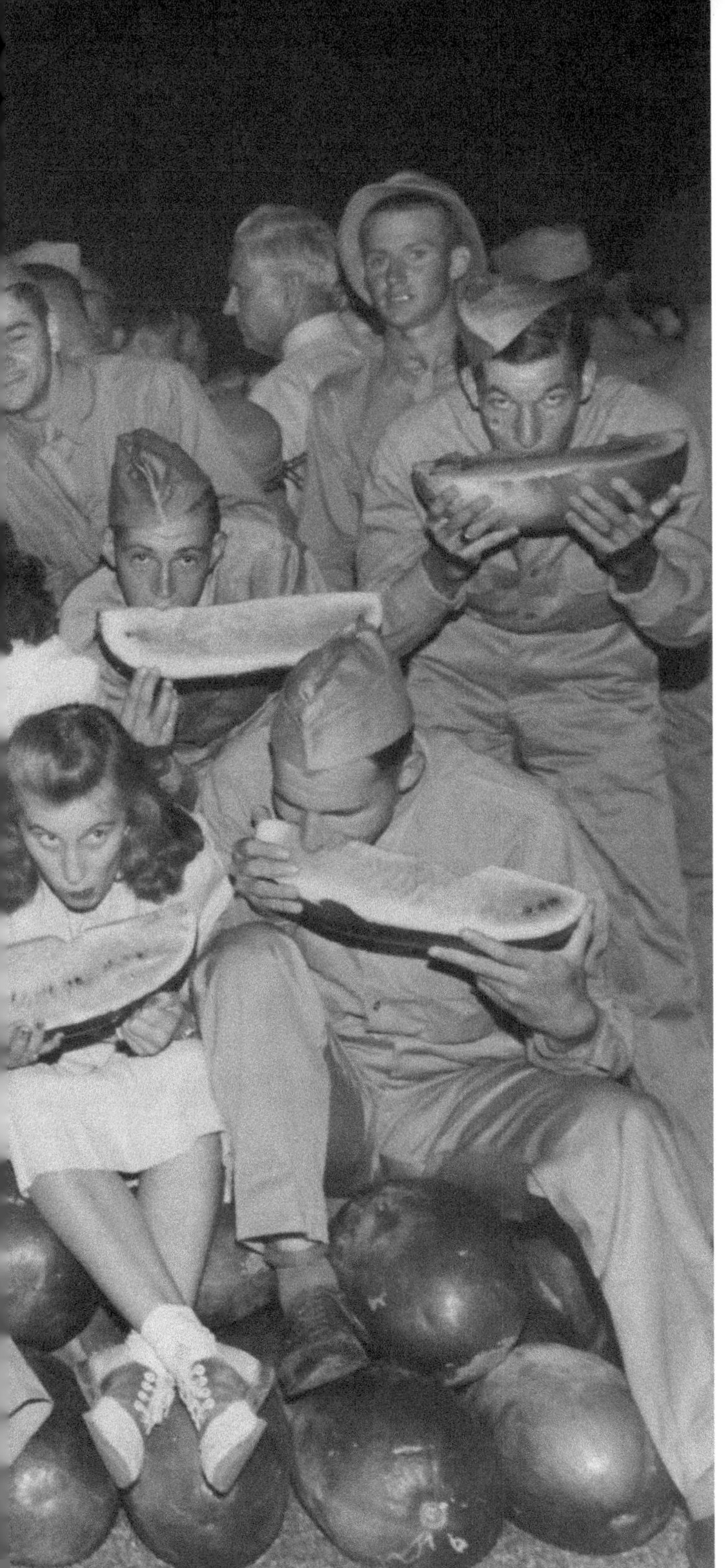

The Tucson Patriotic and Civic League hosted a watermelon party for 385 soldiers from Davis-Monthan Air Base on July 31, 1941. In addition, there were games and dancing on the women's athletic field at the University of Arizona.

Southern Pacific employees gathered to honor C. P. Kramer on his forty-fourth anniversary as an engineer with the railroad in April 1944.

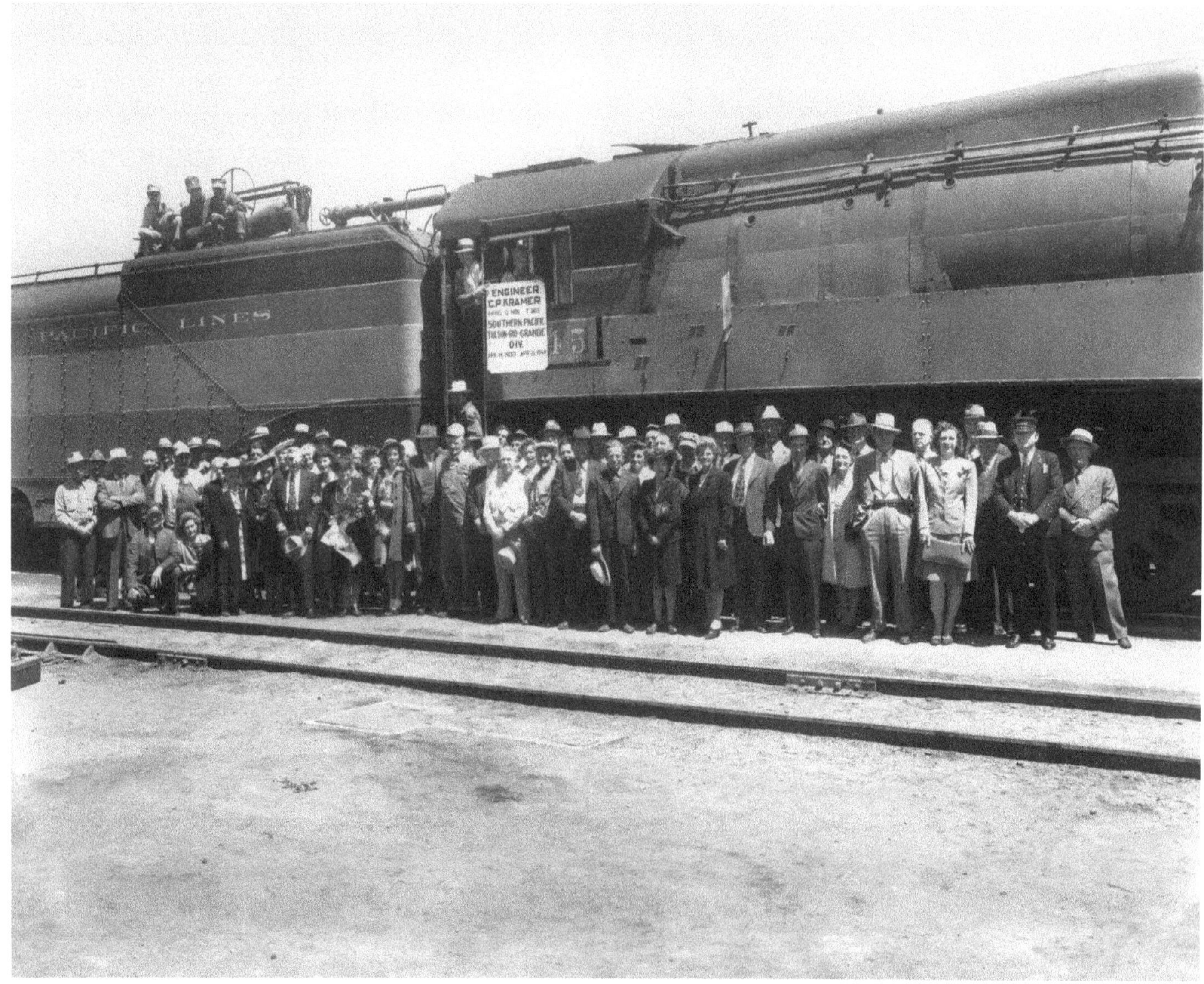

President Eisenhower joined Arizona's newest Senator, Barry Goldwater, at the Davis-Monthan Air Force Base on January 15, 1957.

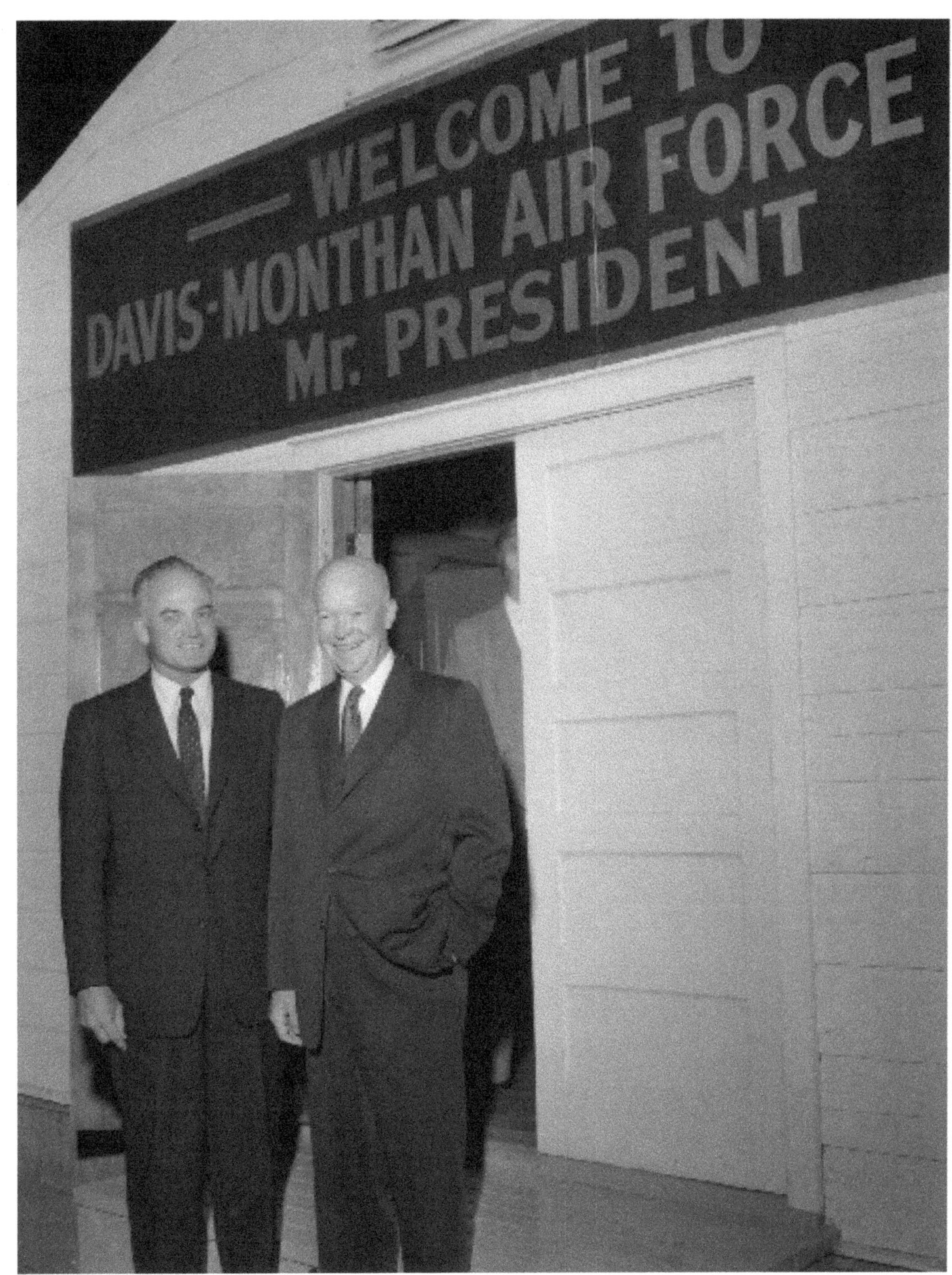

These riders brought a silver-studded elegance to the Rodeo Parade of 1964.

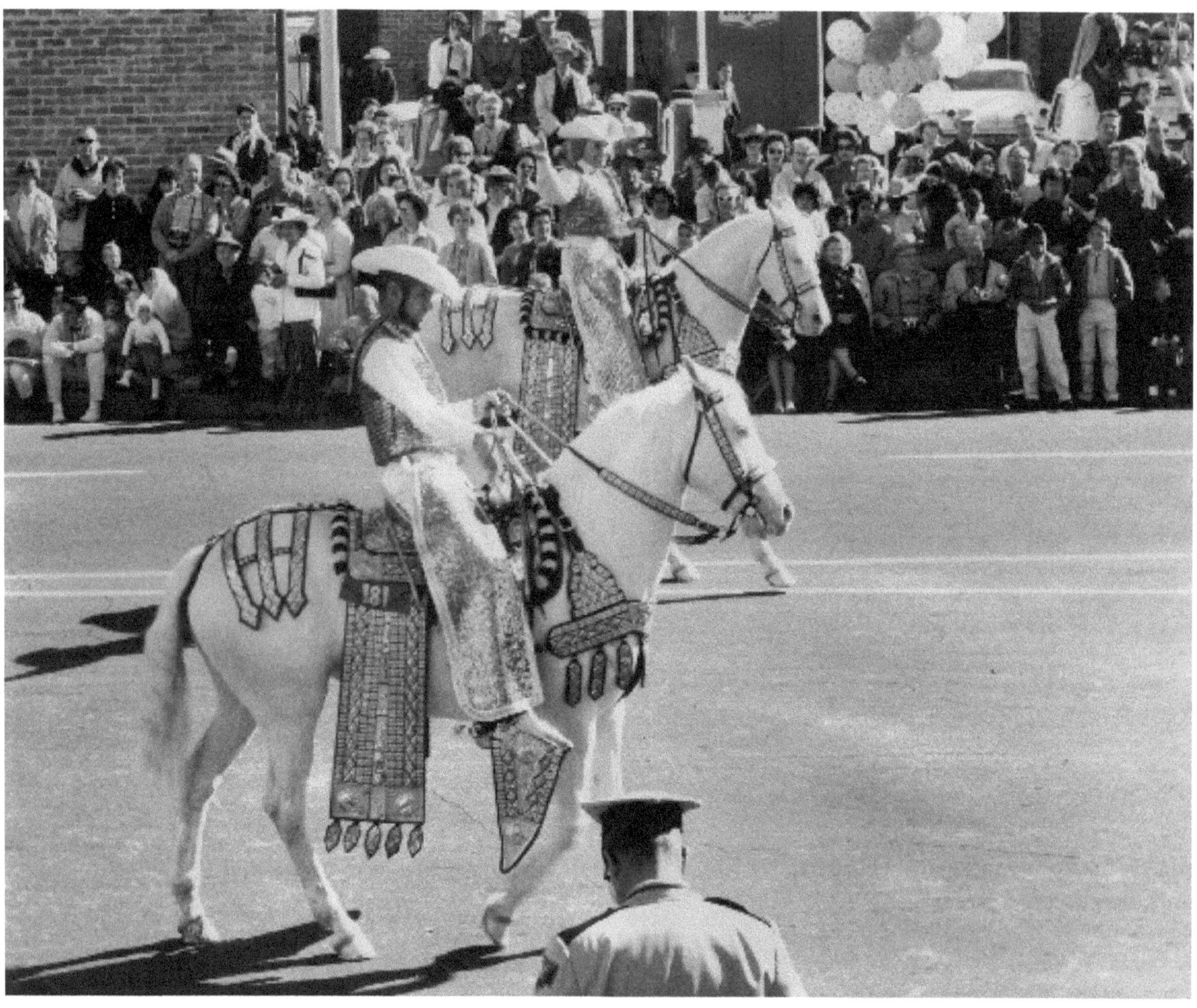

Ammonia gas tanks explode during an April 7, 1970, fire at the vacant Pacific Fruit Express Ice Plant near downtown. The fire burned for twenty-six hours before firemen were able to extinguish it.

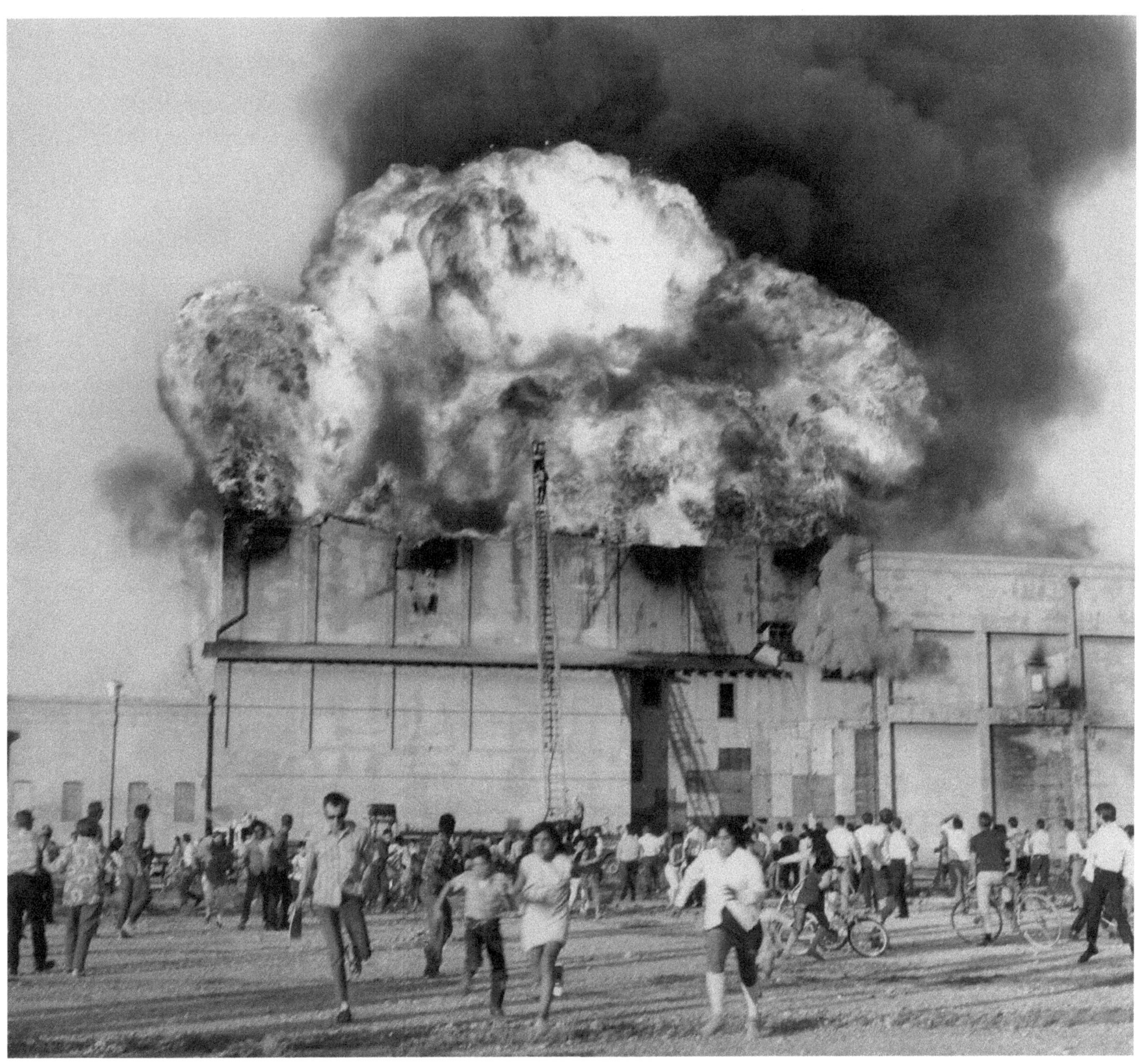

Notes on the Photographs

These notes, listed by page number, attempt to include all aspects known of the photographs. Each of the photographs is identified by the page number, photograph's title or description, photographer and collection, archive, and call or box number when applicable. Although every attempt was made to collect all available data, in some cases complete data was unavailable due to the age and condition of some of the photographs and records.

II **Santa Cruz Valley**
Arizona Historical Society
B#32742

VI **Armistice Day Parade**
Arizona Historical Society
B#39384

X **Mission Complex**
Arizona Historical Society
B#201770

2 **Mission Ruins**
Arizona Historical Society
B#109477

3 **Fort Lowell**
Arizona Historical Society
B#80337

4 **Fort Lowell Hospital**
Arizona Historical Society
B#93875

5 **Fort Lowell Band**
Arizona Historical Society
B#91376

6 **Riders With Horses**
Arizona Historical Society
B#111274

7 **Main Street**
Arizona Historical Society
B#200238

8 **Railroad Engine**
Arizona Historical Society
B#93528

9 **Arizona Citizen**
Arizona Historical Society
B#109358

10 **San Xavier Hotel**
Arizona Historical Society
B#207748

11 **San Agustin Cathedral**
Arizona Historical Society
B#111391

12 **San Agustin Backyard**
Arizona Historical Society
B#200202

13 **Cosmopolitan Hotel**
Arizona Historical Society
B#39845

14 **Sonoran Railroad**
Arizona Historical Society
B#109331

16 **Congress Street**
Arizona Historical Society
B#200235

17 **Congress Street School**
Arizona Historical Society
B#207749

18 **Main Street Parade**
Arizona Historical Society
B#207854

19 **Black Beauty**
Arizona Historical Society
B#44267

20 **San Xavier Del Bac**
Arizona Historical Society
B#111432

21 **San Agustin Cathedral**
Arizona Historical Society
B#27070

22 **S&P Reading Room**
Arizona Historical Society
B#124

23 **Federico Ronstadt**
Arizona Historical Society
B#111188

24 **Expanding Tucson**
Arizona Historical Society
B#200223

25 **East Congress Street**
Arizona Historical Society
B#286a

26 **San Xavier Del Bac**
Arizona Historical Society
B#203225

27 **Church Interior**
Arizona Historical Society
B#201772

28 **Rooftops**
Arizona Historical Society
B#109347

29 **Hose Company**
Arizona Historical Society
B#94485

30 **Chemical Wagon #1**
Arizona Historical Society
B#94484

32 **Carnegie Public Library**
Arizona Historical Society
B#33336

34 **Congress Street**
Arizona Historical Society
B#91768

35 **Railroad Employees**
Arizona Historical Society
B#109149

36 **Music Float**
Arizona Historical Society
B#109101

38 **Loading Ice**
Arizona Historical Society
B#89447

40 **Congress Street**
Arizona Historical Society
B#111211

41 **Park View Hotel**
Arizona Historical Society
B#113602

42 **Congress Street**
Arizona Historical Society
B#18832

43 **Owl's Club**
Arizona Historical Society
B#89385

44 **Botanical Laboratory**
Arizona Historical Society
B#32736

46 **Santa Rita Hotel**
Arizona Historical Society
B#32370b

47 **Touring Cars**
Arizona Historical Society
B#32454

48 **View from Santa Rita**
Arizona Historical Society
B#92128

49 **Convent Street**
Arizona Historical Society
B#207839

50 **Volunteer Wagon**
Arizona Historical Society
B#205197

52 **Ramona Hotel**
Arizona Historical Society
B#38418

53 **Baseball Team**
Arizona Historical Society
B#94395

54 **University of Arizona**
Arizona Historical Society
B#200945

55 **Saint Mary's Hospital**
Arizona Historical Society
B#38129

56 **Nuns and Nurses**
Arizona Historical Society
B#38827

57 **Smoothing Concrete**
Arizona Historical Society
B#62097

58 **Silver Bell Mine**
Arizona Historical Society
B#89572

59 **Union Shaft**
Arizona Historical Society
B#89574

60 **S&P Depot**
Arizona Historical Society
B#32404

61 **Santa Claus**
Arizona Historical Society
B#32390

62 **Congress Street**
Arizona Historical Society
B#111400

63 **Trip to San Xavier**
Arizona Historical Society
B#89406

64 **Cabinet Club**
Arizona Historical Society
B#93521

65 **Exploring the Desert**
Arizona Historical Society
B#109330b

66 **Crossing the Rillito**
Arizona Historical Society
B#203267

67 **Congress Street**
Arizona Historical Society
B#93896

68 **Tucson Furniture Co.**
Arizona Historical Society
B#89551a

69 **San Agustin Ruins**
Arizona Historical Society
B#200271

70 **Trolley Tracks**
Arizona Historical Society
B#89553

71 **Football Team**
Arizona Historical Society
B#200686

72 **Stone Avenue**
Arizona Historical Society
B#32942

73 **Paving Crew**
Arizona Historical Society
B#38381

74 **Paving the Concourse**
Arizona Historical Society
B#32263a

75 **Railroad Park**
Arizona Historical Society
B#89545

76 **Paving Congress Street**
Arizona Historical Society
B#32475

77 **Congress Street**
Arizona Historical Society
B#32956

78 **Congress Street**
Arizona Historical Society
B#89551b

79 **Freight Trucks**
Arizona Historical Society
B#89356

80 **Automobile Accident**
Arizona Historical Society
B#32313

81 **Hotel Tucsonia**
Arizona Historical Society
B#38482

82 **Santa Cruz River Flood**
Arizona Historical Society
B#93468

83 **Hotel Orndorff**
Arizona Historical Society
B#89899

84 **Fort Lowell**
Arizona Historical Society
B#89217a

85 **Horse Racing**
Arizona Historical Society
B#93467

86 Auto Racing
Arizona Historical Society
B#32784

87 Eddie Rickenbacher
Arizona Historical Society
B#93465

88 Congress Street
Arizona Historical Society
B#89552

89 Decorated Float
Arizona Historical Society
B#113331

90 Tucson City Hall
Arizona Historical Society
B#39401

91 World War I Parade
Arizona Historical Society
B#89635

92 First Police Bike
Arizona Historical Society
B#32032

94 Liberty Bell Float
Arizona Historical Society
B#89631

95 Troops Marching
Arizona Historical Society
B#32189

96 Military Band
Arizona Historical Society
B#32185

97 Liberty Bonds Rally
Arizona Historical Society
B#38155

98 Race Car Driver
Arizona Historical Society
B#89491

99 Broadway Boulevard
Arizona Historical Society
B#200555

100 4th Of July Float
Arizona Historical Society
B#30307

101 Sixth Avenue
Arizona Historical Society
B#202876

102 American Legion Float
Arizona Historical Society
B#202962

104 Mount Lemmon
Arizona Historical Society
B#204447

105 Flying V Ranch
Arizona Historical Society
B#201387

106 Stylish Cowgirls
Arizona Historical Society
B#201588

107 Tucson Citizen
Arizona Historical Society
B#32377

108 Newspaper Boys
Arizona Historical Society
B#32028

109 Rodeo Parade
Arizona Historical Society
B#27207

110 Rodeo Parade
Arizona Historical Society
B#200005

111 Hotel Arizona
Arizona Historical Society
B#39187

112 Wright Home
Arizona Historical Society
B#205203

113 Harold Bell Wright
Arizona Historical Society
B#24901

114 Congress Street
Arizona Historical Society
B#39451

115 Rotarians
Arizona Historical Society
B#38726

116 Flooded Front Yard
Arizona Historical Society
B#33211

118 Swimming Pool
Arizona Historical Society
B#35887

120 Congress Street
Arizona Historical Society
B#27898

121 Refurbishing Tracks
Arizona Historical Society
B#203783

122 Rodeo Parade
Arizona Historical Society
B#110065

123 Congress Street
Arizona Historical Society
B#32457

124 Barbershop
Arizona Historical Society
B#62396

125 Christmas Train
Arizona Historical Society
B#35566

126 Albert Steinfeld
Arizona Historical Society
B#203799

127 Southern Pacific Band
Arizona Historical Society
B#32182

128 Stone Avenue
Arizona Historical Society
B#89556

129 Charles Lindbergh
Arizona Historical Society
B#93742b

130 Spirit of St. Louis
Arizona Historical Society
B#93724a

131 Standard Airlines
Arizona Historical Society
B#22105

132 Fokker F-VIIb
Arizona Historical Society
B#39027

133 Commuter Airline
Arizona Historical Society
B#204610

134 San Augustine Cathedral
Arizona Historical Society
B#207711

135 El Conquistador Hotel
Arizona Historical Society
B#29010

136 Hotel Corral
Arizona Historical Society
B#203033

137 Gathering Guests
Arizona Historical Society
B#203028

138 Rodeo Parade
Arizona Historical Society
B#116108

139 Firestone Airplane
Arizona Historical Society
B#35195

140 Motorized Floats
Arizona Historical Society
B#109977

141 Consolidated National Bank
Arizona Historical Society
B#7663

142 Congress Street Parade
Arizona Historical Society
B#110138

143 "The Big Trail"
Arizona Historical Society
B#35340

144 Mickey Mouse Club
Arizona Historical Society
B#35337

146 Santa Rita Hotel
Arizona Historical Society
B#24153

147 Arizona Daily Star
Arizona Historical Society
B#35113

148 Arizona Inn
Arizona Historical Society
B#203053

149 Central Station
Arizona Historical Society
B#205198

150 Central Station
Arizona Historical Society
B#205193

151 Bowen-Sime Motor Co
Arizona Historical Society
B#200586

152 Tucson Valley
Arizona Historical Society
B#200400

153 Art Class
Arizona Historical Society
B#203223

154 Captured Rattlesnake
Arizona Historical Society
B#38128

155 Scott Street
Arizona Historical Society
B#23505

156 Citizen Paperboys
Arizona Historical Society
B#33267

157 Pioneer Hotel
Arizona Historical Society
B#202953

158 Karston the Magician
Arizona Historical Society
B#41488

159 Halloween
Arizona Historical Society
B#34294

160 Stone Street
Arizona Historical Society
B#24701

161 Archery Class
Arizona Historical Society
B#33429

162 Police Motorcycles
Arizona Historical Society
B#29346a

164 Montgomery Ward
Arizona Historical Society
B#200607

165 Armistice Day Parade
Arizona Historical Society
B#204500

166 "Carefree Carnival"
Arizona Historical Society
B#35414

167 Fox Theater
Arizona Historical Society
B#24251

168 Movie Parade
Arizona Historical Society
B#24371

169 "Footlight Parade"
Arizona Historical Society
B#29474

170 Daily Star Fire
Arizona Historical Society
B#207550

171 Roscoe Ates
Arizona Historical Society
B#27413

172 Jean Harlow
Arizona Historical Society
B#34815

173 Bicycle Contest
Arizona Historical Society
B#27340

174 Women's Air Derby
Arizona Historical Society
B#20775

175 Hotel Congress Fire
Arizona Historical Society
B#34509

176 Dillinger Gang
Arizona Historical Society
B#28163

177 Harry Pierpoint
Arizona Historical Society
B#29104

178 Dillinger Gang
Arizona Historical Society
B#28161

179 Pima County Courthouse
Arizona Historical Society
B#5274

180 Palace hotel
Arizona Historical Society
B#200241

182 North Fourth Avenue
Arizona Historical Society
B#34715

183 Horse Racetrack
Arizona Historical Society
B#40070

184 American Legion Float
Arizona Historical Society
B#207646

185 Santa Rita Hotel
Arizona Historical Society
B#28159

186 Potholes
Arizona Historical Society
B#24022

187 Arizona Inn
Arizona Historical Society
B#27129

188 Outdoor Movie Set
Arizona Historical Society
B#204562

189 Movie Scene
Arizona Historical Society
B#204565

190 Fox Theater
Arizona Historical Society
B#27703

192 San Xavier Del bac
Library of Congress
HABS ARIZ,10-
TUSCO,13-1

193 Dillon Ford
Arizona Historical Society
B#25158

194 Watermelon Party
Arizona Historical Society
B#9219

196 Southern Pacific
Arizona Historical Society
B#20687

197 President Eisenhower
Arizona Historical Society
B#214f77

198 Rodeo Parade
Arizona Historical Society
B#185f7

199 Gas Tank Explosion
Arizona Historical Society
B#72573

HISTORIC PHOTOS OF TUCSON

Tucson is an American city quintessentially founded upon change. From its birth to the present, Tucson has consistently built and reshaped its appearance, ideals, and industry. Through changing fortunes, Tucson has continued to grow and prosper by overcoming adversity and maintaining the strong, independent culture of its citizens.

Historic Photos of Tucson captures this journey through still photography selected from the finest archives. From its annexation from Mexico as part of the Gadsden Purchase in 1854 to the twenty-six-hour fire of April 1970, *Historic Photos of Tucson* follows life, government, education, and events throughout the city's history.

This volume captures unique and rare scenes through the lens of hundreds of historic photographs. Published in striking black and white, these images communicate historic events and everyday life of two centuries of people building a unique and prosperous city.

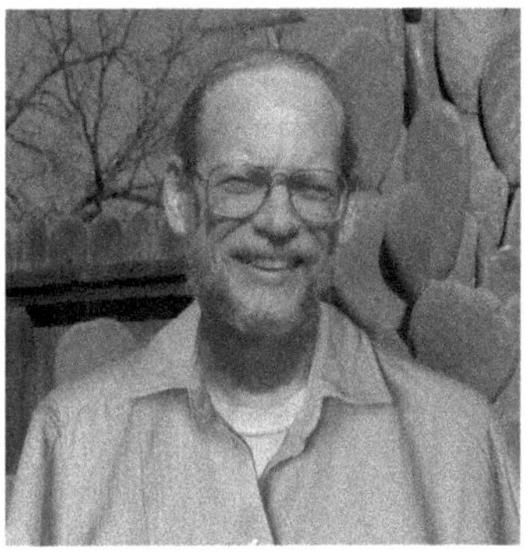

Mike Speelman received a bachelor of arts degree in history from the University of Arizona in 2001 and is a member of Phi Alpha Theta. After a brief encounter with grad school, he began doing freelance historical research in Tucson on projects both big and small. Mike has researched and written labels for exhibits at the Arizona Historical Society Downtown Museum. He contributed research to the Canoa Ranch Historical Designation, to the Tucson Origins Heritage Park reconstruction projects, to an upcoming *American Experience* program on Geronimo, and to the documentaries *Lalo Guerrero: The Original Chicano* and *Inside Deep Throat*. He has also done research on Tucson homes and local people. At the 2005 Arizona History Convention, he received the Friends of Arizona Archives award for a paper presented on African American pioneer Samuel Bostick. Mike lives in present-day Tucson.

WWW.TURNERPUBLISHING.COM

www.ingramcontent.com/pod-product-compliance
Lightning Source LLC
LaVergne TN
LVHW060607110826
845154LV00003B/50

* 9 7 8 1 6 8 3 3 6 9 5 8 5 *